THURSTON MOORE

WE SING A NEW LANGUAGE

D1198545

Thank you to the many people who have shared
some part of their lives with me these past years: it's been a
privilege and an honour to hear of your courageousness in
creating and putting work out into the world.
A further thank you to LiveNirvana –
I'd not be writing without you.

NICK SOULSBY

THURSTON MOORE

WE SING A NEW LANGUAGE

OMNIBUS PRESS

London / New York / Paris / Sydney / Copenhagen / Berlin / Madrid / Tokyo

Copyright © 2017 Omnibus Press
(A Division of Music Sales Limited)

Cover designed by Michael Bell Design
Picture research by Nick Soulsby

ISBN: 978.1.78558.136.6
Order No: OP56650

The Author hereby asserts his/her right to be identified as the author of this work in accordance with
Sections 77 to 78 of the Copyright, Designs and Patents Act 1988.

All rights reserved. No part of this book may be reproduced in any form or by any electronic or
mechanical means, including information storage or retrieval systems, without permission in writing
from the publisher, except by a reviewer who may quote brief passages.

Exclusive Distributors
Music Sales Limited,
14/15 Berners Street,
London, W1T 3LJ.

Music Sales Pty Ltd
Level 4 , 30-32 Carrington St
Sydney NSW 2000
Australia

Every effort has been made to trace the copyright holders of the photographs in this book but one or
two were unreachable. We would be grateful if the photographers concerned would contact us.

Printed in Malta

A catalogue record for this book is available from the British Library.

Visit Omnibus Press on the web at www.omnibuspress.com

Contents

Contents

Contents

Contents

Contents

Contents

Contents

Contents

Contents

Contents

Introduction

There's a secret history threaded through the three-and-a-half decades of Thurston Moore's career. Moore has been rightly feted for what he achieved alongside Kim Gordon, Lee Ranaldo and Steve Shelley as part of Sonic Youth; a band that did more than any other to pierce the staid genre boundaries of rock'n'roll, allowing it to gulp down the creative oxygen of fresh structures and sounds. Building their music upon a bedrock of New York's no-wave scene, on both The Ramones and The Grateful Dead, on minimalist composers working with the material of rock music, the band was invigorated by a creative scene in New York which embraced boundary-crossing collisions of art, film, literature, theatre, poetry and music as a day-to-day practice. Collectively the band was both cheerleader for, and supporter of, the entire underground community; talking up favourite performers, wearing their T-shirts, taking them on tour, sharing stages and releases. They championed engagement across the full gamut of the creative arts —wrapping their releases in visual works by leading artists, referencing poets and authors, embracing multimedia performance long before it became commonplace. Bands like Nirvana would point to Sonic Youth as their concept of 'success'; then having reached the pinnacle of rock stardom, they looked to them again as the quintessential model for how a band could exist in the mainstream, while remaining uncompromising champions of the values that ignited the underground.

Much homage has been paid to Moore's achievements in Sonic Youth. Some of the commentary, however, suffers from a severe myopia, ignoring a substantial part of the music to which he has dedicated his life. It's no conspiracy: given Sonic Youth were deemed barely acceptable to mainstream

1

tastes, the focus on that sole communal entity seems entirely understandable. Where it becomes unfortunate is that it relegates Moore and his colleagues merely to interlocking components; pieces of kit that are of value only when working in conjunction with one another, rather than full-throttle hot rods in their own right.

The definitions applied to their work outside of Sonic Youth seem to imply it shouldn't be taken seriously. Except where it incorporates pop-punk tunes, then it is dismissively tagged as a side project at best, or otherwise as a curio, demo, leftover, try-out, slumming or moonlighting. That's when it's noted at all.

There's a deeply regressive and conservative mindset at play when the door is firmly slammed on non-mainstream subcultures and traditions. Sonic Youth arose at a time when rock music had already begun to ingest its own history, to recycle rather than to expand. The band offered something thrilling: a chance to bust open the formulae of rock, to breach genre barriers and draw fresh blood into the glutted vessel. A creeping conservatism has since rejected their questing vision, accepting that only the most gently tweaked, turgid facsimiles of what has come before can be categorised as music, let alone 'rock music'. The British music tabloid *NME* represented this attitude perfectly, attacking Sonic Youth's embracement of improvisation and avant-garde music (and specifically their improvised performance at All Tomorrow's Parties in 2000) with the headline 'Goodbye 20th Century, Goodbye Talent'. *We Sing A New Language* is not an attempt to reposition Thurston Moore's work outside of Sonic Youth above that band's prodigious discography. It seeks only to correct the neglect of his vibrant discography, to recognise him as an artist in his own right with an existence outside the context of a single group. Its aim is to provide a window onto the constantly evolving artistic passion concealed within his labyrinthine recorded history; to explore one of the most creatively voracious discographies of any modern musician and the vast wealth of scenes, sounds and artists that constitute it.

Moore arrived in New York City at a time of personal turbulence. His father's death in 1976 had been followed by Moore's departure from college and a burgeoning frustration with the dearth of creative opportunities in his hometown of Bethel, Connecticut. A chance meeting in a New Haven record store provided him with the opportunity he was seeking. Invited to join The Coachmen, a art-rock band, he learnt his craft over two years spent playing the circuit of lofts, clubs and art spaces that incubated the NYC underground. Moore absorbed the sounds and images of the faltering punk scene; the multichannel provocations thrown down by 'no wave'; the conservatory-bred minimalism that Glenn Branca and Rhys Chatham were applying to rock; the blunt trauma of hardcore.

When The Coachmen terminated around August 1980, Moore wasted no time in seeking new opportunities. He played briefly with Stanton Miranda at her loft, jammed with Ann Demaranis, stood in with Elodie Lauten's Orchestre Moderne, played bass for one show with a band called Apostles, and began working with a group under the temporary names Male Bonding, The Arcadians and Red Milk. By the time Moore organised the Noise Fest event between 16–24 June, 1981, Red Milk would become known as Sonic Youth.

While that group was firmly established as Moore's primary concern by the end of 1981, this didn't mean the cessation of all other engagements Coinciding with Noise Fest, Moore participated in Branca's *Symphony No. 1* on June 18–19 and would continue to perform as part of the ensemble right through to Branca's *Symphony No. 4* in May 1983. This was not his only exposure to new music composition, as he also guested on Rhys Chatham's seminal work *Guitar Trio* during this same period.

In the background, punk band Even Worse had morphed into an outfit designed, by founder Jack Rabid, to deliberately bait hardcore kids with verbal sniping, excessive tuning, instrumental noise and off-kilter punk rock – a comedic revenge for hardcore's supplanting of punk. Moore's expanding vocabulary of wild techniques was deemed a perfect fit and he became their guitarist for over a year and a half, until the band's demise in the fall of 1983. As well as fulfilling his desire to play in a full-on punk band, there was an additional incentive in that it got him in the door at hardcore shows (including a support slot for Minor Threat in February '83). Moore's impressive stamina – to this day, he maintains a touring, performing and recording schedule that would fell a musician half his age – was already on display. Across 1982–83 he was also serving as an on-off bassist with Michael Gira's Swans, while his friendship with Lydia Lunch led him to play bass and co-write songs at the November 1982 sessions for her *In Limbo* album. His extra-musical activities expanded when he made his first spoken-word/poetry appearance with Lunch, founded a fanzine, *Killer*, then kicked off his one-man label, Ecstatic Peace!, with a cassette split between Gira and Lunch in spring '84. It's easy to forget that, at the time, the music of Sonic Youth – with its brutal volume and almost physical harshness, its lyrics sometimes alluding to serial murder or Charles Manson – was most readily associated with that of extreme figures like Lunch and Gira, who were both friends and musical fellow-travellers with similar interests in sex, darkness and violence, mitigated by the possibility of transcendence.

In this DIY scene – in the absence of much attention, let alone remuneration – the onus was on enthusiasts like Moore to build their own buzz while aiding friends and allies wherever possible. By the middle of the decade, he had passed this cultural apprenticeship to become an established and significant figure on the fringe of modern music.

From 1987–88, other possibilities began to open up. Sonic Youth were experimenting with other musical genres, instrumentation and equipment. The band's long-term viability felt increasingly assured, thus providing its members with the space, time and confidence to try ideas outside of the core unit. Moore's close friend, Byron Coley, claims that the first solo Thurston Moore show took place in spring 1988 at a benefit for *Forced Exposure*, the underground magazine and distributor. Moore played embryonic renditions of new songs alongside solo interpretations from his back catalogue. Similarly, he was part of a live jam with former-Velvet Underground drummer Maureen 'Moe' Tucker in March 1988, but still wasn't quite ready to abandon the sturdy structure of rock music. Having grown into an avid consumer of experimental music, he respected its performers and therefore didn't want to appear a dilettante.

Coley, alongside Forced Exposure's Jimmy Johnson, decided to intervene. They set Moore up with Don Dietrich and Jim Sauter, saxophonists from the uncompromisingly intense trio Borbetomagus, for a fully improvised recording session on Thursday June 16, 1988 at Fun City Studios. Moore says the two instigators were fixated on the idea of 'saving him' from the limitations of composition. The results, released as *Barefoot In The Head*, were varied, evocative and satisfying; a vindication of their faith in Moore and in the potential offered by free improvisation.

Even when Sonic Youth signed to a major label in 1989 and established their place in the vanguard of what became the 'alternative rock' revolution, Moore never relinquished his other interests. Jam bands like Two Virgins and Tusk quickly came and went, while he also played with The Velvet Monkeys and no-wave scenester Rudolph Grey's The Blue Humans, taking on production duties for both outfits. 1990–91 saw a significant ramping up of releases on Ecstatic Peace!, as Moore used the money from his main group to fund material by other artists. It was in this period that Moore's love of record collecting went far beyond a mere passive consumer fetish. Not only did his discoveries produce many an opening outfit for Sonic Youth tours, but he also devoted time, money and energy to releasing and celebrating music he adored. In collaboration with Coley, he compiled and financed a major retrospective boxset for Destroy All Monsters, the band joined by Ron Asheton after the demise of The Stooges. Then, having already supported Grey's re-emergence as an active musician, Moore showed his respect for another New York icon by luring Richard Hell out of semi-retirement to form Dim Stars.

Nirvana's explosion rearranged the musical furniture. Suddenly, music that had been derided and ignored a decade earlier became the motivational force behind America's most acclaimed acts. Thurston's response was typical of a record obsessive; he began evangelising the artists he respected and believed that the world had missed out on. From 1992–94, he contributed cover songs to tribute albums paying homage to Beat Happening, The Minutemen, Suicide and Greg Sage & The Wipers, as well as issuing a cover of the entirety of hardcore band Seven Seconds' *Skins, Brains & Guts* EP. Sonic Youth itself released an EP consisting entirely of covers of Washington DC hardcore band Youth Brigade, covered the song 'Nic Fit' by fellow DC hardcore band Untouchables and invited DC hardcore catalyst Ian MacKaye to play on their 1992 album *Dirty*. It was a love note, a memo to self of the values bequeathed to the band by their heroes long before they themselves achieved prominence; perhaps also a gesture of defiance, declaring, 'We were here long before you cared', to a mainstream that was acting like the US underground began with Nirvana's *Nevermind*.

Something else had changed, however, arising again from Moore's addiction to record collecting. Over bagels and smoothies at a Stoke Newington café, he would describe to me sitting in Kim Gordon's parents' house in the mid-eighties, poring over her teenage collection of jazz recordings; going off on tour with a dozen mixtapes he'd asked Coley to put together, to introduce him to the "primary jazz recordings"; spending months acquiring books in order to ground himself thoroughly in the history of jazz, John Litweiler's *The Freedom Principle: Jazz After 1958* being particularly crucial.

Thurston admitted he "became rabid" in his vinyl-collecting habit. On tour in 1990, he estimates he bought 3,000 records and stashed them all over the tour bus. He would "go to every single used record store in America and wipe them out! Luckily it was at a time when I could find these Sun Ra private press records, pennies per pound, that later became as rare as hen's teeth."

It was extraordinary. Most people accept or reject new sounds near-instantly, merely on a gut feeling. What Moore was describing was a lengthy process of deep immersion in all aspects of a musical form. There's a long history of Caucasian musicians appropriating African-American music, taking what's hot among the minority populace then serving it up to the mainstream as something exotic: this was something very different. Jazz, by the late eighties, still had a critical cachet but had lost much of the mainstream appeal it ever possessed, while its most electrifying exponents were straying ever further from popular tastes. Moore went there anyway and, moreover, devoted himself to it with an all-encompassing fervour.

As in 1988, Moore's respect for the music meant there would be no embarrassingly crass borrowings tacked onto standard rock/punk/pop tunes (no 'D'yer Mak'er'/'The Crunge' here). His friendship with improvisational drummer Tom Surgal led to an earnest encounter with William Hooker, an exponent of free jazz and boundlessly energetic iconoclast. *Shamballa*, released in 1994, documented their dual performance and served as Moore's coming-out party as a free-improvising musician.

Thurston's discography began to burgeon with records recorded in free improv settings. At a time in his career when he could have luxuriated in top dog status — playing only with the rich, the famous, or artists who deferred to him — he chose instead to seek out teachers, to become a student and willingly serve out a new apprenticeship with individuals who might challenge him, or help him grow. He would play with everyone from Daniel Carter to Evan Parker; from Wally Shoup or Joe McPhee to Nolan Green's The Grassy Knoll. He would appear with the London Musicians' Collective, a force in the European improvisational music scene, indicating his desire to experiment with other aspects of avant-garde music. Moore's vocabulary would grow beyond his roots in punk rock to incorporate a wealth of musical languages.

The wider context was the state of rock in the mid-nineties. The hope that Nirvana's rise would open the door for the more original extremes of the underground proved unfounded; while edgier bands were being dropped from their labels, the charts were dominated by reheated seventies nostalgia dressed up in grunge fashion. Many felt that the things they had loved about the underground — its imagination, its diverse takes on rock'n'roll, the tight social connection between performer and audience — had been sacrificed.

Thurston Moore himself hit his 40th birthday in 1998. After nearly two decades in music, his sound had been whittled to a unique tone recognisable amidst even the most violent storms of electronic spit and squall. Many musicians simply didn't have the imagination, or the education, required to continue to grow. Moore, however, fortified by his appetite for creativity in all its forms, began what would be the most productive period of his life, lasting all the way to the present day.

Having made nearly 40 appearances on records outside of Sonic Youth in the 14 years from 1981–94, Moore would manage over 150 in the 14 years that followed; there would be nearly 100 more in the period extending from 2008 to the present day. The expansion of his discography wasn't just an indication that he was writing and releasing more; it reflected entirely new layers of activity, whether that meant in-studio improvisations, live sets, remixes, experiments conducted through the post/over email, guest appearances, film soundtracks or collaborations with visual artists or filmmakers. Moore was not rejecting the musical confines of Sonic Youth (which continued as a creative unit until its final shows in November 2011); his path from here on in was a case of more, *more*, not either/or.

His work developed along numerous axes. Moore's willingness to pay tribute to favored artists, his penchant for forming on-off bands and his increasing status as a musician, all coalesced in the recording of songs by The Beatles for the film *Backbeat* and The Stooges for *Velvet Goldmine*. Alongside these, he contributed solo work to the soundtracks of *Score* and *Bully*, supported filmmaker (and close friend) Richard Kern's projects in the 2000s, and artist James Nares' film, *Street*.

In the late eighties, Sonic Youth examined how their sound might work alongside hip hop and drum machines. In the late nineties, Moore reacted to the rise of electronica by exploring how his guitar might fit within its new context. Improvising alongside electronics – whether Phil X. Milstein's tape machines or Christian Marclay's turntables – was one facet of this activity; the other was the incorporation of Moore's work into compositions by artists like DJ Spooky or Black Pig Liberation Front, who approached from within DJ culture rather than the experimental sound scene. Instead of being scared of the possibilities, Moore committed his work to others, curious as to what might emerge when people rewired and reworked it. He was also an active participant in an invented scene, NeMocore, in which the rules were no drums and no acoustic instruments – electronics only.

The *Root* project of 1998 straddled his interest in electronica and his desire to engage with other creative artforms. Moore contributed a series of brief solo guitar pieces which were then distributed to a range of musicians and visual artists, allowing the simultaneous creation of a remix record, an art-gallery show and an accompanying artwork brochure. Within this component of the discography, one also finds the *TM/MF* project with Marco Fusinato, musical contributions accompanying Georganne Deen's poetry readings on *Season Of The Western Witch* and a score for the London Sinfonietta, created at the invitation of artist Christian Marclay.

By 2000, Moore was a recognised elder statesman. Via his sincere and constantly evolving tastes, he had successfully transitioned from the luminary of a scene that arose in the eighties to a patron and supporter of a plethora of new musical genres. It was quite a feat to avoid being pigeonholed or genre-tagged, to instead carry sufficient credibility for the mainstream to respect what he had to say about obscure new artists. In a way, this kind of cultural hybrid was reflected in Moore's own life: having moved with his family to Northampton, Massachusetts, he ping-ponged between an apartment in New York, nationwide tours and appearances abroad, while also becoming a catalyst for the local scene at art spaces and venues like The Flywheel in Easthampton.

Just as Moore had reacted to the nineties by seeking renewal beyond rock music, a new underground had developed which was a step or two removed from rock'n'roll. This community adopted a number of practices – large numbers of label compilations, a reliance on a recognised network of underground venues and supporters in order to stage gigs across the country – which were familiar to Moore from the eighties' underground. He continued to provide patronage to underground labels, often purchasing their entire catalogue at a single visit to provide funds for their future releases. And as the musical focus changed, he changed with it. 'The band' as the centre of activities gave way to the freewheeling openness of sharing stages and releases with guests and friends. Moore's name would increasingly appear alongside those of numerous other musicians or under a plethora of one-off band names, adopted for particular collaborations or else simply on a whim. The catastrophe inflicted on the music industry by downloading and mass theft demolished the opportunity for the majority of musicians to gain support from a label, or even to make a living from music. DIY became both an aesthetic choice and, simultaneously, a necessity. The direction of the underground changed fundamentally, as an indie label meant relatively little support and progress to a major became near-impossible. The arrival of CD-Rs supplemented (but never replaced) the underground's ongoing focus on cassettes, so many bands began to document nearly everything they did – not just for private archives, but in order to have material to sell on the road or online, or to trade with other artists and labels. It made sense now for small labels to release only as many copies of a record as they could guarantee would sell out.

One result of this was that, in the mid-2000s, recordings of the performances and temporary line-ups in and around Thurston Moore's home in Northampton became a major new component of his discography. There was Nipple Creek, Dapper and Peeper, his guitar duos, The Bark Haze and Northampton Wools (with Andrew MacGregor and Bill Nace respectively), and not least, the resurrection of the Mirror/Dash duo with his wife, Kim Gordon. Some discs – such as *Kumpiny Night*, taken from a January 2007 festival – recorded a one-off event as a souvenir for those who were in attendance. As the Internet made music increasingly impersonal this kind of local activity restored a sense of individual uniqueness that bordered on folk art, at a time when music was increasingly seen as merely data. Moore would continue to experiment not just with his musical surroundings, but with his own art. For a spell in 2010–11, his fascination with the long history of the UK's underground folk scene led to a flurry of records documenting his accomplished ability on acoustic guitar, alongside collaborations with Michael Chapman and John Russell. Similarly, his longtime devotion to poetry made him a regular at Naropa University's Jack Kerouac School of Disembodied Poetics, his work anthologised in various independently published volumes and, since 2013, on records released by Fast Speaking Music. In 2014, in a long overdue move, Moore's well-documented interest in black metal led him to collaborate on an album in that genre as a member of Twilight.

It has become a cliché to speak of Moore as 'youthful', though the description is entirely apt when referring to the energy he exhibits. He has forged a unique path that distinguishes his entire life in art; while many stars seek youthfulness via airbrushing, skin-tucking, gym, diet and chemicals, Moore found his answer lay in creativity itself. It's his boundless enthusiasm for new discovery that makes him the eternal teenager of legend. Meanwhile, his support for younger musicians and willingness to give his energy selflessly are exemplary; their impact cannot be overestimated.

When contemplating how to approach Thurston Moore's discography, a selective oral history seemed the closest to a definitive medium, as it best reflects his relentless focus on collaboration. Moore readily cedes the spotlight to others, leaving his star power outside the room. He has embraced an ego-less desire to learn from and interact with his peers, taking pleasure from a wider hum of ideas rather than seeking to dominate the musical conversation. Working out where he can buoy up his fellow performers; when it's time to lead and when to follow.

A biographical study, isolating Moore entirely, seemed inappropriate when the music under consideration is an expression of what creative individuals can unleash together in unison. The voices of those who shared these moments with Moore will also walk the reader through the music that they brought into being (brief biographies of each participant are provided for reference in the 'Contributors' section). William Hooker gifted me with a dictum to keep in mind as I worked: "Don't get enamoured." *We Sing A New Language* is not intended as a hagiography. It was, however, forged in a spirit of deep affection and admiration for a mind able to avoid the sad path of the typical rock star. That which raises a rock star to prominence may also become a millstone around the neck; everything thereafter is seen in comparison to the commercial or critical high point that put them there in the first place. In the same way that sportspeople pass their peak by 30, every rock star faces the question: 'What comes next?' Dissipation is a common answer. The music fades to repetitive, pale shades of past glories; the artist pouts and hip-thrusts all the way down to the nostalgia circuit, the reformation jaunt, the greatest hits tour. Now far from the cutting edge, they snatch at the new *zeitgeist* in the hope it will pull them along in its wake. Some disappear into mansions; others are never off the red-carpet circuit. Many spend years trying to recall what motivated them to play before they found fame; for others, fame is the only answer they have. Thurston Moore, by contrast, has never granted any critic the licence to use that dreaded cliché about 'a return to form'. His work has never stood still. Throughout the 160 interviews making up this oral history, the word that recurred the most was 'enthusiasm'. His reason for being a musician was always to learn, to create, to indulge an unquenchable thirst for music. He's a 'lifer'; music is not merely what he does, it's who he *is*. Sonic Youth's success seemed to whet the appetite for performing and recording; Moore used success as a chance to reach out to the world, to discover more, to play more. The result is a discography that continually refreshes and reinvents itself; where surprise is not just occasionally possible but consistent and inevitable.

Failure To Thrive
The Coachmen
(New Alliance Records, recorded 1980/
released 1988)

J.D. King: At the time I was living in Providence, Rhode Island. I'd graduated from art school and over Christmastime, December '76, I was home in Connecticut and went to a record store in New Haven. I was going through the Velvet Underground bin and this kid pops up next to me. We start talking about The Velvet Underground and he's really into this stuff that's going on in New York – he was telling me about The Ramones. We swapped addresses and that's how Thurston and I started corresponding. I started a little band, mostly with Rhode Island School of Design students plus one Brown grad. A few of us moved to New York in September 1977 and my ambition was to either be a cartoonist or get a band going. So I contacted Thurston and asked whether he wanted to come down and jam. We recorded some songs on a cassette one afternoon,

J.D. King, Bob Pullin, Dave Keay and Thurston on the roof of 85 South St, c.1979.
Credit – Elodie Lauten

11

including 'Rumble' – I think it's the first song Thurston was ever on – and we became The Coachmen.

A few of us got a loft downtown at 85 South Street, just the other side of the World Trade Center, the tip of Manhattan – it was about $400 a month, we split that three-four ways. Where we lived downtown was so far off the beaten path, we had to walk almost to Chinatown to get to a supermarket. For a lot of meals we just went to local coffee shops to get sandwiches or sodas. Our building had been a warehouse and never should have been used for housing. The floors were just boards running one way, then a space of a few inches, then boards below that – there was no insulation between the floors. If the toilet in the loft above overflowed then it'd flow through your loft, across your floor and down through the loft below, and the one below that. No sound insulation. North of us you got into what's now called Tribeca and above that was SoHo; an art scene. The manufacturing was moving out of SoHo. I remember graffiti in a men's room: 'SoHo Sucks. Bring Back the Trucks.'

Michael Gira: Watch the movie *Taxi Driver* and you might get a sense of what New York was like then. The city was in a state of decline, which meant cheap rents and culturally it was quite vital – there was a lot of great art being made and music was closely associated with that. It was very difficult to survive, but the cheap rent was a plus and there were opportunities if you were headstrong and had, first and foremost, some talent.

David Keay: The subway cars, and walls everywhere, were covered in graffiti. Salsa blasted from cars, bodegas and tenement windows. Mentally ill people accosted you with zany observations and requests for money. You might get a light bulb thrown at you, or garbage dumped on you, or just get called an asshole when you passed someone on the street because they didn't like your hair, or your jacket, or the way you walked. Nobody went west of Ninth Avenue or east of Avenue A.

J.D. King: Thurston was just a kid living in Bethel with no one to play with. He was bored, I remember him telling me that all anybody wanted to play there was Doobie Brothers songs. We were an outlet for him. He probably would have liked something more straight-ahead punk but it was still a band and we got to play out. Thurston would come down on weekends. I was 26, he was 19. At the beginning it was all these college guys, so it was cool having an official teenager. When Thurston got his apartment, late '78 or so, East 13th Street between A and B, I visited him and remember thinking it was a scary block.

John Miller, our original bassist, left for CalArts, so I recruited Bob Pullen – he'd never played before. The drummer, Danny Walworth, had never played before. Danny quit, so we got Dave Keay. Thurston and I were just starting out on guitar. It really was that punk ethos of if you want to play, then just pick up an instrument.

David Keay: The Coachmen were tall, shy, awkward-looking guys exuding sincerity and vulnerability. The chords, chord changes and guitar interplay were beautiful and inventive. The rhythm guitar rocked and swung, the leads were subtle and delicate, the bass parts wonderfully complementary – my new favourite group. At the end of the night, I introduced myself to John and Thurston while they were packing up. John told me that their drummer, Danny, was leaving and we exchanged phone numbers. No more than a week later, J.D. called and I was a Coachman!

We practised maybe twice a week and gigged maybe an average of once every two or three weeks. I was usually the first to arrive. We'd play for two or three hours and then hang out and talk for a while, perusing J.D.'s record collection, which he kept in fruit crates on the floor. He had all the records in thick plastic protection sleeves and he never broke open the sealed plastic on gatefold or double albums. "Weren't you ever curious to see the inside of this?" Thurston once asked, holding up a Paul McCartney album.

Gigs at clubs like CBGB and Max's Kansas City often had us randomly billed with some very uncomplementary bands with far more of an affinity with Kiss than The Clash, let alone DNA. There was no particular camaraderie among unknown, struggling bands, and once a band finished its set they immediately packed up and split. If an amp or drum head broke, guys in other bands were sometimes reluctant to help you out. It was an environment where a bunch of 35-year-olds in black leather jackets might tap you on the shoulder and say, "We're Magic Smoke, and we just got off a tour opening for The Psychedelic Furs, man. We're not on the bill tonight, but mind if we get up and play your shit for a few numbers?"

Jack Rabid: Even all those CBGB bands, in their early days, were living out of each other's pockets. No one thought it was an odd bill when Talking Heads opened for The Ramones a half-dozen times, but a couple years later their crowds hated each other. People compartmentalise everything, it was much more healthy when people felt anything new and original could fit together in the underground.

J.D. King: We played Max's Kansas City once. We played Tier Three once. We had some bookings at CBGB but it was a real chore – you'd have to call, get a busy signal, call, get a busy signal, over and over. Then you'd get through to this guy Charlie: "Hi, I'm from The Coachmen, we'd like a booking…" "Call next week." *Click.* When we played there we often got booked with bands we had nothing in common with.

The best gigs we had were at an art space called A's in the Lower East Side. It was an art crowd, people drank and danced. We'd gotten better, more experimental, noisier, a good rhythm section – we'd get a loft full of people dancing. We played there New Year's Eve '79–'80; we were playing as New Year struck. That was the happiest time. Once, at Jenny Holzer's loft, we played with Glenn Branca's band, The Static, the first time Glenn heard Thurston play. Also there was a place called The Botany Talkhouse – I don't know what it was by day, it was in the floral district, it was a rock club at weekends. We played there a couple of times with Flux, Lee Ranaldo's band, the first time Thurston and Lee met.

David Keay: A Space – run by Arlene Schloss – where art wasn't a dirty word, where poets, performance artists, comedians and groups of all kinds performed. The audience was appreciative and open to anything.

J.D. King: There were no stage antics with The Coachmen: Thurston just strumming away, none of us jumping around like Peter Townshend. We just wore whatever we wore – no rock'n'roll outfits, just presentable… I remember trying to get Thurston to sing, handing him the microphone, but he'd just move his mouth and not make any sound. I remember the first time he came to New York to visit us, he had something he'd written called 'Monkeys From Hell', a little punk-rock song we never played or recorded. But I could tell he had a natural ability, when we were working on material – if I came up with a chord pattern he'd come up with a complementary lead. He had a good, supple wrist for strumming.

David Keay: J.D. was the main songwriter, so 'Thurston's Song' was just that, an exception. It was a breezy, joyful, soulful tune that – maybe with a horn section – could have been a smash for Otis Redding or Archie Bell & The Drells. "Thurston's getting cocky," remarked Bob one day, with a smile.

I doubt Thurston was in standard tuning for any of the songs but the sonic aggression to come would have been completely alien.

J.D. King: *Failure To Thrive* was recorded at a little studio in midtown, a low-end professional studio on two-track. The guys doing the recording were just 'guys', they had long hair and beards – tech guys, not punks. It was our demo tape and it would never have been released if Thurston hadn't gone on to fame and fortune. It was released as a historical article when we'd been broken up for eight years – a pleasant surprise. To put out a seven-inch took a certain amount of money and we just didn't have it.

David Keay: I would estimate the cost of releasing your own record, in relation to the average working-class salary in 1980, as pretty similar to today. It was, and is, pretty doable, but not if everyone involved is a skint kid with a part-time job. Bob was doing graphic work for magazines and J.D. sketched a living as an illustrator. Thurston at some point was working at Todd Jorgenson's Copy Shop. I got a part-time job at a bookstore, working only 20 hours a week, surviving on that for five or six years; buying records, going to the movies, seeing bands. I just couldn't afford drinks in clubs, which necessitated getting a big head start on the cheap beforehand and then repeatedly exiting for trips to the nearest deli, followed by chugging on doorsteps.

Martin Bisi: There wasn't a big recorded canon of alternative music – everything before my era, the seventies, all of that was big-budget, big-production stuff. There wasn't a lot of multi-track, 16-24-track recording of what you'd call 'alternative', that wasn't major-label funded. Literally, when I started in 1981 multi-track recording had been around six years and was hugely expensive. Even at that time, bands still tended not to go into the studio unless a label was present. People had been doing recordings with two microphones on a cassette but there wasn't much DIY until this era. The big revolution was easy multi-tracking, where you'd be able to throw stuff down as you felt it. The equipment just started to turn over in 1980–1982. And there was no canon of what to refer to sonically, or even musically; not a sense of how these bands should sound and what should happen in a recording studio. There was no culture of recording this kind of stuff. Also, there weren't really any avenues for doing much with the recording unless there was a label. So without a label, bands just didn't go into studios – there was no reason to.

Byron Coley: People's ears were tuned to something that was much more polished. So I had a lot of live tapes, I'd play them for people and they'd say, "It sounds great, but it's just not good enough to be on record." People thought that, to be on record things had to be professionally recorded, otherwise it was a bootleg regardless of how it was marketed. It required a sea change for people to appreciate that. Eventually, people came to like records that didn't sound quite so pro, people got used to it, they felt like they'd cracked the code and the secret messages had become clear to them.

J.D. King: The first time we played out was winter '78; the last time was August 1980 at an art gallery called White Columns. At that point my life was starting to change – I had a new girlfriend and I was moving out of the loft. The band just wasn't going anywhere. I was putting a lot of work into it: finding the bookings, finding the car to get the gear to the show; since I lived at the loft it was up to me to move all the equipment back upstairs.

David Keay: With the likes of the New Romantics and neo-ska bands dominating the press's attention, the lack of kudos or offers, and a new breed of indie rockers on the horizon – like The Minutemen or The Meatmen, whom only Thurston would have related to or concerned himself with – we all understood when John decided to fold The Coachmen.

J.D. King: That last gig though, Thurston had just been starting a new band that included him, Kim Gordon and Ann DeMarinis…

Just Another Asshole
'Fucking Youth Of Today'
Thurston Moore (no label, 1981)

Jack Rabid: New York was really broke at the time… people were moving there to live on rice, beans and air, and spend all their time in this creative scene. It was really a cross–pollination. The primary feature of that scene was that the music piece was considered an art attack, so it inspired people who were in fact artists, not musicians, to take a hand at it.

Lee Ranaldo: *Just Another Asshole* was a magazine that Glenn Branca and his partner, Barbara Ess, were doing. Every issue was a different format.

One issue was a paperback book by a whole bunch of people – I had a story in that one. I think the LP was Glenn's idea; to ask however many artists to do audio pieces – maximum 45 seconds long. Glenn and Barbara organised it and everyone they knew was invited so it was a real reflection of the community at the time; in the same way that *No New York* defined one person's view of the no-wave community, *Just Another Asshole* encapsulated what Glenn and Barbara saw as their community at the time. All three of us – Thurston, Kim and I – contributed to it. I recorded a piece called 'Shift', Thurston's was 'Fucking Youth Of Today' and Kim's was 'Working Youth' – the titles of each of those cuts were in the lyrics of the song, 'I Dreamed I Dream', that Kim and I sang together on the first Sonic Youth record.

Rhys Chatham: The way ideas got transferred was we all moved into the same neighbourhoods. It was the same in the fifties; where society went to dream was Greenwich Village, that's where my parents met, you had the beatniks, then that moved in the sixties to this area called SoHo. So in this 20-block radius you had choreographers, musicians, dancers, filmmakers. By the mid-seventies it had gotten expensive there, so everyone was living in either the East Village, SoHo or Tribeca. Back then in the East Village my apartment was $60 a month. Nobody had to pay a high rent so you could support yourself by doing your waitress gig, your bartender gig; then nobody needed to get up at nine in the morning. That's why performances didn't even start until 10 p.m. at CBGB. Your partner could say to you at 11 at night, "What do you feel like doing tonight?" So you'd see an Yvonne Rainer performance then walk down to the Puerto Rican breakfast place, and Steve Reich and Philip Glass would be there talking about it over coffee. Someone else would do a performance and you'd all end up at this bar called Puffy's and everyone would be talking about it.

Noise Fest
'Untitled'
Sonic Youth (ZG Music, 1982)

Wharton Tiers: It was the spell when Max's and CBGB were no longer the satellite places – people were starting to set up their own kinds of shows.

Noise Fest was a great time – it pulled together a lot of people from that art/music scene in addition to some of the earlier punk stuff. I had friends playing almost every night.

Josh Baer: I personally underwrote Noise Fest. I wanted to get my dollars back from selling beer but the port authority police, my landlord, closed that down. Cover charge was maybe $4 and that went to the performers. A lot of people helped with all the labour; Kim and Thurston did the promoting; the staff was me and, part-time, Anne DeMarinis. It was a non-stop party that was so word of mouth even John Belushi showed up one night… four hours too early. My girlfriend at the time, Rosetta Brooks, had a magazine in London, *ZG*, and as we had recorded all the music we edited a tape.

Lee Ranaldo: Ten nights across the summer of 1981, a very hot summer, in this gallery space at the western edge of SoHo. It was Thurston's idea; wanting to showcase the broad crowd of people who were doing things downtown. Kim and Barbara Ess curated an art show to go in White Columns during Noise Fest.

White Columns was all the way at the west end of Spring Street, on one of the last blocks before the river, very desolate and deserted. It had about a 100- to 150-capacity and had big glass windows all along Spring Street. The audience really was the community. Three or four acts a night plus the artists in the art show – everyone turned out. Most people were there every night, it really solidified this community. As for the name 'Noise Fest', the owner of this fancy punk disco called Hurrahs was asked why he wasn't booking New York bands and he said, "There's not much good stuff and all the rest is just noise." Something like that. Thurston chose to embrace the term and call it the Noise Fest as a fuck-you, punk two fingers to the guy at Hurrahs. Everybody came out. There was this sense of 'Here's our community – who are we? How are we? Where are we?' Everyone from quirky rock bands like Sonic Youth or V-Effect to the art-music of Jeff Lohn, Glenn Branca and Rhys Chatham. Dan Graham was in full effect; Borbetomagus was there. It included the slightly older crowd who had been known and written about a bit, like the no-wave acts, and then the young upstarts like me, David Linton, Thurston, Kim.

I played there with Glenn; Thurston and Kim played with a nascent Sonic Youth. David Linton and I performed together as a duo, Avoidance

18

Behavior – we had this romantic notion at the time that we'd be a sort of radical New York update of Simon & Garfunkel, not in terms of the songs or the singing but just by being a duo, and we started recording all these tracks and took all these evocative pictures on the old rundown Westside Highway at sunset which could have been a cover for a Simon & Garfunkel LP, except we were doing all this weird tape-loop stuff. That Avoidance Behavior show: first I played solo guitar and I had my guitar strung with these piano wires that Glenn Branca was using at the time in his early symphonies; David was back at the soundboard doing a Brian Eno-style tape loop and feeding the loop of the guitar back into the mix. Then we switched and David played drums while I did the loop of the drums at the soundboard. Then, the third part was that we played the two loop tapes together – a drum loop with a guitar loop, with neither of us on-stage.

It was during those nights... I was talking with Kim and it came up that David and I had dropped out of Plus Instruments to stay in New York and she said, "You should try and play with Thurston, I think you guys would play really well together." And almost the day after the Noise Fest ended, Thurston, Kim and I rehearsed together in the White Columns space...

Symphony No.1 (Tonal Plexus)
Glenn Branca
(ROIR, 1983)

Michael Gira: I saw Glenn Branca perform several times and that, to me, was the pinnacle of what music could achieve – the ecstasy of it, so transcendent.

He asked every punk rocker in town to play in his band; I wasn't chosen specially, so I played in just one performance and I recall it being a tortuous affair, because he'd written out these scores which were just numbers: "Hit this string so many times, then hit this string so many times," and it was really hard to follow for someone with no musical training. And he was playing his staircase instruments that he'd built which were two by fours with a pick-up on, a bridge, then six strings strung across, and each string would be just one note that you could play with chopsticks, like a dulcimer, and it would resonate. I was so impressed, that's someone with a will to power in the good old sense. He had an instrument maker build these beautiful keyboard instruments shaped like a very long grand piano. So when the three keyboard players pressed on a key, a fly wheel that was spinning all the time would gently graze the string and it would make overtones. I don't think it had the full octave range of a piano but certainly three or four octaves, and when these instruments were played they sounded like the music of the spheres. Then he had the bass, a couple of guitars, two or three of us doing the staircase dulcimer instruments, then a drummer.

We went to rehearsals – it wasn't enough, I remember that! – then we went to this prestigious hall, the Brooklyn Academy of Music, the first time I'd ever been in such a place. His approach was anathema to classical music at the time, I imagine it was mainly other musicians and artists in the room, but it was full. Glenn conducts, waves his arms up and down for dynamics – he's counting with the drummer and guitarist – conducting very dramatically, I must say. I didn't look up, I was just so terrified. To me he was a paradigm of sorts because he's so uncompromising and such a visionary. Searching for an epiphany in sound, that's rare; he's really looking for the moment where your mind explodes with light and people who reach for that are few and far between.

Wharton Tiers: Glenn called me up, saying, "I'm doing this symphony and I know you play all these different things, so I want you to be a part of it." Thurston had to play these steel drums, like a barrel, that he would whack with a two-by-four and Jim Fouratt, who was booking a lot of music at the time, was sitting right in front of the drum and his eyes, when Thurston first hit it, they shot up! I'll never forget. It must be such an extreme sound to be sitting directly in front of that.

Glenn was really good at finding these alternative venues to get his stuff out there – this was at the Performing Garage in SoHo, which was pretty much a garage with some bleachers, a big square space. All that concrete gives you a great swirl of sound – if you're doing instrumental music it works to your advantage.

Glenn Branca: Mike's mention of the power of my music, I would assume, came from the way I used various tunings and stringings that created a gigantic sound that even I had not expected to hear. My work had always been experimental and, when I came up with this particular sound, I was hooked and wanted to see how far I could take it.

20

The effect and experience of this sound was what I would eventually refer to as 'acoustic phenomena', due to the fact that, depending on the acoustics of the room, sometimes you could hear sounds like choirs, even orchestras playing, all at the same time in a kind of interpenetrating harmony that can't really be described. But I did know that this sound was being created by close harmonies at rock volumes.

There was a transition in my music from the rock song bands to the symphonies. In between came a number of one-off instrumental pieces between 1979 and early 1981. This band of four guitars, bass and drums was eventually referred to as The Ascension Band. We did a lot of touring in both the States and Europe. The idea of an even larger band, a virtual orchestra, came to mind on a flight home from one of these tours. It came into my head to call it a symphony, thinking in terms of a full evening show instead of just a set of separate pieces.

For *Symphony No. 1* I expanded the size of the group to 16 musicians. I added three horns and a sax as well as a piano and an organ, a variety of percussion instruments (in one case a giant oil drum played with a two-by-four), and various guitar stringings and tunings, including a couple guitars that were strung with untempered steel wire from a hardware store. I used to hunt down every used guitar store in Manhattan and Brooklyn, looking for cheap old guitars.

Symphony No. 2 (The Peak Of The Sacred)
Glenn Branca
(Atavistic, recorded 1982/released 1992)

Glenn Branca: In this case there were 12 musicians, but I was also using pre-recorded tape through a quadraphonic PA system. I used the tape because there were some sounds that I wanted that couldn't have been played live and had been specifically written for the quad set-up. The live instrumentation was mostly 'mallet guitars' or 'tabletop guitars', most of which were built out of cheap materials and cheap guitars. All of them were played with sticks like a dulcimer. But my design included a third bridge in the middle that allowed the pick-up to hear only the sympathetic vibration on one side of the string, thus giving a very resonant, sustained sound. These were also sometimes used with slide bars to get a 'harmonics guitar' sound. The only instrument that was played like a conventional guitar was the bass.

Symphony No.3 (Gloria)
Glenn Branca
(Neutral, 1983)

Glenn Branca: *Symphony No. 3* was, yet again, entirely different. There were no guitars of any kind in this one, with the exception of a bass. This piece was commissioned by the Brooklyn Academy of Music. It was also the first time I ever got any kind of grant. It was $5,000 specifically to build instruments. I designed six electric harpsichords, all using the same third bridge as the mallet guitars. The keyboards were built by David Quinlan for the entirety of the grant money and more. He actually gave me an amazing deal. The reason I needed these was because I was now using a harmonics series tuning system that required as many as 64 notes to the octave in the high range. None of the intervals are the same in the harmonic series. I also got a clavichord, an instrument that can be tuned one string at a time, and designed a retrofitted organ as well, built by Perry Brandston, that could be tuned to the system and a new large mallet guitar. In those days, 1982, the only electronic instrument that could be tuned in this way was a Kurtzweil [synthesizer] that went for $50,000 just for one.

In this piece Thurston was playing a keyboard and Lee was mainly on the mallet guitar. They had to read off of primitive parts with the number of the harmonic that was marked on the key or beside the strings – and then the number of beats written above each note. Although John Rockwell of *The New York Times* trashed it, we still sold out the Saturday show in the freezing, pouring rain to a great audience. Later, Rockwell retracted his comments about the music when the record came out.

I might as well mention the fourth symphony since Thurston was in that one too. I was still using the harmonic series tuning system, so the instruments were much the same except for the addition of two conventional guitars played by Lee and Thurston. Although they played mainly open strings tuned to the intervals of the series. *Symphony No. 4* was only ever heard in Europe. We did 20 shows in 13 cities in a month. There were 13 musicians and two roadies with a truck full of amps and large heavy keyboards. It was the most monstrous thing I've ever done. While I was writing it I was also booking all of the gigs, hotels and trains with the help of Axel Gross, who luckily spoke three languages fluently.

To give you some idea of how ridiculous this was, Lee and Thurston volunteered to do all of the tuning for each show. Tuning this many instruments to this microtonal system was a horror. At that time, in 1983, the best we could do was a sine wave generator. There were no tuning machines. So they had to set the thing to the right frequency then tune each string by ear, listening to the beating of the harmonics. It took them around three hours before every show. They were incredible, never a complaint and the tunings were perfect.

One of the gigs was in Amsterdam for Dutch TV. We were on the bill with a Dutch orchestra playing Webern. After we played, the Dutch musicians refused to go on because they claimed we were playing out of tune. Ironically, we were playing in perfect just intonation – meaning we were more in tune than they were. It was a scandal in the press the next day. Fuck 'em.

Lee Ranaldo: What we wanted out of a rock band was the beauty and the grandeur of what Glenn was doing – especially with the four-guitar line-up I was involved in with him – and what those no-wave bands were doing, deconstructing rock to the maximum like DNA or Mars. Add in Talking Heads' art-rock, the ferocity of Television or Patti Smith or The Voidoids, the repetitiveness of The Ramones. It was a vision of what a rock band could be that incorporated all of this stuff; side by side with Steve Reich and Philip Glass. The descriptive boundaries between the 'new music' crowd – as exemplified by Glenn, Rhys Chatham, Steve and Philip, La Monte Young, Charlemagne Palestine – were much smaller, there was a lot more overlap; everyone was young and just starting out so nothing was canonised; you'd go and listen to minimalist electric guitar music one night and Steve Reich's 'Drumming' the next. It was an enterprise we entered with almost more of a conceptual mindset – I mean it was very immediate, it wasn't all concepts, but we had a lot more information behind us, being 23 to 26 years old and deciding to start a rock band. It was a different thing than if we'd all been 18; we had different ammo in our arsenal.

Rhys Chatham: One time, I was living over on East 3rd Street and was sat out on the street, drinking a beer, and Sonic Youth went by. I said hi – they were off to play at the Pyramid Club. I said, "Great, you guys are doing really well!" Thurston, joking around, quipped, "You and Glenn had your turn – now it's our turn!" We all busted out laughing. We were all family. Thurston performed with me a couple of times to help me out. I did *Guitar Trio* in various venues and sometimes a regular member couldn't do it, so I'd ask Thurston and Kim if they could make it. They would come when I needed a guitarist – not permanent members but good friends, and there when I needed a substitute. I just taught them the piece the way I did everyone else and it's like riding a bike, you don't forget.

'Leaving'/'One Night Stand'
Even Worse
(Autonomy Records, recorded 1982/released 1988)

Jack Rabid: Post-punk was much more exciting to people after the first wave of punk bands waned – by which I mean got too popular to play in little clubs. Talking Heads, The Ramones, Blondie – none of them were playing clubs after '78. By summer of 1980 Television were gone, The Dead Boys were always breaking up, all The Heartbreakers' shows were: "We've broken up but we'll play one more time." Labels weren't interested because punk rock had died – in their opinion. We'd get derisive press from *The New York Daily News*; 'What are these people still doing here in 1981? Punk rock's gone. Didn't anyone tell them?' Which is ironic, looking back. The Stimulators and Bad Brains were the two big bands; The Mad were the third one; that was our post-CBGB punk scene. I graduated high school in June '80 and we started Even Worse the month before; David Stein, my best friend, plus two New Yorkers, Nick Marden and John Pouridas. We played our first gig May 2, 1980 at Tier 3. The bassist and guitarist shared an entire bottle of mescal, so got lost inside 20 seconds of the start of every song, meaning every song ended up about eight minutes long; total chaos.

That version of the band splintered after two exciting gigs with Bad Brains in December 26-27, 1980. The second Even Worse – me, Bobby Weeks, Eric Keil and Rebecca Korbet – had all the biggest gigs; six sell-outs at Max's Kansas City. Bad Brains gave us all their opening slots and their gear after gigs – on two occasions they literally finished then got back up on-stage and said, "Hey, we want you to stay and hear a couple songs by friends of ours, Even Worse, who are going to play for you and by the way they're playing next week, go see them." We played our last gig on March 27, 1982 opening for The Misfits. Version two of Even Worse pretty much walked out on me after the gig because they couldn't stand me anymore. I've always felt bad about that – they didn't want to play the first version of the band's songs anymore and I wasn't as sensitive to that as I should have been. They had their beefs but I was doing everything; I was booking all the gigs, doing all the publicity. And I decided I wanted to keep it together for reasons I don't understand when I look back at freshly-minted, 20-year-old me. But I didn't want to do the band exactly as it was because I didn't want to be this punk-rock band playing the hardcore scene.

The third Even Worse was hatched between me and Tim Sommer. I told him that if he got a bass then he could join the band, though I knew he couldn't play. I didn't think it mattered anymore. I just wanted to put out something that would piss off the hardcore kids. We went out hunting for a couple of guitar players and zeroed in on Thurston. He was a presence in this new emerging noise scene that seemed to be the heirs to no wave. I picked up a copy of *New York Rocker* where Thurston listed his favourite records and there was a Germs record in there, early Black Flag, a Crime single – I thought, 'This guy really knows his shit. Nobody has Crime records except for us!' So we approached Thurston at a gig at The Peppermint Lounge: "Have you ever played in a punk-rock band?" and he said, "No." So I asked him, "Would you like to?" "With Even Worse? I LOVE Even Worse! I get to play in Even Worse?"

Thurston fitted perfectly because Thurston was a goofball – in all the best ways. He kept us laughing all the time. Never remembering the songs – every rehearsal he'd fuck up every song we had in some way. It was kind of brilliant. We learnt to enjoy it and just say, "Actually, that's better, you just carry on. Do what you do!" The trouble was that Thurston was so busy that it became apparent that if we were ever going to play any kind of regular schedule then we needed a second guitar player. So Tim drafted in Steve Waxman. It was often hard to get Thurston to rehearsal but we managed because we used to rehearse a block from his house, in a tiny basement on Grand Street and Bowery, so we made it real easy on him.

We did a gig at Tramps where Steve Jones, the ex-Sex Pistol, came up and played with us. So we said to Thurston he'd need to leave the stage for two songs we'd written while he was away on tour. He said, sure. So, when we got to that point, Steve Waxman said, "Okay, Thurston, here's those two songs you don't know," Thurston replied, "I know them!" Steve argued, "You've never heard these songs, we only just wrote them," and Thurston just said, "No. I know them." So I interrupted: "Oh you do, do you? Hey Tim? Steve? Make sure you put your backs to Thurston so he can't see what chords you're playing!" I counted out, "Onetwothreefour!" Thurston comes in right on the first note with no idea what he's playing and just carried on all the way from beginning to end, both times. That's

25

the quintessential story of Thurston's time in Even Worse and we let him do it, because that's what made it fun in a scene I hated. It was all hilarious to him – and that rubs off in all the right ways.

The line-up lasted from spring '82 to fall '83. The hardcore scene had kicked most people out we admired and the Warhols and Jarmusches didn't want to be part of this kiddie scene. The underground sculptors and poets, the indie filmmakers and painters, they'd all disappeared. It was all slam-dancing and people dressing alike and acting violent while talking about how the scene was really important.

Thurston is the only guitarist on 'One Night Stand', the B-side, because I wanted to document how we were really trying to get abused by hardcore kids and they obliged. It's a song Thurston wrote; half of it is just him tuning and making this horrible racket, then the song itself is a minute and a half. The song starts off with people screaming obscenities at us, telling us how bad we are and how bad we suck. 'One Night Stand' is Thurston doing his version of hardcore, which is really fast and crazy; our singer, Kenny Tantrum, doing droll lyrics about his own sexual ineptitude and unreliability – it's a really funny song. They hated this noise we were making and I loved it. I'd yell, "Take your time, Thurston, tune another five minutes!" To me that was the only successful thing you could do inside the hardcore scene, basically telling those people that they'd ruined everything and to present a mind-fuck version of punk for them. Kenny was great at saying horrible things to the audience in this snide way. I'd sit there at my drums with my arms folded, smiling broadly. Kenny leapt out in the crowd once and got beaten up. When he got back on-stage he said, "I've just had a meeting with the New Jersey intelligentsia and may I say they carried themselves very well."

Body To Body, Job To Job
Swans
(Young God Records, recorded *c.*1982–85/ released 1990)

Michael Gira: I wasn't thinking about career – I just wanted to make something happen. So I gathered certain people around me. I learned how to play bass in a rudimentary way from the composer Rhys Chatham – he taught me how to play and in fact he gave me my first bass. On a humorous note, Rhys gave me his bass and I used it all the time. Eventually, I decided that the frets were bothersome so – probably under the influence of one substance or another – I got some pliers and pulled the frets out, then filled the holes with wood clay and sanded it down. Then, lo and behold, it turned out the bass was a loan and Rhys called me to say he was coming by to pick up his bass and I handed him this thing with no frets. He was furious – I'm sure the animosity is long gone and we've exchanged niceties on Facebook, but I haven't spoken to him since. The look on his face was priceless...

I started figuring out – I'm not sure you could call them songs, but 'things' that one might sing or scream to, then Jonathan Kane would add a rhythm; then I got another bass player. So we had two bass players but the other bass player kept rotating. And I had various rotating second drummers who would play metal and extra toms and things. The second bass player would activate these tape loops we had running on cassette in time with the rhythm. Anyway, one of them left; I had become friends with Thurston through my association with Kim, whom I had known at art school in Los Angeles, and I think we just had a few rehearsals then did some gigs.

There was no style involved. Thurston's tremendously musical and a very supportive friend, but the bass parts in that era might be a line that went '"pur-do-do-KAH – pur-do-do-KAH...' So one-two-THREE maybe would be the accent – while the other bass would play a chord that would emphasise that accent or the downbeat on these chords I devised which would be the octave, the note itself and a flattened fifth between it, which would make it 'the Devil's Note' basically. It adds dissonance and makes it a little more abrasive.

Neither one of us had regular steady jobs, so when we weren't working we would hang out and we used to play Pac-Man a lot at a local bar. Thurston and I used to go to the hardcore matinees all the time. He liked it much more than I did. I guess I was a punk rocker – I was in the LA punk scene and I was a devoted acolyte, I felt that was the music gist of the era and I was really involved in it and loved it. But when I started going to the hardcore shows, the sense of experimentation, the whole sense of expanding the palette, it was the opposite. Hardcore was shrinking. To me it was just a bunch of post-adolescent males who might as well have been football players. It was entertaining for a while and there were good groups here and there. Thurston liked it, I think he saw it as a sociological experiment.

Hard Rock
Michael Gira/ Lydia Lunch
(Ecstatic Peace!, 1984)

Don Fleming: Thurston put out his first Ecstatic Peace! cassette; one side was a fucked-up spoken-word piece by Michael Gira and the other side was Lydia Lunch doing a short story. I was living in Washington DC and had a cassette label. I was friends with Calvin Johnson, who had a cassette label in Olympia called K Records and had similar ideas. Well, he knew someone in New York who needed copies done of the *Hard Rock* tape so I ended up doing some. I was printing them up myself, I got them made, sent them back and I think that was [to] Thurston – but I had no idea who he was because he wasn't one of the people on the cassette, I just thought he was this guy with another cassette label.

Michael Gira, JG Thirlwell and Thurston dine at Catherine Ceresole's apartment, NYC, June 16, 1984.   *Credit – Catherine Ceresole*

Byron Coley: Thurston started sending me things when I was in LA doing a magazine called *Take It!* and we started corresponding around the time he was doing the *Killer* fanzine. In those days everything was correspondence based – anyone doing fanzines or records got up early and spent a few hours writing letters to everybody, you'd answer mail, send tapes, trade records. Even phone calls could be expensive, so everyone wrote and you expected it to take a long time to hear back. It was a simpler, more gentle time.

Originally he was only going to do Ecstatic Peace! as a cassette label, but at a certain point he realised certain things might be better on seven-inch. This stuff was cheap to do – for a time the economics were in our favour; what you could do on the cheap. Later, there were Ecstatic Peace! records I paid for entirely; it was a very permeable barrier between people who hung out together and knew each other and worked together – we'd just say, "Maybe this would be better on your label." It was kind of loosey-goosey.

Michael Gira: We recorded sitting on my bed with Lydia. I'd shown my stories to Glenn [Branca] and his then wife Barbara Ess and they were quite taken with them, which was encouraging but I'd never considered doing spoken word. I was writing quite a bit and showed them to Thurston – so I'm guessing he thought it was a good idea to record it...

That tale had to do with the kind of abjection I experienced in working for other people and I found that an entirely unacceptable proposition, to waste my time on earth being, essentially, a slave to someone else because I view time as the most valuable commodity that there is. A lot of that had to do with the inner sense of humiliation and anger at finding myself in that position and I made a baroque version of what I was experiencing as a wage slave. Specifically, I think that story had a lot to do with my inner turmoil at being inside that experience for so many years. I still feel that, though a lot of people have no choice, having to do something that does not fulfil you personally and that does not actualise yourself while on earth is a magnificent waste of one's existence. It's gotten much worse now there are computers and the Internet, which I view as even more mindless. Not that I don't partake sometimes, it's like a glass of arsenic-laced laudanum sitting there of which one can partake at any time – and it's easy to get sucked into it.

Jim Sclavunos, Lee Ranaldo, Thurston and Kim Gordon backstage at Danceteria, NYC, February 12, 1983.   *Credit – Catherine Ceresole*

In Limbo
Lydia Lunch
(Doublevision, 1984)

Lydia Lunch: Thurston and I saw each other for quite a long time before we came into contact. We would see each other on the subway and we only lived one block apart, but it wasn't until I had left New York in 1980 and gone to LA for two years, then London for two years, that I actually met Thurston. I'm really not sure how *In Limbo* came about. Thurston mentioned we auditioned him with a slow dance in a basement because I wanted to make one of the slowest records ever created and wanted him to play bass.

In Limbo was very different from *Queen Of Siam*, or from Teenage Jesus & The Jerks, or from 8 Eyed Spy. I'm always looking for a new language to express the same dilemma. That's the difference between me and

Sonic Youth – they've had a particular trajectory of sound and once they developed it they took it as far as it would go, while my work is a lot more schizophrenic. Working forever with the same group – that's brain death to me. I'm a conceptualist, I come with the idea then I decide who would be the appropriate collaborators, then I find out if they would have the time or the energy to do it. I never think, 'Who do I want to work with?' I think of the concept and then, 'Who does it ask for?'

Jim Sclavunos: On the *In Limbo* record I played sax, because I was invited in after Lydia had already put together a line-up that included Richard Edson on drums and Thurston on the bass. Lydia and I had explored the idea of extremely slow, heavy and dark sounds in her band Beirut Slump, in fact as far back as the Teenage Jesus song 'Baby Doll' we had a structure based on alternating very slow, non-metrical verse sections with very strict up-tempo, marching instrumental interjections. *In Limbo* was the next iteration of that idea. Lydia never said, "Play this line." All my own parts I came up with myself. The band came up with a basic structure and it would get elaborated on as we went along. We played at least one live gig doing the *In Limbo* material as well. I remember rooming with Thurston and him jumping up and down on the bed like a teenager, which I found charming.

Paul Smith: Edwin Pouncey wrote a piece for *Sounds* about Nick Cave and Lydia Lunch's *50 One Page Plays*; I thought it was something we at Doublevision could realise as a video. I tracked Lydia down to south London, but she had split up with Nick only the week before, so that idea died on the vine. But she did want to go back to New York and had no money for a flight. I asked my contacts at Rough Trade if a record by her would sell; they said it would. She literally had the two-inch multi-tracks for *In Limbo* under her bed. She went up to Sheffield to Cabaret Voltaire's Western Works studio and they mixed the tracks.

Doublevision bought her the air-ticket, she runs into Thurston on the street back in New York, mentions she has met me and at least I wasn't a total dickhead – a high compliment from Ms Lunch – so Thurston sends me a cassette of the nearly finished *Bad Moon Rising*. There were maybe two, then very rare and expensive, transatlantic phone calls with Lee Ranaldo who tended to look after the business side of Sonic Youth, then maybe a couple of letters: one for the contract, another sending them the test pressings.

Honeymoon In Red
Lydia Lunch
(Widowspeak Productions, 1987)

JG Thirlwell: At the time you don't think, 'Oh this is a scene,' you always have contemporaries you hang out with and collaborate with and there'll be other people doing things in the same or similar areas you're interested in. Sometimes you're coming out of similar places geographically or culturally, so you share some common ground – but it's something observed in retrospect. New York was the exact opposite of London. I lived in London from '78 to '83. London is very geographically dispersed and New York at that time was very East Village-centric. You could walk everywhere, it was 24 hours, while London stopped at midnight and then you still had to get across the entire city to get home.

Lydia Lunch: There are many artistic cycles either when a place is completely bankrupt or decrepit, or when a war has just happened or is about to happen. We could talk about Paris in the twenties, Germany in the early thirties, Chicago in the forties, Memphis in the fifties, Haight-Ashbury in the sixties, LA, New York and London in the late seventies, Berlin for a while in the eighties. Artistic movements – they're never movements at the time, they're just things that happen, usually coming together for economic reasons, and technology has blown that out of the water now. There are all these huge festivals people focus on going to now and they're connected by the Internet, which means there is no real centre or city that people seek out at this point as there once was. It's only a movement in retrospect; when you're there and doing it, you're just doing it – there's nothing more to it.

JG Thirlwell: When we came to do *Honeymoon In Red*, that was drawn from sessions that Lydia had started with The Birthday Party in '82 – they cut the initial tracks and it was never finished, but Lydia got the tapes back and decided she wanted it to be mixed and finished and she wanted me to do it. On one track we didn't have the multi-track so we had to use the rough mix from a quarter-track.

Lydia Lunch: I did *13:13* in LA and wrote *Adulterers Anonymous* then ran back to New York, I was taking *13:13* to London and The Birthday Party were playing – nobody was there of course, it was their first gig. I

32

immediately went up to Rowland S. Howard, he knew my work, and I told him I was moving to London immediately. The show with The Birthday Party was my first improvisational, illustrative word show. Rowland and I went on to do 10-minute intros for The Birthday Party then, after a two-year stint recording *Honeymoon In Red*, I went back to New York, started setting up spoken-word shows, met Thurston and he did my first spoken word show with me. I brought quite a few people to the spoken-word stage for the first time – Nick Cave, Vincent Gallo, Ken Stringfellow of The Posies – I'm the cattle-prodder. So, when I met him I asked him to go for a walk with me and I told him a horrible story, a made-up story – I write fiction very rarely, most of my stuff is true – and he just kept saying, "Oh my God, really? Oh I can't believe that, that's terrible." And I said, "Well, we're doing that as a show tomorrow night at a small café and you're doing it with me." It was un-mic'ed so it's like Chinese whispers and we're walking around, telling the story, and people are only hearing snatches of it. He played the straight man to my horrible story. Years later, I was going to be doing some shows and I invited Thurston and said, "Look, I'm doing some spoken word, why don't you get on the bill and open for me?" And he asked if he could use any collaborators – "Absolutely not, guitar and poetry, that's it." And it was fantastic!

The Crumb
Lydia Lunch/Thurston Moore
(Widowspeak Productions, 1988)

JG Thirlwell: *The Crumb*, that came about because there's a track on *Honeymoon In Red* called 'Dead In The Head' and it has this ending that's just repeating this riff that slows down. As we were mixing it I found that really hypnotic – I liked that, the feel of it, this lumbering thing. Really simple, really insistent, punishing. A chunk of rhythm. I said to Lydia that I'd like to turn that into a different piece as an extra track or something. That's when we enlisted Thurston – I wanted other stuff on top of it. So we asked Thurston to do some vocals – he had a bunch of writing with him, stuff he was working on.

Martin Bisi: The song 'The Crumb' was about a sick, criminal individual – for a lot of his early songs he takes on these evil personas, he doesn't try and humanise them, it's almost like a film, he just presents them flatly. I've always resented that people in film can explore characters without it being seen as a direct expression of themselves, but musicians are generally expected to always be just an honest expression of what they are. That angle worked well for Thurston, he was interested in the whole Manson insanity and the ironies of Charles Manson. That's familiar territory, lyrically. Also, Thurston has the most cryptic, figurative lyrics of Sonic Youth – Kim and Lee are more direct, earnest, less furled within something else.

Lydia Lunch: To me, Thurston's words have always been extremely sexy and abstract at the same time – that's unusual, a fantastic combination. I don't think there's a big difference between how he started out and how he writes now but he does a lot of stream-of-consciousness, which is the most exciting form of writing to me. Where Henry Miller has written passages that go on for pages that's what I go back to every summer.

JG Thirlwell: Next he put guitars over it. I took those pieces, processed it, cut it up, added sounds and made the whole thing fall apart and come back together again – that's what *The Crumb* is. It's very mixed, very processed, very arranged. I'm sure it didn't take long to lay down Thurston's part though. It starts with a loop and then goes back to the loop in the middle, it's a lock-in from guitar or voice, I had it locked into a delay – that was done with editing because the rhythm track didn't go long enough so it was a matter of overdubbing on the rhythm track, then making different versions of that and then editing that together so it slows down then comes back in fast, then slows down again, then comes in at different tempi because its edited in different places. It's really a studio piece.

Martin Bisi: Jim ran the show; Lydia is a big picture motivator; she doesn't like a lot of noodling in the recording studio. She'd do her parts, set an agenda and let Jim haggle with the details. Jim is about big picture, but multiple takes, multiple noodles and ideas and a lot of time in studio. Different values, both intensely valuable though. If the world was left to the noodlers it would be boring. But if the big picture people ran it, with no noodlers bringing the quality up, it'd not have much communication of subtlety. I think Lydia and Jim were a great pairing because they did respect each other though they came from those poles.

When Thurston came to record on *The Crumb*, he sat down with me and Jim and he seemed to need to get off his chest that he felt *Sister* was a step sideways, his words, rather than a step forward. There are different kinds of studio professionals; there's production and doing overdubs; or there's a focus on gear. A focus on gear can go hand in hand with a garage aesthetic because you're mostly just messing with what you run sounds through. The reason they went to Sear Sound was Walter Sear, the owner, was an old-school engineer-maverick and very gear oriented – Sonic Youth wanted to focus on what vintage gear could do for them. It's not something Jim or I cared about. We weren't interested in pure sound, we liked lots of layers, processing, what gear we captured it with was a minor concern. So after the more garage-style experience of *Sister* he comes to work on *The Crumb* with Jim Thirlwell and it's much more about ideas of what you can do in a studio, not just about capturing a performance, using the performances as a vehicle for something else you create.

Barefoot In The Head
Don Dietrich/Thurston Moore/Jim Sauter
(Forced Exposure, recorded 1988/released 1990)

Jim Sauter: If there was a scene it was created by the press, artificial to some extent. In the eighties, New York improv was dominated by Eugene Chadbourne and John Zorn. There was also Elliott Sharp, who we liked and respected. With Eugene and John, though, there was an unspoken turf war. The New York press was really interested in composers, heavily into Rhys Chatham and Glenn Branca – then when Zorn became a composer, they were all over him.

Lee Ranaldo: It wasn't that we were unaware of it, but we were resistant to participating because we wanted to be a rock band – so we didn't want to do improv. It wasn't on our map at that time. By the late eighties, we could finally, actually, see a future doing what we were doing, which put a lot of things into a more stable perspective. Living in New York, even when Sonic Youth were regularly working together four afternoons a week from noon 'til six, even with us regularly hanging out, we still felt we could participate more in these scenes and that we'd developed a unique voice, each of us, that we could bring to playing more improvised music at that point.

Byron Coley: Around that period we had put on Thurston's first solo show as a benefit for *Forced Exposure*. We thought he'd play free but he didn't – he brought some things along; it was the first time I heard 'Kotton Krown', he played this early solo version. Lee, at that same show, was doing his guitar improvisation and spoken word. Thurston could do that but he chose to stick more with structure for a while – I think he was psyched out by it.

I went over to his house when he moved to Lafayette Street and he told me, "Man, you've got to listen to this!" He'd gotten a voicemail message from Cecil Taylor, a message from Milford Graves and a message from Borah Bergman – all wanting to play with him. He was excited but also feeling, 'Oh my God, what am I going to do exactly?' He would get really hung up on whether the guys wanted him to read music, which freaked him out. One of the things we'd talk about was that he didn't want to seem like a dilettante. If you're going to play with somebody who has spent their entire life working on their music seriously, you don't want to just walk in like an asshole. You want to have your shit together, whatever that means. I think it held him back for a while until he realised that it wasn't a problem, they saw him as a lifer in the way that they were – "It's what I do" – and they could relate on that level.

When the CD era really started in earnest, a lot of records that were extremely rare and hard to hear suddenly became available. It was true of a lot of jazz stuff that people had never been able to find, as much as for psych records and stuff like that. At *Forced Exposure* I was the jazz editor, which didn't mean anything, but we tried to write about free jazz in the same sort of way we did rock or punk or anything else. To us they all touched the same nerve; if you liked really aggressive punk then there was no reason you wouldn't like Borbetomagus or Peter Brötzmann's *Machine Gun*. Anybody with a record collector mentality is always trying to find something that the next person hasn't quite heard yet, so it became a race to hear as many weird things as you could – I think that was really important. A lot of these guys from the New York 'loft jazz' era were still around and active. It revived a lot of careers after years where it had been tough for guys like Jemeel Moondoc, Jamil Nasser and Joe McPhee to get a gig in the States. All of a sudden somebody would want to put on a show.

Nels Cline: When I was living in Santa Monica in the eighties, Thurston came by with his brother Gene, who was really into jazz guitar. I was really embarrassed because here's Thurston and I've got a *Bad Moon Rising* poster,

36

a *Daydream Nation* poster and so on all over my office. Thurston just said, "Ah don't worry, I'm the same way about Dinosaur!" As soon as he arrived, he started poring over my record collection the way I've now seen him do in record stores; he's magnetically drawn to records. This was when I realised that his knowledge of free jazz and avant-jazz was not just burgeoning, it was already well developed. It was no surprise that, as soon as he started feeling more confident as an improviser, he dove head first into performing it.

Carlos Van Hijfte: At some point in the eighties I didn't have a clue about jazz music, but Thurston was all over it. Whatever catches his eye, he dives in 120%. You're standing next to the guy, he's a preacher too, he wants to tell people about it and I was an easy victim because I was keen to learn.

Byron Coley: There was a feeling with Jimmy Johnson [Forced Exposure] and I that structure was a potential hazard in music, in the same way that technique is. Jimmy and I were always prone to telling people they needed to listen to a different kind of music for whatever reasons: "You're listening to too many vocal records – you need to get the words out of your head!" or, "You need to get away from structure, it's killing you, get rid of all these songs!" I'd gotten Jimmy into Borbetomagus but he'd had an epiphanic hearing of Coltrane, that's all he listened to for a while. Thurston was obviously interested in the same kinds of stuff, just getting into collecting free jazz – we thought he should be playing it. We were very into Borbetomagus, I was always trying to get people to play with those guys but nobody would. We thought Thurston would be good, so we proposed the idea and he was into it.

Jim Sauter: I played piano as a kid and saxophone in public school, that's where Don [Dietrich] and I met. We both lived in Rockland County, a suburb of New York City 16 miles up the Hudson River – lots of exposure to New York radio but we were definitely not city kids. Living up here gave us some perspective on what was happening. Up here, if you played sax, your teacher would tell you, "Go listen to Stan Getz."

The birth of the Borbetomagus sound came in 1979. Donald Miller was a student at Columbia University at the time and was doing a weekly radio show playing Brötzmann, Derek Bailey, Evan Parker. Don called me and said, "You've got to listen to this show! He's playing all the stuff we've always wanted to hear! This is what we're doing!"

37

Carlos Van Hijfte and Thurston at Traumzeit Festival, Landschaftspark, Duisburg-Nord, Germany, June 23, 2013. *Credit — Eva Prinz*

Don Dietrich: I was fortunate to catch Donald's show. He was playing these unbelievable sounds: *Topography Of The Lungs*, *Metal Machine Music* (occasionally simultaneously) and the FMP and ICP catalogues. I turned Jim onto it and he too was blown away, so he called the station one Friday and told Donald, "Hey, my friend and I really like what you're playing – we play sax." So Donald replied, "Hey, I play guitar," and invited us down to jam. It was instant magic from the minute we got together; we knew immediately this was like nothing we'd ever heard before. Jim and I were playing saxes with the bells together – Donald was playing laptop guitar with files and sheet metal. None of us had heard anything like what we played that afternoon. We were floored from the first blast.

Jim Sauter: 'Bells together', where we put the bells of the two saxophones together, is our unique technique that we came upon through natural exploration of the possibilities of the saxophone in high school. We informally patented the technique. We create a sound chamber where the sounds are glancing and deflecting off each other and we stagger our breath – we watch each other and alternate breathing – so we can get this continuous sound. Opening certain keys releases the sound and we're working our embouchures, mouth, lips, to change the tone and pitch. Different combinations of instruments can alter things as well. You lose yourself in the music when you're doing it. You have to be conscious of making sure the bells do stay together; sometimes you don't have the right reed so it's not working quite right, so we don't stay with it long. It requires a fair amount of lung power and I guess it's good cardiovascular exercise. On *Barefoot In The Head* we used it extensively. I was playing bass sax – how did it feel after the session? I can tell you how I felt, exhausted. That's a lot of air to pump through that thing, and you're pumping it against Don pumping air through his horn so you're in a face-off, pressing against each other.

Don Dietrich: *Barefoot In The Head* is Thurston's first foray into purely improvised music and, from a different perspective, it was Jim's and my first exposure to playing in a trio setting with a guitarist other than Donald Miller. It was an experiment. This was the brainchild of Jimmy Johnson and Byron Coley of Forced Exposure – their fingerprints are all over it. They were Borbeto-fans as well as friends of Thurston and had this idea, a gleeful perversion on their part, to see what would happen if they threw Thurston into uncharted waters – and if they took Don Dietrich and Jim Sauter, then replaced Donald Miller with Thurston. Byron's liner notes are telling, the secret to the session is in there: "Two free men meet a slave. Everyone goes home barefoot." The slave is a slave to the beat, that's my take on it. It was a very cordial situation fuelled, for Jim and I, by a lot of Rolling Rock beers. I remember we kept running across to the Bodega to fuel the project. There was no tension, this was a comfortable situation. Wharton Tiers was a very accommodating recording technician.

Wharton Tiers: What made it happen for me was I was working with this landlord on real estate stuff and there was a space that he couldn't rent – it had a little flooding problem – so he said if I wanted to use it to go ahead. Then, right at that point, Tascam came out with their lower-priced tape decks – probably two months later I was doing Sonic Youth. It was the basement of the building but it was half above ground; the low part of the studio was immersed in the rock of Manhattan, which probably had something to do with the sound. Plus the construction – it was built around the 1900s and the basement had this fascinating brick archwork throughout, even though the rest of the building had been renovated.

My recording style always involved just getting people set up and playing as fast as possible, then just rolling tape. There wasn't much budget so it took less than a week to do everything. In 1988 Fun City was all there, so it was easy for anyone to show up and just play almost immediately. You try and capture as much sound as possible and while you might have some bleeds, parts that aren't 100 percent, at the same time you're getting this brilliant feeling of how things are unfolding, so you go with that. I was a fan of rolling tape as people worked, so you catch people informally when they're hashing through things.

Jim Sauter: You actually hear some of the guitar sounds that were a part of Sonic Youth, that shimmering guitar. None of us went in knowing what to expect; no charts, no preconceived ideas. My attitude was, 'Let's see if anything comes out of it, you never know.' It was about trying different configurations of the instruments, Thurston would throw out a riff then we would think, 'What would work on that?' We were there maybe four to six hours, no retracking or overdubs. We tried to make sure we had a variety of lengths of things and instrumental combinations. On 'Concerning The Sun As A Cool Solid' you'll hear a certain sound, that's what Don calls 'mouth wah-wah', I'm blowing air through his sax and he's shaping his mouth at his mouthpiece to let the sound come out...

Don Dietrich: …Up my horn, then out my mouthpiece, and I modulate his horn sound with my mouth. Got that? I can change the sound of his horn because it's in my mouth. It's another extended technique.

Playing with Thurston, whose approach was so radically different from Donald's – more impressionistic, shimmering textures, repetitive vibes, on the first piece he was banging the strings with a drumstick – was quite challenging. If somebody plays something you can ignore it, play against it, or play with it but, in this case, what Thurston was doing, we actually dealt with it and it set up new musical expectations. I'm playing more rhythmically than in a Borbeto-situation. When you've got an emphatic rhythm, like in the first piece ('All Doors Look Alike'), it makes more sense to work within it, off it, through it, round that structure – but not to ignore it.

Byron Coley: I don't think he really thought of playing in a hardcore band, or a Sonic Youth show, or working with Borbetomagus as different things in most ways. In general he would use slightly different approaches, but he seemed to get swept up in the process of doing it and that would erase any hesitation there might have been.

Jim Sauter: Thurston's separated from the herd here, he's on his own and he's up against two guys who've been doing this a long time. This did seem to be one of Thurston's first outings into improvising and that was very significant; once he started he never stopped – the genie was out the bottle, no putting him back!

Dave Markey: Two Virgins opened up a show for Shonen Knife in Los Angeles in 1989. It just so happened that Kurt Cobain was at that show, this was before we had met. It was a band consisting of myself, Thurston and Bill Bartell – who was also known as Pat Fear, the guitarist and singer for the southern California punk band White Flag. There was no real gear there; we didn't have equipment, let alone songs planned! Thurston either borrowed a guitar or brought one with him. I went into the kitchens at the venue and got their largest cooking pots to use as percussion. We knew we were playing, Two Virgins was officially on the bill, but there wasn't even a call beforehand where we worked anything out. Robert Hilburn of *The LA Times* gave us a rave review, as if it was something laboured over; it wasn't, it was completely off the cuff. It was a short performance, sort of like songs with Bill and Thurston trading vocals. Bill revived the name for a piece on a Suicide tribute ['Speed Queen' – *Your Invitation*

To Suicide, Munster Records, 1994] that he had Thurston and me play on – to evoke the memory of that gig the best part of a decade earlier.

I played with Thurston in another improvised band around that same time, August-September 1989. It was a gag band I had called Tusk. I booked a tour of my films showing on the East Coast, mostly around NYC, and Thurston was on board to do shows with me. There were no recordings made but it was while playing in Tusk that the song 'Mildred Pierce' surfaced, which appeared a year later on the *Goo* album. I remember Thurston showing me the riff and telling me, "Yeah, this was an early Sonic Youth song we never did anything with." It was a case of something from these other activities and collaborations he was doing feeding back into Sonic Youth.

Joggers And Smoggers
'Gentlemen' – The Ex
(Ex Records, 1989)

Anne-James Chaton: The rock scene seems to make it very difficult to do things that are not strictly 'rock', probably due to the industry, labels and managers; they're less open than the artists they produce and even their public. And that's the strength of artists like The Ex or Thurston Moore: they connect these scenes, build bridges between the publics, between each universe. To me, The Ex or Moore do not leave one scene to enter another; they run from one to another, always bringing a part of their audiences with them. They initiate their audience into different forms, inviting them to discover other sonic horizons.

Andy Moor: I moved to Holland to join The Ex. What I noticed when I got here was that [compared to the UK] there were many more possibilities to play; many more non-commercial places. When we started travelling around Europe I really noticed it. More recently England has changed; The Ex are playing there and we're being treated quite decently compared to before, when we'd get 100 quid, sleep with our heads in the kitty-litter tray, pay for our own food and only ever get stale beer. That's changed. In the past there was far more structural funding for musicians on the continent. A lot of English musicians in the improvising scene have to come to Europe quite often, they have to travel to earn their bread and butter – they're not getting enough to survive locally.

I wasn't with The Ex for *Joggers And Smoggers* and Thurston wasn't either. It was a project the band had where they asked lots of musicians to participate and Thurston was one of the ones who chose to send over a recording. They took his part and then created something around it. The first tour that Sonic Youth made in Europe, they slept in Terrie (Ex)'s house – there was a strong connection for a lot of years. Later on The Ex opened for them, the four of us in a van with our gear, and they arrived in two coaches – one for the band, one for the equipment – but when we got on-stage we were all doing exactly the same thing in two totally different ways. It was still nice to feel that, when we were on-stage, all the things that grow around a band became irrelevant; we felt like we were the same again.

Rake
Velvet Monkeys
(Rough Trade, 1990)

'Rock The Nation'/'Why Don't We Do It In The Road?'
Velvet Monkeys (Sub Pop, 1991)

Special Kiss
Gumball
(Paperhouse Records, 1991)

Don Fleming: I moved up to New York from Washington DC in '87. I'd come up a lot when 42nd Street was completely insane! It was really rough – but by the time I lived there it was starting to change. We lived in Tribeca, it hadn't taken off yet; there were still artists, musicians, able to stay there. The big difference was DC was truly local, where you knew everybody; bands could play with each other despite being completely different. New York always seemed split; it never gelled into something like the no-wave scene – there was a lot of different music but people didn't connect much outside of their bubbles.

Jay Spiegel had come with me, he was the drummer for Velvet Monkeys in DC; Mark Kramer and David Licht had been in a band called Shockabilly and Kramer had a studio in Tribeca. So we were making records together as Ball and at a certain point did shows with Sonic Youth. We really hit it off with that whole crew of people; it was this time of us flitting in and out of each other's bands for a while. Ball broke up, I revived Velvet Monkeys and both Thurston and J Mascis were in it with Julie Cafritz [Pussy Galore]. I think it was a time of throwing a monkey wrench into the works, having something more spontaneous, chaotic. It was like, "Hey, on Friday let's do this!"

We did most of this recording around that time in a little studio on 14th Street called Waterworks. At the time 14th Street was a great location, a slice of the old, seedier, New York. We were above a place called Dizzy Izzy's Bagels and the whole street was full of transvestite hookers – you'd come out at night and there'd be 50 of them on either side of the road, working it as people drove down the street. It was the Meatpacking District – it's where Stella McCartney is now, it's been completely changed over. The guy who ran it, Jim Waters, he was a perfect engineer who would just get the job done. And it was very inexpensive; for making indie records it was my favourite place. He didn't even have great gear but he knew how to get great results from it; he had a good ear, patience, he enjoyed working with freak musicians. You'll find most producers will work at one place, or one or two, because you want to avoid a learning curve when you're trying to track a band. You want to know where you're going to put the drums to get the best sound.

On some things we've done, Thurston wanted me to be the lead guitar player and for him to be the rhythm player. He doesn't have a big ego; he doesn't need people to know he's the best. In Velvet Monkeys he played bass because he felt we had enough guitar players. Working with him is fun because he'll defer to people, let them take the spotlight – you don't always see that. He makes it enjoyable, he puts his all into it but he'll always share the stage.

Dim Stars **EP**
Dim Stars
(Ecstatic Peace!, 1991)

Don Fleming: The era got diluted more and more – people got disenchanted once they saw what being on a major label was about. It did change. But it was a healthy and fun time, for a while. That's where Thurston was at when he came up with the idea of Dim Stars. It was a case of wanting to collaborate more with people he thought a lot of, mentors; where, even if he felt it would be difficult, it would be worth the journey to work with them. To get Richard Hell to make a record, then to get him to call up Robert Klein and get him to join in, it was great as a musician and also [created] a positive environment, which I felt throughout the sessions and always do with Thurston. It's like he has a karmic medicine-man vibe. I know people who do that, they get up on-stage and go into a strange zone where they're almost tripping out. They make it a space for what music is about. Thurston's never lost that, he goes there very easily. It's a mix of primal ways of making music with a record collector's sensibility. That's part of the fun of hanging with Thurston for me, we're both record collectors and we'll talk on that level of geekdom, discoveries, where we say, "How did they make that sound?" "Don't know!" "Let's try to make that!" That's the fun of it.

Thurston had come up with the name Dim Stars two or three years before the band came together. He'd put the name in his adverts for Ecstatic Peace!, but he hadn't decided at all what it was going to be. Then suddenly the idea became to get Richard to do it. A guy named Sonny Vincent – a New York guy from the late-seventies punk scene – was doing a record and it was me on guitar, Cheetah Chrome on guitar, Richard Hell on bass, Sonny on guitar and bass, with Scott Asheton on drums. Richard hadn't played in years, sounded great, but halfway into the session his fingers were bleeding because he had no callouses; he probably hadn't picked the thing up in a decade. Within a year or so we did Dim Stars. Thurston wasn't close to Richard, so it was a gamble – you never know beforehand if someone is going to turn out to be a complete freak who starts yelling at everybody. Richard wasn't like that. He was nervous but convinced enough to give a couple of songs a shot.

Richard Hell: I hardly went to clubs or to see bands at all by the early eighties; I was burnt out and having a lot of problems. It was personal, though, rather than some kind of problem with developments in the scene. I wasn't committed enough to music to maintain interest once that first moment was past and I realised what would be required of me to continue – I just wasn't interested anymore. I quit music entirely, more or less, in 1984. I did actually experiment with a new band for a few months in around 1986, but we only played maybe three gigs before I realised I still didn't like the life. Being a working musician is a full-time job and I didn't like the demands, especially touring. I never ruled out recording if someone made me an irresistible offer, but mostly I'd get offers to play live and that just didn't appeal.

So when Thurston asked if I'd be interested in making a single with him I didn't hesitate. I didn't know him at all, had never met him, but I was a fan of *Daydream Nation* and had reviewed *Goo* in *Spin*. The set-up was ideal by my lights. We'd go into the eight-track studio, record a couple of obscure punk covers and he'd release the results. Thurston had the personnel in mind: Steve Shelley is one of the best guitar-band drummers alive and Don Fleming is one of my favourite people, an inspired musician and tremendous producer.

We ended up writing a new song, too, and the process was ideal: we jammed on some chords of Thurston's for many minutes, I listened to that, picked out a stretch of it and wrote words to that, then recorded the vocals. This was 'Dim Star'. We casually jammed around on the structure of my ancient song 'You Gotta Lose' too. I must have been just fooling with the bass and played the 'Gotta Lose' pattern and everybody joined in and we just kept playing, as usual. The eight-track was always taping as we played, but I was surprised and kind of aghast when he added like 20 minutes of that to the EP. But the overall experience was great and I loved the songwriting method – jam on good chord changes, take home, pick three minutes to write to and then sing – so within a few weeks I suggested to Thurston we do a whole album of new material that way.

Dim Stars
Dim Stars
(Paperhouse Records, 1992)

Richard Hell: The whole *Dim Stars* album was composed, recorded and mixed in three weeks. It was always understood that we wouldn't play live; this was simply a one-album project, like you'd make a movie or something. They're all laidback people, completely loose and unpretentious, so it was pure pleasure. We worked a full schedule for three weeks. The usual programme was we'd jam on someone's chord changes, fooling around, for a long time and then do it again for someone's different set of changes, all on tape. I'd take home a cassette of a fast mix and write lyrics. The next day we'd jam to different ideas and I'd also lay down singing of my new lyrics to a song or two: like that. There were a few exceptions to this procedure, but 80 percent of the album was done this way. There was an occasional overdub, maybe a solo, but the mixing was as casual and quick as the recording.

The exceptions to the 'jam/select-stretch-from-jam/write lyrics/sing' were when we did covers and the songs I'd already written. 'Downtown At Dawn' was on my *Destiny Street* album. I wanted to try it again because there were things missing from the original recording. 'She Wants To Die' and 'All My Witches Come True' came from the mid-eighties, when I was briefly fooling around composing songs on a cheap home four-track. As I recall, for 'Baby Huey' I just had the music in 1992; I wrote the lyrics for the Dim Stars release – the song is actually about the first Gulf War.

Don Fleming: Richard had stuff he'd been holding onto for quite a while. We'd have been happy to just do all his stuff if he'd had enough material – we'd have loved doing all his songs! With the Dim Stars sessions it was so fun to be in the room with Richard and with Robert Quine at the same time. Not only cutting stuff with them live, but sitting there watching them interact. They were such a team. To be witness to them back in the room was my favourite part. Richard was really serious about his takes, the words, getting it to sound good – but we all enjoyed the process, no stress, he did too. Thurston and me, we were in heaven, we couldn't believe we were doing this, seeing it come together.

We didn't have a master plan at all, it was always a surprise to get to the next stage. We did one show, a benefit or something, and Richard was super-nervous. I realised he couldn't do it every night because while he hadn't been uptight in the studio, now he was *really* uptight. Once he was onstage he was amazing, he bounded across the stage the whole time, played bass – but before going on there was this anxiety. We would have liked to make another record but it was probably a case of laziness, other things coming up, whatever. I think, for Richard, we took a lot out of him – maybe we should have pushed to go back and do more but… I saw him last night at a book release party, he looks great. He could do it again!

Mask Of Light
Rudolph Grey
(New Alliance Records/Ecstatic Peace!, 1991)

Clear To Higher Time
The Blue Humans
(New Alliance Records, 1992)

Don Dietrich: Rudolph Grey was the original rock'n'roll/free-jazz crossover. He was associated originally with Mars, then left to perform under his own name with a band as The Blue Humans. He would hire free-jazz drummers like Beaver Harris and saxophonists like Arthur Doyle. We met him as far back as 1980–81; there was the Noise Fest music festival arranged by Thurston and he invited us. Arthur Doyle had recently gotten out of jail in Paris and had just gotten off a plane to come over and play

Alan Licht and Thurston at Sonic Youth's last CBGB show, NYC, June 13, 2006.
Credit – Angela Jaeger

with Rudolph, who told me, "Yeah, Arthur's been up for three days – no sleep."

Tom Surgal: Rudolph and I would play on these ridiculously incongruous bills at CBGB, where more times than not the soundman would turn off the PA halfway through our set, even when Thurston sat in with us. Talk about no respect! I remember after one show when Thurston jammed with us, a particularly clueless member of the audience accosted him and told him that he looked "a lot like that dude in Sonic Youth", assuming that a celebrated rock star of his stature would never stoop so low as to perform this kind of music. Thurston responded to the guy by telling him, "Yeah, I get that a lot."

We all started to perform at this club called The Cooler, located in the Meatpacking District, then the exclusive domain of hardcore leather boys, transgendered hookers and butchers cleaving their bloody carcasses. The Cooler was an improvement in terms of it having more adventurous programming but, although The Cooler had a good and eclectic booking policy, you still got treated like shit.

Don Fleming: Thurston, Tom Surgal and I produced a Rudolph Grey single. Rudolph is another guy like Richard Hell who lives in New York, really didn't do much music anymore at that point, and Thurston just thought, "Let's get him out! Let's do a record!" What was so amazing, Alan Licht played guitar on it, Jim Sauter played saxophone, but they got [John Coltrane's drummer and noted free-jazz innovator] Rashied Ali to play drums on it – so there we were, recording Rashied. That moment came out of a record collector's mentality of 'It'd be the coolest thing if we could put together a band to record a Rudolph Grey single'. Thurston liked bringing guys out of their apartments into a studio. Opportunity struck, a phone call was made...

Wharton Tiers: Thurston had a lot of interest in the way things were sounding; he wouldn't be saying, "Change the EQ 10Db," or whatever, he would just let me get something together then comment on it; especially when we were mixing the tapes, he'd sit there with me and work the faders and he seemed to get more interested as it went along, he came to embrace the process. I can remember one instance where we'd been trying to mix a song for four, five, six hours, then he went home and at about three in the morning he called me up, yelling, "I know what the mix needs!" And all I could reply was, "Thurston? Go back to bed – we'll sort it in the morning." He'd probably been sat there listening to all the mixes over and over until he had his realisation. When I think of Thurston what always occurs to me is enthusiasm; he's an enthusiastic musician, he's enthusiastic about pretty much everything. He's helped so many musicians get recordings done, get records out, go on tour.

Tom Surgal: It was Thurston who first recommended me to Rudolph. That's kind of a funny story. I was helping out Thurston with the drum production on the record that Rudolph was doing with Rashied Ali at Waterworks. They finished recording an album's worth of material and Rashied was basically out the door, when Rudolph remembered that Gerard Cosloy had asked him to do something for a Matador Records compilation. Rashied – who had only brought a pair of drumsticks to the session, which he had already deposited back into his stick bag – looked at Rudolph with an expression of incredulity and announced that he was all packed up and proceeded to leave. It was at that point Thurston volunteered my services, much to my dismay, as he had only ever heard me tooling around my kit at home. My music career was born. Rudolph just wanted to revive the name The Blue Humans, which was cool because we eventually started to play with Arthur Doyle, who was in the original configuration. So we did some quartet shows with Arthur and Wilbur Morris and then we started doing trio gigs with Charles Gayle on drums.

Alan Licht: I was just shy of 22 years old in late 1985 or early 1986. I bought the Tellus cassette *All Guitars*, compiled by Live Skull's Tom Paine. The last track on the first side was by Rudolph Grey; I'd never heard of him but I really liked the high energy of the piece. Not long after, an issue of *Forced Exposure* magazine came out with an Ecstatic Peace! advertisement announcing an upcoming EP by Rudolph, calling him 'Ex-Mars/Lydia/ Branca Guitar Killer'. That made me even more intrigued. Eventually I got in touch with Rudolph and invited him up to be a guest on my college radio show and later interviewed him for a fanzine. In getting to know Rudolph I gave him a cassette of my guitar playing, then he asked me to play bass with him and David Linton at The Knitting Factory in August 1989 on a bill Thurston had set up under the name 'Thurston Moore's Rock 'n' Roll Circus' – Thurston played solo, just doing what would become material on *Goo*, not improvising yet. That was the first time I met Thurston; the first time I played an NYC club.

Thurston was a producer in the sense that it was his idea to do the albums; he organised the studio time, he was there to keep things on track. But I don't think he had any preconceived ideas about what the material should be. There wasn't very much discussion of technical stuff. *Clear To Higher Time* is one guitar in each channel and drums in the middle for the entire album. Rudolph had the structure in mind for *Clear To Higher Time*, which was based on a show we played at CBGB which was released as a seven-inch [To Higher Time]. The rest of it was just improvised in the studio with the idea of having another 20 minutes' worth of shorter tracks. On *Mask Of Light* Rudolph also had the structures in mind; 'Implosion 73' was sort of a tribute to an old Ray Russell guitar/drums duo on Ray's *Secret Asylum* LP, while 'Flaming Angels' was adapted from a show Rudolph did at The Kitchen in 1982 with a nine- or ten-piece ensemble. He had each player come in one at a time with a tape of slowed-down animal sounds underneath.

Ecstatic Peace! was going through New Alliance for both *Mask Of Light* and *Clear To Higher Time*, so obviously it was different than when it was just Thurston doing it out of his apartment; or later, when he was having Forced Exposure manufacture and distribute it. Thurston would conceptualise and organise what was going to come out, but then it was up to New Alliance to release and promote it – there was probably more lag time with New Alliance than with any of the other arrangements. The recording sessions were fairly simple: a day for recording and a day for mixing. Rudolph did the cover art and layout.

Shamballa
William Hooker/Thurston Moore/Elliott Sharp
(Knitting Factory Works, 1994)

Byron Coley: Thurston was playing in a lot of different situations without recording it – he would play all the time in different groups and with a lot of people. Once we were walking along, Sonic Youth had a show that night somewhere pretty big, and we ran into [noted jazz saxophonist] David Ware on the street. Thurston asked him, "Hey, do you want to play while people come into the theatre for our show? Be over at six o'clock." He had whatever amount of dough he could offer him, so Ware just headed over, set up and started playing.

William Hooker: Thurston came down to the St Peter's Church on the East Side of New York with his friend Tom Surgal – that's where I first encountered this gentleman. I guess they were interested in my form of playing and the scene that was being created in terms of free-form improvisation and the music we were doing. So he introduced himself to me and told me he was a member of a group. I was fascinated that he was a very open and gung-ho type of guy. Especially when you think of the kind of crew I associated with over there, because there do seem to be certain camps – like there's a free-jazz camp, a free-improv camp, a black camp and a white camp… I tended to be crossing the boundaries a little bit [or] a lot actually. I invited him to a studio I was rehearsing at and when he turned up he just set up and we played. We enjoyed each other and each other's company. Unless I have a gig, I don't invite a whole bunch of people over because I have to pay for session time, so I don't want to pay for people to just practise. I had no conscious awareness of this group he was playing with; I just trusted that he was somebody who was interested in playing. When you find honest people who aren't trying to make moves for their careers, for their resumés – we just like music, the history of it, the collecting of it. It's a creative connection, it trumps the entire situation.

We played a couple of gigs together and I was kind of astounded by this scene he was associated with; I liked it – people were open to noise, to loud music. A lot of these jazz-heads, they weren't so open to experimentalism, to making mistakes, to things that were abstract, because sometimes mistakes create the greatest successes – they preferred something that's in a box, easy to define, that had easy frames of reference. What Thurston and I were doing didn't have a frame of reference; you either liked it or you didn't. The audiences in Thurston's scene were into taking chances; it was a mutual thing, each of us opening doors for the other and to the music.

Obviously he had no idea of what kind of stuff we were doing, so it opened him up to things beyond the music associated with a backbeat drummer. This stuff is obviously much more exploratory, freer; extended improvisation takes time to get into and the more you get into it, you'll find it's a very fulfilling way, something beyond spending a minute-and-a-half improvising on a song that's still only four minutes long. There's a different range you have to immerse yourself in. There's the test of who can keep up, who's for real. That's a whole other level of acceptance – when you get that deep into it, if you can't keep up then, "Sorry." If you can't keep up it means you're not playing anything; you're staid; you're

52

not going anywhere creatively. These are some rough customers here in New York – they can play, they're not fooling around. Excitement is about personalities, this is about people's musicianship. With Thurston specifically, I think his musicianship improved based on our relationship and his relationships with others. I even think that the shape and the direction of his main gig changed – it was evident and it was a good thing. Nothing to be afraid of, confronting audiences with something completely new. It's like when Stravinsky played *The Rite of Spring* and people were jumping out of windows. Thurston's choices about who to play with, these were some serious, honest people – playing with musicians like that makes you better. Many of his choices have been the ones that make you learn.

Carlos Van Hijfte: Your audience gets a little bit predictable. You want to challenge them. On the other hand, I remember a show in London where Sonic Youth had an improv noise unit, guys with beards, making music – and the audience got aggressive. It was so stupid! When Sonic Youth were on doing all these long noise pieces, people were cheering! They couldn't make the bridge from the noise Sonic Youth made to the noise these other guys made. The rock world is a bit of a cliché and I don't think Thurston is the kind of guy who wants to be clichéd. But he understands that by playing the big festivals and shows for 5,000 people, it pays the bills even if it never made them rich.

Lee Ranaldo: It was through Thurston that I met William Hooker and seeing Thurston play with him started me playing with him. It felt like all of us were active simultaneously; that there was a freedom that opened up where we felt we could balance the work we were putting into the band – which was substantial – with doing other things. We were finding that we had established enough of a space, enough security, around what we were doing as a band that there was time to do other things and the opportunities presented themselves. We were playing with other people, bringing those ideas back into what the band was thinking about. I always said that it was an opportunity for each of us to isolate certain small aspects of what Sonic Youth had in its mix and to expound upon them in a different setting.

William Hooker: There are things that I study, separate to music, that I try to bring to my work. *Shamballa* appeared as the range I wanted to use for that record; that's the way I approach my work; it's another one of the ways I wanted to interpret what that particular improvisation was about.

53

It was the way I wanted to brand my efforts to be creative – it keeps me grounded. Some take it for granted, look it up in some spiritual dictionary then move on; 'Okay, next.' I like things to have a context, and that was the right context for my relationship not only with Thurston but with Elliott Sharp as well.

Byron Coley: People who had just been interested in underground rock began to perceive similarities of vibe, ineffable qualities that weren't easy to describe but they could see were shared – non-doctrinaire creation and approach. Rock guys no longer thought jazz was off limits, though I don't know how much that worked from the other side. The big news in jazz at the time was 'the young lions', the Wynton Marsalis kind of stuff, these guys with bow ties. It was good realising that there were people like William Parker out there – guerillas scuffling around in the same way as the noise-rock bands, they're not putting on tuxedos and playing at a Lincoln Center. It was an awakening to the possibilities, and there were a lot of great players in New York at the time who weren't really valued in the jazz scene. When Sonic Youth had Sun Ra open for them in Central Park that was a huge deal – seeing bands willing to share the stage with these great improvisers lent the latter a degree of hipness among young white audiences that may not have ever run into them anywhere else.

Backbeat
The Backbeat Band
(Virgin, 1994)

Don Fleming: Even during this time, with major labels involved, we never felt a pressure – it was more of a Wild West mentality, with people assuming we knew what we were doing. In my case, as a producer, my mentality was that the records I grew up on, especially '71–'74, were all about this analogue way of recording that was particular to that time. That was the thing in my mind I wanted to do as a producer, that was the sound I wanted to discover in the studio. It brought more of a rock sound to things that I did because I wanted it to sound like a Badfinger record, that aesthetic was an influence.

The Backbeat Band was the first thing we did for a film. Don Was came to Thurston to try to put together a band for this idea. The idea was we would record live Hamburg-era Beatles songs and it was meant to be raw, in the style and sound of that stuff. Then the actors were going to lip-sync to this, so it had to be made before the film was done. Thurston's aesthetic was right on the money, we would come in and do it in two days. No learning ahead of time. We'd just go in and figure them out one by one, do two takes – done, onto the next. Don loved the idea: "Sounds fine! Let's do it!" Thurston pretty much wrangled the band together. It had the right pre-planning, a method that worked fine, that created the sound we needed which was this idea that we were only just on the verge of playing them correctly. We knew everyone coming in could handle it pretty well.

Monster
'Crush With Eyeliner' – R.E.M.
(Warner Bros. Records, 1994)

Thurston Moore: I went to LA to play in The Backbeat Band's only live performance, which was at the very first MTV Movie Awards. As *Backbeat* was a movie, they thought they should invite us. So we were flown out to LA – me, Dave Grohl, Greg Dulli, Don Fleming – we had a great old time. We were put up in the Chateau Marmont, we each had a car they'd rented for us, we had fun being feted as this movie company paid for it.

At the same time, R.E.M. were recording *Monster*. Mike Stipe was staying in Chateau Marmont, I ran into him and he asked if I wanted to come by the studio and do something. Courtney Love was there too – I hadn't seen her since Kurt died, so we had a long talk. I did backing vocals which were based on an Iggy Pop song. No guitar.

Our Band Could Be Your Life – A Tribute To D. Boon And The Minutemen – 'Shit You Hear At Parties'
Thurston Moore
(little brother records, 1994)

Thurston Moore: I was so big into American hardcore seven-inch records – that was my primary interest in music at the time. Possibly it was this nostalgia for that period in the eighties when Dave Markey was very young and that Mike Watt and Dez Cadena had been a part of while I was in New York in this art-rock band, but ensconced in what was going on. I did that thing with Even Worse, so you could say I was 'hanging out' with the hardcore scene. It meant so much to us – it was really defining for us.

David Markey: Thurston and Mike Watt became very close. D. Boon's death was a turning point within that music, that world, that scene. Watt was devastated, unable to leave his house afterward. Thurston convinced him to come visit New York City while Sonic Youth were recording *Evol* and had Watt record on a track or two. Thurston really reached out to Watt to give support, he was really concerned to help Watt keep playing music. When someone dies suddenly in a freak accident, at a young age, it creates a giant void, one that's harsh to deal with, and there was a period where Watt didn't even know if he could continue to play, his only experience of music was what he'd made with Boon.

Thurston invited me to play on the track he contributed to a D. Boon and The Minutemen tribute record. That was put together by a guy called Mike Hogan, who ran little brother records up in Oregon. It was already nearly 10 years after D. Boon's passing, and I think it took that long for people to process the tragedy of his loss and to deal with it. The compilation was a democratic way to pull together like-minds and to let them be heard together, as a cohesive declaration of the emotion he sparked. Compilations were a huge part of the hardcore scene – sometimes that was the only time bands were documented.

Skins, Brains & Guts
Society's Ills
(Ecstatic Peace!, 1994)

Dave Markey: The whole hardcore scene really inspired Thurston when Sonic Youth was forming, in terms of attitude and the vibe. It really showed up later though, during *Dirty* in 1992, when Sonic Youth covered 'Nic Fit' by The Untouchables, a really early Washington DC hardcore band, and they had [Dischord Records and Minor Threat founder] Ian MacKaye guest on the record. Before, Thurston liked it, he'd go see all these bands, but he couldn't bring it properly into Sonic Youth. It took a decade of knowing all these records back-to-front before he found a way to make it part of their music. Remember this is all post-Nirvana, it was a very odd time – all these obscure eighties bands were suddenly being pushed into mainstream consciousness.

Thurston Moore: The 7 Seconds seven-inch ['Skins, Brains & Guts'] was almost a blueprint template of what an American hardcore record release was. I knew the songs really well, I had all the lyrics printed out and it was a really funny session. Dez knew 7 Seconds, he had stayed with them at their house in Reno, Nevada – it was a famous crash pad for hardcore bands. It was Kevin Seconds' mother's house, so she was known as 'Ma Seconds.'

Dave Markey: Personally, there are a lot of records I would have chosen before that one. Thurston had a boombox and a cassette with the record taped onto it. He'd play a track, we'd sit and listen to it, sort of learn it; then we'd record it instantly. The whole record was done in one afternoon on into the evening. Usually we had just one or two attempts at the song before we recorded an actual take. Sometimes we'd not even listen to it, we'd just press play on the tape deck and 'Boom!' We'd just play and record what we were doing. Some of the takes on the Society's Ills record follow the original songs pretty closely while some of them are something else all together. Thurston even took the original record sleeve, covered the 7 Seconds logo and used the same artwork – that's pretty bold. It's an audacious concept: 'Who did that?' It was still paying tribute, but it was something odder.

We were all together in the same studio to record 'Shit You Hear At Parties' with Thurston, then we came back, without him, and did one single under the name Chop, performing Blue Öyster Cult songs. You can tell because at the end of the Society's Ills EP you hear a slow-speed take of 'I'm On The Lamb But I Ain't No Sheep', so Society's Ills was either done right before or right after we did Chop. The reason we were recording that was because Blue Öyster Cult was Mike Watt and D. Boon's favourite band as teenagers.

Dave Travis' sister is Vicki Peterson of The Bangles, so we ended up recording all of this at her home studio out in Calabasas, California. I'll always remember when all this was done because it was just after the North Ridge Earthquake in January '94, and all the time we were playing these big aftershocks would hit and we wouldn't even stop playing. There'd be a 5.1 aftershock and we'd just play over the top of it. That happened right through the Society's Ills sessions. Everything we did together was tributes – even Two Virgins, the moniker itself, was a tribute to John Lennon and Yoko Ono.

Germs Tribute – A Small Circle Of Friends – 'Now I Hear The Laughter'
Puzzled Panthers
(Grass Records, 1996)

Dave Markey: Our work together just mushroomed out. People always had some project or other they were doing – friends were always working on compilations. Bill Bartell put together a tribute to The Germs record and asked a bunch of friends to play on it. Sonic Youth couldn't do it but Thurston wanted to, so we put together a band just to play on it – Puzzled Panthers – which was me and Thurston, Mike D of Beastie Boys and Kira Roessler from Black Flag. She was an amazing bassist, it was an honour to be playing with her. Mike Watt produced it in The Beastie Boys' G-Son Studios with Mario Caldato Jr., who was their in-house producer. We chose the song 'Now I Hear The Laughter' – even the band name was from a lyric by Darby Crash: 'I came into this world, a puzzled panther waiting to be caged, but something stood in the way.'

'I Hate The Nineties' / 'Tube Tops Forever' / 'Cellphone Madness'
Rodney & The Tube Tops
(Sympathy For The Record Industry, 1997)

Dave Markey: Rodney & The Tube Tops was a tribute to Rodney Bingenheimer. Being in Los Angeles, for me Rodney was a crucial figure. He was the first person to play underground music on a commercial radio station. The radio could care less about all of this music but Rodney turned a lot of people onto it; he was the John Peel of LA.

We knew, again, it was just going to be a one-off thing, nothing that would tour, nothing that would last. We wrote the songs in the studio, rehearsed a few times and then we recorded – there wasn't an intense amount of labouring over it. The record was brought together by the artist Cameron Jamie and was a direct result of his friendship with and respect for Rodney. Cameron co-wrote the lyrics to 'I Hate The Nineties' with Rodney, it was just a funny track bagging on the culture of the time in a humorous way.

[It was] Thurston, Bill Bartell, Eric Erlandson, me: Cameron phoned me up and said, "Last night at Canter's Deli, Rodney and I wrote this song and I think we want to bring it into the studio – do you want to play?" That coincided with Thurston being in town. We didn't have anything together for the B-side so I had the concept of doing something using the chords D-G-C, because both Eric and Thurston were signed to that label at the time. So that became the song 'Tube Tops Forever'. There were a lot of those jokes going on at the time – Sonic Youth had the label Goofin Records, which was another direct reference to Geffen.

Thurston, Steve Shelley and Tim Foljahn overlooking Canal St, NYC, summer 1995.

Credit – Dave Markey

Psychic Hearts
Thurston Moore
(Geffen, 1995)

Tim Foljahn: My music thing was somewhat normal; I played a little bit in high school and stuff like that. Then, when I went off to college, I got in this band called The Spastic Rhythm Tarts who were later known as Abiku, Strange Fruit and a couple of other things. It was basically a noise band; there were shows in basements where I was shaking gravel around in a big tin tube and stuff like that – we made a lot of racket and we could clear a house party pretty quickly. But we made a record and it turned out Thurston heard that because he was a rabid seven-inch collector. It was exciting but it wasn't a total surprise when Thurston asked me to record with him. It was sort of natural. I was around, I was available, and I fit the bill for what it required to do that particular music.

After high school, I met up with Steve [Shelley] because we were from the same hometown. Kalamazoo was where I pretended to be in college and that band down there really needed a drummer, so Steve came down. We remained friends after that, so, when I came out to Hoboken, Steve was playing with Jad Fair and he invited me along – I ended up playing in Half Japanese for a couple of years. Next I ended up playing with The Boredoms because they needed a driver and then suddenly they needed a guitar player. I had started doing my own music with Steve, while Steve and me were playing with Cat Power by now; the joke was we'd become the punk rock Sly and Robbie, that we were just playing with all these other people as this rhythm section. But, in the nineties, a rhythm section didn't include a bass player.

I think that Thurston's deal was that he wanted to do something that was sort of straight-ahead and pure. These were also his ideas of pop songs. But more than that, I don't think people realise how much Sonic Youth was a collaboration. My impression was that if somebody brought a song into that band, it really got worked over; it would get thought over every six ways from Sunday. I think he was itching to do something where he got to bring it in and that's what it was. There were two kinds of songs on this record – that's sort of generalising, but I think there were the 'pop songs', if we can call them that; I think he was itching to do this simple heartfelt thing, to get right to the heart of things, even though they're very poetic. His lyrics are just very surreal. And then there are the longer things where he's clearly coming from a minimalist, modern composer thing. An obvious reference would be Branca, but I think older stuff might be even more appropriate, like [Terry] Riley and even the jazz guys, Ornette Coleman. A composition born of improvisation, frozen but still flexible, and of course passed through the sieve of punk.

We had been gigging this material for a while so it was just a matter of going in and throwing down. Thurston stayed and put bass on some of the stuff and he did overdubs, but the actual sessions were one day. Most of these songs were three takes at the most, we were pretty tight. When you listen to the record you can tell that they're all very live takes. It was a very minimalist experiment. On 95 percent of the stuff on this record – and the Male Slut work – my part was doubling Thurston's guitar part. He would come in with these songs complete in form; then they might change, especially the longer pieces, until he got it where he wanted it. Most of the time I was playing exactly what he was playing. So I was providing a wobble. At the time we were all into this idea of 'What is improvisation?' and improvising within very narrow parameters. Like there's a lot of talk about 'pulse'; and just being able to pulse really well – we could do that, we could lock in. Thurston plays really straight and his tone is like that too, there's nothing making it cloudy. I'm more, like, dirty. It gives it that wider thing that I think he was going for. There were definitely long passages of noise freak–out and soloing within parameters, but it was all stuff that we could do in our sleep. It was more like a function of a large moving chord than 'Look what I can do'. Even on the shorter stuff, you'd lock so tight that there really wasn't much room to think about anything.

The shorter songs were much more angular, so it was not intuitive as far as 'I'm a guitar player, this is what a guitar player would play'. I really had to be in the moment, which made it really fun for that reason. Thurston was totally in control the whole time. He brought it in. He told us what to do. His instructions to me were often, "Play it dumber. Dumb it down. Don't be clever." And, of course, that is totally in my wheelhouse. As far as the sort of explosive sound of the record, a lot of what you hear is just the sound of Thurston and Steve when it's opened up – there's a lot of thump in their sound, a lot of low end, a lot of bang to that. If you stand right in front of them when they're doing that it's pretty heavy. I think you can get a real sense of the sound of the band in the longer parts because they're basically live, they're just exactly what was happening.

'The Church Should Be For The Outcasts Not A Church That Casts People Out'/ 'Thoodblirsty Thesbians' Male Slut (Stomach Ache, 1995)

Tim Foljahn: It was funny, this period; Dim Stars had happened and Thurston was just really prolific at this point – he was writing a lot of good songs. It was really shocking, because it wasn't as jammy and sprawling as Sonic Youth was. It was definitely smaller, it was very poppy really. But I don't think people knew what to think of it. We would do tours in conjunction with the leg of a Sonic Youth tour, odd nights in smaller places. But it was strange because we were either the indie-rock band with a bunch of noise people, or the noise band with a bunch of indie-rock people. It was always fun – nobody knew what to expect. We were pretty tight so we'd come in and launch that thing and it always worked.

Thurston Moore: The 'Male Slut' name came from Julia Cafritz of Pussy Galore – it's how she referred to [bandmate] Jon Spencer and, though I forget what the conversation was about, she called him "a male slut!" I thought that was such a great name for a band:"I'm taking that!" There was this idea that *Psychic Hearts* was going to be by Male Slut and it really is, it's the same trio, but I made the sensible decision of putting it under my own name instead. I do remember seeing a Guided By Voices gig in Seattle at a small club, and Robert Pollard called me and Steve out while on-stage: "Male Slut's in the house tonight! You know about Male Slut, right? It's Thurston, Steve and Tim but Geffen refused to put it out under that name." Which isn't exactly true but it's a good story.

Tim Foljahn: So we had this body of work which included the pop songs and it included this one song called 'Super Christ'. 'Super Christ' would have been the only song that was a literal outtake of the *Psychic Hearts* sessions. But there was always a new modern composer-style piece going. So, every once in a while, we'd go into the Magic Shop studio or the Noho studio and cut a bunch of stuff. I remember it all going down very live: "Was that a good one?" "Yes." Done.

We opened for a secret show of The Black Crowes at Irving Plaza. We got there and we saw dudes, predominantly dudes, lined up around the block with beards (back in the days when beards weren't cool), flannel, beer bongs and pizza. We get in there; The Black Crowes' gear is up on-stage all covered in tie-dyed sheets, we get backstage and everybody from the old guard is there. We're getting a kick out of this – there's nothing wrong with the band, it's just not somewhere any of us would ever go. They're joking around up there about all the goofy things they could do to raise hell. We get down to the stage and there's a sea of dudes all chanting, "Male Slut! Male Slut!" So we go out there and Thurston has a joint and he's joking about Chris [Robinson] from The Black Crowes dropping acid in his eye. He starts singing a little bit of a Bob Seger tune; everybody's like, "Woooo!" The whole crowd's into it. So he's up there smoking the joint and then he says, "Okay, I'm going to pass this down here and I want it to go all the way around the room, then come back up here and I get the last toke," and it's a huge room, balcony and everything. This is all ridiculous buffoonery and I'm trying to keep it together because it's already pretty funny. So we launch into it and they're eating it up – they're going wild. We're thinking, 'What the hell…?' So we go on a while, do four or five songs, they're rocking, it sounds great in there and we'd not played through such a big sound system before. Then we do 'Super Christ' and my instructions for this song became – probably because it was my tendency anyway, or I had some kind of mental block – to never accurately learn it. It had this really off-kilter thing and I always played it wrong. By the end of that song the whole place is yelling in unison, "You suck!" and the ice and full beers are hitting the stage like nothing I've ever seen. It was a barrage of shit hitting the stage – we're batting cans back with our guitars, it's bedlam. They hate us now. "Thank you, good night!" It was a great feeling – them hating us was more fun than them loving us.

Milktrain To Paydirt – 'Asleep Sneeze'
Trumans Water
(Homestead, 1995)

Kirk Branstetter: We met Thurston at the Irving Plaza in New York at a show that had Trumans Water opening for The Boredoms. We talked and somehow ended up opening for Male Slut. Soon after, Thurston wrote me a letter and sent a cassette which had some guitar sounds on it. He said it'd be cool if we added some Trumans Water guitar; I recorded some and sent it back to him. The plan was that he would send the Thurston/Trumans Water guitar sounds to Evan Parker, who would add sax; then, naturally, an album would be released. That plan never panned out.

In order to pay tribute to the influence Thurston provided to our band, I thought it would be sweet to have Thurston's name involved in some form of collaboration. So I wrote and asked if he would mind if I used that joint recording for a Trumans Water release instead. He said that wouldn't bother him at all.

Kevin Branstetter: For *Milktrain To Paydirt* we had just relocated to Portland. My brother and I, being northern California boys, had become tired of perpetual summer and wanted to move somewhere with actual seasons and where houses had basements. We had definitely overstayed our welcome in our San Diego neighbourhood; practices were kept short knowing that the cops would be there within a half-hour of hitting the first notes. The main motivation for the album was simply to keep the ball rolling. The challenge was we were doing it as a three-piece for the first time as we couldn't talk Glen Galloway [lead singer] into coming north.

Klangfarbenmelodie And The Colorist Strikes Primitiv
Thurston Moore/Tom Surgal
(Corpus Hermeticum, 1995)

Tom Surgal: It was another swampy night at The Cooler – someone once joked that it should have been renamed The Warmer. It's hard for me to enthuse too much about those early recordings, because I'm so down on my own playing from that era. It was early in my career and I was still struggling to find my voice and the right gear, but Thurston sounds great and the vibe was good. We first started playing together when I asked Thurston to sit in with me for a set, opening for some friends. Thurston's improvisational skills were fully formed right from the get-go. I saw his first improv gig and he was great. Thurston is no virtuoso, but he has developed his own highly personal language that is unlike anybody else's and he has a real flair for sonic dynamics. I think I'm the insufficient one on those sessions. For the record, our individual

Thurston and Tom Surgal backstage at Baby's All Right, Brooklyn, NYC, May 1, 2016.
Credit – Brian Turner

methodologies are diametrically different. Thurston never practises and I never stop practising.

Not Me
Thurston Moore/Tom Surgal
(Fourth Dimension, 1996)

Tom Surgal: That was a board tape or video source recording of us in duo at The Middle East in Cambridge, MA. Probably the record company asked Thurston for something and he extracted those bits. I was never consulted, Thurston just showed up one day with a box of records for me!

Piece For Jetsun Dolma
Thurston Moore/Tom Surgal/William Winant
(Les Disques Victo, 1996)

William Winant: I knew Kim Gordon since high school. She was one of the people who turned me onto free jazz and improvised music. I was into English blues then; through that, I got into American roots music and progressed into jazz and free jazz. Then, toward the end of high school, I started getting very interested in contemporary avant-garde music; so as well as drums, I started studying classical and contemporary percussion. I built my technique up by going into the classical and new-music worlds. In the eighties and the early nineties I was mainly playing with new-music composers and playing contemporary classical music, or even with traditional orchestras. At the same time, I was working with Anthony Braxton, David Rosenboom, my own improv groups – so I always had a foot wedged in both doors. It wasn't until I was in my forties that I started to work seriously with a rock band, Mr Bungle.

Thurston was asked to do the Festival International de Musique Actuelle de Victoriaville in Quebec, and the promoter wanted him to play with more than one other person. So, on Kim's suggestion, he called me. I was on tour with Mr Bungle in Europe but I was totally up for it. I'd always wanted to work with him but was too shy to ask. We got together and it turned out to be the perfect grouping – I knew Tom, I'd seen him play, but I'd never worked with him. He turned out to be my favourite free jazz drummer – he has a unique style and there's a nice flow to his playing. It gelled well because we all had that same interest in music and were listening to the same things, whether it was free jazz or experimental pop music or new music. We had the same record collections. It felt totally natural up on-stage.

Thurston Moore: Jetsun Dolma was a female Buddhist deity I read about at that time, so it was an instantaneous decision to call it that. William is a remarkable percussionist – he was John Cage's percussionist in his last stage of life, the first chair percussionist in the San Francisco Symphony Orchestra; also a scallywag. He's the kind of guy who'll come out on the orchestral bandstand with a skull and crossbones T-shirt and a Mohawk. He's always been really contrary to the formalism of classical music. We really connected – we were talking a lot about free jazz, especially free-jazz drummers, and he knew everything.

Lost To The City/Noise To Nowhere
Thurston Moore/Tom Surgal/William Winant
(Intakt Records, 2000)

William Winant: *Lost To The City* was recorded at Taktlos Festival in Switzerland in the spring of '97, when we played in Zurich, Basel and Bern. Taktlos was similar to Victoriaville, an improvisational, free-jazz music festival put on by three different spaces and run by a collective. What they did was they put it together and then they'd do one concert each night in each city for three or four nights, with all these groups switching around. A label sprang up in relation to the festival called Intakt, and so that record with Thurston and Tom was recorded in Zurich. Our performances were completely improvised. Every time we play it's been like that: no 'Let's do this', 'Let's do that', just open form. I try to keep an open and clear mind, try not to preconceive anything, just go out there and try to play as hard as I can, whatever I can add to the music but starting from this clean slate, fresh, for the first time.

Senso
White Out/Thurston Moore/Jim O'Rourke
(Ecstatic Peace!, 2009)

Tom Surgal: I guess Lydia Lunch was my first friend in a band. The first guest list I was ever on was for her *13.13* project. I had been the production designer on a no-wave film entitled *Vortex*, which Lydia starred in and Richard Edson and Adele Bertei did the score for. In the process of making the score, Richard enlisted the services of Thurston, which is how Lydia and Thurston first met, and it was through Lydia that I met Thurston. It was through Richard that I met Lin Culbertson. So it's kind of interesting that this truly crap movie spawned all these salient artistic connections.

Lin Culbertson: The inspiration for White Out was my acquisition of a Pro-One analogue synthesizer. It's really that simple. I bought one and was playing it and Tom joined in on drums. We were like, "Hey this is kind of hip," so we recorded a little cassette and gave it to a few friends that included Thurston and Byron Coley. We got a lot of positive feedback so we thought we should play some shows. Tom and Thurston were serious record-collecting buds, so when White Out made an actual studio recording, Ecstatic Peace! was the most logical label choice to approach. Thurston was always really supportive of the project. There was no label 'admin' at all! No contract, no advertising, no money, just a way to get the music out.

There was almost no one doing this kind of experimental music during the mid-nineties in NYC. There was the jazz scene that always operated as a giant cooperative, with everybody sitting in with each other, so I think we modelled ourselves after their example. The people that I can remember on the scene that played this type of crossover free-improv were The Blue Humans, The No Neck Blues Band, White Out, Test, K Salvatore. I was always reticent to leave the city for fear of missing something. There were always new clubs and art galleries opening up. I attended roving outlaw parties that took place all over the city – like the abandoned railtracks where the High Line is now – and hip-hop parties that happened on rooftops till dawn. There were not as many genre boundaries, and there was tons of cross-pollination happening between scenes. That was my favourite thing about that time: the art and music scenes were exploding with symbiotic support of each other. I think Giuliani's reign as mayor started the downward spiral of NYC club life. He would harass club owners with frequent visits by the fire department and continual fines. This was all part of a master plan to 'Disneyfy' NYC. As the chain stores moved in, all the old neighbourhoods started to lose their local character and rents went sky high.

William Hooker: I think there's less openness because of the economics. In the case of myself and Thurston, playing together wasn't our main project, those were our side projects. His bread and butter was Sonic Youth, mine was jazz and free jazz – so if we came together we did so to do things in idiosyncratic places for people who were open to it. I find that's definitely going backward or simply becoming 'less' – I'm just speaking of New York. There aren't that many clubs to be able to do this anymore. I think the time has passed. People are a little more toward catering for the audience and for those that are the producers and club owners. There were more places open to it before; there was no money in it but that was okay. People aren't taking chances now. They're playing music I heard in 1970, rehashed seventies-type music. And that's kind of boring. I can remember when this music was done in people's lofts, in squats, but now nobody can afford a loft in Tribeca unless they're a millionaire. It's a hollowed-out city – as a musician you become a person who doesn't even live in the city anymore. The people who buy the drinks, that's an important part of the equation; it's gaining more and more relevance sadly.

Lin Culbertson: White Out had been performing and recording with Jim O'Rourke for a while as a trio. So we thought, 'Why not add Thurston to the mix?' I think we only played about three shows with both of them before the *Senso* performance. There was never any pre-gig conversation about what would transpire. I like not knowing what's going to happen, even though it's a bit nerve-wracking.

Senso was two separate 40-minutes pieces, one piece from set one and one piece from set two, at Tonic on the night of December 18, 2004. This night was just one of those instances when the connection between us was strong and it resulted in something greater than the sum of its parts. Maybe we could just hear each other. During the quiet sections there was rapt silence, not the distracting background chattering you usually hear at a live gig. The thing about improv music is that there can be a special intensity to the live shows that won't necessarily come out in a studio setting. The adrenalin rush created by performing in front of a live audience without a safety net of song structure, or anything preconfigured, gives the music an additional element of excitement. Whenever I played with Thurston I was always impressed with his mastery of dynamics and his showmanship. He knows how to draw people in. I look up from my keyboard and all eyes are on him. I hardly even have to be there except to make the occasional *blip* or *bleep* sounds! It's always really effortless to play improv with Thurston because he creates this open sea of guitar wash that you can float on the surface of, or deeply immerse yourself in.

Instress Vol. 2 – 'Just Tell Her That I Really Like Her'/'Deirdre Of The Sorrows'
Loren Mazzacane Connors/Thurston Moore
(Road Cone, 1995)

Loren Connors: I come from the sixties and my inspiration was blues and the abstract expressionists. I didn't do anything publicly until the late seventies. Pretty much the only way to get music heard back then was through college and community radio stations. There was a small abstract

Loren Connors and Thurston playing the Stone, NYC, July 14, 2012.

Credit – Kurt Gottschalk

scene, but they weren't like me – their roots came more from jazz. People started connecting more with my music around 1990, with the growing independent music scene. I met Thurston Moore one night, in the early nineties, and was surprised that he already knew all about my music. Mike Hinds of RoadCone was doing a series and he wanted the two of us together. We each didn't know what the other was going to do. My song, 'Deirdre Of The Sorrows,' was taken from the work by the Irish playwright John Millington Synge, which was in turn based on folklore.

MMMR
Loren Mazzacane Connors/Jean-Marc Montera/ Thurston Moore/Lee Ranaldo (Xeric, Numero Zero, 1997)

Wharton Tiers: When Sonic Youth got the studio together they were all recording different solo things and a couple of times a week I'd go down there. Lee had called me up back when they were planning to put a studio together, suggesting I get involved. They wanted my help in setting it up in terms of getting it wired. They had ordered a bunch of crazy gear, the craziest of which was this Neve console – a broadcast console from maybe the early sixties, that had come out of a truck – and all the faders were backward. So when we first turned it on and pushed the faders up, there was no sound; we had to work out you had to pull them down. It had more relays in it than any console I'd ever seen in my life and it was hard to change without running into all kinds of problems – so it became a nightmare to reset things and to get back to where you wanted to be. When it was working right it had a great sound though, and you just don't find that in consoles anymore. When they started working with Jim O'Rourke, he hated the console – so that's when they took it out and shot it.

Lee Ranaldo: From the moment that we had our own serious studio we were off the clock, allowing each composition to reach its pinnacle. We'd had our own studio before; around the time of *Experimental Jet Set, Trash And No Star* we bought an eight-track reel-to-reel machine and a small mixing desk and were in a rehearsal space on Mott Street. We realised that was the way to go for us because it took us so damn long to write songs – it made sense that we should be recording our rehearsals for reference

71

and, ultimately, release. The Lollapalooza tour in '95 paid for all the Murray Street studio gear. We took a lot of our earnings that summer and invested it. We could have just divided it all up but we realised we needed to establish a studio that would serve us – and that has served us right through from then until now.

We showed up so often – normally around four afternoons a week – and we usually played in the afternoons so our evenings were free. Some days it'd just be exploratory playing and we'd make these amazing tapes in a more spontaneous manner. Without all the time-intensive development and brouhaha that would surround our next 'proper' album, we could now put out more experimental records on the side, records we could create quickly and release simply, for those interested to hear them. The studio was a very big deal; at that point you could invite friends in. We could see people around us, all these young artists, releasing not just their one big record a year but doing other stuff as well. People were figuring out how to self-release records – it was the beginning of a flood of small-label pressings. We wanted to get in on that!

Jean–Marc Montera: The first time I saw Thurston and Lee was in 1996 when Sonic Youth performed in Marseilles. Philippe Robert, who had a fanzine called *Numero Zero*, arranged a meeting and acted as the go-between. Robert had read an interview that took place in one room of Thurston's apartment. There was a photo of Thurston sitting in a chair and, behind him, the entire wall was upholstered with LPs. Philippe enlarged the photo until you could read the title of one of the LPs, because he recognised it was on the HatHut label. The record was *Mante* featuring Jacques Diennet, who was the composer and played the synclavier, Joe McPhee on cornet, André Jaume on bass clarinet, Irène Jarsky singing, Martine Pisani doing readings, Christian Tarting was the writer, and I played guitar and mandolin.

Philippe informed Thurston that I lived in Marseilles and organised a visit. The meeting was brief but very friendly. Thurston said something like, "Let me know if you come to New York, we could play together!" I thought he was very polite, very empathetic, but wasn't convinced that one of the leaders of Sonic Youth would find a couple of hours to spend with me. Sometime later, however, Thurston approached Philippe and my friend, Marie-Pierre Bonniol, to organise it so we would visit New York in January 1997 and record at Sonic Youth's studio. Thurston proposed the idea that Loren Mazzacane Connors would join us – it was a dream come true. Lee was busy for a lot of the week, doing production for a Spanish band, but he joined us while we were recording. We also did a concert at The Cooler with DJ Olive. It was an unbelievable, a truly unforgettable week.

Loren Connors: Everything happened easily. It was sort of a jam session. It's a conversation. It's not about picking a note to go with a note. It's about mixing vibes, laugh for laugh, sorrow for sorrow, blow by blow. I often have a directedness in my playing and people sometimes like to work with that. It was very casual. I never even knew it was going to be a record until it came out.

Jean-Marc Montera: In the early seventies I played rock music in a quartet with school friends. A friend of mine, both older than me and better educated, was an actress in a theatre company. One day she took me to a concert of improvised music; the Barre Phillips trio with the French guitar player Raymond Boni; the precise date my musical life changed. Since then, I've been really influenced by Derek Bailey's book *Improvisation: Its Nature And Practice In Music*. I consider free improvisation a working practice for the playing of music – and I make a clear distinction between improvisation in idiomatic music and free music. The improvising music which began during the sixties in the UK – AMM, The Scratch Orchestra, Derek Bailey – is not a musical style; it's a practice in the sense of being a new way of playing, fed by the diversity of musicians the practice inspired. They came from jazz, from contemporary music, from composed music, and each one has been an incredible source of wealth for this emerging music. Different music groups and artists rapidly appeared – mostly in Europe, such as MEV in Italy, Free Music Production in Germany – wherever musicians were shown the path. This attitude, the open door, to this very day it provides musicians with opportunities.

Les Anges Du Péché
Jean-Marc Montera/Thurston Moore/Lee Ranaldo
(Dysmusie, 2011)

Jean-Marc Montera: We created GRIM (*Groupe de Recherche et d'Improvisation Musicales*) in December 1978 as four musicians living in Marseilles. We all came from different spheres of music but we had one goal in common, to stage concerts of free music in our city. We went on to create the associated music label in 1983 and, after 1986, I directed the project alone. It's been a lengthy and perpetual battle to keep GRIM alive. In France, cultural associations (of which we are one) need justification in order to realise their activities. So, each year, we have to meet various people from the local authority's cultural department, and write responses defending the project's funding.

A couple of young musicians from St Etienne and Grenoble, Christian Malfray and Pierre Faure, have a duo called Nappe that I've invited to perform several times. Once was in 2010, when I played with Lee at GRIM. They created a record label and asked me to permit them to release the performance Lee and I had put on. An LP, however, requires two sides, so I suggested maybe we could use the duo between me and Thurston recorded in 1997 that had never been released.

The Only Way To Go Is Straight Through
Loren Connors/Thurston Moore
(Northern Spy, 2013)

Loren Connors: That was our live performance at The Stone. It was like an oven in there that night. I never sweated so much in my life; had to take off my shirt. It's a small place. People were sitting all around us on the floor. Thurston's style is much different from mine. He's more active and I'm more minimal. He doesn't stampede the person he's playing with, though. It's not a practising, rehearsing thing but it's not a jam session either. I wouldn't call it improvisation, even though it is 100 percent improvised. It's a coming together to compose something. I'd say we're both spontaneous composers, and that's why it works.

Piece For Yvonne Rainer
Thurston Moore
(Destroy All Music, 1996)

Thurston Moore: Working with Yoshimi [P-We, drummer with The Boredoms and founder of OOIOO] and Mark Ibold [bassist with Pavement and then with Sonic Youth], that was a session done in a rental house in

Amherst, Massachusetts, when Kim and I were investigating living up there. We decided, before we bought something, to rent a summer house. We went through the bulletin board of the University of Massachusetts and there was some professor's modest house available for rental. People would come and visit us; we would have cookouts and stuff. There was a great basement I'd postered. That's where that was done. Yoshimi plays mouth harp, then Mark and I jam with her.

I was reading a book about the history of the Judson Dance Theater, which was based at Judson Memorial Church in Greenwich Village. Yvonne Rainer figured very significantly – I was very enamoured by that history. In the book there were some photos and there was one of Yvonne dancing which became the cover of the release. I thought it was really provocative – I loved everything going on in the photo. This guy is contemplating without daring to gaze, this woman is actually gazing, this guy is thinking. Her stance is really remarkable. I thought, listening back to what we did, that it could stand as an instrumental dance piece, so in a way it was a gift to Yvonne Rainer.

Byron Coley: Coco and my daughter were born two weeks apart, so Kim and Thurston were trying to figure out what they would do, because their apartment was fine but it wasn't that big – the room they could use as a nursery wouldn't be big enough for a teenager, for instance. They got money for re-upping with Geffen, started looking in New York, but all the places that were big enough, they didn't like the neighbourhood. So they were here and saw this house in one of the real estate books they put out. So, when they left, my wife Lilly and I went and looked at it, decided it would be cool. It meant they could keep their place in New York, as well as buying this place and doing it up. Then by the time Coco was ready to go to school, she could go to school out here rather than in New York – it's a standard problem, people in New York are always wondering about schools.

Please Just Leave Me (My Paul Desmond)
Thurston Moore
(Pure, 1996)

Ron Lessard: I was running a thriving mail-order service and Thurston's was just another order I had received. I asked him to do a CD on my Pure series because, what the heck, he was a customer and I figured the worst that would happen is he'd say no. The written text included with the CD was submitted by Thurston and though I never asked him about it, I think it's just a note he left to a friend saying it's cool if he takes that stack of records but 'please just leave me my Paul Desmond records'. The original concept of Pure was to release a series of 50 budget-priced CDs over the last five years of the 20th century. On January 1, 2000, I officially retired the series, stopped using the card-stock Pure covers I made and repackaged my remaining stock as RRR titles. I chose the title 'Pure' because I was planning on doing only pure noise/extreme noise in the series; unfortunately, I lost focus on my original concept and ended up releasing titles that were more experimental, avant-garde – it's safe to say the *Paul Desmond* CD falls into the latter category. Also, I got caught up with the ease of releasing CDs and ended up releasing 55 titles over three years.

Thurston Moore: Ron needed something for the liner note and I had this poem I wrote, 'Please Just Leave Me My Paul Desmond', Paul Desmond being the saxophone player in Dave Brubeck's band – I thought it was a cool jazz record, 'take all my records but please leave me that'. I was in my little office in the apartment Kim and I had on Lafayette Street and I had a tiny amp and my guitar plugged in, so I did this instantaneous feedback piece for a certain period of time, up to the point where somebody buzzed the door – I decided that was the end of the piece. Very Dada, do something in the moment and send it away.

Ron Lessard: The image of the smiling man is Paul Desmond; I clipped it from the back cover of one of his LPs. I did not make the original design for the Pure series, it was by my friend Timm Williams – he was sort of my in-house design guy, he did many an artwork for RRRecords and my various sub-labels. The front-cover image is a photo of a peanut vendor standing in the aisle of a hockey game, there is a bit of fog rising from the ice – the back cover is the moon with my address.

There's also a record that's only available – *strictly* only available – to people who visit my shop for the sole purpose of buying records. The only way people can find out about them is if they visit my shop and look at the bin of my own RRR titles. It's not intended for collector types who want an exotic limited-edition LP with their picture on the cover; whenever I sell a copy, I ask the buyer to never write about it, blog about it, talk about it on the Internet. It's strictly for my customers and they've been really good about keeping it on the down-low. Each record is an edition of 100 copies and each copy sold is named after the person who buys the record and requires me taking six Polaroid photos of the person in my shop. So, if you came and bought a copy, then the name of the LP is *Thurston Moore: The Nick Soulsby Album* – I write the title on the front cover and the record label in black marker. I then take four of the Polaroid photos of you holding the record, one against each of the four walls of my shop, then I glue these Polaroids to the front cover. I then take two more Polaroids of you holding the finished product; one I keep for my scrapbook of every copy sold and I mail the other Polaroid to the artist for their scrapbook of every copy, so we each have a document of every person who bought a copy. About two years after the first release, Polaroid ceased production – fuck! It's now impossible for me to buy fresh Polaroid film and I can only find film that's past its expiration date, which means the photos are no longer sharp and clear; they're all faded and riddled with defects – which is kinda okay in an artsy-fartsy way but wasn't the intention.

When I asked Thurston to do the LP I specifically asked him to make the noisiest, most abrasive LP possible. He basically gave me his *Metal Machine Music*, a big, thick wall of guitar noise. Incidentally, I still haven't sent Thurston his scrapbook. I was waiting until I had a bunch of photos to put in it before giving it to him, but then he moved and I haven't been in contact with him since. Oh, and if I didn't say it enough, there's no point calling me to ask about it either. You want it? You visit the store. End of. Okay?

Electricity Vs Insects
Prick Decay/Thurston Moore
(Chocolate Monk, 1996)

Dylan Nyoukis: Prick Decay was myself and Lisa [Nyoukis], aka Dora Doll. Blackburn, West Lothian boredom gave us bellyache, so we started fucking about with cassette tapes. We were both out of high school, none of us in uni, the friend circle was starting to dissolve as people started to move onto 'better' things and we just ended up falling more and more into the underground. Stuck in the backwoods, we were lacking cultural sustenance.

I had heard about punk rock, well after the fact, in my earlier years; it sounded braw, then I heard it and it was so deflating: pub-rock-plod, maybe you had to be there? Anyhow, the punk aesthetic stuck with me even if the music left me limp. So I would record tapes for my own amusement with handmade covers but never thought there was anyone to push this crud to. Then, via some fanzine, I came across tape reviews for a few labels and made contact with the OSKA Products label. Turns out it was also a young man in his bedroom making sounds, and his muck did make me jig! His name was Jod [Russell], he lived in Patcham, East Sussex, and his wiggle made me realise that I could make some magic and some mungs would come. Finally, a year or two in I discovered *Bananafish* fanzine, and my brain was well and truly fingered. The Chocolate Monk label started to ferment in my brain...

Prior to that, I had the usual childhood wonk of creating little, handmade, one-off pamphlets, tapes and so on. I think all kids have that desire, and many adults also have that desire, but the capitalist system from school onwards is designed to kick that shit from our soft eggshell minds; creative guff is meant to be a hobby, unless you're one of the very lucky who are ordained to be 'entertainers', you know? Otherwise it's 'Get back to work and wake up!'

Thurston sent Chocolate Monk a letter. He had apparently picked up some Monk tapes in Rough Trade in London and he wanted to know what else was available. I think there might have been an Ecstatic Peace! list included – hawking for a trade, the bastard. I sent him all I had, he sent me some Ecstatic Peace! shit in return and a connection of geekdom was made, like a sickly little protein dribble. Then, sometime early '96, Prick Decay got an invite to open for Sonic Youth at Glasgow Barrowlands. We cobbled together a 'big band' featuring myself, Dora, Neil Campbell, Richard Youngs, Andy Bolus, Sticky Foster – and others including my six- or seven-year-old cousin on table-top guitar. It was a fair racket! I had a dance off backstage with the singer from one of the other bands; jigged his ass into oblivion.

At the time there were a lot of people just sniffing about for something to get the old juices running again. Rock was burnt out after the grunge thing, had been for years, but folks now were happy to dip their wick into the wilds – Sonic Youth were wet for that from the start.

Lee Ranaldo: In the wake of Nirvana, just a few years later, we, and many others too, were looking around for other avenues. You were being bombarded by all these supposedly credible rock bands that were being signed; a glut of pretty bad or at least uninteresting music, so much of it that I think a lot of artists turned their backs on that and started thinking, 'Well, let's make noise music for 45 minutes with no words or breaks in the music,'

78

taking inspiration from wherever – Cage, Stockhausen, The Grateful Dead, Terry Riley. This whole other investigation began opening up that was right up our alley, given how much we had explored various musical spaces.

Dylan Nyoukis: The seven-inch, that was a real pain in the ass. The whole idea came about back at that Barrowlands show. "Let's collaborate!", that was the shout. I can't remember who suggested it, but I do know that it was a common yelp back then. So the rough idea was laid right there in the grotty Barrowlands green room. Hands might not have been shook but the dude from one of the other bands sat exhausted in the corner, just looking on in defeat.

Anyhow, back to the record. Well, originally Thurston wanted to call it *Sunday Sport* after the shitty, titillating newspaper, I said, "Naw, man!" I later decided on *Electricity Vs Insects* after reading the William T. Vollmann novel *You Bright And Risen Angels*. The record was made via the post, no live recording together – I wanted the big lank to get back to doing some wonk. I had told him and Lee to sell all their guitars and replace each one with a Walkman; they seemed keen but never followed through. Wankers. So anyway, for Side A of that seven-inch there was some strange score that we had devised, a simple grid and dice scam, we threw the bones, Thurston was to pull a record and play an excerpt for a designated time and send us the tape. We received the tape of Thurston's sounds and then we did some kinda sherry-fuelled flip of the numbers and used those digits throughout the whole Side A. Side B was a different beef. There was some kind of cosmic octagon score we had devised – we were really smoked out – and the idea was to remove as much of the sounds of Thurston and Prick Decay and replace them with the sounds of the Glands Of External Secretion. We rolled and rolled 'til we got near absolute perfection.

Thurston Moore: The Prick Decay record is a mispress. It's always been a really annoying record! One side is me, the other isn't me – it's a guy called Seymour Glass who published *Bananafish* magazine. I'd sent Dylan tracks but my B-side piece, I don't know what happened to it! I asked Dylan and he just said, "I dunno!"

Songs We Taught The Lord Vol. 2
Phil X. Milstein/Thurston Moore
(Hot Cars Warp, 1997)

Songs We Taught The Lord Vol. 1
Phil X. Milstein/Thurston Moore
(no label, recorded 1996/released 2015)

Phil X. Milstein: I had known Thurston since the time I was in Uzi. When, some years later, Lee Ranaldo had to back out of a mini-tour he and Thurston had booked for two dates in Massachusetts, Thurston invited me to take his place. I was obviously flattered.

Musicians who play more conventional instruments have the entire range of their abilities at their disposal at any time, but part of the challenge of playing the instrument that I did was that I was limited to those sounds that already existed on my tapes. Thus it was always very important for me to have a wide range of sounds at my fingertips, and to have an intimate knowledge of exactly what sounds were at what spots on those tapes. That preparation was key to being able to succeed at what I did. I had dedicated cassette boxes, mini-suitcases that were slotted for the storage of cassette tapes. I had the spines of the tapes labelled extensively, with all sorts of info squeezed in there in increasingly tiny writing – not only shorthand prompts for what sounds the tape contained but also indications of where on it a particular sound was located. My tape parts were all carefully worked out in rehearsals, so ordinarily live performance was simply a matter of doing it.

Prior to the first show, I'd never played improvisationally. Not in public at least. The technique I worked out was to listen not just with my ears but also my imagination, and then reconcile what I was 'hearing' with the materials I had on my tapes. I'd been hoping to get a sense from Thurston in advance of what sorts of things he planned to do at the shows, but he said no to rehearsing or even to discussing it. As much as I wished otherwise, I respected his approach – after all, they were his gigs and he was an experienced improviser. I understood that I had to go with the flow but I also knew I had to refamiliarise myself with my tapes as thoroughly as I could, so that I could make choices that were more than mere guesswork or chance.

Those shows were fuelled, for me, by a lot of adrenalin, which I needed to stay as alert as I had to be. But Thurston made it easy by playing stuff that happened to fit well with sounds I had at hand. After a while, in fact, I began to feel confident enough to drive the collaboration here and there, rather than only respond. There was only one other band member, so I had a lot more sonic room to fill which led me to run two tape decks simultaneously for the shows. Not only had I never run more than one machine, even in practice, the second machine, which was a rental, was a model I'd never used before. I had just a few minutes with which to familiarise myself with it but, like two competing computer applications that do essentially the same thing, that was mostly a matter of figuring out what the different functions were called and where they were located. Running one machine, even with four tracks available to bring sounds in and out, I was still limited to what was on the tape that was running at the time; those tracks were all temporally locked to one another. Two machines, on the other hand, permitted a vast expanse of possible sound combinations.

The time onstage was mostly a blur; the most memorable aspect of the mini-tour was John Fahey opening for us. As someone who had scarcely paid any dues as a stage performer, I was mortified that I, in effect, was headlining over such a great and venerable artist. The one part of what we played that sticks in my mind is the 'tail' I came up with at the end of a show, as Thurston faded his guitar out. It was a bit from some sort of automobile instruction tape, a thrift-store find from a few days earlier which I hadn't yet had a chance to listen to. It was even cued up to a random spot and yet, as I brought it into the mix, it fitted perfectly, an ideal wrap-up.

The original plan was to release each of the two shows, but for some reason the first record never came out; thus we were left with a *Vol. 2* without a *Vol. 1*. I kind of liked it that way, though I also liked the recording of the first show and so, 20 years or so after the release of *Vol. 2*, I finally 'released' *Vol. 1* myself on my Probe downloads site.

Legend Of The Blood Yeti
13 Ghosts/Derek Bailey/Thurston Moore
(Infinite Chug, 1997)

Andrew Clare: I started a cassette label back in '86. I'd been running a little fanzine since I was just into my teens, so I was connected to all these people sending me tapes and zines. I was just this switched-on kid in a small town reaching out to an international community of weirdoes through any medium that worked – mail art, zines, tapes, flyers. It was a natural step to start messing around with tape recorders. I remember the first time I heard 'Brother James', I was so inspired but the only means I had available to me at the time to respond to that was plucking on an elastic band that was wrapped around the built-in mic on a dictaphone. Infinite Chug grew out of the tape label, again from a kind of 'What happens if I do this? Can I get away with it?' approach. It was a really good time to be putting records out, there seemed to be something of a blooming at the time of people from the lo-fi tape scene making tentative steps into vinyl. Distributors and shops were receptive, even supportive – anything seemed possible. What actually catalysed me to put the first single out was I'd sent a cassette by my band, I'm Being Good, to John Peel, and, out of the blue, he phoned me up and told me how much he liked it. I guess that was all the encouragement I needed.

The *Legend Of The Blood Yeti* album grew out of a process of everyone just pushing their luck. Ben [Switch] and Alex [Ward] were already working with Derek Bailey on and off and were keen to get him on board. Somewhere along the line I remember reading an interview with Thurston where he was enthusing about Derek's playing; around the same time someone gave me Thurston's fax number, and we thought, 'Well, why not drop him a line?' I'd never even used a fax machine before, had to go to the post office. It all felt so flimsy and tenuous that this was ever going to actually happen.

Alex Ward: Thurston had a free daytime during Sonic Youth's three-night residency at the Kentish Town Forum, so we booked a rehearsal studio in South London and brought down our own recording gear. Thurston showed up and plugged straight into the rehearsal-room amp, we played for a couple of hours. After that, the next time I bumped into Thurston was at Taktlos Festival in 1997, and then our paths didn't cross for another 15 years...

Andrew Clare: We just turned up, plonked some mics in front of things, hit record, and played for a few hours. We did okay to get the sound we did with our hastily positioned, borrowed mics mixing straight to stereo. We all seemed very comfortable in a practice-space environment and there was no third-party engineer glaring at us from behind a double-glazed window the whole time – had we gone down the studio route, the performances would have been very different. We didn't take much time out for actual conversation beyond discussing the task at hand. We took a breather at one point and stood outside in the sun for a while, then jumped back in and went nuts. It was the strangest thing ever but also completely natural, but stranger still because of how natural it felt. So, kind of a high-intensity vortex system caused by a cold front of strangeness meeting a warm front of naturalism.

Pillow Wand
Nels Cline/Thurston Moore
(little brother records, 1997)

In Store
Nels Cline/Thurston Moore
(Father Yod, 1997)

Nels Cline: It'll sound self-deprecating but I think I'm pretty objective about the fact that, by 1984, I was a full-blown Sonic Youth obsessive. I wished, in a way, that I could unlearn all the things I knew about music so I could participate in something that had that feeling, that sound. I became a real fanatic.

I was working at Rhino Records, except for a brief run at a record distributor, from late '76 until '85. I decided to start putting on in-store meet 'n' greets with Sonic Youth because I knew there was a lot of interest in them. But then it also meant I got to hang out with them. I had first met Kim and Thurston in '83. Thurston was shopping and somebody said they wanted me to talk to him, because Sonic Youth were looking for more places to play in Los Angeles. I thought that was really odd because I couldn't even get gigs in Los Angeles at the time and I wasn't playing anything like Sonic Youth's music. I was playing in an acoustic chamber jazz group; I was playing with a man in New York named Julius Hemphill, a saxophone/woodwind player; I was playing nylon-string guitar with Charlie Haden. I didn't know what I could possibly tell Thurston Moore. Anyway, he called me up, we chatted, then he came into the record store with Kim to visit, gave me a *Confusion Is Sex* T-shirt and was super nice.

It was when I started playing on and off with Mike Watt years later that Watt asked me why Thurston and I had never played together. I said, "Well, we are friendly, but I'm just a psycho fan. Who wants to hang out with a psycho fan?" Watt replied, "Well, I'm making my record with all these people so I'm going to enable you." I recorded a bunch of tracks for *Ball-Hog Or Tugboat?* [Watt's solo album released in 1995] in Los Angeles. I came out to New York for one session to record with Lee, Steve, Thurston, J Mascis and Watt on a few tracks. I think it was when I started playing and touring with Watt that Thurston and the others started to view me differently. Maybe they felt that anyone willing to get in the van with Watt was way more hardcore than they'd assumed. I started playing on tour for Watt in 1995 and our paths crossed a lot. Thurston and I discussed the idea of what we started to call the 'Dream Guitar Project'. We didn't mean that the dream was the two of us playing together; we meant the music was going to be super dreamy and minimal. The idea became *Pillow Wand*. I came up with the name from a particular type of eye-shadow applicator I remembered from a TV commercial in the seventies. I thought that the Pillow Wand was a really good metaphor for dream guitar because it looked kind of like a tiny guitar and we were into this feminine energy, Thurston and me were both into feminism and there was a lot of 'riot grrrl' stuff going on too.

Kim and Thurston used to come to LA every Christmas to visit her family. So it was one of those times that Thurston and I got together to record. We went to my friend Wayne Peet's garage studio in Mar Vista, West Los Angeles. Wayne's studio is literally in his garage; he's literally sat next to you as you play, no isolation or anything. Thurston and I spent maybe two hours creating this really minimal music with almost zero discussion.

Later in the evening, we had an in-store appearance set up at Rhino Records where I used to work. They had a small, low stage – even Nirvana played on that stage in the *Bleach* days – and mostly people just stood in the aisles. We headed over there, taking the same equipment and guitars we'd just recorded with. We set up and as we were about to play, I realised my friend Wayne, who we had just finished recording with, was there setting up his stuff. "Wait a minute, what are you doing here?" And he said, "Oh, David Crouch asked me to record it." "But we only just left your house!" David was the manager and knew how excited I was to finally be doing something with Thurston. So, behind our backs, he and Byron had decided they were going to put out whatever we played that day.

The CD of *Pillow Wand*, I believe, reflects the sequence in which we recorded the music. The first thing and the last thing on the disc are the most minimal pieces – and I had written the piece called 'We Love Our Blood' that basically consists of an opening statement from me, then this repetitive arpeggio with Thurston letting loose over the top of it. That's the closest we got to structure, to having to learn a piece. The one called 'Tommy Hall Dragnet' happened because Thurston really liked the tremolo on my little amp he was using, so he just cranked it up and started doing stuff then I responded. Tommy Hall was the jug player from The 13th Floor Elevators. Thurston and I both decided there was something about

Thurston's sound on that piece that reminded us of Tommy playing the electric jug, so we had this idea: 'Where is Tommy Hall?' This was before the Internet told us everything, so we just wondered, 'What's he doing?' That informed the track title.

While *Pillow Wand* was this deliberate plan to get together and make a record, we had no agenda to make a recording with *In Store*, it was just a live gig. It possesses elements from *Pillow Wand* because we were working off the same set of ideas, but we allowed it to go wherever it felt like going. Some really great improvising happened and I was really excited.

On *In Store* I used this looping device I've had since the mid-eighties and that I'm still using. On the recording, if you hear backward things, strange loops, stuff like that, that's me. Other than that I think one of the most enjoyable aspects of both these recordings, for me, is that the sound is just one big guitar. Good improvisation for me is where it keeps finding new areas; it doesn't just stay in one place. Thurston is capable – if he's playing with Mats Gustafsson or somebody like that – of staying at a high level of intensity for most, if not all, of the improvisation. What happened with *In Store* is what I enjoy, a dynamic performance where ideas don't outstay their welcome, where the sound keeps developing. I think some of the areas we explored are literally gorgeous. It's crucial though to know when it's done. With *Pillow Wand*, when we stopped, Thurston simply said, "Yeah, that's it." I nodded and we just knew we had what we were looking for.

Since then, when Thurston and I have played together, we've taken to calling the duo Pillow Wand. It's basically a chance for me to go into that sound–world, a place I feel so close to and admire so much, then try to live there as long as I can. Probably my greatest strength as a player is improvising. I meet people halfway at least, find common ground and work in that area. I'm not pushing an agenda or sticking to playing only what I know.

Kerouac: Kicks Joy Darkness – 'The Last Hotel'
Patti Smith/Lenny Kaye/Thurston Moore
(Rykodisc, 1997)

Thurston Moore: I went to the Kerouac Festival in Lowell, Massachusetts by order of a magazine to interview Patti Smith. I was in La Guardia

Airport and Lenny Kaye was sitting there, so we flew to Boston together. He kind of had an inkling of who I was, but he didn't really know – I could tell. But I definitely knew who he was. When we got there Patti asked me, "Why don't you play with us at this reading?" So they secured me an extra acoustic guitar, we figured out what we were going to do and I got this great poster signed by everybody. That's where that recording must come from. I played with them again at St Mark's Church in the Bowery for a New Year's Day poetry reading – they do a marathon poetry reading every New Year's Day.

'Telstar'/'Sputnik'
Don Fleming/Thurston Moore, Experimental Audio Research
(Via Satellite, 1997)

Don Fleming: I was really into Joe Meek. As a producer I loved his stuff and loved that song ['Telstar']. So I was approached by the label to perform a cover and I asked Thurston if he would join. We recorded on a little multitrack I had at home; it was a little home-brewed thing, just one of those things: "If you wanna come over tomorrow I'm recording this." We asked them to put a postcard inside that had a picture of a tuba made by Walter Sear, from Sear Sound.

Foot
Foot
(God Bless Records, 1998)

Jim Dunbar: Foot formed in 1997. The three of us had been jamming a little as a threesome and we were feeling good; talked about playing a gig. Thurston showed up one day and said we can name a band after anything. He pointed down to a guitar case on the floor on which my friend, the painter Charles Miller, had written 'foot' in fluorescent paint: "We're Foot."

Don Fleming: We had been doing a series of improv performances at a friend's loft apartment, Jim Dunbar's. He was down on Canal Street, we set some gear up, people would drop by and we'd flick everything on. We called it 'NeMocore'. It was a loft project where there was just a bunch of synthesizers and gear set up.

Jim Dunbar: Jimbo's pad was located at 363 Canal Street on the border of SoHo and Tribeca. My part of Canal Street was, for all intents and purposes, a truck route connecting Brooklyn to Manhattan to New Jersey. Canal Street at night was already noisy. The trucks would rumble by and the whole building would shake; the building shaking was the Canal Street sound. My spot was the top floor, six steep flights up. Before I moved in I put down three layers of insulating foam over the old floor and then covered the foam with half-inch plywood and then laid down wall-to-wall carpet. I was trying to soundproof in a crude way.

Don Fleming: All the NeMocore bands worked to simple rules: no drums; no electronic drums because they were mimicking the drums; no acoustic instruments allowed; it had to be improv based on electronics. Over time that developed into a thing with several bands – My Fork, Turbulence, Bus, The Dolman, Three Way Split, Broken Chair. It was like the cassette label thing back when I was in DC, where there were a dozen bands on it that no one had ever heard of. We came up with the term 'NeMocore' almost as an internal joke.

The Foot stuff was just Thurston and I showing up at Jim's place and jamming, then someone wanting us to do a show. Our rule was that we wouldn't play clubs or places set up to be musical. We'd play art galleries mostly but we also played at a library. There was no rhyme or reason – people would just get in touch and ask Thurston if we would do a gig. He'd decide if it sounded good, then, as we didn't need a PA because we had no vocals, we'd just show up with our gear.

Lin Culbertson: The NeMocore session was a very fun night after a show. We went to Jim Dunbar's house and had a massive synth jam, with all this cool old vintage gear that he had been collecting over the years. Jim had secured a lot of his gear from auction lists, so some of the instruments had crazy backstories to go along with them. Afterward we watched this wild animated Kraftwerk video, if memory serves.

Gene Moore: When we did the recording for NeMocore at Jim Dunbar's apartment, Patti Smith happened to stop by – we had been to her show earlier and this was around one in the morning. She asked if she could sit in with her clarinet but one of the guys said, "This is an electronic gig, you'll get drowned out!" So she shrugged. Later we looked at each other, wondering, 'What the fuck did we just do?' Blew it! Ha!

Jim Dunbar: We went to the New Year's Day Poetry Marathon at St Mark's Church. Patti was intrigued about what we were doing and came back with us, and brought along Oliver Ray who was playing guitar in her band. She brought her clarinet and wanted to jam but we told her she had to plug into something, anything. She just wanted to play clarinet. So we told her she could go onto Canal Street and play the clarinet through the intercom. She looked at us like we were crazy and went home.

Kim Rancourt: Recordings were over before you knew it, on purpose. I was invited to Jim's loft and Don told me to bring the Casio sax. He and Jim recorded me in the vestibule of his building, me playing the sax into the speaker that you spoke into to gain admittance after you buzzed the buzzer − they recorded it off the intercom speaker in Jimbo's apartment. I and guitarist Bob Meetsma also recorded a cassette of sounds at his place of some guitar stuff and, I think, a blender. Then they took all the contributions and mixed them into the masterpiece *This Is NeMocore*. As followers of Captain Nemo, we created our own movement. We had to follow him. Music was imploding; we had to seek a master who could peel paint with just his vibe! Nemo music that had shivering ovaries and a salute to everyone and our future; music not contained by guilt or profit; but just for Him.

Jim Dunbar: We had a philosophy about the music we called NeMolodics, which was based on the NeMocore ethos of electricity/no drums and Ornette Coleman's harmolodics. The three of us would start out in our own improvisational spaces but over the course of time those three spaces would become one; we called that moment the NeMolodic convergence. 'Electrical Storm' was recorded during a thunderstorm with the windows wide open and a mic picking up all the sounds through the intercom to the street. 'Symphony For Dog' was recorded shortly thereafter. Don was hitting notes on his ARP Axxe that only a dog could hear. Notice on the CD that all the running times are about the same? We recorded on the Marantz four-track and wouldn't hear it shut off when it reached the end of the cassette.

Velvet Goldmine
Wylde Ratttz
(London Records, 1998)

Don Fleming: The drummer from Ron Asheton's band in Detroit had sought me out to come and produce them – that was the beginning of the chain. Shortly after that, the idea came up where they needed a Stooges soundalike band for one song in this movie. So I said, "Let's get Ron – he's available." Things just started to fall into place. Steve and Thurston immediately seemed like the rhythm section, Thurston had played bass for The Velvet Monkeys, but we changed and got Mike Watt in on bass so Thurston was on guitar. In the first session we brought Mark Arm in to do this Stooges song, 'TV Eye', they needed. But like other things it turned into a case of, 'Wow, this is fun!' So we ended up doing a second session and knocked out a whole bunch of songs. Sean Lennon came in for the second session; that was another one that was sheer coincidence. He'd just been in the studio working and we ran into him and thought we should bring him in. Again, the idea, maybe it's overkill but it was the fun of throwing in new elements to keep everyone on their toes. They didn't even use Mark's vocal on the movie, Ewan McGregor re-sang it, though Mark's version did get used in *School Of Rock*, the Jack Black film.

Jim Dunbar: The first night at Sear Sound, Ron, Watt and Mark came straight from the airport and we jammed out on the first two Stooges records. Epic jams! Twenty-minute versions! This was the first time everyone was in the same room together and it was magic from the first count-off. I asked everyone to be prepared to write. Ron showed up with some lyrics penned by Niagara [from Destroy All Monsters] and day two, we cut 'TV Eye' and started to work on original songs. Ron and Mark got together and wrote 'Be My Unclean' and we cut it right away. Thurston sang 'She's Like Poison', which was Niagara's one-note "Have Thurston do this." Michael Stipe was one of *Velvet Goldmine*'s producers and we were told he had some lyrics for us; we never saw them but he did stop by. So we were having all these songs messengered to the *Velvet Goldmine* office and we kept recording; new songs, new jams and extended Stooges' riffage. Don and I started putting together CD-Rs of the best stuff and making cover art. By the end of day two we had created a couple of 'albums'. Day three,

Todd Haynes, the director, wanted us to record 'Gimme Danger' but Ron refused. He still had bad feelings about how Bowie's management treated him during that period of The Stooges. The film folks offered us some extra dough to do the song and we took the bones so we could pay Sear Sound; we never told them Ron wasn't on it. Ron came back when we were finished and we cut 'Fun House' with Sabir Mateen on sax. We packed in a fortnight's worth of recording in three days.

Ewan sang to our instrumental track in the film but for just a brief moment. The people in charge wanted a full version of 'TV Eye' for the soundtrack and we booked time at Sear Sound but he was a no-show. In Ewan's defence, he never knew about the session; he was doing *Star Wars* and was double booked. Finally, he had time to do a quick one in London and I was sent to produce. I had an hour with Ewan, which is crazy – his people treated it like he was dubbing a line. Not his fault.

Don Fleming: J Mascis came by but we were maxed out on guitar so he didn't play – but not long after he did his Stooges thing, a few shows with Ron, which led to Iggy Pop hearing what Ron was doing and deciding that the Asheton brothers could still do the songs pretty well. That's another reason we didn't put the record out – why bother putting out Wylde Ratttz if The Stooges are back together? Mission accomplished! It was a mess anyway, tied up with the movie, and we'd all moved on.

This Is NeMocore
(Instant Mayhem 1999)

Jim Dunbar: It was Don who started recording everything; any music that survives is because of Don. Thurston would wrangle a crowd and I provided the space. Don and I were in a heavy krautrock phase and were especially influenced by The Cosmic Jokers. The records started out as acid-party jams that were edited into larger pieces and this is what we tried to do with our CD-R. There are 21 different musicians in countless combinations edited together on that release; it was a conscious decision on our part to make this 'scene' a collective.

But here's the truth about the 'scene'. [Brit journalist/musician] Everett True came through town and, after a few drinks, Don, Everett, Bil Emmons [engineer at Sear Sound] and I ended up back at my place and we jammed. Afterward, as we drank wine, we told Everett what we were doing in terms of recording and looking to make a Cosmic Jokers' 'sci-fi party' style record which would be all electric and "free from the fascistic constraints of timekeeping".` We called our music neo-modern but tongue in cheek; it was Everett who coined the phrase NeMocore. He then proposed writing a short piece in *Melody Maker* about the 'Canal Street scene'. Don and I made up a bunch of band names and a movement was launched; whenever we had a jam we would take a name from the list and say, "These people are now Turbulance!" We would tell them before we started recording, "You are now in a band."

Jeg Gleder Meg Til År 2000
'Armageddon' – Foot
(Universal, 1999)

Jim Dunbar: We did another recording that Thurston hooked up. Universal Records in Norway released a compilation of bands covering songs by the experimental Norwegian band Holy Toy. We covered 'Armageddon'. We recorded our vocals through the intercom on the street; only time we ever sang.

Live At The Cooler
Foot
(Breathmint, 1999)

Jim Dunbar: When we played out we felt that a Foot performance began when we all gathered at Jimbo's Pad. We'd drink a couple of beers, smoke some American jazz cigarettes and plot our performance. Sometimes Chris Grier would be there to drive and hump gear. On the way to the club we'd stop and try to shanghai someone like Bebe Buell, or go into some shitty tourist bar and drink whisky while we explained the NeMocore manifesto to the bartender. We had swagger! We'd tell strangers we were New York's premier noise-improv band, the founders of NeMocore. It was rock-star theatre.

Thurston Moore: There was a Foot performance at the Flywheel in Easthampton. Mat Rademan [Breathmint label founder] has this solo thing, Newton, and he asked if Foot would play with them. Don Fleming was visiting, Tom Verlaine was visiting, J Mascis was around, so we went and did a Foot gig. I created this thing where we got in my Volvo and did this performance happening. I had filmed Jim O'Rourke doing his version of yoga exercises on a yoga ball and I had one of those TVs that took VHS tapes right in the front. So I brought the TV into the space, there were maybe 30 noise kids hanging around in the middle of the afternoon with all the lights off. I turned the TV on and started showing this; people are wondering, 'What's going on?' Then I got a really long cable with a microphone, took the microphone out to the car with the cable plugged into the PA, then put the microphone in front of the speakers of the car radio. So, in the car is me at the steering wheel, Don Fleming in the passenger seat, then in the back are Tom Verlaine and J Mascis. Jim is on top of the car, on the ball, doing yoga exercises. We start revving the car and as I rev the car it makes this great sound through the car radio system, all this noise that was pouring into the space. Every once in a while I'd lean on the horn. So people were coming out of the club, seeing this car with all of us inside and O'Rourke on top. We do this for about five-ten minutes, then some guy in a wifebeater and his pants comes out and starts shaking his finger at us: "Stop blowing your fucking horn!" Time to go! Jim jumped off the roof, got in the back and we sped off – the microphone flipping out of the window. That was our performance.

We did a Fluxus show event for the release of Al Hansen's book *Playing With Matches* – he's Beck's grandfather. All these Fluxus performers were there. Marianne Faithful was playing and there were sections where they were doing classic Fluxus performance pieces. I was asked to be involved; I thought it'd be good for Foot so we thought, 'What can we do?' We decided to get a male stripper to perform while we played. I knew this guy, called him up, asked him if he knew where we could get a male stripper. "So you need someone like one of the male go-go-dancers who dance on the bar down in Chelsea? How about I take you guys out and we'll go find one?" So, me, Don and Jim, with this guy who was a habitué of all these places, went on a bit of a crawl of all these go-go clubs and gay discos, guys in cut-off hotpants and no shirts with people sticking dollar bills in their crotches. We got fabulously drunk and at the last place we just said, "That guy there'll work." We approached him, told him if he showed up at this time tomorrow we'd give him $50, that we'd be performing for five minutes.

Jim Dunbar: At the reception, Thurston started telling people that Foot was an acronym for 'Fluxus-Orientated Oscillating Thrash'. It was a mixture of high society and art-world celebrities; front table had Gwyneth Paltrow and Kate Moss, next table over sat Yoko.

Thurston Moore: Our stripper showed up and he was amazing. After all this relatively polite and pleasant improv stuff, we had the amps on 11 and went for a barrage of electronic noise as this audience just sat there at their tables like, 'What the fuck…?' Then out comes the go-go dancer and starts doing his slow-writhing go-go thing as if he's on top of a bar with sexy disco records playing.

Jim Dunbar: We crunched. Loud and free wailin' with Leo gyratin'. We hit our NeMolodic convergence and I remember looking up and seeing Kate and Gwyneth with hands over ears and pained expressions. When we finished Yoko stood up, clapping and shouting, "Bravo, bravo!" Like Orson Welles in *Citizen Kane*. Afterward, Yoko came to the dressing room and told us we were truly Fluxus and "the best". The next day Ann Powers reviewed the event for *The New York Times*.

Thurston Moore: The article said that it was all fairly staid except, "The only true Fluxus moment was when Foot came out." We knew we were the miscreants of the night. We were so proud. Yeah… Foot had its glory.

Fringe Benefits
The Walter Sears
(Instant Mayhem, 1999)

Jim Dunbar: Besides *This Is NeMocore*, Don and I also put one out by a group we named The Walter Sears, called *Fringe Benefits*. *Fringe Benefits* was a sexploitation film that Walter Sear produced and Roberta Findlay directed back in the seventies – I believe there was a poster in the studio lounge. Not NeMo, this overlaps with the Wylde Ratttz as The Walter Sears were Tom Smith and Rat Bastard from To Live and Shave in L.A.,

Steve Shelley, Sean Lennon, Thurston, Don and me. I put this together from tape sources I can no longer remember at Sear Sound, when we were waiting around for Ewan McGregor to sing his vocal on 'TV Eye'. Ewan never showed up, so Don and I overdubbed a couple of things and mixed the track. A few months later I worked on a film called *Committed*, which starred Heather Graham. There's a scene where Heather's character comes home to a loud party raging in her apartment and screams, "Turn that shit off!" The song playing in the released version of the film is 'Fringe Benefits'. We're in the credits.

Riddim Warfare – 'Dialectical Transformation III (Soylent Green)' DJ Spooky (Outpost Recordings, 1998)

Paul D. Miller: There was a lot of resistance to what I was doing, it was warfare! That's where I got the album title from. It was incredible how much bitter anger was levelled at me just because I was doing something different. And this was from people you would think would be more progressive, more flexible. Critics who supported what Sonic Youth were doing in rock would rain hellfire on me because of what I was doing to rhythms.

The conversations me and Thurston got into had a lot of 'What is an instrument?' Is the turntable an instrument? Can the guitar be deconstructed after traditional tuning systems have taken hold? The guitar has a tremendous amount of legacy that the turntable doesn't. Thurston is also one of the few people I can go toe to toe with about limited–edition–records; I collect vinyl. There was this one museum exhibition at a space called Exit Art on the history of the record cover sleeve. It was curated by Carlo McCormick and they had some of my record collection, some of Thurston's record collection, John Zorn's record collection. That's when we realised there was a kindred spirit, it was a pleasure to talk about information and ideas. With most musicians it's usually a drag; a lot of musicians don't know about art and a lot of artists don't know about music. The Sonic Youth guys, they actually think, they knew about all of that.

The concept behind *Riddim Warfare* was 'world as mixtape'. Thurston was really into mixtapes, so am I. This is where the metaphor of collage becomes the basic substrata of how I think about things. I wanted to think of Thurston's guitar solos as collage material, so we printed his pieces to vinyl and I did scratch routines based on the noise of the guitar, then mixed that with beats.

Subliminal Minded: The EP – 'Dialectical Transformation III Peace In Rwanda Mix' DJ Spooky (Outpost Recordings, 1999)

Paul D. Miller: I tried to figure out a cool, fun thing that would open up the door to conversations about change and permutation. The 'Peace In Rwanda Mix' title, that was because it seemed like an example of an impossibility. The track is called 'Dialectical Transformation' because dialectic means a conversation. If you go back to the beginning of western philosophy, dialectical process is how philosophy moved forward. I don't see any point of closing down when I'm making a track – no beginning, middle or end – that's why I called the track 'dialectical', because it can go in many different directions. I see albums as snapshots, they're not about having finished versions, so I try to put that out there. People resist that, they want a finished thing, because it suits labels, because they're processing a specific something they can sell. Whenever I do something it's always iterative, I don't do anything that's just one thing – I want multiple approaches. The implicit logic is that everything can be changed; doing electronic music, you have to be open to the fact that anything you do, remixing is just a part of the process. The hard part of being experimental is there's no path in front of you, you're making the path as you go.

The Secret Song – 'Known Unknowns' DJ Spooky w/Mike Ladd (Thirsty Ear, 2009)

Paul D. Miller: Another overlap between me, Thurston, Lee Ranaldo; it's the idea of sound as a secret world, as a political dimension. This time we're in, we're facing an extinction of languages, of species, a consolidation of the human genetic map; McDonalds of the mind. People have been straitjacketed into very narrow concepts of what they think of as culture. When I was coming up in the nineties, The 'illbient' scene in NYC was meant to be an insurgency about sound, about removing the boundaries between genres. Now we live in an era of algorithms, Spotify and SoundCloud zombies, so anything goes but it's all algorithmically driven. You can do anything with a computer but most people are being railroaded straight into Facebook, Twitter, it's all about particular formats and it really governs their whole aesthetic. People absorb an implicit sense of rules without being told; it's a Pavlovian reflex. Most people are using 4/4 rhythms, it's pretty much standard worldwide, which is eerie. I'd be willing to go toe to toe with psychoanalysts to argue that it's all about a fear of complexity. Most people are struggling to live, let alone to thrive; simplicity gives people a sense of a little more peace. It's kind of like that phrase "religion is the opiate of the masses", we can easily say that digital media is the new opium, the new poison. People fear complexity but noise is one of the most complex things the human mind can conceive of – it makes people go crazy, it makes them flee. Noise purifies the mind, and me and Thurston were into those issues – me from a hip hop and African-American perspective; Thurston, meanwhile, is a pretty white-bread guy. That's healthy, mixing and having different perspectives, that makes humanity move forward – no reductionist bullshit.

Root
Thurston Moore
(Lo Recordings, 1998)

Jon Tye: In the early days Lo Recordings was very much about collaborations, experiments to see what would happen when a musician from one area or era worked with someone from a different area or era. We did a whole album of collaborations and one track involved Lol Coxhill. I saw that Lol was doing a gig at The Jazz Café in Camden with Thurston Moore and Lee Ranaldo and various free-jazz luminaries under the banner 'Nuclear Jam'. The gig was great, people got really offended by the music and were shouting and leaving in droves. By the end of the concert the venue was a quarter full. I went backstage, ostensibly to chat with Lol. I saw Thurston and asked if we could have a brief chat; he said. "No!" And then,

"Just kidding." I asked him if he'd be interested in doing something for the label. He said "Okay, I'll send you some stuff. If you don't hear from me, you can hassle me," and gave me his fax number, so I started sending faxes saying, "I'm hassling you (you said I could)." Eventually, a DAT tape arrived with 30 one-minute guitar pieces. As I recall, Thurston went into the studio and, as soon as he had a sound he liked, he'd play and ask the engineer to hit record for 30 seconds. As soon as he had 30 pieces the session was over. The initial idea was I'd give them to Graham Sutton but, after a year or so, Graham still hadn't produced anything so I started to think of other ideas. Gradually, the idea evolved to send the recordings to visual artists as well as musicians; the list got longer and more ambitious. Eventually we had a plan. I emailed Thurston (it was a year later and I had email but was still very new to it and used to mail him entirely in CAPITALS, until someone pointed out that this was considered rude and akin to shouting) and he seemed to dig it. I took the idea to Jon Forss.

Jon Forss: Jon met me for a drink one evening and told me about the DAT from Thurston, and that he wanted to send out the 30 tracks individually to about 100 or so recording and visual artists as a starting point for new musical compositions or, in the case of the visual artists, as inspiration for artworks of some kind; any kind. Jon asked me to design an invitation that would appeal to a pretty diverse bunch of creative individuals. Of course, this meant I was under quite a bit of pressure to come up with something that would stand out amongst all the other stuff the folks on the list might get sent to them each day. Jon suggested we call it *Seed*, which made sense given it suggested some kind of starting point.

I soon found myself with one last Sunday to work on it before Jon would be expecting to see something. I was at a loss. Everything I tried seemed like a dead end. And then my girlfriend at the time called me to see how I was getting on. I told her in desperation that it felt like I was working in a vacuum. And then it struck me exactly what we should do…

The next day I told Jon that we should go and buy 100 blank, generic, vacuum-cleaner bags and silkscreen-print the invitation onto the front using the kind of typographic layout you might see on those kinds of bags. We could then prise open the sealed end, fill each bag with fluff and dust, drop in the DATs, seal them up and send them out in clear mailing bags. The core idea was that the DAT had somehow been vacuumed up off Thurston's studio floor and he was sending them out to his friends, bag and all. I also suggested we change the name from *Seed* to

Root. I liked the double meaning of 'root' as a starting point and 'root' as the action of digging around to find something – in this case, the DAT in the bag.

Jon liked all this apart from one important detail. He said there was no way on Earth he was going to send bags filled with a stinky mixture of fluff, human hair and dead skin cells to his list of VIPs. He had a point. We needed to find something far more sanitary. So we got hold of a bunch of yellow-coloured, blank, generic, vacuum-cleaner bags, I designed the invitation which was silkscreened onto the bag in a deep-red ink, and then we settled on kapok for the filling. Kapok is a fluffy, organic material used for stuffing teddy bears and suchlike. It's not exactly the same as the contents of a real bag of fluff and dust but it was close enough to convey the idea and, more importantly, it's clean.

Jon Tye: Usually a copious amount of beer helped the thought process. With David Bowie we mailed a package to his management with my home phone number on the bag, and one day he just phoned up and said, "This is David Bowie..." Even Yoko Ono said yes, but unfortunately her schedule didn't give her enough time. We tried to persuade Gilbert and George; they said they didn't have anything to play tapes on so we bought them a Walkman and delivered it to them in person – maybe they couldn't figure out how to work it as we never received anything from them, but generally the response was amazing.

Stuart Braithwaite: Mogwai were wee guys still living at our parents' and couldn't believe everything that was happening. These were the days when we had no money and getting free records was a big deal, so getting some CDs through the label, we were happy with that. It gave us a bit of a spring in our step because we were such huge fans that, even though it was pretty tenuous, having some kind of connection with Thurston was definitely exciting at a time that was already super-exciting. We were getting a lot of offers to be on compilation albums, but this was a little bit different. Someone at the label sent us out a tape of weird noises and we made some other weird noises and mashed it together. There's something about remixing – it's not quite a collaboration but you get to look behind the curtain of how someone works and it's nice to see, with your own music, how people interpret it. We recorded something specially; layered feedback, this weird, overwhelming noise panning from left to right which we were doing by adding loads and loads of feedback.

Jon Tye: There were instructions on the bag but they basically said that the person was free to respond to the piece in any way they wished. There was certainly much hilarity and a certain amount of hysteria involved, it was a lot of fun but became quite stressful. The project grew into an exhibition and the orders for the CD and vinyl increased steadily – at one point we had to hand-package 4,000 CDs, each into a vacuum cleaner bag that then went into a 'film front' bag, which was then stickered and individually stamped.

Claire Robins: I was invited, I think, because I had a solo show at the Commercial Gallery. I felt that the whole project was very 'male' and perhaps was implicitly working with a whole load of values: the rock star; the artist as genius. In a way I think my response, both in the sound piece and the sculpture, sought to gently undermine these conceits. From guitar feedback to radio tuning – a sort of domestication of sound. The wax casts of cow tongues – I had been making these anyway and the project allowed me to play around with combinations. Some play on words, 'licks', also with more gendered references to the inevitable adoration. I had no idea that the image on the cover of Thurston would feature his tongue! I imagine this was serendipity rather than cross-referencing.

Waren Defever: I didn't know Jon very well at the time – I have a vague recollection of having had him thrown out of the dressing room at a His Name Is Alive gig – and I assumed it was some sort of practical joke. Then I received a DAT with one minute of classic *Sonic Death*-style scrape-skronk and immediately recognised this was the real deal.

Chris Gollon: They just said, "Do with it what comes." So when I received this 52-second piece it straight away reminded me of Native American burial grounds – it sounded like chimes, quite haunting notes. At the time I'd seen a mainstream film called *Jeremiah Johnson*, starring Robert Redford. One of the opening scenes was where he rode his horse through a burial ground, so I re-watched the film just to get that part in my head.

Also, I had a studio on an island on the Thames and you could only get there by boat or over a little footbridge. It was a listed island because there were old hangars there that they used to keep Swordfish aeroplanes to protect Hampton Court during World War Two. They turned the hangars into studios for artists and for recording. The Spice Girls were doing their recording there – I remember being there on a weekend and seeing one Spice Girl coming over the bridge, then another one, another one, with all their minders and so on. But there was also a tiny studio, a two-man firm, that made prosthetic arms and legs; they used to hang them from a washing line and they'd blow in the wind. That started reminding me again of Native American burial grounds and the music Thurston gave me.

I'd recently been to Toledo Cathedral and what they have there is that they hang all the cardinals' hats from the ceiling and let them rot – some of them are a thousand years old. All of this started to come together for me into what I could do for my piece of work. I used to go to the Glasgow Print Studio and they had a crossover exhibition about death. The boys from Glasgow sent all their little drawings of skulls to Mexico and the Mexicans sent their death masks to Glasgow where they put them all round the walls. I used one of those.

So when you go back and look at the picture you can see the cardinal's hat hanging from the top; there's all the chiming going on, then I use the mask. I was reading about the Kingdom of Sleep, or the House of Sleep, it's a place where Thanatos (death) lived with his mother, Nyx (or night). Sleep itself has wings, the same as death, and it's also a dwelling place as described in Ovid, visited by Morpheus, the God of Dreams, which is where we get morphia (morphine) from. I imagined Morpheus to look like a Mexican death mask.

It was painted on a large panel of wood but I realised I was going a bit too far away from Thurston's piece of music, so I cut the panel in half because one side was working quite well but the other was too far from what I was trying to do. I started replaying the music and I realised that some of the picture was going too far into the Kingdom of Sleep, so I just got rid of that part and solved the other piece properly. I wasn't struggling with time, given that decision to cut it in half – I wouldn't have attempted that if there was a deadline because I'm not the best carpenter in the world and I'd have had to start again if I hadn't got it right!

Too often one art form tends to exclude another, and it's not like that with artists – you get conceptual artists, painters, musicians and so on, they're all friends and they don't see any difference... since I did *Root* with Thurston I realised I quite liked collaborating with musicians, that was the first time and I've done it ever since.

III
The Grassy Knoll
(Antilles, 1999)

Nolan Green: It was the winter of 1997, just a month before Thanksgiving. My project The Grassy Knoll was recording our third album, *III*, for Antilles. I had initially chosen Nicholas Sansano to coproduce the album because he was involved with so much music that inspired my thought process: Public Enemy, Ice Cube, his production work on *Daydream Nation*, damn! What I soon found out was that Nick was one of the most incredibly beautiful humans I had ever met. *III*, recorded at Greene Street Studios in NYC, was a month and a half of complete joy even though I knew the album would be canned once it came out. The writing was on the wall; Antilles wanted at least two tracks to contain vocals and at least one song to be over 130 beats per minute – an outrageous request to ask of an instrumental downbeat artist. So we forged ahead to make the best Grassy Knoll record to date.

Jane Scarpantoni: I dealt with Nick [Sansano] and Bob [Green – co-producers], we discussed their project through a series of phone calls to set up the date, and I may have even had a face-to-face meeting with Bob before actually going to Greene Street, which, at the time, was well known for rap and hip- hop – a kind of underground, windowless music cave of sorts in NYC's SoHo district, when it still had some art galleries but was transitioning to its later, unfortunate, upscale boutique phase.

Nolan Green: All the sequenced and arranged tracks were dropped down to two-inch tape and the areas where we needed the musicians to perform were mapped out. I had three tracks in particular that needed some noise, guitar noise to be more specific. I made the request to Nick that we rent a Marshall stack to produce some feedback and he suggested that we call Thurston instead to see if he was game. I was beyond excited the day he came to lay down his parts. We recorded his parts on three songs in approximately three and a half hours. His shining moment on the album occurs on the track 'Every Third Thought', guitar noise weaving around a subtle melodic phrase – a bomb dropped, beauty in utter darkness. The two other tracks were 'Thunder Ain't Rain' and '112 Greene Street'. At one point during the recording of '112 Greene Street', Thurston says, "Why does everyone think all I can do is play feedback, I can do so much more!" I thought it was hilarious.

No Music Festival
(Entartete Kunst Records, 2000)
This six-disc collection features members of The Nihilist Spasm Band and invited guests (including Thurston Moore) performing in a range of improvisational line-ups.

John Clement: My memory is that, off and on over the years, I had said we should do a No Music Festival here in London Ontario but I never did any more than talk about it. Then, one day, Ben Portis came up with the idea of doing this. He had a number of contacts and some ideas about who to invite, which was discussed with the members of The Nihilist Spasm Band, who agreed we'd like to do this.

Alan Bloor: When I began Knurl in 1994 in Montreal, there was a small scene of artists that I hung out with. They weren't necessarily into 'noise' per se, but liked what I did. These were people who enjoyed seeing someone ram large metal rods into typewriters and smash toasters while creating an unrelenting barrage of noise. A friend of mine, Jason Kushner, put me in touch with Ben Portis, the artistic director for No Music Festival, so I gave him a call. I told him about my noise project, Knurl, and after some convincing he decided to let me play.

Terri Kapsalis: I was trained as a classical musician. In my early twenties, I had an automobile accident and severely injured my left hand. After I met John [Corbett], I learned about free improvisation and found there was a way to return to my violin with my new hand while drawing on my earlier classical technique. In Chicago there was never an extensive audience for free improvisation, in rock terms, but the early-to-mid-Nineties was a kind of renaissance period for free music in Chicago; there were lots of small places to play.

Hal Rammel: John [Corbett] Terri, and I played as a trio called Van's Peppy Syncopators, named after a band Terri's father had led in Wisconsin

102

in the thirties, though we were a freely improvising acoustic trio and definitely not syncopated: acoustic guitar with preparations and extended technique, violin and text, and my original invented instruments – the triolin, snath, palette.

John Clement: The realisation that we could do something toward bringing others the pleasures and challenges of more full-throated and complex improvisation led to the idea of No Music Festival. We all were involved in billeting the visiting artists and I think that Hugh McIntyre, Murray Favro, Art Pratten and I somehow came up with the idea of the two-part structure, where the first part of the evening was performances by various people upstairs at the Aeolian Hall and the next part of the evening was held 30 minutes after the main evening and consisted of Hugh choosing who should improvise, then setting and enforcing a time limit of five to ten minutes. This last part went on into the wee hours of the morning and spread the improvisation message out into the experimental/ noise world. It made it all a much less precious thing, one not dependent on who was famous or better, but relying upon the quality that the whole group could achieve in collaboration.

Alan Bloor: It wasn't until the night that I learned there would be a jam afterward with the other musicians. This was in a smaller room at the back of the venue. I'll always remember Hugh being the timekeeper; he would come up on-stage and tell people when to stop playing. At the end of the evening there was one great big jam with all the performers.

Jamming with Thurston was cool. I liked how he left a lot of room for me to improvise with his sounds. He was pretty laidback and I stayed relatively mellow as well. I remember it wasn't a full-blown noise assault, which is good, because I find it can just lead to a mass of sound that doesn't go anywhere and becomes tiring. I thought the jam went well, considering this was my first time improvising with noise. Usually when I'm improvising with other musicians, I play an actual instrument, be it a violin, bass or piano. There are usually silences and room for other musicians to interject. I wouldn't really call that 'noise'. I found the jam with Thurston and Jojo Hiroshige [guitarist and founder of Japanese group Hijokaidan] to be more intense and the sound fuller and louder; which is not a bad thing by any stretch of the imagination; just a different kind of improv.

103

Terri Kapsalis: The festival had a dynamic energy, folks were enthusiastic and welcoming. I was a bit green when it came to that kind of music and, before the festival started, I remember walking to lunch with Thurston. He mentioned his wife and I asked, "What does your wife do?"

The Nihilist Spasm Band folks were more 'jammers' than improvisers, and jamming was a form I was not so experienced with. But I loved their passion for the music and the years of commitment they brought to their playing. Thurston approaches improvisation in ways with which I was more familiar. I remember having the immediate sense that he was a sensitive listener and open to responsive interplay. Thurston is so good at modulating feedback that our improvisation was a hovering, floating play of harmonics with Hal on musical saw. A nice palate cleanser between all the crunch and aggression.

John Corbett: We were playing very quietly and I remember that, at the soundcheck, Thurston played a solo very loudly. We walked away and Hal was terrified, thinking we were doomed. During our set, I think we called what we did 'quiet noise' and it was an especially nice performance, with short pieces and some text including Ivor Cutler poems read by Terri. After our set, we went to the parking lot to chill out and a little group of teenagers, clearly Thurstonians, were huddled around, smoking. One of them hollered over to Terri, "Hey, you guys ROCK!" She looked at me and Hal and said, "Did you hear that? We ROCK!"

Hal Rammel: I really enjoyed introducing The Nihilist Spasm Band that final night, and concocted a story about my parents being big fans of their records and how it took me longer to come around to appreciating their music. Truthfully, I'm about the same age as the members of the band. John Clement, Bill Exley and Hugh McIntyre got the joke, but I'm not sure anyone else did.

My one amplified contribution to No Music Festival was a specially-made, amplified palette directly inspired by The Nihilist Spasm Band. Palettes are amplified with a contact microphone and this version included a single string attached to a chair leg extending out from beneath the board. It looked like a guitar, though I played the wooden rods mounted on the board with a bow like a normal amplified palette. My set with them was a disaster; all that volume fed back through my palette. My only recourse on-stage was to look around, as they all were, as if I had no idea where all that feedback was coming from either. Afterward, I sat backstage behind the curtain as Jojo, then Thurston, took their turns sitting in. Thurston rushed back there when he finished and proudly exclaimed, "Now we can say we've played with The Nihilist Spasm Band!" Very kind and generous sentiments from someone whose presence at this festival made it the huge event it had become.

John Clement: I just remember all these people playing so well and such exciting sounds and being so engaged in listening to it all. We were trying to spread the word and expand the size of our 'sandbox'. We were trying to have more fun; real fun is engrossing, deeply satisfying and meaningful.

The Promise
Thurston Moore/Walter Prati/Evan Parker
(Materiali Sonori, 1999)

Walter Prati: I first worked with Evan Parker back in 1987, thanks to a commission from Biennale di Venezia requesting a composition for saxophone, trombone and live electronics. After that, I was performing with Giancarlo Schiaffini for a few years and thanks to Giancarlo I stayed in touch with Evan – that's what led to this first opportunity.

The Promise is a very special project because it combines the improvisational sessions, completely free playing, with 'post-composition' created by me through sound editing and processing techniques in the studio. It was a way to integrate improvisation and composition. It was quite easy to think of live electronics as a new dimension alongside traditional musical instruments for both improvised music and polished compositions.

Martin Bisi: Innovation in music technology is a gigantic factor – and innovation in music is beholden to there being innovation in technology, in the available tools. You can see it over and again; it takes the electric guitar to define and inspire rock'n'roll. It took computers to define and inspire electronic dance music. Even if you look at heavy metal, it takes distorted basses and huge amplifiers. Without the new tools you're just creating new hybrids or little variations. For an across-the-board revolution, with countless artists moving in a new direction, the only way is with new tools and [it's] dependent on how revolutionary those tools are. What can we do without them? Music is tough, there are only 12 notes – to blow that out of the water requires something revolutionary.

Walter Prati: As for Thurston, I had met him at the Victoriaville Music Festival when I was playing with Evan Parker's Electroacoustic Ensemble. The night before our concert Thurston performed. His work reminded me of my original starting points: the experimental psychedelic rock of Jimi Hendrix, Pink Floyd, Vanilla Fudge and so on. I was always impressed by the sound itself and its possible evolution, so I put in a lot of hard work in order to bring about a recording session. The results themselves were fantastic – precisely what I expected. Thurston's electric guitar gave that feeling of acceleration to all the music. On the one hand, the instrument itself brings a certain weight, a punch, but overall I think it's more about the way Thurston plays, that's what releases this energy. I had the same feeling during one concert where he played an acoustic guitar; even then there was this big impact. I can't imagine anything finer than bringing together the sax energy of Evan and Thurston's sonic-guitar explosion. They're very complementary performers, they each improvise in a way that's pure energy and *The Promise* was transformed by that.

'G.Neurus'/'Super Tuscan'/'Super Tuscan Deisonic Rmx: Sollo Un Minuto' Deison/Thurston Moore (Loud! Sin, 1999)

Cris Deison: I was very young when my passion for music drew me toward an independent radio station in my hometown. From 1990 I had a weekly slot, giving me the space to broadcast everything from avant-rock to the avant-garde to the most extreme experimental forms. I started to listen to the Italian noise scene which wasn't just 'the underground,' it was an ultra-underground world focused on self-production, a method I've always loved and practised because of the artistic and expressive liberty it offers. I was fascinated by the intensity of the sounds being produced; the natural, frenetic and sometimes confused spirit of the artists.

I became part of a network of correspondence, first only in Italy, then with foreign musicians and labels all exchanging cassettes, fanzines and catalogues. The tape network was very active in Italy and even inherited a history from the eighties, consisting of artists who had experimented with electronic sound and became well-known for their unsellable product which, today, is cult material. Everything was so much slower then: awkward parcels full of cassettes; photocopies and handwritten letters; endless queues at the post office. It was all much more artistic, spontaneous and stimulating. That's how I created my personal network and micro-label, Loud! I released about 20 cassettes, trying to mix a range of musicians on each release, creating themed compilations. Almost daily I had to do photocopies; experiment with different types of paper; assemble, cut and glue the graphic material to get the final definitive cover. I never made more than 100 copies per batch and they were all handmade, recorded and assembled by me. The virus spread around the world and I received weekly orders from far and wide, becoming the centre of a spider's web, an alternative distribution outlet running parallel to the official ones.

One day, a letter arrived from New York containing praise for my work plus money to buy some of my cassettes. I sent them to the postbox number provided along with a letter asking the writer to send some of his work – he'd mentioned he was a producer too. Perhaps there'd only been initials, I hadn't paid much attention to the name or the signature on the letter, but you can imagine my surprise when I received Thurston's *Foot* project: *Piece For Jetsun Dolma*; the *Goodbye 20th Century* vinyl. This time I looked a lot closer at the letter and realised it was really him!

After exchanging a few letters we decided to do something together, and the idea of a seven-inch seemed the most likely as Thurston had just gone into a studio to record a new track ('Super Tuscan'). At the time of recording I didn't have any material ready so I wrote a track especially for it and, seeing as I had another minute to fill, I disassembled and reassembled the sounds from Thurston's piece as a 60-second remix. For the cover picture I used a photo negative that I had taken of lights; the colours and the shading looked like a monster. Everything flowed so naturally, problem-free, Thurston was so helpful, so calm. I don't think he even asked for a minimum number of copies, he only said, "Tell me when it comes out."

The following year, Thurston played a concert in Venice with Walter Prati and Giancarlo Schiaffini. I joined a queue of rowdy kids waiting for his autograph and had a dozen copies of the record with me to give to him, I thought I'd sent him too few.

Opus: Three Incredible Ideas
Thurston Moore/Walter Prati/Giancarlo Schiaffini
(Auditorium Edizioni, 2001)

Walter Prati: I'd been collaborating with Giancarlo all the way back in the seventies and we have had numerous musical experiences together; collective compositions, touring as a duo in Italy, then out across Europe, America and South America. *Opus* was the result of circumstance, an opportunity. I had wanted to do a project as a quartet with Evan but we couldn't reconcile dates so we – Thurston, Giancarlo and I – began planning a series of trio concerts. Thurston and Giancarlo knew each other by reputation and through one another's music.

Giancarlo Schiaffini: I met Thurston for the first time in Chicago during a festival at the Empty Bottle – he immediately told me that he was a collector of my LPs! Then he invited me to play with a trio in New York, for a festival organised by William Parker. We found a good connection, as performers, almost right-away.

Walter Prati: More than experience playing together, an improviser needs the ability to listen and to empathise with the music and with their fellow performers – that's what creates good music when it comes to improvisation. We spent a whole day exchanging our views and our impressions of music. That evening we headed out to the first concert and, right there on-stage, we found how we could express those opinions, how to exchange perspectives with one another live and in the moment. It was a mini-tour consisting of four concerts: Milan, Venice, Bologna and Rome – every night we said something more, something new through the music we created.

The *Opus* recordings are extrapolations from those concerts, particularly from Milan and Venice. No post-production, just live material, the exact opposite of *The Promise*; two completely different experiences that were deeply significant for me.

Giancarlo Schiaffini: The environments were different: theatre, club, social centre. It worked perfectly, completely free performance, just as we planned. There was a great response from the audience, even the people who had been attracted by Thurston's presence and were expecting some kind of rock show. I used a multi-effect Digitech TSR24, Walter had a Kyma Workstation, while Thurston had several standard pedals. It was all so easy and immediate – no rehearsal, we'd just head out on-stage and there was never a problem achieving togetherness.

I think it's difficult to explain the mechanisms of improvisation in an exhaustive way, but to improvise you need four things: talent (of course); memories of what one has experienced and heard; practice, so you can adapt to any kind of sound or urge. The last thing is error – the opportunity to make a mistake allows you to find unexpected paths, things you wouldn't plan or that you would instinctively self-censor.

While American free jazz is strongly rooted in jazz – for example, in terms of sound and the role played by different performers, front line versus rhythm section – there's a marked difference here, an 'Italian colour'. I started playing professionally in the early sixties – bebop, standards, switched to free music in the mid-sixties, and we were quickly aware of the existence of various national schools in free and improvised music. The British way was different from the German one and they were both different from the French approach. I think that Dutch musicians were the most similar to the Italian. While the seventies saw the development of a strong underground following, there were plenty of ups and downs, particularly in Italy. I found Germany and France were far more consistent in terms of their appreciation for music based on improvisation and not necessarily bound up in a jazz vocabulary.

'Apple Seeds'/'Inverse Ratio Or "The Vanishing Voice"'/'Halloween 99'
Golden Calves Century Band/Dr Gretchen's Musical Weightlifting Program/Thurston Moore
(Polyamory, 1999)

James Toth: Following the grunge feeding frenzy things returned to being more DIY, but this was probably more out of necessity and circumstance than any grand 'back to the roots' movement. Pre-Internet you had to find people out there via letter writing, tape trading, touring, reading zines. *Muckraker* magazine doesn't get nearly enough credit for connecting a lot of those dots. Founder Patrick Marley seems to be a neglected figure in a lot of people's recollections, but without Marley, Clint Simonson [founder of the De Stijl label], John Olson [founder of Wolf Eyes and the American Tapes label] and Chris Freeman [founder of the Fusetron label], I'm not sure this network would have existed in the same way, if at all. Everyone was doing something different, but that's what unified us; you didn't really have 'noise' bills, or 'ambient' bills, or 'psych-folk' bills. You had bills made up of bands who shared tastes and aesthetics, maybe owned a lot of the same records, but were executing a unique vision. It wasn't until you started seeing indie-rock gatecrashers that the scene started getting wider mainstream attention and by then, of course, it was already over. Underground movements are often co-opted, diluted and inevitably destroyed by the meddling of mainstream tastemakers so, in a sense, it was a more nourishing and accommodating scene in the late nineties because it was autonomous, self-sustaining and didn't rely on banner ads, soundscans, sync licences.

Tovah Olson and I started Polyamory when we met as freshmen in college. We were ex-hardcore/punk kids who'd just gotten ahold of *Muckraker* and *Bananafish* magazine and found that noise/drone/experimental music was just the new kick we were looking for. Coming from punk, where we often found ourselves face to face with the bands we admired, we thought nothing of writing to our new favourites to ask if they'd like to release something on our new label. Maybe that was audacious but it seemed natural to us. Everyone was accessible and everyone was cool.

In some ways the LP was the beginning of my relationship with Thurston. It began with him just agreeing to do the record and then sending us the master tape, but he'd go on to write the liner notes for the first Wooden Wand LP and I'd go on to record two albums for Ecstatic Peace! The Golden Calves portion was recorded for a planned full-length, but when we had the idea to include Dr Gretchen's Musical Weightlifting Program and Thurston we just scaled it way back. Thurston's contribution is outstanding. I still have yet to hear him do anything else like the sort of mutant free-jazz/*musique concrete*/folk-song hybrid he does on this LP.

Getting to know him just made me an even bigger fan, which is historically the opposite of the way these things usually go. He's one of the least jaded people in the 'biz' that I have ever met. Every time you see Thurston he's off to catch a house show by some noise band called Billygoat Fuckface or something, or telling you about some new tape label out of Tel Aviv. That guy never sleeps, man!

Hurricane Floyd
Toshi Makihara/Thurston Moore/Wally Shoup
(Sublingual, 1999)

Toshi Makihara: Wally and I drove my 93 Corolla from Philadelphia to Boston through the most extreme weather on the day of the performance. A wild experience indeed. When we got to the venue, I was tired but I guess I got a second wave of energy. I think the weather affected my playing, but it was more driving over 500 miles in eight hours in a serious storm that did it. We each brought something to the performance; I was the landscape; Wally brought the lightning; Thurston was thunder.

Wally Shoup: Hurricane Floyd was raging. Toshi and I drove in torrential rain. It was harrowing, the windshield wipers could barely keep up. The rain finally let up when we got to Boston, but signals were down and traffic was

Wally Shoup and Thurston setting fire to Tonic, NYC, Sept 16, 2006.
Credit — Stefano Giovannini

111

crawling. We didn't know if we would make the gig or even if the gig was still happening. But we got there – a huge church with high ceilings – and Thurston's fans came out in droves. He played an acoustic solo set then we played as a trio. It was true improv in the sense that we had never played before as a trio. Given the circumstances, however, there was a heightened sense of anticipation and excitement. Free improvisation takes place in real time; each and every decision happens spontaneously and, over the course of the session, music takes shape. It's all in the musicians' hands. Thurston gets this and is quite adept at mixing it up with others. He has a great command of guitar tones and textures, which he uses judiciously and at the service of the overall sound. He also has a firm sense of 'form', both structured and free, and a quick ear. He's intense, but there's also a sense of humour and play in his approach.

TM/MF
Marco Fusinato/Thurston Moore
(Freewaysound, 2000)

Marco Fusinato: Thurston's an incredible guitarist; he can go from pandemonium, dissonant shred, to forensic string analysis within a second. He's good to hang out with because he's an enthusiast, a collector and/or archivist. For me they're the best musicians because they're not 'chopaholics' who buy *Guitar Player* magazine and get tortured by technique. They learn their craft by being obsessive collectors of the cultural artefacts of their industry, like records and books. From the records they digest everything, [from] the cover art, to the liner notes, to every groove of the LP. By absorbing all those sounds and attitudes, they invent their own language. I think Thurston is a distillation of his collection. Now that's insane!

My interest in noise-guitar came more from ideas found in visual art, primarily 20th-century avantness – say Duchamp, the futurists, Fluxus – and where it crosses over with anarcho-punk and hardcore/industrial/noise. At the time I was exhibiting regularly and I was working through a series of monochromatic 'speed' paintings. They were paintings all made using the same colour (signal red) on standard-size industrial materials: masonite, signwriters' steel and so on. I would apply the paint using whatever was lying around in the studio. The paintings were titled according to the duration it took to cover each of the panels, no more than a few minutes.

As with my guitar playing, the paintings were an exercise in 'non-technique' as technique. I wanted to explore this idea further and collaborate with a sympathetic musician to harness the art/music connection. I asked Thurston if he'd be up for the collaboration, which he was.

I usually set up a template and use a set of self-made rules as 'controls' for experimentation. Consequently a lot of my work is serial, as if I'm demonstrating a thesis. *TM/MF* was made specifically for exhibiting in a gallery. Thurston was filmed in the studio making short improvised guitar pieces, all different from one another. Some are feedback-drenched while others are pedal crunch. The videos were then sent to me. Back in my studio I had 10 panels all the same size, the idea being that I would attempt to cover the surface of each panel within the time of each of Thurston's pieces. One take; whatever happens, happens. The pieces vary in duration, the shortest one being one minute and the longest three minutes, 44 seconds. I used a different implement for each painting. For example, for one of the pieces I taped together an inexpensive five-piece paintbrush set to make a large brush – it was so bad that all the hairs fell out. On another I used a plastic shopping bag tied around my hand; just whatever was lying around.

The thing that stands out now is how raw it was. This was made at a time when brick-size digital tape was just entering the market and VHS tape was still the standard. The quality of Thurston's footage and his sound matches the roughness of the paintings. I remember it being difficult to hire monitors to play footage in the gallery. Technology was limited and expensive then. Consequently, one monitor was used to present all 10 of Thurston's pieces, with my paintings in a row around the gallery walls. If we were to show that today, because technology has moved [on] significantly I'd rest the 10 paintings on the floor with a large flatscreen monitor next to each painting and have all of them playing at once: full blast; total cacophony. That'd be more in the spirit of our actions.

Fuck Shit Up
Christian Marclay/Thurston Moore/Lee Ranaldo
(Les Disques Victo, 2000)

Christian Marclay: Catherine and Nicolas Ceresole, a Swiss couple who lived in New York in the early eighties, used to organise dinners at their apartment uptown. It was like a salon where musicians would hang out.

113

Catherine cooked in this tiny kitchen – in those days people were happy just to get a free meal; I think I met Thurston at one of those dinners. I was trying to be an artist, not a musician. I grew up in Switzerland, started art school in Geneva, then got accepted at the Massachusetts College of Art in Boston and that's when I started getting involved in music. While there, I applied for a semester-long exchange programme with Cooper Union in New York. Living in the East Village, I got exposed to a lot of music and I ended up staying the whole year. I went back to Boston to finish my studies and returned to New York during the summer of 1980, and stayed. As a visual artist I had no outlet; there was a moment there when I gave up on the art world and became totally involved in music. It was also how I survived financially at the time. As the art world became more commercial, all this other stuff like performance, that didn't have a market value, was ignored; that's when the art world slowly separated from the experimental scene.

When Lee and Thurston asked me to play with them in Victoriaville I needed more records, so I went to a junk shop, a car-boot thing, and bought records and a turntable that had been covered in graffiti by some teenager. These drawings were later used for the cover of the CD, and the words used for the titles. 'Diane Allaire' was written on the turntable – this unknown person's turntable – so we dedicated the recording to her: 'Pour Dianne Allaire'. During the concert a guy in the audience shouted, "Fuck shit up!" You can hear it on the recording and that's how the album got titled.

The only preparation for me was to select records which I thought would work with two guitars; to either contrast or imitate. Lee and Thurston's performance style involves projecting a lot. The guitar is an instrument that becomes your body and you move with it. The turntable is very static, there's nothing very theatrical about it – it's a lot of small gestures and micro-movements within the groove. While Lee was dragging his guitar around and Thurston embracing the amp to generate feedback, I was stuck behind my turntables. Often because the sound engineer doesn't have a visual cue to what I'm doing, I get mixed in the background. If I remember well, on this live recording the sound guy understood that I was part of the sound and mixed me as an equal instrument, not just in the background.

I remember the concert was fairly chaotic, it was hard to hear who was doing what – but there was a great energy. The audience was really into it and you feed from that. It was a good experience to be performing with these two rock'n'rollers in front of a big audience; it was very loud. Most of my performances are for small audiences, but in Victoriaville we had a full house of people screaming. If you're a rock star you're used to it, you rely on the energy of your fans; outside of the rock arena you never get that kind of adulation.

Evan Parker: I think the great blossoming I was aware of was at the Victoriaville Festival in Quebec. Here I first heard the term 'the Thurston Effect'. This effect was that Thurston's interest in and approval of free jazz and free improvisation more generally increased interest and audiences.

Thurston and Christian Marclay having a beer at the Cooler, NYC.

Credit – Stefano Giovannini

115

Kill Any/All Spin Personnel
Beck Hansen/Thurston Moore/Tom Surgal
(Freedom From, 2000)

Tom Surgal: That Beck session was a hoot. Thurston just ran into Beck on the way to The Cooler and dragged him along to play the gig. The set concluded with Beck disassembling my drum kit, piece by piece, while I was still playing it. All my friends were chiding me after the set, saying how you know you've really made it when rock stars break down your gear.

Matthew Saint-Germain: Thurston had been super-generous throughout the years, had gotten me backstage to a ton of gigs and even a few festivals, so it was pretty natural; I just asked him to do a tape and he said yeah. I'd asked him for something solo and this is what he sent on a gold CD-R. Thurston gave no real specifications for the artwork and left it up to me. I took orders before it was ready then had trouble getting it transferred. I know it seems stupid today but I had zero means to convert a CD-R to a cassette back then. So people got super-pissed on the Sonic Youth mailing list; I copied all their angry emails, photocopied the editor list from *Spin* and made that the cover, with sprayed fake blood covering it.

New York – Ystad (aka *Black Box*)
Mats Gustafsson/Thurston Moore/Lee Ranaldo/
Steve Shelley
(Olof Bright, 2000)

Lee Ranaldo: This project came out of a two-week period we spent at an artists' residence at the village of Ystad in Sweden. Mats Gustafsson had something to do with setting it up – a friend of his was the director of the museum. We were doing all kinds of things there, they had a print shop and I was spending my days making etchings and prints. In the evening we presented programmes where each of us would perform a song solo, or combine into various improvising groups; Loren Connors performed a solo set one night, another night there were dancers performing to a film. The concept for the *Black Box* was that it would house works by the various artists to celebrate those two weeks and inside it were all kinds of things: I had a limited edition art print in there, Loren contributed some of his drawings, Leah Singer had a die-cut silhouette, everybody who was there contributed something.

Mats was a like-minded traveller. It was a phase when we were starting to connect with this more international set of people who were at the same place we were in terms of what we were aspiring to do.

Mats Gustafsson: *New York – Ystad* came about at the Kultur Bro 2000 – 'Culture Bridge' in Swedish. There was a huge event that took place in relation to the opening of the bridge between Denmark and Sweden. We went over to New York a year before the event happened and recorded at the studio on Murray Street. We recorded a couple of tracks while Kim wasn't available that weekend, so that's why the title is 'Without Kim'. That material was then included in the *Black Box* produced after the event as a 100-copy cardboard box. I love doing these kinds of limited editions. Thurston contributed a fanzine about music and feminism; Kim provided a text; Jim gave a solo CD which is unique. I think there were two full CDs, five EPs, a lot of printed materials, original artwork. Me and Thomas Millroth, the director of the Ystad Art Museum, produced it.

I think it's good to find a mix between unlimited and limited releases. Some music fits the format of 'limited' better. When I do a new thing in studio that I feel is a strong statement artistically and musically then I want to have an unlimited edition. But a special project linked to a time and place, it can be more useful to do a limited run. It's a double-sided thing. In general I don't want to make it too exclusive; usually, if I do something limited, I also make sure that it's available digitally so people can access the music. Some musicians tend to release everything they've ever recorded; it's a trend that's really died off, partly because CD-Rs are a terrible format to store information on… or maybe it's the perfect format, if you go by Derek Bailey's quotation that he was looking for media you could only play one time.

Moonlanding Vol. 1–2 – 'Mouse'
Thurston Moore
(Helicopter, 2000)

John Wiese: When I was in kindergarten, I had this Disney LP that had isolated sound effects on one side and a complete narrative story, told exclusively through sound design, on the other. There was no dialogue or music, only sound effects describing a story of an astronaut landing on a planet's surface and getting into trouble and escaping. I think this idea had a strong impact and influence on me and made notions of sound as a world unto itself very natural to me from the start. I can remember very early on making sound experiments with whatever I had available to me. My sister and I made a radio show recorded to our boombox. I remember taking two boomboxes, facing them together and making a pause-edit cut up of a Prince tape. By the end of grade school, I saved all my money to get a proper stereo with a receiver because I wanted to be able to cut between sound sources by pushing buttons. I made all kinds of weird collage tapes this way. Even my first discovery of feedback was within a component cassette deck, plugging the input into the output and recording it while manipulating the modulation with the record-volume knob. These things were natural – long, long before knowing anything about 'experimental music'.

I moved to Los Angeles in 1998 to study graphic design at CalArts. After making tapes and CD-Rs in St Louis I had finally decided that I wanted to make a seven-inch. Fortuitously enough, after driving three days from St Louis, it arrived from the pressing plant the very day I arrived at my new apartment in LA. For years up to this point my main connection to like-minded artists was through mail and trading. During this time, 1999, the Internet was becoming a better resource, but still pretty crude; the main place to share information was MSBR's 'guestbook' on his website. Now that I had a label it seemed logical to start making compilations. The first *Moonlanding* seven-inch was single-sided with cover printing provided from a friend who worked at Kinko's. Out the door it cost $199 to make 200 copies. I remember Thurston Moore was the second person to mail order that compilation. When I sent it to him, I told him I was making more volumes and asked if he'd be interested in contributing. In no time I received a DAT in the mail.

Naked In The Afternoon: A Tribute To Jandek – 'Painted My Teeth'
Dapper
(Summerstep Records, 2000)

Thurston Moore: *Dapper* was a sixties men's publication with literary pretensions, so there'd be all these photos of nude girls then a Jack

Kerouac piece or something. Byron said we needed to do something for this Jandek tribute record, so we just went in my basement and we recorded. There was a copy of *Dapper* lying around so he said, "Let's call it Dapper."

Dapper
Dapper
(oTo, 2001)

Rob Hayler: oTo stood for 'Ordnance, Tape Only' – there were 50 releases, 50 copies of each, all one-sided cassettes and the inlay cards were made using chopped up Ordnance Survey maps of the British Isles, which meant you got to study a random square of Britain while listening. The only other details on each tape were the artist's name, the catalogue number and a handwritten edition number. I thought the squares of map added to this austere military/industrial functionality. It was more of a sound-art project rather than a record label; I wasn't creating enduring cultural artefacts or product. I wanted to invoke that sense of strolling in a gallery, standing in front of something for a few minutes, forming a judgement and moving on. The tapes and packaging just had to hold the eye and the ear for that moment. Despite (or because of) the uniform look, the tapes weren't meant to be fetishised in the way other rare releases can be. I was put in touch with Thurston by Phil Todd of Ashtray Navigations and oTo/T20 features his band Dapper. Thurston is one of six or seven people who own all 50 tapes.

Live At Easthampton Town Hall
Nels Cline/Thurston Moore/Zeena Parkins
(JMZ Records, 2001)

Nels Cline: When I was recording [my 2000 album] *The Inkling,* the idea was that Zeena was going to guest on a couple of tracks but that it would primarily be a trio recording. When she came in on the second day though, it was one of those things where you meet somebody and you're immediately so ecstatic over how they play. I came up with excuses for her to overdub on other pieces and from then on I encouraged myself to play with her whenever possible.

I knew Thurston was an admirer of Zeena Parkins' work, that he had played with her. So we got a gig together, I think through Zeena, for the three of us to go to Boston and participate in the School of the Museum of Fine Arts' sound arts programme. We played a concert then, the next day, we were part of a panel discussion about sound art before, uncomfortably, Zeena and I had to walk through the exhibition of student works and critique and comment on all their contributions. It was all good fun. After that, we had a gig booked at Easthampton Town Hall so we drove down in Thurston's station wagon, stayed at his house in Northampton, then played the gig. After that we did a show at Tonic in NYC the next day.

Keith Wood: I lived at Thurston and Kim's house in Northampton for two years – Christina Carter also lived there a long time, Andrew MacGregor… they've always had people renting rooms from them. It's a pretty big house – a great house! Three floors with a basement; an upstairs with four bedrooms. When I moved back from England, Thurston said, "If you need a place to stay, you can always stay with us."

Nels Cline: In Easthampton, Thurston broke a string at the very beginning, maybe even [in] the first minute of the gig, so he had to five-string the guitar. I remember thinking it was incredible – it felt electric, intense in the best way. Thurston seemed unsure: "I dunno man, I had to play the whole thing with five strings instead of six." All I could say was, "Hey! It didn't matter. It was great." The venue sounded so good, it was like an auditorium with high ceilings, a resonant space. It was such a contrast to playing in a basement or somewhere more *ad hoc* – it felt like a real concert and it was a more open space, so the sound was fantastic. It was one of those shows where the audience was in the dark while we were all lit up so around us it was all black; everyone was out there somewhere.

At Tonic the next day, we arrived late and headed to a Mexican restaurant two or three blocks away to try to get some food before we played. Over dinner, Thurston said he wanted to play quietly: "At least let's start quietly. It'll be packed in there tonight, people will be expecting it to be really intense. I'd really like to do it this way." We agreed and headed back to the club. He was right, it was packed. We got up on-stage and suddenly, before I'd even got my amp set up, Thurston started totally freaking out on guitar at full volume! That was the only time we ever discussed what we were going to do in advance and it ended up being the complete opposite.

Four Guitars Live
Nels Cline/Carlos Giffoni/Thurston Moore/
Lee Ranaldo
(Important, recorded 2001/released 2006)

Nels Cline: The whole point was that Lee and I were finally going to get to play together as a duo. We'd booked a club called Luxx in Brooklyn; it was super-crazy; really atmospheric, crazy, textured, painted walls. Every weird indie performer in existence was on that night, so it kept getting later and later. We waited ages until Thurston finally said, "Hey, do you mind if we play together, all four of us?" I don't know if he had to drive back to Northampton that night, but we said yes. Carlos was living in Bushwick so it was a local gig for him. I remember it being a shit-storm. Carlos always played really loud, so it kinda started on 10 and eventually made its way to 11! Carlos, at the time, was emphatically into the noise scene in Williamsburg and Bushwick, so he did everything at super-high intensity.

Carlos Giffoni: What happened with that is we were supposed to mix it at Echo Canyon, then 9/11 happened. The studio was damaged and they had to clean it up. A few years later, I was able to come with Lee and work on the recording. The release was meant to go on a different label but then there was financial trouble, the artwork never worked out, there were problems with it. So when I started working with John Brien from Important Records, it finally became easy to get on. My friend Maria Fernanda Aldana, who plays in an awesome Argentine band, did the inside artwork.

For *Four Guitars Live*, as far as the experience, we were all very different as guitar players. With Thurston it's very much about texture, he plays this rock/punk-inspired guitar sound. Someone like Lee is more about these expansive landscapes of sound. Nels is an amazing guitar virtuoso who can do anything but also has a really good understanding of how to take sound and stretch it in real time and do interesting things with it. Technically I'm not very good, but I had that feeling of going more guttural, doing something that was punchy. All of us have very different styles when it comes to what we like sound-wise. It comes through on that recording because at times you can totally tell who is doing what.

'Yellow Label Silence'/'Come Back Archimedes Badkar, All Is Forgiven' Diskaholics Anonymous Trio (no label, 2002)

Mats Gustafsson: That's a record we made exclusively for our Japanese tour. We made an edition of 300 but Jim's edition was stolen from the flight he was on, going to Japan, and no one has ever seen a copy, so they're probably down in a dump somewhere. So there's 100 copies I designed and 100 copies Thurston designed – and a painting by Kim Gordon on each of them. That was a strictly limited run that we used in Japan for trading. We posted online that collectors could bring really rare records and trade with us – and it actually worked! People showed up with really rare, mostly Japanese experimental or noise music, free jazz stuff, and then we traded with them after the concerts. After the concert, people lined up and we'd see what they had to offer. We each took a few copies home to our archives but the rest ended up in Tokyo and Osaka, because we took some of the records left over to the shops and traded there too. The whole edition disappeared in Japan. We are all diskaholics and we needed more records – it was a genius plan that worked really well, no money involved, just trading for whatever me, Thurston or Jim needed. Everyone was happy! As I remember, Jim did all the technical mastering and made sure it was pressed up and ready, it was all pretty fast. I hope we do it again! One track was unreleased and the other is an alternative mix of a track that was released later on *Weapons Of Ass Destruction*.

It was extreme discipline – the most disciplined week of my life. We'd turn up early in the morning at a café in the hotel then, with this vinyl-collecting bible they used to have in Japan, we'd choose the record shops we were going to hit, then hit them one after the other until we absolutely had to go to soundcheck. Our sound guy had already set everything up so we literally just had to plug in, play the concert, trade after the concert, then do interviews late at night. Next day, exactly the same – we bought and traded an insane amount of records, Japan is still vinyl paradise.

Weapons Of Ass Destruction
Diskaholics Anonymous Trio
(Smalltown Superjazz, recorded 2002/
released 2006)

Mats Gustafsson: Jim was a fulltime member of Sonic Youth and they were doing so much around those years there wasn't any real space to find gigs. So it wasn't intentional that there was a gap in being able to hook up. *Weapons Of Ass Destruction* was recorded on our second time at the Culture Bridge project, while *Live In Japan* was from the trip to Japan. We had real difficulty getting the trio together in those years so that was part of the truth, that we wanted to have something released and there was no chance to play, so we released the material from 2002. After that we did the Original Silence projects, which were like an extended version of Diskaholics Anonymous Trio.

Live In Japan Vol.1
Diskaholics Anonymous Trio
(Load, recorded 2002/released 2006)

Mats Gustafsson: My first meeting with Jim O'Rourke in London, 1990, was very important for me. He was the first person I'd met, from my own generation, who had a similar experience of researching other kinds of music, primarily rock and contemporary music. Most others I was working with were primarily focusing on just improvised music and free jazz. The friendship and connection with Jim, of course, brought me in touch with a zillion creative musicians and bands and made me aware of the fantastic Japanese scene.

My first meeting with Thurston, meanwhile, took place where else but in a record shop? Sonic Youth were in Stockholm to play a festival; Jim pointed Thurston in the direction of the best record shop in Scandinavia, Andra Jazz. I was helping out in the shop at the time – I still do. My friend

Harald Hult runs the business in his own, very personal, way and I was always around, putting prices on records, exploring, learning. Thurston and I had a connection; a vinyl connection; shared diskaholism. From there on it has been a very interesting journey onstage, offstage, in an insane number of record shops all around the world.

45'18 – '4'33'
Thurston Moore
(Korm Plastics, 2002)

Dave Markey: I didn't even know Thurston had done that John Cage piece. He just brings the record over and goes, "Oh yeah, check this out." He spliced a piece from one of the tracks on *Society's Ills* and put it right in the middle of a take of John Cage's '4'33'. It's bizarre but it's a way for Thurston to mix things up; to bring together two worlds that were so opposite – hardcore and modern avant-garde composition. It made a sort of sense on an absurdist, Dadaist level.

Live At Tonic
Chris Corsano/Paul Flaherty/Thurston Moore/
Wally Shoup
(Leo Records, 2003)

Wally Shoup: Paul Flaherty is a powerful saxophonist who has kept the 'fire music' aspect of free jazz alive in his playing. He puts his whole spirit into each and every situation. Chris Corsano is, likewise, a strong presence, bringing chops galore and an attention to detail. We played as a quartet at Tonic, a great venue where experimentation and adventurous playing were welcomed, indeed, championed. Thurston's fanbase packed the club and we responded to the energy in the room. Thurston laid down heavy drones, which created an undercurrent of sound that allowed Paul and I to interweave our lines with full intensity. Chris pushed the rhythm and the group sound ebbed and flowed.

Tom Surgal: It wasn't until Tonic opened on the Lower East Side that we all really felt like we finally had an amenable home base from which to operate. Good locale, chill ownership, dope staff, plus the room sounded great. We all bemoan its passing – it was really Manhattan's last gasp.

Loren Connors: In the early nineties, I played a lot at a place in the Meatpacking District called The Cooler. Then it closed, but a new place on the Lower East Side called Tonic opened. That's where Thurston Moore set up my month-long 50th birthday celebration in 1999. Then Tonic closed, but a new performance space in Brooklyn called The Issue Project Room opened – it's an art space dedicated to independent music.

Jane Scarpantoni: The Knitting Factory, and later Tonic, was where the 'scene' was when I was coming up. I lived in the East Village and for me that's where I met most of the great improvisers, not straight-ahead jazz composers [but] crazy avant-garde musicians and performers. We played and went to hear others at these and other places, like P.S. 122, The Kitchen, The Pyramid Club, for a short while Sin-e, The World, the Mercury Lounge, of course CBGB. Then the Knit moved down from East Houston to Leonard Street; Tonic, which opened across from old Meyer Lansky's speakeasy, was going strong as the centre for all things off-centre into the early 2000s, but then came its death knell too, although we came together to try and save it – Marc Ribot was a big activist there – but the inevitable steel-and-glass high-rise landed right on top of it. By that time things were getting squeezed out to Brooklyn, and now even out of Williamsburg into Bushwick, so there you go; the demise of the East Village as the place to be and play and rant. Rent, the huge beast forcing most places we knew and loved to close. Not for lack of good people or music, though. I still count myself lucky to be carrying on, being privileged to have joined some of my heroes, like Lou Reed, who once said to me, "How lucky are we that we get to do this?"

The Roadhouse Session Vol. 1
Chris Corsano/Paul Flaherty/Thurston Moore/ Wally Shoup
(Columbia, recorded 2002/released 2007)

Wally Shoup: Two days after the performance at Tonic, we went into a studio called the Slaughterhouse and recorded six lengthy improvs. Having played several times helped us create cohesive, long-form pieces that rode on the energy that this group could sustain. The studio sessions benefitted from a better drum sound and are, perhaps, the best documentation of this quartet.

Paul Flaherty: Wally had developed a musical relationship with Thurston and on occasion flew from Seattle, Washington to do a few East Coast concerts. I don't know who set the small tour up but I think Chris, [or] maybe Thurston, suggested adding me to two of the three gigs. I joined the band in Boston and two days later in NYC at Tonic. I met and played with Wally for the first time and each concert was totally improvised, no discussions beforehand; I realised that Wally was just as comfortable with this approach as I was. No leaders other than the music itself. Listen and become.

Chris Corsano: Slaughterhouse Studios was in western Massachusetts, not too far from the area where Thurston and I lived. It actually was an old slaughterhouse converted into a recording studio, hence the name. John Truscinski worked there as an engineer; John's one hell of a drummer and plays with Steve Gunn these days. I hung out a lot with John around then, since we lived more or less in the same town, and we'd occasionally get together and play together at the Slaughterhouse. So it seemed like a natural choice for where to record that quartet. A lot of the studios I've played in feel a little stifling for improvised music: the isolation booths and headphones seem counterproductive in terms of encouraging group-think in the music. Slaughterhouse was a big, open room, nothing fancy, and I think that helped the record sound the way it does.

Paul Flaherty: We recorded two and a half hours of extremely intense music. I remember Chris feeling depressed at the end, wanting to continue because he didn't think we'd been wild enough. But we were wild – and shot. I continue to hope that it'll be reissued so people can hear it outside of Japan. Plus the other half of the session was just as strong, so I might as well hope the whole session sees the light of day; the best example of that quartet.

Wally Shoup: What makes Thurston unique as both artist and archivist is that he really investigates his interests. I mean some folks might get into British folk guitarists from, say, 1955 to 1960 and research the best known of the bunch. Thurston, however, will want to know all of them, particularly the ones who were fully committed to the craft and respected by their peers but didn't necessarily become well known. He considers these artists just as important as the ones who got famous and, in some cases, more interesting. So, in the world of free improvisation, he would not only know of guys and gals like me, he would have a working knowledge of what we do. It's a form of breadth that eventually becomes depth. It takes a certain kind of curiosity and a lot of diligence.

And, although he has the 'name' to play with the likes of Cecil Taylor, Evan Parker and John Zorn, he is willing and open to playing with me, Paul Flaherty, Bill Nace and others who are, perhaps, lesser lights but still long practitioners. As long as the music takes wing, ignites a fire or whatever, name recognition becomes secondary to the collective experience that's happening right now, in this moment. That's the core of improvising, to my way of thinking, and by far the best method of becoming a better player. Plus, if you have enough of these experiences you start realising that you gotta have 'em, you need them. I think Thurston loves these moments and assumes his rock audience will, as well. There's a great symbiosis in his doing this – everybody benefits. It's unusual, for sure, but definitely praiseworthy.

G2,44+/x2
Phill Niblock
(Moikai, 2002)

Robert Poss: Susan Stenger and I met as teenagers in Buffalo, New York in the early seventies, I would say that we were and are musical soulmates. In the late seventies, knowing that Susan had worked with Phill Niblock on things like *Four Full Flutes*, I went to one of his legendary Solstice Concerts where I first experienced the magic of his musical/cinematic symbiosis. I recall saying to Susan, "This is rock!" Meaning that, to me, his music had the elements I love about certain forms of music; a visceral, repetitive quality of infinite density; subliminal harmonic messages; an East-West fusion of microtonalism; a timeless, almost geological or tidal majesty.

Susan had a decades-long history with Phill as a performer and collaborator. And my association with Phill dated from the early eighties. We were obvious choices when the guitar piece came about, since Phill knew that we understood and respected his aesthetic, his technique, the subtleties of his music. We both understood the role of the performer in sounding overtones and making microtonal tuning changes, and interacting with the recording and the acoustic space.

Rafael Toral: I was staying with Phill at his loft and he told me he had this idea to do a guitar piece. He asked me to set up my guitar so he could find out what to make of it. The first thing he decided was to use the 'a' and the 'b' strings in standard tuning, because the EBow, a device for sustaining sound indefinitely, could rest on the adjacent strings. He recorded the tones then used them as a starting point. He later recorded more tones from three other guitarists and, when I heard the piece, I loved that he added a low 'e', it brought a lot of power. His approach was similar to pieces he recorded with other instruments, multiplying the tones then detuning them in subtle ways.

Robert Poss: Phill made his pieces by having performers record a series of tones. He then assembled a layered multitrack mix of these sounds, changing their tunings to create a rich harmonic mass. In live performance, the Niblock mix is played back at high volume and the live performers augment it by doubling the parts, and making subtle real-time changes in tuning via string bends or tuning peg manipulation, varying the string or octave and adding back in a transitory human element. The biggest mistake that inexperienced or unserious Niblock performers make is to overplay, to play at a volume far above the playback mix, to draw attention to themselves or to make unsubtle, large musical gestures that separate their participation from the whole. It takes restraint and discipline to play Niblock well.

The focus for performers while recording his music is on the successful execution of the parts; for example, not clanging the EBow against the guitar strings; holding the pitch steady or doing subtle microtonal bends when appropriate. The performers supply the raw materials for Phill's computer pitch manipulations and looping. Phill directs the pitches to be played – these are simple scores – and the other tool besides the recording chain is a clock or stopwatch. Phill always has a duration in mind for the final piece.

Alan Licht: It's fairly simple to play: you start off holding a 'b' note with an EBow, then you move down to an 'a' and then eventually go back to 'b' and/ or move back and forth between those two notes and a low 'e'. I recorded at the studio on Murray Street on a different day than the others. I don't remember how many of the other overdubs were already on there when I was tracking, or even if I opted to listen to all of what was already there.

Robert Poss: I joined the other performers at Murray Street to record with Jim O'Rourke. As in live performance, we listened to playback and added live drones. This session was quite a bit looser than the original recording. I think I may have been the only guitarist in this second version who'd played Phill's music before and was truly familiar with Phill's goals and expectations. Probably as a result, the others departed more from usual Niblock performance practice, his preference for no audible swoops or extreme bends and so forth.

Rafael Toral: I played the piece live several times, the first in Chicago. Phill produced a basic version and to play it live one just adds tones, freely choosing their duration but only using the notes belonging to the piece; then very subtly bending the string to produce beat frequencies, a physical phenomenon that occurs when two or more close frequencies are heard together. The sound would be so loud that often I couldn't hear the tone I was playing, but I could hear the beats changing and I held my breath while making very slow movements with the whammy bar to bend the pitch.

I loved the piece so much that I thought it was screaming to be released. The experience of recording it as a studio piece was quite meticulous and laboratorial, as home studio work usually tends to be. I really had a hard time blending new tracks, they just didn't seem to glue well to the mix – I had this feeling that adding anything to Phill's 'monument' would taint it like bad graffiti. I managed, eventually, to find my way into a subtle mix with the new tracks, adding delicate hues and discreet modulations. I was delighted to create the new version that came out on the record without steering much away from Phill's original. The real thing, though, was getting to play it live; it's like being on the nose of a flying train, deeply hypnotic, enrapturing immersion inside one of the most powerful, beautiful, enthralling sound streams I've ever experienced.

The Good, The Bad And The Ugly – 'South Beach'
Sonny Vincent
(Munster Records, 2003)

Sonny Vincent: In the mid-eighties I moved to Minnesota and discovered, surprisingly, this young and vibrant scene which included The Replacements and Hüsker Dü – the spirit reminded me of how NYC had been a few years earlier. I moved because the scene in New York got too junkied out and a lot of the original resolve got soft. There had been an undeniable dulling of the edge; lots of inane, pointless parties and heroin – a lot of the original 'soul' was sadly missing.

I wrote the song 'South Beach' in Detroit and right away found myself focusing on the darker aspects. I remembered being in South Beach, Miami, hanging in the worst part of town: drug gangs, violence, helicopters, mayhem. My desire was to add chaos and a violent edge to the core of the song, as well as an atmospheric element within the periphery of the sound. I was certain Thurston and company could bring the sharp knife-edge, as well as the brain-swirling helicopters, to the landscape of the song. While in Detroit, I played my guitar core part on the basic tracks with Scott Asheton of The Stooges and Captain Sensible of The Damned. The album had tons of guest guitarists on it and I criss-crossed the globe recording in various studios. I sent the masters of the song to Thurston to continue with Jim O'Rourke. Along with their co-conspirator, Don Fleming, they added a wild, untamed aspect. Later, while at Ivan Julian's recording studio, I added Ivan to the line-up mainly because of his ability to play beautiful, as well as manic, guitar. I was adding all the 'manic' I could find.

'Sweetface'/'Rom Supply Co.'
Mirror/Dash
(En/Of, 2003)

Robert Meijer: En/Of started because I wanted to realise this idea of combining art and music. Certain artistic histories, such as Fluxus, were influences for me – the idea of combining things that were maybe not meant to be together. Sonic Youth had a very strong connection to visual arts, so, even more than being into their music, I wanted to have them be part of my series because of that. I was really excited that it turned into a Mirror/Dash [the duo of Kim Gordon and Thurston] record. That project seemed to fit best because, although there weren't many releases under that name, it seemed to be more connected to both Kim's and Thurston's roots and to their connections in the art world.

We barely discussed the record – actually not at all, I just received the master. But we did discuss art and which artist could fit with their record. That was the exciting part, because normally I approach a musician and artist with a concept. In this case, Thurston gave me a list of artists that he knew personally who we could possibly ask. It was the most insane list, of course – about eight famous artists who I would have been extremely glad to see be part of the series. And the best thing? Thurston just said I could pick one out and he would ask them. That was almost too much; I came out of that candy shop with a huge bellyache! In the end, I decided on Dan Graham. I met him at a diner in New York sometime after and introduced myself. I'm still not sure if he actually knew what I was talking about – either I had more than enough wine in me, or he really didn't know what I was talking about. It didn't matter; he made an amazing edition for the series that connects back to the history and friendship

Kelly Davis, Thurston and Cory Rayborn at the Hopscotch Music Festival, Kings Barcade, Raleigh, North Carolina, September 5, 2014.   *Credit – David Schwentker*

with Kim and Thurston, and is, in itself, a great image. Half of the image is a portrait of Chan Marshall of Cat Power and, years later, it turned out that Dan had also made that a stand-alone artwork for a show at Greene Naftali, New York.

I Can't Be Bought
Mirror/Dash
(Three Lobed Recordings, 2006)

Cory Rayborn: Three Lobed Recordings initially started for me as something that I wanted to try out. I started the label pretty much simultaneously with my matriculation into law school. I had done some booking in college, engaged in a lot of live taping and put out a zine. As someone with no musical ability, tinkering and helping around the edges was where I felt my ability to best participate in the scene and help out some friends. Putting out a release or two seemed like the next obvious step. I had become pretty good buddies with the folks in Bardo Pond after assisting them with a website for a few years – I figured that I could ask them if they wanted to do a release. They did and I took the plunge.

2006 struck me personally as a bit of a change for the label. This little hobby, after-hours activity, had become more serious, a fact [made] obvious because folks – musicians and record collectors alike – were seemingly interested in what I was doing. I actively remember being on vacation with my wife and picking up an issue of *Arthur* magazine, flipping through Thurston and Byron's *Bull Tongue* column and seeing them chat about the then-new Bardo Pond/Tom Carter collaborative release and speaking in generally positive tones about the label catalogue. I couldn't help but feel flattered and, well, noticed.

When the time came to assemble the *Modern Containment* series of CDs, I mentioned Thurston's recognition of the label to a mutual friend, Dave Sweetapple, as a sort of 'out loud wondering' if he felt Thurston might be interested in hopping in on this. I specifically wondered about [him] contributing as Mirror/Dash since I had long enjoyed their first seven-inch [1992's 'Gum'/'Electric Pen'] and kind of hoped they would put more stuff out into the world. Dave was pretty sure that it would be of interest and, lo and behold, within a week he had spoken with

132

Thurston and gotten us in touch with each other. Thurston and Kim were totally on board and into the idea of submitting some material as Mirror/Dash. Only a few months later I had discs containing the audio and the artwork in hand and ready to roll.

'Blues For Proposition Joe'/'Sign Stars'/
'101 On Semlow'/'Seychelles'
Mirror/Dash, Kit
(Nothing Fancy Just Music, 2008)

Vice Cooler: I grew up in Alabama. There wasn't much to do so we got really into records and writing music – I was a record collector from when I was probably 10 or 11. Me and a group of young teenagers started a touring band called XBXRX, which imploded and then reformed after me and Steve Touchston moved to San Francisco. One of the first Bay Area shows we went to there was to see the infamous Friends Forever. They were playing in their van outside of KIMOS in The Tenderloin. Kit started after that particular show, as the four of us were all standing randomly on the sidewalk reflecting on the energy of the night. One of the shows we did was for Washington DC's Quix O Tic and, shortly after, they set XBXRX up a show in DC. Thurston, Kim and Eddie Vedder were randomly in town and happened to show up. Thurston and Kim kept in touch with me.

Me and Thurston vaguely talked about doing a split for a long time. Kit had these alternate versions of some of our songs, along with some improvised outtakes, that were unreleased. Kim and Thurston had a track laying around also. I released them on a split very impulsively. It was as simple as one email exchange. I got the files from Thurston and then put together the Kit side; mastered it with my then XBXRX bandmate, Weasel Walter; scanned in Kim's art with my friend Joey Mansfield – all probably within an hour or so.

I pressed it through my friend at a plant in San Francisco. I went and picked up the pressing a few months later. Once the records were in, I sent them to all the band members and Stickfigure, my distributor. There weren't really any decisions to be made as everyone involved was really relaxed, and almost hands-off, about the whole process. But overall, since it was my release I handled all the labour within it, which is pretty

133

standard. I felt it was more creating a fun thing with my family than a spotlight- or attention-grabbing situation. It sold out in a few months and that was that.

Between Lee, Kim, Steve and Thurston there was always this mishmash of weirdo artists hanging out at their shows – it was always like a family reunion, no matter where in the world I saw them. It still exists but it's just that now it's in a smaller form. I think the communal void is that, like every band, Sonic Youth all had their mutual friends but then there were all these different crews who would roll up – it really was a special scene. I've seen them all play since the break-up, all great shows, but there's something a little absent backstage – it's still a good scene, tons of good people there... just not the same. Their whole career was, and is, one of a kind. I'm really glad they existed as long as they did and that they're all still working on such cool stuff.

A funny memory was when XBXRX and Wolf Eyes toured with them and we rolled up to Las Vegas; this huge sign popped up that lit up all our names – right next to a sign for a Cyndi Lauper show. Ridiculous! We all laughed. Then a friend of ours told us later that, during our set, the people next to them kept going on, "This is the worst thing we've ever heard!" Until Wolf Eyes went on, then they said, "No, wait... *this* is the worst thing I've ever heard. How's it possible I heard two of the worst bands of my life all in one night?"

The Whys Of Fire
Dredd Foole And The Din
(Ecstatic Peace!/Father Yod, 2003)

Mike Gangloff: In the nineties, Jack Rose, Patrick Best and I could be pretty sure that in whatever town we found ourselves, Pelt was the strangest band working that night – at least we felt that way, like we were missionaries of some sort, saying, "This is music too!" But by the mid-2000s, there were a lot more bands exploring the improvised thought-as-sound realm where we lived. It was still a tiny scene, but it felt a lot bigger than a few years before.

Patrick Best: There is always an ebb and flow to outsider art. During the early-to-mid-2000s, noise, drone and folk were swelling with players and listeners. I would like to think that Pelt's early years, from 1995–2000, playing all the weird hole-in-the-wall shows and one-off festivals, seeded that upwelling of interest.

Mike Gangloff: When it comes to *The Whys Of Fire*, I blame Byron Coley! As I understand it, Byron and Dan Ireton were figuring out how to put together Dan's next record and somehow decided Pelt could be The Din this time around. Byron hired us to come up for a night of recording – our pay was to each get a copy of the Charlie Patton boxset on Revenant.

It was a really cryptic session, both at the time and afterward. I'd been on the road for something like 14 hours, driving with Mikel Dimmick from Virginia to Philadelphia to get Jack, then to Brooklyn to get Patrick, then up to Massachusetts, with instruments packed on top of and all around us. We got to Slaughterhouse Studios kind of glazed and crispy.

Thurston was loaning us amplifiers for the session and, while we were setting up, Dan or someone suggested that he play too. He wasn't sure at first if he wanted to, but then joined in. I don't think he had a guitar with him and used one that was in the studio. I remember Thurston said afterward that it was the first time in a long time that he'd played – or maybe the first time he'd recorded – in standard tuning.

Patrick Best: This was a straight improvisation for 20 minutes at a time – we recorded all night. Pelt brought a very limited selection of instruments which, in hindsight, created limitations but we worked with what we had. I remember a lot of give and take from all parties, as well as everyone just head-down attacking their instruments. We all had lots of experience improvising so it just took a little bit of warming up to get in the pocket.

Mike Gangloff: John [Truscinski] ran around trying to decide what to mic, and I think Dan just told us to start playing. He had a microphone and a delay unit and a guitar amp and began roaring. It felt like we played for hours, sometimes in shifts – I remember standing outside with Dan, talking and looking at the stars and getting some fresh air, while people were still wailing away inside.

When we started playing, I wasn't sure if Thurston would join in or not and I couldn't see him from where I was sitting on the floor, playing. We were building down from a big squall when the Thurston stick sound started drifting over my head. I think I just sat and smiled for a while; I'd spent a lot of the eighties listening to that sound.

Jack had an electric guitar that he was using for Pelt shows at that point. It was black with a pointy headstock – a sort of goofy, hard rock-looking thing. He tended to play it lying flat on the ground or on a tabletop, using a bow or EBows, Allen wrenches or pieces of metal wedged into the strings. He was playing it on the floor during the recording session, leaned into it too hard and snapped the neck off mid-cacophony. I'm not sure if Dan or Chris or Thurston noticed – they just kept going. Patrick and I were laughing and trying to cheer Jack on while he held the guitar together, wrestled with the string tension and kept playing it. He ended up breaking the guitar into pieces while everyone kept playing.

Patrick Best: The only weird issue I have with the record is that it does not sound like what happened in the room. Jim O'Rourke mixed the record but he was not present at the recording, so mixing must have been a little weird, plus we were told that the raw tapes had a lot of dropouts that he had to overcome.

Mike Gangloff: My impression of the whole session was one of joy, just abandoning everything except a waterfall of sound that stretched on and on. The mystery to me is that I don't hear that in the album at all – what I hear sounds nothing like what I remember us playing. We all played together just once more, the next night at The Flywheel. Pelt played a short, acoustic opening set and then Dan and Chris and Thurston joined us as we dove into a continuation of *The Whys Of Fire*.

Tribute To Martin Luther King Jr.
Thurston Moore/Moz
(Breathmint, 2003)

Mat Rademan: I established Breathmint in 1995, initially as a fanzine, to showcase music and art that I was passionate about but which wasn't getting the support or exposure I thought it deserved. I had no delusions about making money. I began to trade releases and correspond with people all over the world. Some ran small labels; others were just fans of the artists I was working with.

James Brand (Moz) and I connected through our mutual pen-pal Gary Stevens of the Anti-Everything label. Gary and I met via *Maximum Rock*

And Roll classifieds, where he used to post ads like, 'Bored? Get yourself a cheap cassette recorder. Record yourself, your friends, anybody causing public chaos, mad noise, screamin', bangin' on shit, spoken word, lo-fi, experimental, homemade, punk, noise, whatever. Go the fuck off! Mail it to me with art, words and your address. Why? For upcoming cassette/vinyl projects.' In 2000, James and I began discussing a Moz release for Breathmint. He mentioned he was working on a split with Thurston Moore, *Tribute To Martin Luther King Jr.*, and suggested that Breathmint release it. I had met Thurston briefly several times, but had never had a substantial interaction. At first I was unsure that he would be interested in working with me, but James informed me that Thurston was not only aware of Breathmint and my solo project, Newton, but was a fan. I was floored.

Thurston sent James the master of his track, recorded and mixed by Jim O'Rourke, on cassette. James then remixed Thurston's track and sent me the masters for all three tracks. Originally, I think we were discussing a seven-inch but I couldn't afford it, so we decided to release it as a fan CD, a disc that is manufactured with only a partial silver metallisation. Basically, this means that the silver area of the CD only extends outward partially, not through the entire disc. The result is that a portion of the disc remains clear or transparent.

The Vietnam Songbook – 'Fourth Day Of July'
Thurston Moore
(no label, 2003)

Kim Rancourt: *The Vietnam Songbook* started when Don Fleming asked me to come over to the Alan Lomax Archive to help him organise Alan's book collection. As I was sorting through the bookcase, slipped into another larger book was *The Vietnam Songbook*. It was written by Barbara Dane and her husband Irwin Silber of *Sing Out Magazine*. It was a collection of protest songs against the Vietnam War, not just from the US but from all over the world. Neither Don nor I had heard of it before. We thought that it would make a great live show but first we had to find Barbara Dane. We tracked her down in California and I gave her a call. She loved the idea. We approached the always classy Joe's Pub here in New York with the idea, and they said yes immediately. Then we had to find performers and a core band. Thurston, of course, was high on the list.

We did two complete shows that evening, sold out. It was a magical night; Barbara Dane was thrown into the New York spotlight once again. Every performance was standout, but a favourite for me was Pete Seeger playing Lennon's 'Give Peace A Chance', 'Somewhere Over The Rainbow' and a brand new song he had just written called 'Take It From Dr King'. [Ex-Fug] Tuli Kupferberg whipped up the crowd with sing-along versions of 'Kill For Peace' and 'Cave 64' – he passed out Xeroxed lyrics to the audience! Most of all, though, it was the star, Barbara Dane, who blew everyone away with 'Brother Can You Spare A Dime' and 'Ballad Of Richard Campos'.

By coincidence, this was the weekend that Bush invaded Iraq and there was a giant rally in New York against the war that weekend. So it took on a more political significance because of this. Pete Seeger showed up at the last moment – he had said he couldn't make it – and it was fun to see his face when Thurston blasted into 'Fourth Day Of July'. I think he dug it! Thurston brought along an authentic protest sign painted by Allen Ginsberg that said, 'Down with Death... War is Black Magic.'

Thurston and My Cat Is An Alien's first encounter in Torino, Italy, July 15, 1998.
Credit – The MCIAA Archive

138

From The Earth To The Spheres Vol. 1
Thurston Moore/My Cat Is An Alien
(Opax, 2004)

Roberto Opalio: We entitled a series of releases *From The Earth To The Spheres* to underline the nature of ascension, transcendence and 'vertical perception' within our music; the thing that characterises it and makes it unique. It also related to the primary concept behind the project: to use vinyl as both a container and the chief representation of music, given that music is otherwise the most abstract of the arts, pure cosmic ether or cosmic debris. It's like matter becoming pure spirit, or the inseparable body/soul dichotomy; it's impossible to conceive of it without its vessel.

We gave the artists total creative liberty, no direction or guideline; we would publish any musical piece received from them with complete trust in their talent. It was a spontaneous decision to call on Thurston to open *Vol. 1*. This was about two years after he released our *Landscapes Of An Electric City* LP on Ecstatic Peace! We were rewarded by his immediate and enthusiastic reply; he reinforced our willingness to take this next step with our private label after six years where we had just released CD-R editions; he spurred us on to contact other artists and it was so satisfying to see all of them replying positively.

Maurizio Opalio: Of course, the series meant an extreme financial effort for us. We had seven volumes scheduled but the actual possibility of publishing them depended entirely on whether the first volumes would sell quickly enough to allow us to immediately reinvest all the revenue each time to prepare the next one. Fortunately, our hazardous plan worked!

We then received further good news, as Darren Crawford at the label Cargo proposed reissuing all of the volumes as CDs, a co-release with our label, Opax. Before accepting, we asked all the artists involved and everyone, barring Jim O'Rourke, agreed. We also made sure that the artwork was an exact replica of the LPs and detailed the concept of the original.

Roberto Opalio: One morning, a ring from the postman; a small package with a sender address that was already well known to us. We were pretty surprised it had taken less than 20 days to receive Thurston's material for the split LP. There was an orange sheet of paper, handwritten, stating, 'Hello, here is my side of the split. IT IS RAW! Lots of tape hiss and it is called

"American Coffin".' The words 'Noise Against War' and his signature were followed by a drawing of a pierced heart. We also received an email from him, specifying, 'I recorded it on a cassette player and there is a lot of hiss, which I like. Please master it dark and loud.'

We ran to the stereo, put the CD-R in, pushed the volume up and couldn't believe our ears. My brother and I were very aware of Thurston's solo output so far, everything, but we weren't prepared for the track he had sent us. It left us breathless. It was otherworldly; it still stands as the most extreme and radically experimental work in Thurston's discography.

Maurizio Opalio: Thurston engaged in a free-piano attack referencing figures like Cecil Taylor live at the Maeght Foundation, Dave Burrell's *Echo* LP, Stockhausen's wildest scores. After nine minutes of blasting piano, suddenly you're projected into guitar noise, a wall of feedback only apparently out of control because you know he's manoeuvring it with great skill; then, suddenly, a drum machine disrupts it in the most derailed and ravaged manner while the whole piece is shaken apart by musical collage inserts, abrupt radio broadcast signals, fragments of dance music splattered into crazy rhythms and broken beats, even a clip of a war speech, all permeated with mini-Moog tones *a la* Sun Ra. Finally, a crescendo of guitar howls before a final four minutes where the piano rises once more, this time playing brief, repetitive, melodic chords like Satie or Charles Ives, a surrealist, post-romantic, touching mood; then the piano key release gets lost again in the sonic magma of tape hiss – a shiver running down your spine.

At the time, Thurston seemed very touched by 9/11, by the worldwide hell that followed, all the things that turned for the worse – he even set up a website called Protest-Records.com and on his letter to us signed off with the words, 'Noise Against War'. We were angry at the total lack of understanding of what he created with this track. Thurston called into question the very concept of music and art at the beginning of the new millennium, which began with the US in one of its most fractious political eras. We always wondered if Thurston completely realised the full extent of his statement, but maybe the answer became clear when, several years on, he included the final four minutes of this same piece, still under the title 'American Coffin', on the *Trees Outside The Academy* record.

Roberto Opalio: For the painting accompanying the LP, I used a wood panel and created an acrylic background of different shades of blue featuring sparse, abstract shapes as material reliefs of crystal mortar mixed with glass powder and other materials. It was essential, to me, to create a strong connection between the vinyl's musical contents and the painting visually representing the contents. My *modus operandi* was to find points of contact and interaction between them, something emerging from my subjective perception of the music, its atmosphere, its moods – the invisible electricity running through the entire work. The difficulty was to find time to make the 100 paintings needed for each volume; I had to start and finish each single piece before I could begin the next one. I would have hated it to become a factory-like concept or process, so I often painted in the middle of the night, working by candlelight, because I needed the silence, the inspiration that runs through both inner and outer space at that time. Sometimes I painted quickly, violently, other times I was slow and gentle. Each sleeve was painted as an astral fragment, as cosmic debris. The reward came when the artists involved received their personal copies and responded with tangible joy; likewise when fans around the world understood the spirit of the series.

Maurizio Opalio: Our own piece was entitled 'Brilliance In The Outer Space' and was an antithetical counterpart to Thurston's. We played liquid guitar drones, extended a peaceful sense of calm evolution through the surrounding space, stretching it out, expanding it around the listener. Yet it's just an apparent peace; several minutes in, sparse guitar strings and isolated darknesses become ever more concrete. At one point Roberto picked up a drumstick and began to beat rhythmically, and with increasing emphasis, on the strings of his prepared guitar to obtain a slow yet relentless crescendo of feedback modulations. Old 78rpm classical music shellac by Tchaikovsky and Rachmaninoff played simultaneously, recorded in real time from several gramophones. We perceived the piece as the brilliance of a supernova in the single moment of its explosion; material thrown in every imaginable direction; the listener nearly physically touched by these sonic splinters.

Future Noir – 'In My Room'
Hanin Elias
(Fatal Recordings, 2004)

Hanin Elias: Promise not to laugh? I had made an album called *No Games No Fun* to break free from Atari Teenage Riot. My first idea had been to call the album *Playing With Balls* and to just make collaborations with guys... but I would be the one in charge! *Future Noir* was more planned; I already had an idea of what I wanted to do. I hired TweakerRay to make the album – he was a fan who jumped on-stage while I was playing a gig in Hamburg. Afterward, we were driving in the car and he played us some of his instrumentals, so I started to work with him. Meanwhile, I had first met Thurston in New York when Atari Teenage Riot were playing in a record store called Other Music. He was super-nice, really friendly, and even asked us for autographs. He is a very good friend of very good friends of mine who live in Amherst, so when I was visiting them we would all go by Thurston's house and jam.

Pete Nolan: They had some fun parties at their big mansion a few times. We had a jam in his living room once, and I remember their teenage daughter Coco running around and screaming 'cos she said I was banging on their piano too hard.

Hanin Elias: The album only took four months. I wrote the lyrics while we were making the music and the words just ran out of me. I collected lyrics for a while; every time I had an idea I wrote it down. I'm a very fast songwriter. I think if you have a vision and you're in the same room with a creative person, the vision passes over to them and they understand without needing many words to explain it. I just knew Thurston would get it! You can't be a good artist without knowing what suffering is – and Thurston is an amazing artist.

I remember listening to 'Teenage Riot' when I was a teenager over and over again, it was a big inspiration! The desperate screams and longing for hopefulness, it's just the way Thurston plays it. 'In My Room' is a song about being depressed and empty – that's the feeling I wanted to get across. TweakerRay and Thurston were immediately into that vibe and a friend of mine, Bertil, played amazing drums on top of it at a later date. We were discussing the heaviness of sadness and how it might sound as a song. I played him the unfinished song and he just recorded some guitars on top of it. It was magical! The album was originally intended to be purely electronic but his guitar just blew my mind.

Kapotte Muziek By Thurston Moore
Kapotte Muziek
(Korm Plastics, 2004)

Frans De Waard: The name 'Kapotte Muziek' was given to me by my father, who very much liked classical music. He'd say, "Frans? I have no idea what you're playing – this punk, funk, disco, it's all kapotte muziek," it's all 'broken music'. I thought it was a good name for a band so it kind of stuck and I've been using it since.

In the very early days, I was clearly inspired by a lot of industrial music, noise, power electronics or whatever the term was then. But at the same time I also listened to prog rock, Alvin Lucier or Steve Reich – the scope of interests was pretty big for me, in my late teens. Over the years, especially since we started playing live concerts in 1993, we became ever more interested in playing electro-acoustic music using stuff that we found on the street.

I saw Sonic Youth in 1983 when they played Nijmegen. The support act was a film showing of *Subway Riders*. I went not because I thought this was a great alternative US rock band but because the papers said, 'There's a band in town next week and two of the guys played with Glenn Branca.' Just two weeks before that Branca had been on TV with his guitar orchestra, including Lee Ranaldo and Thurston Moore, playing a symphony which was a big scandal on Dutch television, as it was loud and the official orchestra members walked off because they were furious at the volume. I saw that and thought, 'Wow, this is great.' Then I saw Sonic Youth and shrugged: 'Oh, well, it's a rock band.' I was interested in minimalism and thought they'd be more like Glenn Branca – which they weren't. Later, on another occasion, I saw Lee and Thurston play this noisy, droney guitar-duo thing for maybe 20 minutes, banging guitars and making a furious amount of noise – I thought, 'Wow, that's brilliant! I wish they did more like that.'

In 1993, we were touring with two guys from America called Howard Stelzer and Jason Talbot, Howard played cassettes and Jason played turntables; they were an improvisational duo from Boston. Howard knew Chris Cooper from The Flywheel, so it was one of those things where the five of us would drive there in the car and play music. It was a very small place, it looked very alternative, which I liked because it reminded me of a place near Nijmegen called Exitpool – full of volunteers and

143

people working. It was beautiful weather and nobody came out, one of those concerts where there was only a handful of people. What I do remember is in the audience there were three people that others there knew: first, there was Scott Foust, who is the main man from The Idea Fire Company; the next guy there was Gregory Whitehead, quite a well-known radio guy – he has this very distinct voice and Howard said, "That guy you're talking to, I know his voice! Who is he?" I said it was Gregory Whitehead, to which Howard replied, "Why does Gregory Whitehead head out all the way to Easthampton to see you guys?" The third guy who was there was Thurston Moore. What we did is we played what we always do, the three of us have a suitcase full of stuff we've collected, stuff we find in the streets – wood, metal – and sometimes we scavenge the place where we're going to play and find objects that are too heavy, so we just put our contact mics against them and start playing them. The concert started with us opening the suitcase, getting the stuff out, then we started playing from there – no idea why we did this, it's the only time we did that more Fluxus kind of thing. Then, of course, this was recorded, but I think I sent Thurston a recording from the night after this – [so] maybe it wasn't recorded.

This whole *Kapotte Muziek By* thing, a lot of the music by Kapotte Muziek was to do with the recycling of sound. So we would take sounds and process them into something new, what is now called a remix we would call 'rework' or 'recycling'. When we played in Kaiserslautern, Germany, a good friend of ours, Ralf Wehowsky, who recorded as RLW, came up to us and we talked about how these live recordings could be the starting point of collaborative work. Right on the spot the decision was made to do a seven-inch called *Kapotte Muziek By RLW*, using the recording of that performance. We thought it was a nice idea, so we asked more people we played with to do more seven-inches. Working for [the record label] Staalplaat we had access to cheap pressing plants, so we could get them done. When I left Staalplaat I no longer had access to the pressing plants, and maybe it was just a logical idea to shift toward CDs.

I was talking with Roel [Meelkop – fellow member of Kapotte Muziek] about who we could ask to do another release and he suggested we try Thurston. I just emailed him and he responded straight away, saying, 'That's a good idea – send me a recording and I'll send you something.' Lo and behold, a short amount of time later I got a master. I remember playing it and thinking, 'Hmm, I don't know – is this good?' I was a bit surprised. But then I played it again on my headphones and this time I could hear what he was doing. He didn't use the material as soundblocks to sample; instead, he took the sounds of our performance as they were and used them as a score to improvise, using the dynamics of our piece. So if we went 'up' he'd go up and if we went down then he'd go down, and so on. I thought that was a really good CD.

'Jong'/'New Wave Dust'
Thurston Moore/John Wiese
(Troniks, 2004)

Phil Blankenship: In the nineties, I would put pen to paper and write to any and every address that was included in an album I liked. I traded mixtapes with people at shows and would call college radio stations to find out what weird shit was coming through town. Here in Los Angeles it seemed like there was always a solid core of fanatics; you'd see each other at shows, hang out and drink beers at home, record together. Everything was interconnected and I wanted to help expand that with an online message board. In my eyes, that's when everything really seemed to take off. All of the smaller communities were uniting to form one big one online, shootin' the shit about our interests, sharing ideas, helping book tour dates and more. You'd see the Wolf Eyes guys talking to a kid who just posted his first track, or Thurston talking about hot tapes he got on tour. But, of course, people on the Internet are always terrible and, as time went on, the whole thing imploded with spam, trolls and garbage.

By 2004, John Wiese had already done a lot of releases for Troniks and, through his artist network, had somehow met Thurston. I was sending a lot of my output to Byron Coley and Thurston for review consideration with *Bull Tongue*. I'm not sure how the exact details were decided but John and I were probably sitting on my couch, watching a movie and brainstorming. Considering it was one of my largest releases up to that point, the whole thing was super-simple. Thurston sent his track and a photo through the mail. Wiese did the layout and design, then we sent everything to the pressing plant and printer. The main thing that was really different was that I didn't have any problem moving copies – distributors were eager to take copies and orders came flying in. It was very different to my normal slate.

John Wiese and Thurston at the Museum of Contemporary Art, LA, February 1, 2015.
Credit – Leah Peah

John Wiese: My recollection was that I came over to Phil's house one day and he said, "Want to do a split seven-inch with Thurston?" My piece was something I was working on, not necessarily conceived as a piece for the split. In those days I thought about most things as singles, seven-inch side pieces… Troniks made 1,000 copies, which was a bit more than a typical pressing, so it afforded us the option of making a glue pocket-sleeve, clear vinyl edition, printed labels – all stuff we didn't normally splurge on. Normally those expenses would be saved for making more releases.

Phil Blankenship: Running a label is tough when you're poor – and, if you're running a label, you're always gonna be poor! The biggest godsend that ever happened to me was PayPal. Being able to easily accept instant payment online was a massive game-changer from the days of someone promising a cheque or money order in the mail that might never come. But the immediate nature of online payment was also a curse to a lot of other labels; it helped create buyer expectation that they would be getting a package just as fast. I never really had a problem but I saw slow shipping and customer chargebacks crush some of my competition.

Make No Mistake About It
Carlos Giffoni/Thurston Moore/Dylan Nyoukis
(Gold Sounz, 2004)

Dylan Nyoukis: That was a fun but dumb one. Myself and Carlos had recorded, via the post, *Chewing Smoke*, a vinegar piss of love. Apparently, Byron Coley and Chris Corsano teased Thurston that spring about how much he would jam *Chewing Smoke*, it became a bit of a joke in the Northampton scene. So Bill Nace, who was a big believer in Wiccan cleansing rituals, had this idea that Thurston could purge our racket from his brain with some kind of 'loopage'. So Thurston drove about Northampton while jamming *Chewing Smoke* and letting loose. I think it done his head in.

Carlos Giffoni: The recording with Dylan and Thurston, it's probably my favourite thing we worked on together – it's hilarious. They had an apartment in New York as well, so there was this three-hour drive he'd do really often, I was on a few of them with him. It's a boring ride so you entertain yourself by doing different things. So, one day, Thurston was driving alone and decided to play this recording and started yodelling and screaming really crazy nonsense into his tape recorder while the music was going on. That's what this release is! It's him in his car driving from Northampton to New York with the music Dylan and I made, then him with this handheld recorder talking nonsense. It's completely spontaneous – then it came out on this label. I'm sure some people were pissed off when they got it, because they were probably expecting something like a live performance with the three of us. Still, I feel it stands on its own as a piece of really strange sound-art that I really love.

'Messy Mystery'/'New Vietnam Blues'
Can't/Nipple Creek
(U–Sound Archive, 2005)

Gene Moore: Nipple Creek was done at the New Grass Center for Underground Culture in Florence, a record- and bookstore owned and run by Byron Coley. I believe Byron asked us to do this gig. The actual place was called Yod, I believe.

Byron Coley: Ecstatic Yod really started as a store. Thurston and I would buy a lot of records – really a lot. When we would bring them home, Kim or my wife would ask why and we'd say, "They're for the store!" Really they were just for trading or whatever. So, when Thurston and Kim had the house but hadn't moved in yet, both Kim and my wife Lilly put the foot down and wanted to know where this store was that we were talking about, why our homes were full of piles of records. So we decided to open the store – the Ecstatic Yod Mill Outlet, because it was in an old mill that was used as a bookstore, we got a room there. We put a bunch of records in there, bought more stuff.

Once we were doing that we decided we wanted to put out more records, some of them we'd do together – and those would be Ecstatic Yod, just one of those arbitrary things because there were still Ecstatic Peace! and Father Yod records, but you'd have a hard time figuring out why. One thing was Ecstatic Peace! would have different people distributing it at different times, so would Father Yod – so Ecstatic Yod was a way to get out of some of the distribution networks we had to use. But they were also collaborative records; we did a series which all had fake BYG

Actuel label covers. We were particularly interested in records we could do smaller pressings of, because nobody would be very interested in them and we thought if we did a series then we could get people interested in buying the whole series. It was fun – I don't know how successful it was. Records that I like, I don't care if anyone buys them or not, to tell you the truth. I always tell people who are starting labels to only put out stuff they'd be happy to have sitting under their bed for a couple of years.

'Female Body Inspector'/'Monster Tape' Monster Dudes/Thurston Moore (Deathbomb Arc, 2006)

Jeremy and Venec Miller: Monster Dudes was a father-and-son excuse to travel. A friend introduced us to a two-piece rock band that was planning a tour from the West Coast to the East Coast before they were to embark on a semi-permanent tour of the other continents. The catch was that they didn't have transportation and, since they intended to leave the US, weren't interested in investing. They contacted us to see if we'd like to enter into an agreement where they'd book the tour and we'd provide the wheels across the country. The youngest member of Monster Dudes was four years old at the time.

The first Monster Dudes recording was an EP of pre-made beats, improvised guitar and vocals, somewhere between industrial, tribal and Halloween sounds. For that first tour we enlisted the help of a close friend and put on an improvised, somewhat Dadaesque, show with the EP as the soundtrack. There were costumes, lights, live mics with tons of delay. We wrestled, played catch, rolled around and acted like monsters. If there was ever a drum kit nearby, the youngest would inevitably gravitate toward it – getting home five weeks later, it was clear we needed to invest in one.

On that tour, one show in LA was promoted by Brian Miller of Deathbomb Arc. We had the next night off and Brian invited us to stay and play that night too. Deathbomb Arc were preparing the second year of their tape club; individuals would subscribe, then receive a 10-minute cassette each month. Every instalment had a song by a different artist on each side, so the track had to be as close to 10 minutes as the artists could manage. Brian pitched us to participate and – in a hushed, guru-like way – stated that he had Thurston committed and that we'd be sharing an instalment with Mr Moore. The condition was that it had to be something unreleased. For our 10 minutes we recorded two live improvisations of the band and an improvised, vocal-only track; then we edited the three pieces together, which resulted in something that sounds a lot like goofy sounds and skits over the din of a five-year-old drummer improvising along with keyboards and noises.

D.D.T.
Aaron Dilloway/Charlie Draheim/Thurston Moore (Tuskie Skull, 2006)

Amanda Kramer: On the tour circuit there was this thing where, "You were the guy in Omaha," "You were the girl in Philly," "You were the one in Baltimore," and anytime anyone needed to run the circuit you went to those people. Same with labels, certain people were doing it across the country and they were the people you had to constantly send your music to. There were these points, magnets, and everyone would know where to go, where to send. Anyone making weird music and coming to LA had to go to The Smell – so live music was how we were finding people. People would come through, we'd buy the cassette and it'd have an email or a phone number on the back – it still had that feel of the past to it. This wasn't like the eighties labels though; they were children of the seventies while we were a different phase and cultural mindset. Everyone was in a bunch of little bands and projects, you'd all join forces to make one project or you'd have a project on your own. It was a devaluing of the idea of a band or of a solo career, it made everyone more amorphous and created this beautiful web where there was so much music emerging and everyone was connected via a band, or a friend, or a live set. After a certain point, we became one of the dots on the map and people would write us emails to say they were coming to town, asking us to see them play; all we had to do was be part of our community.

Chris Pottinger: Aaron Dilloway put up with a bunch of questions from me about the logistics of releasing a 12" LP: "Where do you send the master tapes to? What does it mean to get it 'plated'? What record pressing plants do you recommend?" At that time, he was one of the only people I knew who had released experimental recordings on vinyl.

Aaron Dilloway: Growing up in the nineties tape-trading scene, we would just record things, make copies, trade them with friends. When Wolf Eyes started touring that's where I started my label, Hanson Records, and distribution for underground noise cassettes. Whenever we'd meet an opening band – usually just one person playing noise – I'd buy multiple copies of whatever tape they were selling, come back to Michigan, type up my catalogue and try to distribute them. I'd mail catalogues out to this small list of people who had ordered tapes from me. There were magazines like *Bananafish, Muckracker* – I would write to people asking if they wanted to trade. Thurston checked out all those magazines, he knew about our stuff, about all the underground weirdo tape labels. When he invited Universal Indians to open for Sonic Youth, I brought one of my high-school band records to give to him, a band called Galen, there were only 300 copies, but he said, "Oh man, I've already got it – hey, give it to Lee!" I was blown away that he had that; he was a crazy collector of the most obscure stuff.

Charlie Draheim: In 2006 there was a show, Sonic Youth with The Flaming Lips in Detroit. My roommate, Greh, ran the label Chondritic Sound and we had a loft in Detroit overlooking the Eastern Market, which is this big industrial area of slaughterhouses and what-not. We would do shows there. That night, I was at work at the time, Greh called me saying Thurston wanted to play an after-party at our loft. So we headed back after the show. Aaron, Thurston, Kim and Mark Ibold were hanging out at my loft and we decided then that me, Thurston and Aaron would do this. Word of mouth got around, a lot of people showed up – maybe 70–80 people crammed in. It was a pretty drunken affair, people partying, having a good time. Five minutes before we were going to play, we went into my bedroom, thinking, 'What are we going to do?' Aaron had this electronic reel-to-reel tape set-up thing he does; Thurston and I played guitar. Thurston had a bunch of guitars with him. I had this homemade, beat-up guitar I'd built. We played about 25 minutes – somebody's girlfriend at the time had a camcorder, so I suggested to her she record it for posterity. It was fun, very loose, drunk, lot of feedback, lot of guitars being slammed on the ground. I'm sure people in the loft enjoyed it, but it was three drunken guys so I'm pretty objective about what it was.

Two days later I watched the video; it was unwatchable and the audio wasn't that great, but it was definitely something I thought maybe in the future people might want to hear. Three months after that, I went on a mini-tour and I needed some merchandise with me to sell. So I remembered the audio from that show, thought it'd be a funny thing to take it out on the road with me. I made a handful of copies, all on recycled cassette tapes, put it together in my bedroom, took the audio directly off the videotape, ran it through a mixer and a tuner to clean it up a bit. The artwork was from pictures I had of a Patti Smith performance at the Glastonbury festival in 1999 that I went to with a high-school buddy of mine. He had taken this picture of her and I thought, 'What the hell?' So it was a photocopy of that, the initials DDT and I think the word 'live'. When I did the tape I thought I should put a label name and a catalogue number on it just to make it look a bit more official. Tuskie Skull was a label I had; I'd make 15–20 copies of tapes to give out to friends. I'd grown up in a little area called Tuscarora township, we'd refer to the police department as the 'Tuskies', so 'Tuskie Skull' is a joke name I'd been using since a teenager.

My plan was to give the tapes away or sell 'em for three-four bucks. People were intrigued by it, didn't think it was a real thing, that it was a joke or whatever, and I didn't really talk about it so it kept some mystery. I mistakenly gave Aaron the master cassette. I don't even have a copy! I was going to make one to send to Thurston, which never happened – I feel bad about it to this day! He would ask me about it; it almost became a running joke. I played No Fun Fest in New York and the Color Out Of Space festival, and both times he heckled me: "Where's the tape?!"

Blood Shadow Rampage
Dream Aktion Unit
(Volcanic Tongue, 2006)

Paul Flaherty: I met Chris Corsano and Thurston Moore at an improvised concert they both attended separately in Amherst, Massachusetts, featuring me, Randall Colbourne, Richard Downs, Mike Murray and James Chumley Hunt. Thurston recorded us and Chris started buying our records, so we gave him a few more and a friendship with both started. Randy and I played together from 1988 to 1998 almost weekly at jam sessions, but when we decided to take a break Chris was one of the first I asked to jam. We met at a one-room house he was renting in Northampton and the music was so intense that I suspected he was trying to kill me. Then he asked me if we were on our last piece because he wanted to 'drop the bomb'. Frightening! But I survived and realised I'd found a drummer who wanted to play with a similarly excessive energy to me.

Thurston came to a duo gig Chris and I were playing around 2001, and when I suggested that he should have brought his guitar he seemed disappointed. I told Chris this and he invited Thurston to our next gig. It was at a bowling alley that played disco music in the lanes while the balls hit the pins. We played in the side-room restaurant and here comes Thurston, with a small amp and no effects, and we hit it. The drums were muffled, the sound was terrible and mixed with disco and, for some reason, Eugene Chadbourne was in the bowling alley audience and ordered roast duck – what kind of duck gets roasted at a bowling alley? That was our first trio gig and my first time playing with Thurston.

After that we called it The Aktion Trio; soon we'd add Jim O'Rourke and it was a quartet; then at some point it became Dream Aktion Unit and we did some great shows in NYC, Minnesota, Connecticut, Massachusetts and at All Tomorrow's Parties in England. The band seemed to have a lot of potential. At times Matt Heyner joined on bass, but we never recorded and years passed. Finally, we were well recorded in Scotland; it was going to be a quartet with Matt – O'Rourke had moved to Japan. At the last minute, Thurston asked our friend Heather Leigh to join and made it a quintet. This was one of those under-recorded groups that 'coulda been a contender'. I saw it as a perfect union of noise-rock and jazz which I've always wanted to pull off. And we did it... for those who were there. Can't win 'em all.

Flipped Out Bride
Thurston Moore
(Blossoming Noise, 2006)

Thurston Moore: *Flipped Out Bride* and *Sensitive/Lethal* happened around the same time. It was right around the apex of noise culture. Also, I had a burgeoning interest in black metal. This was all during the 10-year period where I was living at Round Hill Road in Northampton. These releases were done in my basement – people would just ask me to do things. This was meant to be the first of a series and I was going to use these portrait paintings that Kim does – but it didn't get beyond this release.

Noon And Eternity
To Live And Shave In LA
(Menlo Park Recordings, 2006)

Tom Smith: My instinct has always been to steer clear of movements, genres, eruptive confluences, and other ephemeral anomalies, including those I might have had a part in birthing. I was *musique concrète* from the get-go, destroying my parents' hi-fi to alter pitch and force the cartridge to jump the groove. My first band, Boat Of, were the first group to use Sugar Hill/Enjoy label tape-edits to create backing tracks – we were the only fuckers in the world doing this, at least in 1980. Peach Of Immortality used live edits and mixed chamber instrumentation, albeit at extreme volume. To Live And Shave In LA harnessed the hysteric qualities of text and edit. When faced with the artificial dilemma of dramatic forward movement versus appeasement, the rock underground will always ask to eat more shit.

I'd liked the forlorn quality of the first two Sonic albums; not much afterward until the *Silver Session For Jason Knuth* disc, which I quite admired. The other stuff was a bit too Perry Como for my liking. It was lovely to record *Noon And Eternity* at their Echo Canyon studio; very relaxed. Don Fleming and Andrew W.K. were behind the board, the dudes were blowing dope through the ventilators, and I wrote the track 'Early 1880s' on the back of an old Sonic Youth tour poster lying on the floor of the vocal booth while lunch was being delivered. All the music was improvised, but certain motifs were selected and expanded upon. The truly sick 'Mothers Over Silverpoint' riff was begun by Chris Grier, but Thurston jumped on it immediately and within seconds we were all screaming, "That's it!"

Horóscopo: Sanatorio De Molière
To Live And Shave In LA
(Blossoming Noise, 2006)

Tom Smith: We had several hours of outtakes from the *Noon And Eternity* sessions, plus fragments of Thurston's tracks, in addition to other things he'd sent me over the years, which comprised his contribution to *Horóscopo*.

More recently, we released *Absence Blots Us Out*, it's about our late comrade Chris Grier. Fucking heroin – you'd think everyone would have received the memo by now. The title of the album came to me a few days after we got the news. We had to define the man as we knew him best, so I sent emails to members of the collective and affiliated friends. I was rather too angry with Chris for dying – I had no subjectivity – so I asked Thurston to pen the eulogy. I assembled the contributions at my home studio and found a motif rather quickly. Extracting Chris' voice from old tour videos and including a reading of an email of his which uncannily prefigured his malaise helped to humanise the freak and reminded all of us of just how much we'd lost.

Insertion/Untitled
Cotton Museum/Thurston Moore
(Tasty Soil, 2006)

Chris Pottinger: Cotton Museum recordings usually consist of rewired thrift-store keyboards, samplers and a small, homemade Theremin processed through plenty of delay and a handful of other effects. After a number of live performances were cut short by having gear fall off the table and getting unplugged, I realised it'd be much easier if I created a system to keep my instruments in place. I used Velcro to fix all my synths, guitar pedals and samplers to the top of a card table which allowed me to become more physical with my performance without worrying about knocking anything off, without any interruption, even when the legs would collapse on the battered card table – there were times I even played it upside down like a mechanic working on the underside of a broken car. Over time, I started to imagine this card table as an instrument all of its own; the mess of patch cables and synths were just the veins and pulsating organs that controlled this weird machine.

Heath Moerland, Jamie Easter and I all moved into a house in Hamtramck, Michigan, which we started calling 'the Get Lost House'. Everyone living in that house was always creating something, spurring each other on. I even had a pirate radio station set up in the attic, broadcasting a Cotton Museum recording made specifically for it, looping endlessly for six months straight. You could tune into the broadcast on your car radio while driving down the I-75 freeway.

Heath Moerland: We had some legendary gigs and parties in that house! The house was shaking and you could hear the jams a couple blocks in every direction. A two-storey house with a basement, except there was a front room under the upstairs porch that we didn't have access to. There was a hole in the floor upstairs you could look through and it was a trash nest of fast-food wrappers and garbage, pizza boxes and beer cans. Legend has it that Rat Man lived there unseen in the shadows. No one will ever know. No one wants to know.

Chris Pottinger: The neighbours totally hated us; they'd mess with us all the time, most likely because they didn't know what to make of the sounds always coming out of our basement. Some dudes would hang out on the steps of an abandoned house across the street and would try to start fights with us, harassing anyone who came over. When they weren't around, we started hiding old rotten food over at that house, pouring tuna juice and old fish guts on the steps. After a while, it smelled so bad it was attracting swarms of flies and stray cats – those dudes couldn't tolerate sitting there any longer. Eventually, we thought they had decided to focus their energy on something else but unfortunately that wasn't the case. Shortly after, the two abandoned houses next to us were burnt down and a car in front of our house was set on fire. We got the message. Sticking around the Get Lost House was probably not the best idea so, sadly, everyone moved out.

I had recently started Tasty Soil and, though I'm not sure how he heard about it, Thurston ordered a Cotton Museum release from me. Thurston's experimental recordings were one of the reasons I'd first become interested in recording my own stuff, so I thought I'd ask him if he was interested in doing a solo LP – I felt this could be a fitting release and, as he'd just ordered one of my CD-Rs I figured it wouldn't hurt to ask. I was surprised when he wrote back saying he'd like to do it, but he thought it would be cool if it was a split with Cotton Museum. Two dudes over six feet tall making a weird record? Sounded perfect to me! I remember being excited and totally stressed out too; I had no idea how to release something on vinyl or where I'd come up with the money to do it.

I started saving up money by working as a groundskeeper for an outdoor concert venue, basically a glorified garbage man. One time I discovered a guy covered in blood, lying on the ground next to a car with some windows smashed in. He looked all pale and didn't appear to be breathing. I poked him with my stick because I was convinced he was dead. Surprisingly, he jumped up in a flash and resumed what he must have been doing earlier, punching out car windows with his gnarled, sliced-up, bare fists. I remember thinking that this had to be a good omen for the record.

I recorded the four songs for my side before Thurston's CD-R arrived in the mail. A few weeks after I finished recording, I received a package in the mail containing a CD-R with the title 'Insertion' scrawled on it with magic-marker. The only request Thurston had was that his side be played at 33rpm or 45rpm, leaving it up to the listener to decide how to experience it. I'm not even sure what the instrumentation is. I'm guessing guitar, but who knows? I probably should have asked.

Unlike the spontaneity I was accustomed to when releasing CD-Rs and tapes, I quickly realised you need a lot of patience when putting something out on vinyl. While waiting for the final recordings to be mastered and plated I spent time illustrating the album artwork, selecting the paper stock for the covers, having the artwork screenprinted, folding the covers, hand-stamping them and numbering them. Creating the artwork and package design for releases on Tasty Soil is a lot of fun. The imagery usually consists of infected mutants and nocturnal beings, drippy and covered in oozing boils. When the records eventually arrived, I spent evenings after work putting all 500 copies together. My local post office grew to hate me for showing up with large stacks of records to ship out every other day.

Free/Love
Thurston Moore
(Throne Heap, 2007)

Tom Moore: Thurston was an early supporter of the label. Shortly after the third tape was released, Thurston sent me a purchase inquiry and requested to be added to the update list. We exchanged a few emails and did a trade or two before I asked him if he would be interested in recording some material for Throne Heap. A few weeks later the master for *Free/Love* arrived. Asking Thurston to join the Throne Heap roster was really a no-brainer.

Thurston provided the image of the nude couple embracing that was used for the cover. I seem to remember him being really specific not to forget to include a '/' between the words free and love. Aside from that, Thurston's only other request was that the release be limited to no more than 200 copies. I was still dubbing the tapes one at a time back then, so I decided on an edition of 90. The artwork was xeroxed onto paper recovered from an abandoned paper factory in western Massachusetts. The toner didn't quite take to the page so I used hairspray as a makeshift fixative. They sold out pretty quick and the Throne Heap email update list – less than 100 people at the time – had first dibs. The recording is supremely raw in both fidelity and approach. The A-side, *Free*, contains a series of brief amp-play feedback meditations; moody and minimal with a kinda *Confusion Is Sex*-era blackness ringing throughout. The B-side, *Love*, is a somewhat more musical affair, 10 minutes of endless momentum, warts and all, guitar shredding.

The Voloptulist – 'Corion Sound For TNB'/ '840 Seconds Over' The New Blockaders/Thurston Moore/ Jim O'Rourke w/Chris Corsano (Hospital Productions, 2007)

The New Blockaders: The New Blockaders largely shaped what is considered 'noise music' today, while not actually sounding anything like the scene it helped to spawn. Most noise musicians ('noisicians'?) now are just that: musicians, using the same old hackneyed clichés of volume, dramatic preconceived performance moves and professionalism for career advancement that have been around since the dawn of rock'n'roll...

In the beginning, it was just about the blockade; that impenetrable barrier between nerve-endings, impervious to everything, ultimate stop-gap. It was about creating a music so fraught with possibilities its darkness gets transformed into a kind of pure light, imaginary fingerings of primary tongues. Music which is not-music, communication which refuses to communicate, art which is not-art... expect nothing. Absolutely nothing. It's your best shot at having everything delivered.

The New Blockaders have always been interested in collaborating with other artists. Working solely with noise can be rather limiting, so collaborating with others can produce interesting results beyond the restrictions of pure noise. When The New Blockaders started in 1982 there weren't many international artists working in the same field – Das Synthetische Mischgewebe in Germany, The Haters in the US, Merzbow in Japan, maybe a few others. There was no noise scene.

158

In 2006, Thurston Moore and Jim O'Rourke were invited to contribute to *Viva Negativa!: A Tribute To The New Blockaders* along with a total of 75 artists. They each submitted a track, 'Corion Sound For TNB' and '407 Seconds Over' respectively. Both Thurston and Jim used raw sounds submitted by The New Blockaders which they fused with their own.

After *Viva Negativa!* was released, I asked Thurston if he would be interested in releasing 'Corion Sound For TNB' as a seven-inch. He was in favour of my suggestion but suggested he do an extended version of the track and issue it as a 12" retitled *The Voloptulist*. We agreed it would be good to include Jim's '407 Seconds Over' on the B-side but Jim also preferred to record a new track, a collaboration with Chris Corsano entitled '840 Seconds Over'.

Black Weeds/White Death
Thurston Moore
(Meudiademorte, 2007)

Pascal Hector: I was involved in the hardcore scene like a lot of noise experimentalists. I played in bands, organised shows, started to book festivals and tours for international bands. Next I created a mail-order distributor and started to release hardcore music.

Then the Internet started growing: Napster, Soulseek, message boards. There was no 'real life' network for us in Germany, just a few nerds around the globe who were doing noise and posting this stuff on message boards – that's where I met Thurston, John Wiese, the Wolf Eyes guys. It was easy to connect with people who were interested in the counterculture but there came a time to transform this virtual world shit into real life. I stopped doing crowded hardcore shows for 100–500 people and started doing shows for The Sunburned Hand Of The Man, Yellow Swans, Lightning Bolt... with 20 people in the audience!

Thurston was a customer of mine and ordered a few tape releases from my label, so I just asked him if he wanted to do a tape. Easy! I think after a month I had the master on a CD-R in my mailbox. I directly put it into my stereo and started to draw the cover while dubbing 200 tapes. A month later it got released. So it was really a fast thing. Easy! The tape sounds like Thurston had a bad day after the shooting of a *Gilmore Girls* episode. He switches on his amp and just tries to destroy the guitar and his amp.

Stereotypical? Thirty percent of copies were given to Thurston, twenty percent to distributors I was working with, leaving the rest to be sold direct over the Meudiademorte website – they sold out inside a couple of hours.

Action/Extra Action
Richard Kern
(Taschen, 2007)

Richard Kern: I'd starting doing some stuff with Lydia Lunch who I met through a friend of mine, David Wojnarowicz. She introduced me to Sonic Youth [in the early-to-mid-1980s] and the band was doing 'Death Valley '69', plus a video for it which had a lot of Charlie Manson references. They wanted to shoot a scene that had something like Sharon Tate's house. They knew I did a lot of cheesy gore stuff for my own movies so they asked me if I'd help them do that part. Some of it was taken straight out of one of my other films called *Submit To Me*. We just put this stuff with Lung Leg in there to make it more street–creddy.

Thurston knew I also shot photos of girls so he asked me if I would give him some photos for his fanzine *Killer*. They had this huge fascination with Madonna. When she first moved to New York she was doing nude modelling and these things were surfacing. Thurston put 'Madonna Nudes' on the front of the fanzine and inside were my photos of girls without their faces showing. Sonic Youth used a photo of mine for the cover of *Evol*, another for *Sister* in the collage; then into *Goo*, I shot the band for that in 1990; then I did another video for them. There was always this back-and-forth.

I quit doing films for about 10 years. I'd been shooting videos of girls rolling around and stuff, but for quite a few years I focused on photography. What happened was the publisher Taschen, I was doing a book with them and they said that they had this new policy of putting out a DVD with each book, so they asked me if I had any footage. All I had was tons of footage of girls rolling around naked or walking around naked, things I would shoot with my video camera occasionally as I was shooting girls for photos. So Taschen asked if I could make them an hour-long video.

Way back when, there was a movie I was going to make called *Strip For Me Now*, which is still unreleased. Thurston had always said he was happy to give me music for it. So when it came time to do this Taschen movie, he sent maybe 20–30 minutes of tracks by email. Just random stuff he had left over from personal projects. The book comes out and Thurston was pretty surprised at the content! That it was like a porno film – it wasn't all porn, a lot of naked girls, but a lot of it is just stuff you don't normally get to see, like girls doing their teeth. The one comment he had was, "I wish you'd asked me for more music, I'd have gladly given you more," because I'd had to use a lot of songs over and over.

Action started me wanting to do more art films like I used to so I started this one, *Face To Panty Ratio*. I had this idea of making a movie that was just of girls' panties and their faces – it ended up also being about their hair. Again I called Thurston, asked if he had any music lying around. I didn't know what I was looking for but he sent me a few clips and I just took one I liked and cut the film straight to his music. I got a commission from Channel 4 in the UK to create one based on that film, so I asked him for more music. It was called *Clean* and Channel 4 took one look at it, even though they told me it could have nudity, and they freaked out. But at least they still paid me. I realised, looking at *Face To Panty Ratio*, that you never see any nudity, but in *Clean* I put a lot in. I can almost picture the exact point they decided they weren't showing this. It's a shot of this girl's huge boobs with soap dripping down them. I'm thinking, 'Right there! That's where they thought they're not showing this…'

Shot/Extra Shot
Richard Kern
(Taschen, 2013)

Richard Kern: This time I didn't want to bug Thurston again, I was asking all these people but it was such a hassle – they'd say I could use this or that, then I'd find out it was on a record label and I'd have to tell them I couldn't just lift it. Or people wouldn't come through – unreliable, legal bullshit. So I called Thurston and, man, just the relationship with Thurston is so mellow; "I'm doing this film, can I have some music?" "Sure! Here's some clips. Do whatever you want." It must help that he's recording music constantly, never stopping. By this point I was listening to a lot of Thurston's stuff, and I did notice parts he gave me, I'd find them in songs in slightly different versions or buried under a lot of stuff on his releases. He'd have the version on the record then 10 other versions of the same song. Different tempos, mixes, words, instrumentals. If there was something I liked on an album, I was able to say, "Hey, do you have another version without lyrics? With fewer lyrics? Different lyrics...?"

With *Action*, it was cut a little bit to the music but it was more like putting the video together then adding music on top. On *Extra Shot*, I had the music and was cutting it to the beat – I was a better editor by that point. I divided the film into individual songs, took the tracks, I'd see what the lyrics were and what might work great with this. 'Groovy And Linda' was a song by Chelsea Light Moving and just the fact it said 'Groovy', I could put anything to that which had girls in it and it'd work. A lot of time I'd turn up the actual sound from the video, a birdsong or the sound of music in the background, and I'd mix that in with the music. There are a lot of jokes woven in. Like one song is called 'Global Warming', so the footage is just of girls rubbing their breasts and close-ups of nipples – all this stuff all the way through to the very last image, which is of a big pregnant belly, and you realise all these boobs are just there for babies, they're not there for anything else.

There's a lot of stuff he sent me that'd be... say your radiator was making a lot of noise. It'd just be the sound of the radiator with a guitar on top of it. And if you've seen him play live at those improvisational shows he does, he's sent me those too. It's noise, electrical instruments not necessarily being strummed. At one period I'd see him play at so many gigs and I was thinking, 'Wow, I'd really like to see him strum that guitar or pick a note.' I saw shows where he'd never play a chord – lots of pounding on guitars, rubbing strings, bending the neck. I had to shoot Sonic Youth for *Dazed* one time a few years back and, while I was shooting Thurston, he just plugged his guitar in and I thought, 'Why wasn't I shooting video?!' I wish I had that. It was like watching Hendrix and I was there getting this private concert. He lives to play, lives to do it.

AM500 – 'Noh Neighbors'/'Noise Complaint' Thurston Moore (American Tapes, 2007)

John Olson: I knew I was going to stop at 1,000 releases on American Tapes so *AM500* was dead smack in the middle, I wanted it to be a big middle point. C. Spencer Yeh [experimental musician and avant-garde lightning rod] worked at this packing place, so he got me these booklets that held 20 CDs; I thought they'd be pretty good for a boxset – the materials governed the release. So *AM500*: a seven-inch, 19 CDs, a DVD, a tape and a poster – it's pretty hard to find.

Thurston is on two of the CDs called 'Noh Neighbors' and 'Noise Complaint'. It was a jam with us, the members of Hair Police and Graveyards recorded in Thurston's basement in Northampton. It was in the summer, right around fourth of July. Whenever Wolf Eyes would come to the East Coast we would stay at Thurston's house in Northampton and we'd always end up playing around in the basement, but that was the only time we recorded: Ben Hall from Graveyards on drums; then all the members of Hair Police; Thurston played guitar and I played saxophone on both. 'Noh Neighbors' was pretty aggressive, then 'Noise Complaint' was a little more laidback. The cops or someone did complain – that's where we got the name from – plus Kim shut it down after I grabbed Thurston's guitar and started playing a blues riff.

When I was in high school my favourite record was *Confusion Is Sex*, and whenever the lyric 'Squeeze your tongue and wrench it out' would come on my mom would sing along with the record. *Sonic Death*, I bought that when it came out and that was a huge influence in terms of documenting stuff real raw, doing versions of songs that don't sound like the songs, very Velvet Underground-ish. That was a big influence on the American Tapes aesthetic.

Thurston curated an All Tomorrow's Parties at Minehead [in December 2006] and people talk about that being the peak of this scene, because right after that is when everything started to die off. A lot of people quit. There were a lot of drugs and a lot of partying going on. There were a lot of people getting ready to go into middle age, getting families. So it was kinda the last hurrah. There was such a tidal wave of homemade releases that everyone got fed up with it. In hardcore they say a good scene only lasts five years, so that was pretty much right. It was a good time for people to go back into the bushes and see who comes out for food.

Touch The Iceberg
Owl Xounds Exploding Galaxy
(Fuck It Tapes, 2007)

Shayna Dulberger: I got my BA at a conservatory in 2005. I couldn't wait to gig fulltime and break free from that world. The scene for weirdoes and egomaniacs is where I feel most at home; it was a natural congregation of outcasts. It was obvious to me that we'd all end up in dive bars and DIY spaces; these are the places it's safe to be extreme, vulgar, crazy... or not. I was as ambitious as I could be, trying to play with everyone in the free-jazz/noise/rock scene. I thought, 'This is it, if I don't make shit happen now it'll never happen!' I felt like I was hanging onto life by a thread. I wanted to play as much as possible and as hard as possible.

I drove up to Easthampton by myself and met the guys there. The ride's only a couple hours. I remember feeling bummed I wasn't going to get to meet up at Thurston's home and possibly meet Kim. I think I had work, or didn't want to drive in the back of a van without a seat or seatbelt. Besides, I like to be self-sufficient. The music itself was pretty noisy, high-energy and focused. I felt like it was a great balance between Thurston's loudness and calmness and Owl Xounds' sweat-flinging propulsion. It was pretty calming to be on-stage with him. The whole ride up, I got pretty anxious – as I do before most events I'm excited about – and then once we were up there on-stage it was no big thing. I felt like Thurston was pretty comfortable with himself and what he was doing; that made me comfortable.

Adam Kriney: Gene Moore, Thurston's older brother, was a member of Owl Xounds, we had been playing guitar with him for quite a while. The decision to play with Thurston was opportunistic. I felt it was something one was supposed to do; if you improvised or made experimental music, at some point you would have your collaboration with Thurston Moore. Because we had already been playing with Gene and because we had a show in Thurston's hometown, I put it out to Gene to see if his brother would be interested. The gig was less than remarkable; however, opportunities being what they are, we got an offer to do a release so I proposed this recording and they agreed.

Shayna Dulberger: The Flywheel had an almost church basement-like atmosphere; low ceiling, short stage (maybe six inches off the floor), sometimes-working PA, and a bunch of incredibly dedicated, talented and hard-working volunteers who put everything into making it hospitable for bands: carpeted floor, fluorescent lights, some stage lighting. Any equipment that worked was usually donated.

Brett Robinson: The cast of board members has changed over the years but there are some consistent members. Chris Dooley has been a huge asset to the community there in terms of booking, organising, training, running sound. He's a true living legend in Western Massachusetts. In this first incarnation, The Flywheel was basically a nondescript room on the outskirts of Easthampton. The performance area was all dark walls, shitty carpet, a couple of beat-up old sofas, no windows. There was a front room, a café area with a busted-up old piano and a few stacked bookshelves which comprised their 'zine library'. People could hang out while music was playing in the other room, which is great because you're rarely going to have to deal with people talking over the performers. The Flywheel, to me, is a little corner of Easthampton where I can go see some weird music then walk home, feeling satisfied with where I live.

Adam Kriney: I think there was a very interesting thing that happened in the late nineties through the first decade of the 2000s with the underground, which had to do with certain key members, like Thurston, opening up the worlds of weirder music to the general public. But I feel the entire process was actually a bubble and it burst. I don't know if there was much to see in it – way too many releases, not a lot of quality, way too little quality control on a lot of the stuff that was coming out. Everybody flooded the market with releases and there wasn't an audience to service it all. It became this very fetishistic and collector-based world that wasn't about the art or the music at all, it was really very gross to see. That's part of the reason I put Owl Xounds away, because I saw there was really no sustenance to this improvisational world; we would get write-ups in *The Wire* magazine but nobody would come to a concert – so what's the point? It seems like there's all this idea that things are happening but, in reality, nothing's happening at all. There was definitely an exciting moment but nobody was taking care to make sure there was any longevity to it. Perhaps it was all about that moment, I don't know, but I'm glad to have been part of it despite the mistakes made.

LP
The Bark Haze
(Important, 2007)

Pete Nolan: Apollo Grill [where this record was recorded] is just some restaurant in an old factory building in Easthampton where Ecstatic Peace!

had their headquarters. I believe it may have been still daylight when we played. I think Thurston wanted to really immerse himself into a fully improvised wash of guitar sound and Andrew [MacGregor] had a certain melodic sensibility to his playing that kept it from being just total harsh noise. There was an openness and sense of direction to the pictures they painted. I think Thurston's work with Bill Nace in Northampton Wools was a continuation of this desire to do the two-guitar thing but it was way harsher and less inviting than what the Haze were doing. I was stoked to throw myself into this rhythmic guitar wall of sound. I had chops as an improvising drummer and I felt I could push their jams along and freak them out a bit. Thurston plays with a kind of rhythmic intensity that's super easy to lock in with for a drummer. I thrive on Teutonic repetition and gradual heightening of experience in my drumming style. Byron [Coley] was working the door at this gig. He was always hassling me! He asked me what kind of music we would be playing and I told him avant-garde jams. He said he thought that was a rather clunky classification.

I think there was something special about the time period, specifically 2000–2010 or so. Lines became quite blurry when the ethos of free improvisation that was always present in jazz started to blend with free rock music. It made perfect sense for anyone who was involved with this scene of music to jam with anyone else. There were bands, but they weren't thought of in the old-fashioned sense of promoting songs or promoting a brand or whatever. If someone had a band in this scene they were promoting some kind of intense vibe or new sound form.

Total Joke Era
The Bark Haze
(Important, 2007)

Andrew MacGregor: The Bark Haze... the name comes from the name of the sixties band The Bar-Kays. We came up with it after Thurston was misquoted in a magazine article, so there was always a playful element involved. The Bark Haze played around the Valley as well as a show and in-store in Boston, one in Austin at SXSW, one in NYC as well as one in England at All Tomorrow's Parties, which he put together. It was more if we were both around and someone asked then we would play; if not, he would play in another configuration or whatever he wanted to do. I think that I initiated the NYC show because I knew we would both be in town and it was convenient because we would likely be going to the show.

McCannabis
The Bark Haze
(Arbor, 2007)

Pete Nolan: This tape is a recording of a Bark Haze performance at the Thurston-curated All Tomorrow's Parties that featured sets by The Stooges, Negative Approach, The Dead C and every American noise band that ever was. I was asked to go to perform with Magik Markers and as a guest in The Bark Haze. As a performer, the ATP festivals were completely debauched; this was the festival where Wolf Eyes had a party in their chalet that was so big that the deck broke free from their apartment and was utterly destroyed. I had a party in my tiny hotel room with at least 100 people. Anyway, on Sunday at noon, when The Bark Haze was taking the stage, I was still asleep in my room. I awoke to the sound of Ecstatic Peace! partner Andrew Kesin shouting my name through the window to wake up. On the *McCannabis* cassette you'll find that the first 10 minutes of the performance are *sans* drums. There could well have been 3,000 people packed into the hall as I ran toward the stage with The Bark Haze, making an absolutely beautiful racket. When I finally reached the drums I pummelled them with an intensity brought about by a particular rush of anxiety and adrenalin that I may have almost missed the entire gig.

Lee Ranaldo: Festival culture is great if you're of a certain age or mindset and you're there for the spectacle of it. And from a musician's point of view, it's great because you get paid well and there's a lot of friends backstage you haven't seen in ages. But, like the Internet age in general, it was an era of increased preoccupation – people would watch you for two or three songs then go off to watch something else, because there's 10 other things going on and you don't want to miss anything. It wasn't about the music or any individual artist present, more of a morass, a hive. I'd heard stories that in the 1910s, 1920s, the surrealists would go to a movie theatre and watch 10 minutes of a movie then go to another theatre and watch 10 minutes of another and so on – it felt more like that, interesting in and of itself but not giving any single artist their due. It was a spell where, even as giant festivals continued to happen, a certain quotient of people realised that it wasn't the most interesting way to present or experience music, and maybe a club with 50–100 people is a more satisfying experience – or 1,000 people as opposed to 10,000 people. The perception shifted for people who weren't looking for commercial success to begin with.

One For Merz
The Bark Haze
(Three Lobed Recordings, 2008)

Cory Rayborn: Having run a couple of multi-artist subscription series – a way for me to feel like I am making my own little effort to assemble a greater snapshot of the underground scene at any one particular time – I felt like I needed to give it yet another whirl. That need led to the *Oscillation III* series. Having had a good experience with Thurston the last time out – and having had a good on again/off again email dialogue with him over the intervening time – I wanted to ask him. I had been enjoying the few Bark Haze releases that were out there at that point, as well as a few additional live recordings that I had been able to track down. It seemed like a fun ask for the set that was already starting to come together.

The response was quick and enthusiastic. Like the last time out, the music and artwork came in due order and were, of course, great. With *Purposeful Availment* (a previous subscription series), I was still learning how to run a record label. I went for EP-length submissions as that made sense to me at the time in a number of ways, including pushing up to the boundaries of what I felt I could ask for from people without a lot of track record. *Modern Containment* was a big step forward and then the collection of full album-length material in *Oscillation III* just really seemed like a more comprehensive scene statement.

Basement Psychosis
The Bark Haze
(Ecstatic Peace!, 2008)

Andrew MacGregor: I don't remember ever feeling bad about a live performance or recording with Thurston; to be honest, playing live or recording improvised music is such a joy that, even if certain aspects go poorly, there is likely to be something that feels good to hang one's hat on. When I was playing regularly in different formats, I would often be overwhelmed with a feeling of joy that there was an audience who was in that space and I was doing exactly what came into my body/mind in terms of sound/action. To me, a very important part of making music is being in the moment and available to move with time, space, emotion, whatever. The Bark Haze was very much like that.

Monolith: Jupiter
The Bark Haze/Traum
(Music Fellowship, 2008)

Andrew MacGregor: When playing music, especially improvised music, I am trying to reach a point where thought and ego cease to exist and it is all action/sound. Thurston and I maybe discussed The Bark Haze in terms of sound really once, which was during a practice before our first show and that was likely an effort to be comfortable, having never played together before. Of course, the show was totally different than what we had discussed; after that I never really thought much about it during the time – maybe he did, but we certainly didn't communicate about it verbally. I get bored with playing the same way, not necessarily the same thing, but the same way. For the longest time I didn't really know that bands were often putting on an act, a theatre event really, playing the same set the same way each night when they played a live show. I can't imagine how painful that would be – just the thought of it makes me cringe.

Wild And Free
The Bark Haze
(no label, 2009)

Andrew MacGregor: The artwork on *Wild And Free* was done by me. At the time I was dedicating a decent amount of time to painting. I used the same process as I would use for improvised music, mixing paint and applying it in a somewhat haphazard fashion with non-traditional tools, hoping to pull something out of the moment that can be made sense of. I find visual art very appealing in many ways because it is often less intrusive than sound and people tend to have a less opinionated or violent response to visual art they don't like, appreciate or understand.

'Can We Just Talk Instead?'/'Sadnessfinalamen' The Bark Haze/Our Love Will Destroy The World (Krayon Recordings, 2009)

Alan Read: Krayon was always an open platform for the artist to present their work how they wanted with minimal label interference. The idea for the split seven-inch series was thought up by a friend who I ran the label with at the time and, from there, we contacted some of our favourite musicians and asked them if they'd like to be involved. I believe it was Thurston who wanted this release to be a double A-side with Kim Gordon artwork for the Bark Haze side. Campbell put together the artwork for the Our Love Will Destroy The World side. All of which I was ecstatic about. The release of the split seven-inch was the point where Krayon changed from pretty much only existing as a merch-box at gigs plus a webstore into a global record label. It was the first release which already had a fanbase and that shops were actively interested in. Unfortunately, financially, seven-inch singles are really hard to break even on. I would have liked to have continued with the series but I couldn't afford to keep funding the shortfall out of my own pocket.

Campbell Kneale: I have always had an open-door policy as far as my involvement with labels and have welcomed whoever turned up at any given moment. It's more fun that way, or perhaps I just never reached that rung of the rock'n'roll ladder where a label would actually want to keep you! Krayon just miraculously appeared as I was ready to start putting out the first Our Love Will Destroy The World material. I hadn't heard of The Bark Haze and just let Alan – who was so obviously a first-class kinda chap – make the aesthetic decisions; if he thought the pairing would work then I was more than happy to play along.

I had some seven-inch-sized tracks lying around in the hard-drive, sent a track and it appeared one day on a record – no mess, no fuss, no major emotional drama at all, which I was delighted about because the dramas of running a record label from an isolated country like New Zealand had well and truly knocked all the joy out of almost everything, except actually making music. To have this all happen so easily was exactly what I needed at the time. Everything seemingly happened in another realm and appeared on my doorstep one day in the form of a nice little box of pretty records. I went to bed happy that night. I was happy to be surprised about what was happening on the other side, and I was finding out that the magic happens when you let go of these things rather than tenaciously clinging to them. It seemed like the best way to get new perspectives on the music I was making – and the music I wanted to make in future – was to give up and let go. So I did. And it worked. My attitude has always been that 'technique' is interesting but it's always subservient to something bigger. Music is a result of a commitment to magic, not the other way around. 'Being' something trumps 'doing' something. The force behind the music, the overarching composition, the 'why' you do this is of far more consequence than a great deal of the audible component. The point where you become invisible as a performer and where the listener is taken beyond knobs, dials, pedals and cables is the moment you shine brightest.

Northampton Wools
Northampton Wools
(Bonescraper Recordings, 2007)

Jeff Hartford: When Thurston lived in Northampton he started playing with local guitar mangler and improviser Bill Nace. On Pleasant Street there was a knitting store called Northampton Wools, from which they drew inspiration. It was not uncommon to see them shredding in local basements for a number of years. Their live output was diverse and explored everything a six-string had to offer. My favourite moments of their shows were always when they would attack their instruments, causing the volume to grow and expand; raising the blood pressure of the audience.

After one such performance I approached them, told them I wanted to release a double tape, whatever length they wanted, but it had to be harsh. I didn't want to hear any noodling. They handed me four 12-minute sides of blistering, harsh guitar noise and feedback edited from a live studio jam in Thurston's basement. I asked Lauren Pakradooni, who lived in the Valley at the time, playing under the name PAK, for the two cover images I used. At the time she drew a lot of people covered in hair and I enjoyed her images. I made 100 copies.

Thurston and Bill Nace, Northampton Wools at Coco 66, Brooklyn, NYC, January 30, 2010.   Credit – Louis Caldarola

Valley Of Shame
Northampton Wools
(Open Mouth, 2009)

Bill Nace: We played together for about six to seven years. We only used that name as a duo but we performed in a lot of different combinations over that time. As a duo I think we were kind of under-documented, especially compared to how many shows we did together. The tapes don't really do the duo justice in my mind. I don't really know how many times we've played together but it's a lot, probably up there with the most I've played with anyone.

Thurston played a huge part in my development. For one – and he's done this with a lot of people – there's something very nurturing about someone who is older and more accomplished who kind of accepts you as a peer and acts like there is as much for him to learn from who he's playing with as they have to learn from him.

For the performance captured on *Valley Of Shame*, Thurston came into the movie theatre I worked at. I was scooping some popcorn, turned around – and Thurston was standing there. Ha! He asked if I wanted to play with him so we did a show at Flywheel with, I believe, Can't and Cotton Museum.

Chris Pottinger: I booked a Cotton Museum tour with Sick Llama and asked Thurston if he'd set up a show for us. He booked us into a club called The Flywheel, opening for Northampton Wools. That was the duo of him and Bill Nace, such a great project; two guys mangling electric guitars through a pile of effects pedals, creating sounds you'd never imagine were coming out of just two guitars. They sounded totally destroyed, raw and frantic.

A few days into the tour I got an email from him saying he was sorry but he thought he wouldn't make it to the show. We showed up to the gig anyway, expecting to be playing alone, but surprisingly Thurston ended up making the drive out after all. It was totally packed, one of the bigger audiences I had played for at that point, and at the end of the night Thurston insisted on giving us his cut of the door money, even after he'd driven all the way from NYC just to play the show and not let anyone down.

Jeff Hartford: There are a number of people who either grew up in the area or came here for school and stuck around. There is also a fluctuating group of students that add new energy every other year. I wouldn't say that any one particular person, venue or band made the scene. Venues and bands tend to change with the seasons due to so many of the active participants coming and going, but these things keep the local scene fresh with ideas and constantly evolving. During the 2000s there were some quality bands, creating challenging sonic output, that made this community what it is: bands like Fat Worm of Error, BenGeorge7, Beltone Suicide, Son of Earth,

Magik Markers and Ben Heresy; on the punk side of things, bands like Relics, Orchid, Vaccine, Potty Mouth and Ampere have contributed to making this scene great. Now there's a whole new crop of bands contributing to make the Pioneer Valley a cool place: punk and hardcore bands like Hardware, Urochromes, Chemiplastica and Gay Mayor; noise bands like Scald Hymn, Gastric Lavage, God Cage, Egg,Eggs, Curse Purse, Sam Gas Can and Phurrne.

Untitled
Paul Flaherty/Thurston Moore/Bill Nace
(Ecstatic Peace!, 2007)

Paul Flaherty: I'm a free-form improviser; learned the sax in the school's classical music system; played in the closet with jazz and rock recordings from age 16 to 23, and then found my voice improvising freely with my 18-year-old cousin, Daniel Flaherty, doing sax and drum duos. We had one gig only and were barred from the club after that. We played everywhere we could – parties, mountain tops, traffic jams, a strip club which we were thrown out of quickly. I did play one sax/drum piece freely with another drummer before Daniel and I began jamming. His name was Jim Polenza and we did this piece at Jack's Bar in Rockville, Connecticut. Jim kept a loaded shotgun next to his drum kit and told the audience they weren't going to like me but to "Shut the fuck up and listen". I never have had a better intro. To this day he rides his motorcycle with the Hells Angels in New York City.

My own sound seems to have always been there. A combination of a sad howling cry that, at times, becomes truly insane and, at times, turns into a spiritual prayer that expresses itself in full-blown release or a softer walk through a dark passageway. In essence, it's all about releasing to the music – I ask it to take me. I surrender to it, whatever it is that's there to take over during the process is what I surrender to. I don't know what God is but something amazing holds this reality together, and something much deeper than what I think of as myself is what grabs hold of the sax when it's time for music to reveal itself. I've always looked for and seldom was lucky enough to find musicians who could play at extreme energy levels and lift a room, a spiritual essence that draws people to music and lets them become inspired. I've seen Thurston look for this in other players as well – inviting and being invited to perform with players of all styles.

He's been called the anti-rock star; a down-to-earth character who interacts with everyone. But it's the energy and uplifting quality that attracted me.

So, this was a recording at Paranoise studios near Amherst, Massachusetts that I organised with two things in mind... that became three. Bill had been asking me to try a duo recording session and I wanted to do it, but Thurston was in town so I asked him to come if he could, thinking we'd do the duo if he didn't make it. When he got delayed because a pipe in his basement broke, we recorded most of a duo LP while we waited which Thurston released on Ecstatic Peace! as *An Airless Field*. Then, when he got there, we recorded 70 minutes of music and used it all on the nameless trio release. When he left to take Kim out to dinner, we went back to recording the duo and by chance a singer named Laila Salins showed up. So she joined Bill and myself for 30 incredible screaming minutes. And that, along with some duo material, was released as a CD, *Broken Staircase*.

Trees Outside The Academy
Thurston Moore
(Ecstatic Peace!, 2007)

John Moloney: The first time I played with Thurston was 2005 at The Flywheel. He had emailed, asking me out of the blue if I wanted to do a duo with him. Thurston was doing a lot of gigs with Chris Corsano at the time, then Corsano started playing drums in Bjork's band, or he moved to the UK, so he wasn't around. So Thurston asked me because I was there – of course I said yes. "No practice," he said. "We'll just show up and go for it." And I thought, 'Oh my God...'

The night before, I went out to eat with a girlfriend; I got savage food poisoning and woke up with it on the day. I was in bad shape but there was no way I was going to cancel the show. We played about 40 minutes – we blew it out. That whole first show he had his eyes closed most of the time, on his own planet, just taking it all in – one of the best guitar players I've seen in my life, let alone played with. At the end I thought, 'Oh he must have hated it,' but no, it worked out because then he called me back.

In 2006–07, I was still living in Boston and he asked me if I wanted to come out to play drums on some of the songs that ended up being *Trees Outside The Academy*. He basically tried me out for the drum position; we ran through a bunch of the new songs in his basement. I was so nervous. He said to me he was thinking about having a different band, he thought it'd be cool – so he had Steve [Shelley] in mind but wanted to try me. I even said to him, "Why don't you use Steve? I'm just going to play like him!" Steve was an influence on me and when you play with Thurston you realise that's the sound, some kind of telepathy he had with Steve about the drums.

Justin Pizzoferrato: *Trees Outside The Academy* was done at J Mascis's Bisquiteen Studio. It's in his house and he doesn't really let just anyone record there.

John Moloney: By 2007 I had moved to Northampton and moved in with Thurston and Kim. So I got a call from Thurston: "I've got one more song, Steve isn't here – do you want to come over and play drums on it?" He gave me a burn of the song, 'Language Meanies', I tried to practise it but had a hard time then went over to the house to join Thurston. J lives in Amherst, next town over basically – there's a river that separates Amherst and Northampton with a little town in between called Hadley, it's about seven miles. He put me in a room in J's attic in front of this giant drumkit – the largest drums I'd played in my entire life. We did three or four takes, I was there for maybe 20 minutes; I felt I'd screwed it all up, then, after I got some coffee, I got a text from John Agnello, the producer, saying to come on back and check it out. What he'd done is take the best bits of my takes and made a song out of it.

Built for Lovin'
Thurston Moore
(Lost Treasures Of The Underworld, 2008)

John Moloney: I call it Thurston's basement tapes – it's all stuff from Thurston's basement around 2006–07. There's a piece on the record, uncredited, with Thurston and Steve Shelley working out some possible version of something from *Trees Outside The Academy*.

When I went up to Thurston's to try out, Mark Ibold was up there; he was trying Mark out for whatever he had in mind, but Mark couldn't do it because he was having a baby. Me, Mark and Thurston played some kind of improvised hardcore-esque stuff, some version of a hardcore band – that's where the piece with us on the record comes from, from the day I tried out.

176

We did one show too, a one-off where we did a Misfits cover with Matt Krefting [Easthampton-based musician and founder of Idea Fire Company] on vocals.

Kumpiny Night
Elisa Ambrogio/Ben Chasny/Zac Davis/Dredd Foole/Kim Gordon/Gown/Matt Krefting/ Thurston Moore/Bill Nace/Jessi Leigh Swenson (no label, 2007)

Brett Robinson: The Kumpiny Night gig was just another show at the Yod space. It's basically a room, 15 chairs and Byron's usually making food. It's a studio in an old factory building that's floor-to-ceiling 15 feet high, with records. A beautiful sight. This particular show was mainly a collaborative guitar event with a few other performers jumping in. Performer names were drawn from a hat and the sets were timed to five minutes exactly, at which point someone (Matt Valentine, I think) pulled the plug on the amps. It was a very intimate and chill environment, everyone eating food, laidback and chatting. Not sure who had the idea to draw lots, but these were all individuals who had mostly performed together before in some combination, so it wasn't anything too adventurous; just a fun game for friends.

I videotaped the entire evening; I've never shared the footage, but I did make 13 CD-R copies of the audio and gave them out to performers. One of them, Zac Davis, re-pressed it as an edition of 113 copies on his Maim & Disfigure label without my permission or that of any of the performers. A recording of me taking a piss happens in the middle of it. Thurston told me, "Nice piss!" one time in reference to it. I never stopped recording so the entire thing is just one long uninterrupted track.

Thrash Sabbatical – 'Unzipped'/'Petite Bone'/'Creamsikkle'
Thurston Moore
(Deathbomb Arc, 2007)

Amanda Kramer: The *Thrash Sabbatical* thing was all Brian Miller – a very dear friend. At the time Britt and I were in this crazy band called

177

Barrabarracuda. It was never really meant for primetime, we'd just go insane. Grace Lee and I would play this weird drum kit together where we both banged on things and screamed about weird stuff. Brian loved it, so he told us he was doing this record and wanted us to be on it. We gave him a joke song, 'Stone Cold Steve Austin At The Cold Stone Creamery'.

Britt Brown: Brian pitched us his unconventional vision for the release – multiple split-vinyl releases in a silkscreened pizza box with an insert and some campy holiday objects – and it sounded extreme and ridiculous, and pure Deathbomb Arc, so of course we agreed. I named it *Thrash Sabbatical* and drew the original artwork but, other than that, the release was Brian's doing! Deathbomb Arc is definitely part of a lineage of fringe capitalist curators picking and choosing a new way to operate, with new principles and new aesthetic concerns. Brian's gone from noise rock to rave jams to rap tapes; he's run split cassette clubs and digital singles clubs; he's traded music for canned goods and slept in a minivan; he's organised shows where bands in other states performed through cell phones. The goal isn't to replicate the model of major labels, or indie labels – the goal is to go your own way and work with people you respect and not get burned out. However that manifests, and wherever that leads, is how it was meant to be.

Brian Miller: I had invited Thurston to do music, a single 10-minute track, for a cassette series called the *Deathbomb Arc Tape Club*. When he sent in his music for it it was more material than would work for the club, so I suggested doing a multi-vinyl boxset that also helped bring attention to LA artists and he loved the idea. The only thing Thurston insisted on was that Britt and Amanda from [the label] Not Not Fun be involved. They're old friends, so it was a natural fit. The art was entirely of Britt and Amanda's design. I consulted for what would be reasonable and then I did all the labour to spray-paint, silkscreen and assemble them.

To me, the lasting highlight of *Thrash Sabbatical* is that Men Who Can't Love were involved. I think this may be their only release even though they were such an important aspect of the cultural DIY landscape in LA at the time. After the two brothers in Rainbow Blanket (Jeff and Greg Witscher) met more like-minded young noise musicians, they formed Men Who Can't Love. Essentially it was a bunch of young solo noise acts that would set up their tables of gear in a circle around the crowd and then tag-team five-minute noise sets, one at a time. It allowed lots of acts to play one show, to tour together, without worrying old-school bookers/venues that too many acts were on the line-up.

Amanda Kramer: At the time we wanted to give people so much art – there was no strategy other than, 'How impressive can we make this release? How artful can we make it? Can we hand-draw this? Can we glue this? Can we silkscreen this? Can we get good, interesting, weird bands to do this? Can we get people to come up with supergroups and side-groups?' It was a pleasure-based thing for friends of music, period. No one was making anything off of this or expecting anything other than to make the people listening happy. We weren't aiming for a legacy.

Brian Miller: I started Deathbomb Arc in order to work with the musicians from a Bay Area band called rRope. Coincidentally, Thurston Moore was one of the few people really celebrating them. In 2001, things took a sudden leap forward when a friend helped me make the first Deathbomb website. Until that point, I had no idea how to reach a fanbase for cutting-edge sounds. Pretty much as soon as the website went live, people started coming.

The size of runs for Deathbomb releases really varies. I think the best part about there being so many mediums to release in, from digital to cassette to CD to vinyl, is that a release can cater to its situation. Fifty copies of a tape can help an unknown act reach the right people, like in the case of the rap group Clipping I put out. I showed their cassette to a friend at Sub Pop and a few months later they were signed! At this point Deathbomb has a sort of vague Motown thing going, with lots of the same musicians working with each other and helping each other out under various names and combinations.

The First Original Silence
Original Silence
(Smalltown Superjazz, 2007)

Mats Gustafsson: It was usually six of us on-stage – sometimes five because Jim O'Rourke could not make it: Thurston, me, Terrie Ex from The Ex, Paal Nilssen-Love from The Thing, Massimo Pupillo from Zu. It was really spectacular, that kind of open playing in a more rock setting. If there are a lot of instruments it gets more complex, but that's a challenge which can turn into something positive. All six of us had the same feel, the same drive. It made it very fluent; with six on-stage, if you play freely without any preconceived material, it is difficult. But that's the beauty of it.

I'm amazed we managed to get the six of us together to tour. Mini-tours can work around the schedules of a band like Sonic Youth and everything we were all doing. But you need to do four shows to make it economically worthwhile because the costs of bringing everyone together in one place are so high. Massimo is not a normal bass player and no one in the group was a normal guitar player, so we were all trying to make the instruments work in a different way – none of the guitars is doing any riffing, it's an organic body of sound. The saxophone I use sometimes for riffs, so it's not just on top of everything. Same with electronics – it has to interact and to be within the mix. With Original Silence, what I liked was each instrument had its independence. It's like conversation; if you're in a group of people there'll always be one or two people who say something to which everyone else really responds. It'd be stupid, though, if the same person was making a statement each and every time with all the others simply reacting. You need to be humble, unselfish, then it might work – it's about trust and respect, without those nothing will work.

Massimo Pupillo: This show was in a classic Italian theatre so people were sitting while we were extremely loud, so it was all very surreal. There was a strong feeling of excitement among us and the performance was electric. For me, it's very challenging to be part of a large ensemble of improvisers – I've never tried something as big as Original Silence ever again. When you improvise in that way, without words, it's like diving into a pit not knowing if you'll meet water or stone down there. It felt like being among a flock of birds, no one leading, all moving and changing direction at the same time.

When I mixed one of the two albums I discovered I was actually directing the entire sound of the performance through the mixing process. Focusing on one instrument rather than another would create a totally different narrative within the piece. For example, Jim O'Rourke was playing this glorious EMS synthesizer and his textures alone could fill the room and the entire spectrum of frequencies. But due to acoustics and to how we were lined up on-stage, I realised I was only uncovering them via the mixing stage. You could isolate him and Thurston to create this weird, droning, ambient, textural album. Otherwise, if you focused on my bass and Paal Nilssen-Love's drums, what you now had was a more frenetic, spastic dance. Taking everything all together, that again was another story.

The Second Original Silence
Original Silence
(Smalltown Superjazz, 2008)

Massimo Pupillo: We played only five shows together: four in Italy; one in Norway. In the beginning the idea was we would release them all, but probably two albums was enough. It was an easy tour: eight people in a van; six musicians, one soundperson, one recording engineer. We kept it very simple, given all of us were aware that touring with such strange music was already a success in a way. What I recall best was how easy it was to spend time together, the humorous mood among the group, all of whom were equally at ease in a posh theatre or in a squat. I consider Original Silence a sort of improv-punk band, at least that's the attitude.

This gig was part of the RomaEuropa Festival so the audience was very mixed: punks, free-jazz people, art people. Rome is always a strange beast for me because I come from there and at the time I was still living there. I felt lots of eyes on me and my only reply had to be a complete commitment and abandonment to the music.

Now And Forever
The Thing
(Smalltown Superjazz, 2008)

Mats Gustafsson: The Thing is a very close collaboration between two Norwegians and a Swede. We started as a Don Cherry [tribute] project, exclusively playing his compositions, but that came out in a way that we thought was very interesting so we decided to make the group permanent. The Thing quickly developed into using musical elements that we like to listen to like garage rock and psychedelic, [or] free jazz.

So we try to make our own group language of our inspirations. Over the years we've had a lot of guests – it's an important process in this group that every year we have one or two guests coming in and fucking us up in different ways which teach us something we can take to the next project. It's very seldom that we sit down and discuss "Next year we should invite…" It's quite spontaneous and emotional; we'll hear something and think, 'We've got to play with them!' and even if it's a weird idea in the beginning we'll get in touch and ask if it's possible and, if it works, then maybe it continues for a while and you develop the music together.

The *Now And Forever* boxset came about because we wanted to make our first two records available again – they had sold out really quickly. We had a recording with Thurston from the Norwegian Øya Festival which we felt really worked, so we wanted to get that out there. Then there was a longer improvisation from the *Action Jazz* [2006 album by The Thing] session that we put in. We thought it'd be more fun to put those recordings all together in a box because we didn't want to take attention away from the next studio release.

Live
The Thing
(The Thing Records, 2014)

Mats Gustafsson: A live recording has to be very special for us to think about releasing something, and the level of interaction on this one was quite amazing. We were touring our record *The Boot*, the harshest, most rock-based material we have in our book. So it was a natural thing to invite Thurston to Café Oto for the performance.

The key to music, to art in general, is you need to develop your own voice, your own technique, at a high level, so there's no doubt who it is playing. You develop your library of approaches which is, in a way, a mirror of who you are as a person, then you communicate that in the moment with someone in a musical situation. You hear it by the sound, the colour of the sound, the way you use a technique. That's a long-term process – it takes a whole life to develop the language on a musical and philosophical level. And that's so fucking beautiful, to be able to share your life experience, musically, with someone else who is willing to share.

When that's there, the audience really gets it. No one is pretending, no one is trying to play louder or stronger than the other – you just share the moment together. Thurston and I have an advantage there in that we didn't go to music school or university, we went the long road round; we developed on-stage with our friends and didn't have teachers telling us what to do. We had to develop our musical language ourselves. You have to be aware that all techniques and structures are a good learning – but nothing is true; you have to make it true yourself. When I understood, on a deeper level, that I will never be fully taught, then a weight on my shoulders was gone and I could really get creative.

Live
Zac Davis/Thurston Moore
(Maim & Disfigure, 2008)

Thurston Moore: That record is just Zac and me playing in my basement and Zac left with a tape; he's notorious for not telling anybody what he's doing!

Amanda Kramer: One thing I've always looked up to Thurston and the Northampton community on is there was a point where everything was being released – all the thoughts and sounds. What it felt like was this overwhelming glut, but what I recognise now was a sort of historical logging. You can look at that and tell exactly what was happening at that place and time. That was so influential on us – we also wanted to log our journey and our portion of the underground. You end up fetishising community and the now and the beating heart of what everyone's doing in the moment – it becomes so visceral that you can't stop yourself from spreading what you can everywhere you can. It becomes an imperative to document. There's less of that now but it was a driving force for years.

There's something alluring and sexy about a time when people were so un-selfconscious about being musicians. Now everyone is a brand and you have to really think about the best time of year to drop a single or a record, or you have to be doing these distinct moves. Back then it felt like things were pollinating! We were collecting as much as were releasing; we were fans as much as we were artists. I felt very much a part of something that wasn't stale, wasn't stagnant. Maybe some people now have never had a chance to feel that way. We're insanely jaded, very cynical, very pessimistic sometimes! But never about the music. Never.

Maison Hantee – 'Chamber 20'
Mike Ladd/Alexandre Pierrepont
(Rogueart, 2008)

Gene Moore: 'Chamber 20' was recorded in Thurston's basement in Northampton. Not sure how this came about, most likely Thurston got asked to do this project.

John Moloney: Thurston, Gene, Bill Nace and I were over at Thurston's house. We were recording as a group in his basement, jamming, screwing around. I was living in the house, so if he wasn't on tour with Sonic Youth and I wasn't on tour with Sunburned Hand Of The Man then we'd be hanging out, jamming a lot. The basement was huge; the music room was very comfortable; he had a lot of records down there – set up like a record store where most of his records were in bins that you could browse through; there was a room just full of Sonic Youth back-stock; he was a noise cassette collector, thousands of them on these shelves. There was a show that night at Time Machine, a short-lived record store over in Easthampton, so Matt Krefting joined us and that becomes the Peeper record.

Time Machine
Peeper
(Manhand, 2008)

Bill Nace: Peeper was like, someone just wrote me and said, "Oh, we're all hanging out at Time Machine. Come down if ya want to play."

Gene Moore: Time Machine was a very cramped space. People were standing in the doorway craning their necks to check it out. I played a baritone guitar running through a wah-wah pedal and an echo. Matt Krefting played a very weird synth to haunting effect.

Lee Ranaldo: The Internet and other technology allowed bands to document everything they did. On the one hand, it's a very Warholian concept: "Document everything – art equals life." Throbbing Gristle did that too, cassettes of every rehearsal and show, and the psychedelic culture starting from the tapers surrounding The Grateful Dead then extended to all these younger jam bands like Phish, where there'd be people taping every single show and trading it like some priceless currency, and that becomes everyone from Pearl Jam to Bruce Springsteen having every gig available 10 minutes after the show is over.

Shayna Dulberger: The whole Internet mentality sort of permanently destroyed any barriers between genre at this point in history. The filters in culture that used to exist out of necessity are done. Everything is just everything now. I think this reflects more on the progress of general society rather than some kind of progression in music or the people who listen to it.

Britt Brown: The contemporary reality of the Internet seems to foster splintering and subdivision more than confluence or commingling. Location has certainly ceased to be an organising agent in any capacity; people live and exist more online than they do in their own city. This fact is reflected in the detached way many labels operate, and by people's generally erratic and web-dictated tastes.

'Western Mass Hardcore Rules OK'/'Untitled'
Paul Flaherty/Thurston Moore/Slither
(Not Not Fun, 2008)

Chris Pottinger: In 2005, Heath Moerland and I were in a band called Odd Clouds. Heath and I discovered an interest in playing woodwind instruments together and began using horns while performing. During this time, the band would sometimes infiltrate other local gigs unannounced. We'd sneak our acoustic instruments in and squeeze into the club's bathroom to do impromptu performances, freaking out whoever was in there at the time. We called these types of guerrilla sets 'Slither'. Shortly after, Heath and I were leaving on a tour out east under our solo projects. In addition to all our regular electronics, Heath brought his clarinet and I brought my saxophone. We started playing our horns together to transition between our two solo sets. Slither performances graduated from the stinking, cramped stalls of club bathrooms, crawled out and found their way on-stage.

We recorded our side of that record at the Get Lost House downstairs at Heath's place. We had a little recording studio set up in his bathroom. Looking back on it, maybe we were subconsciously trying to capture some of the original Slither bathroom vibe?

Heath Moerland: The studio moved locations at least 10 times. At one point it was in my windowless 18' by 18' basement bedroom, another time down in a mildewed, boulder-filled, stone-wall Michigan basement that was also a makeshift darkroom and laundry/furnace hangout. Due to circumstances, HAM Studios would almost have to convert to being Quiet Studios because of neighbours and paper-thin walls, towers of tape decks, organs, reel-to-reels, instrument pile, stereo receivers, four-tracks, boombox, Casio SK-1, reeds, permanent marker, drum kit, synths, tape synth. I wanted to build a rotating Leslie speaker out of box fans and VCR/VHS machines for audio manipulation, but those attempts resulted in setting the studio on fire and having to relocate once again.

Finding gear on the street and at thrift stores kept things cheap. The blank tape warehouse was just down the street. I acquired a CD burner and decided to release those as well as cassettes. Mail order, record stores and playing gigs got word out about the label and the crazy amount of creativity coming out of Michigan. American Tapes, Hanson, Gods Of Tundra, Chondritic Sound, Tasty Soil; everyone and their grandma had labels!

Britt Brown: In summer 2007, Thurston invited Pocahaunted and Robedoor to play with Sonic Youth in Berkeley before their performance of *Daydream Nation*. I remember Bethany (Cosentino, who did Pocahaunted with Amanda) immediately being like, "Well, we obviously have to say no, right?" It felt unreal. We typically played crouched on the ground, in intimate art spaces and all-ages venues, to very modest crowds; the idea of 3,500 legacy-rock fans watching us doing the EBow drones and moan through delay pedals seemed insane.

Amanda Kramer: Bethany and I, at the time, would play for six-seven minutes, feel like we'd played for 40, then just stop. People would feel cheated, they'd be shouting, "Keep going!" and we'd be saying, "It's all we have." Part of our routine was anti-vanity, where we'd just talk to the audience for a while, make some jokes. We were an anomaly: we were two women crouched on the ground making these vocals, not singing lyrics, playing out of tune guitars. At the time nobody understood and we didn't either. Thurston saw something and Britt persuaded me that we would do it. We actually practised for it, so it's not one of our most emotive sets; we were so nervous, so it was antithetical Pocahaunted, we sat and worked through what we were going to do, which is something we never did. The night itself, the theatre was gigantic, so many people there – I was sick to my stomach. I wanted to play it so cool and just couldn't. I was too young and too in awe.

Britt Brown: Afterward we hung out a bit backstage, eating pizza with Mark Ibold and Jerry Harrison [guitarist of Talking Heads and member of The Modern Lovers], feeling starstruck. When he reached out again later that year to ask Pocahaunted to come open his solo show, we felt even more honoured – it meant we couldn't have sucked too bad at Berkeley. He even emailed us his cell number, which ended up being useful because our car broke down on the way north so we had to get towed the rest of the 80 miles to Visalia. We called to let him know what was happening and he was chill.

From 2005 to 2010 we ran a split seven-inch club called Bored Fortress, where subscribers would receive two records every other month for six months. Since Thurston had been a subscriber to both previous years of the seven-inch club, we thought it seemed like an apt time to invite him to participate. It was inspiring to see someone who you'd admired so long remain so committed, humble and enthusiastic about the simple pleasures of playing music. You can be in your fifties and still enjoy jamming fuzzy noise in the basement of a house party, then sharing a beer in the kitchen with music fans half your age. Music isn't about youth – it's about meaning. To continue to derive pleasure in adulthood from something most of us are taught to disown or grow out of seems, to me, slightly heroic. Thurston has never ceased being a fan of music and that's a life-giving quality. Spreading his support and fanship to lesser known musicians is a huge gesture for a person in his position. He knows how much it means because he's felt the same way himself many times.

Amanda Kramer: Eric Shaw did the cover art, he's an amazing artist. Thurston has never given a lazy, "Oh here's some bullshit" – if he gives you a track it'll always be something very cool. The deal was that you got the full series, amazing music from all these different people, you couldn't cherry-pick things. The Thurston single was one of the ones where you saw strangers, for want of a better word, emailing, asking if they could just take that. It was definitely bringing buyers to us who probably wouldn't have taken a chance on our label – not enough money to go on vacation with, though, and it doesn't mean those people stick with you for the next thing.

Brett Robinson: Paul and Thurston's side was recorded by me on February 25, 2007 at The Flywheel. I would go on to see Paul and Thurston play alongside each other in different groups many times, but this remains their only duo performance that I know of. Not many people were there that day: me and the bands; the venue staff; maybe another person or two. I shared a DVD of it, which eventually made its way to YouTube, then, in conversation with Thurston, I realised he had sourced the recording from that YouTube video. I mostly record for my own personal posterity purposes, so fidelity isn't a concern because I don't document with the intent of releasing a commercial product. Obviously Thurston didn't care, since he sourced his seven-inch from YouTube! I believe he did a similar thing with the AA Records Mirror/Dash lathe cut [a 2007 untitled seven-inch].

Guitar Trio Is My Life!
Rhys Chatham & His Guitar Trio All Stars
(Radium, 2008)

Rhys Chatham: I hadn't seen Thurston in 20 years, I was playing at SXSW and the head of the record label I was on came over, saying, "Guess who's here? Thurston's here! He says he wants to sit in on *Guitar Trio*." I actually got nervous; you never know what fame does to people, right? Then Thurston comes in looking like he'd just stepped out of the station wagon coming from Vermont or someplace, like a guy from the country, and just as sweet as I ever remember him – he hadn't changed.

The first time we played *Guitar Trio* in a rock venue was at Max's Kansas City in '77. I was scared to death. At that time in the punk scene, if people liked you they'd throw beer cans at you with the beer still in them; but if

188

they thought you were posing you were lucky to get out with your life. I was worried we'd be too arty, I was worried about getting lynched. While we played though, people kept heading over to the soundboard and asking, "Hey, where are you hiding the singers?" They were hearing the overtones and, whereas in an art context people might think of it as a new strain of minimalism, in the rock context people were thinking of it as another version of 'wall of sound'. People were hearing it differently depending on their background and the environment they heard it in; they'd all hear a different melody because, if you're listening to something serial where you can hear the overtones coming out of repetitive e-string, what you hear depends on air pressure, where you are in the room. If you're trained to hear harmonics then you'll appreciate that, but if you're not trained you'll hear heavenly choirs and voices. The main thing is I was glad I got out of there with my life.

I was doing performances in Atlanta, Georgia at the behest of Jeff Hunt who owns Table of the Elements. Jeff had heard me talking about the original version that was 45 minutes long, so he suggested, "Listen, why don't you do a special performance where you use the guitarists from here in Atlanta and do the original *Guitar Trio*?" It was glorious. So Jeff decided, "I'm going to hook you up with a booking agent called Gina Green and she's going to book you a US tour doing *Guitar Trio*." She ended up finding us 14 shows and we brought a sound engineer with us who recorded all the concerts. Jeff decided to go crazy and put out a three-CD boxset.

Byron Westbrook: I toured with Rhys in fall of 2006 as part of his Essentialist metal ensemble, where we performed new collaborative work and ended with an encore of *Guitar Trio* every night. At a show in Ohio, when Rhys asked if the crowd would like to hear us encore with *Guitar Trio*, someone in the audience yelled, "*Guitar Trio* is my life!" That story influenced the idea for the separate *Guitar Trio Is My Life* tour that followed in 2007, including different performers of the piece in each city, of which I performed in the January 26, 2007 performance at Issue Project Room.

Guitar Trio is a piece with very simple, explicit instructions for the guitar player; it leaves virtually no room for personal expression, or assertion of identity, by any individual guitar player. Any difference between any two guitar players playing the piece would be extremely nuanced and virtually undiscernible. The place where identity is apparent is the rhythm section, mostly the drummer, as the piece is the constant repetition of a short rhythmic pattern. A good drummer can make or break the performance.

Colin Langenus: Issue Project Room still exists, but in a different space. It's a long-standing avant-garde venue, like a non-profit cultural space for the weirdest of the weird. The space at that time was in an old silo, so a circular room; it wasn't that large a space and the band and the audience were all crammed in there. Drums and bass were in the middle; five guitar players on each side. No false starts. One shot. Live like a gig. One, two, three, four – go.

Rhys brought in each guitar one at a time, but after that everybody was playing the same thing – other than their strumming position on the neck, which was up to the player. The guitar has certain places on the neck that produce overtones: the fifth, seventh and twelfth fret are the most prevalent. So while we are all playing the same rhythm at the same time, we are all on different places on the neck, creating different harmonics, and while I think Rhys has orchestrated this in the past, we were allowed to play on whatever fret we wanted to, creating clouds and fields of harmonic motion.

Alan Licht: Hearing *Guitar Trio* and *Drastic Classicism* really helped me connect the dots between the minimalism of Young, Riley, Glass, Reich and the underground rock I was listening to. *Guitar Trio* is a bit like playing Phil Niblock's *G2,44+/x2* piece in that you only have a few notes to deal with, but it's much more forceful, more an extension of rock-guitar playing.

Rhys Chatham: Every city was a different group. In New York we played with Jonathan Kane on drums and a bunch of great guitarists, all my friends who I asked personally to play. In Chicago we had the guys from Tortoise – I was scared to play with them because they're such fine musicians – who turned out to be sweethearts. In each city we wanted to get set up with bands people knew about there; Gina told the promoters in each city to find local acts who would cause a stir, unless I knew someone then I'd ask them personally. For that tour, *Guitar Trio* was divided into two parts – the first 20 minutes was just with the hi-hat, then the second 20 minutes was essentially the same piece but with the full drum kit. The performances were very different; the first would be quite minimalist, then, when you add the full kit, it becomes a rock performance.

New York was special; it was part of a festival the night we were playing. It was a small space so we just needed light amplification on the drums; everyone's guitar amplifiers were positioned so we didn't need more on that; we had an adequate soundcheck, something like two hours, and the soundcheck was also our rehearsal so I taught the piece. Each person had the score beforehand so they knew the form of the piece; I didn't run through the entire piece but I ran through all the sections, the transitions. Then we all hung out – people I hadn't seen in years showed up – and did the concert, an absolute blast.

Blindfold
Thurston Moore
(Destructive Industries, 2008)

Thomas Mortigan: One of the main focuses of starting this label was to take things back to a more DIY level. My black metal band Octagon had been signed for a few years, had pro-pressed CDs and such, but the labels were very hesitant to agree to cassette releases in fear of them sitting on a shelf somewhere and never selling. I have always felt proudest when doing things by hand: dubbing the tapes, folding and cutting out the covers, cutting and pasting. Having to ship your work to a plant where most all of that is out of your hands once it's shipped off feels a bit invasive. What if they royally mess up the process? What if the prints look awful? What if it ends up sounding super-shitty? Dubbing tapes became ritualistic for me. Every day, wake up and dub; dub while packing orders, dub while getting ready for bed. That was a creatively fantastic time, but unrealistic in terms of solidity. One month would be financially abundant, others barely scraping by. Digital downloading was becoming a big thing at the time so people got lazy about buying physical releases and started stealing people's work more.

The first time I met Thurston was at a Ramleh show in Brooklyn, New York back in 2007. He was just hanging outside, drinking a beer out of a brown paper bag; I introduced myself and we talked for a bit. When I got back from the trip, I emailed him and told him about my label and that I was interested in putting out a release for him. He kindly agreed and the next thing I knew, I had the CD masters for *Blindfold* in my mailbox along with the artwork for the cover.

To me, the tape always felt intimate. It was carefully controlled and almost, though in an improvised way, composed. He could have made blistering guitar noise and shrill feedback, but the gentle sounds of a bowed guitar, radio static and suchlike felt more personal and thought-out to me. I feel a release such as this one deserved more than a tiny limited release. It's a gift to the underground. He could have easily worked with just about any label he wanted to, but was kind enough (as he has been many times) to keep his ear to the ground and work with a DIY label because he is still a fan of music. He was even kind enough to mail a signed picture LP to my younger sister, Rhianna, for her birthday when I told him how big a fan she was. When I told her I would be putting out something for him, I think she was even more excited than I was!

Thurston is good friends with Richard Kern and the track is entitled 'Martynka', which is actually the name of the model on the cover, Richard's girlfriend at the time. I think he may have chosen that photo in relation to the label's aesthetic with previous releases, but it may just be coincidence. There is a very fetishistic and objectifying vibe about the *Blindfold* tape.

I distinctly remember getting the *Blindfold* master CD-R in the mail, calling into work and claiming I could not come in due to sickness, opening a bottle of red wine and turning off all of the lights. I blared that CD-R over and over and just smiled the entire time, shit–eating grin from ear to ear. No one on this earth, no matter how hard they try, can ever 'sound' like Thurston does with the guitar. If an artist can be that good with an instrument they compose on, imagine how amazing the results of them experimenting with it can be. *Blindfold* will forever live in my mind as one of the greater examples of such a piece. And wherever Martynka is out there... I hope she is doing well.

Sensitive/Lethal
Thurston Moore
(No Fun Productions, 2008)

Carlos Giffoni: No Fun Productions began after No Fun Fest. I invited people to that music festival because I felt there was this scene that was not being represented properly through the media. I had this idea that if I did one festival, three days, and got as many of those people as I could then it'd be really amazing – firstly for people who like that music, they could hear a load of it in one place; secondly, hopefully it'd make people notice it more. The best thing about it was that people with ideas spoke to one another, all in the same room, for the first time. Unexpected connections and new ideas happen when you have creative people in one place for a time – the ability to connect these people, I felt, was a really strong push for experimental music. In the process of selection for the label, I always went for things that, to me, were unique – one-of-a-kind representations of what an artist was doing, something that hadn't seen the light of day before. Even when I did the solo CD for Thurston it was the type of thing he hadn't done before at that level. I loved working on that label – unfortunately, financial situations and time meant I had to stop doing it, but it was something insane, 50-60 releases in a period of three years. So I think there's plenty there that will stand on its own and be remembered.

Keffer Gordon Moore
Kim Gordon/Leslie Keffer/Thurston Moore
(Ecstatic Peace!, 2008)

Leslie Keffer: I met Thurston because he had been getting cassettes of mine from somewhere and he emailed and asked if I would like to play No Fun Fest with him. I kinda thought it was a joke or something because it just seemed to come out of nowhere. After that, I played a show with Thurston in Columbus which was very 'Ohio-style': a nice, dirty dive with endless amounts of Miller Hi Life beer, stoners, drunks, punks and the freaks. It's all the elements of home. The show and our sound was very grimy, high-energy punk. We were terrorising people with the volume and the energy was excitable and vibrant. We just hit it off. I love Leos and I felt when we played together we were brazen, bold, and just rocked out together and had tons of fun.

The *Keffer/Gordon/Moore* cassette was released on Ecstatic Peace! and I didn't have to do anything for this release! It was so interesting to see what recordings they picked for it and what the artwork would be. When I saw the cover I almost fainted. Kim had painted a portrait of me. I melted! I wrote her to thank her and tell her how much I loved it, and she told me she was trying to capture my 'wild beauty'. Seriously, probably one of the best moments in my life.

'Noise Virgin'/'CCTV Laceration'/'Free Twisted Filth'/'I'/'II'/'III'/'Spirithenge'
Kylie Minoise/Thurston Moore/ Tusco Terror/ Wether
(Insult Recordings, 2009)

Lea Cummings (Kylie Minoise): I am predominantly interested in noise, distortion and overload as techniques for accessing the subconscious and achieving higher spiritual states. I also enjoy pissing people off at some level. I really fucking hate mediocrity and banality, which is spiritual murder. I value spontaneity, instinct and synchronicity. Everything that I do contains this spirit at its core and is then refined. The refining process can be a challenging balancing act to make sure the purity of spirit is not buried under the weight of logical thinking and problem solving which extinguishes that spirit. I also value humour.

When I started in the mid-nineties it was incredibly difficult to connect with like-minded people. I used to buy every fanzine and interesting record that I found and write to all the addresses – a very long process. We pressed around 500 copies of the first EP from Opaque [Scottish noise group] and I must have sent out at least 300 of them to addresses that I'd found without knowing if they were a complete waste. One of the addresses I sent the EP to was the Corpus Hermeticum label in New Zealand, whose address I got from a CD by Thurston Moore and Tom Surgal [*Klangfarbenmelodie And The Colorist Strikes Primitiv*]. I was so excited when we got a letter back from Bruce Russell saying that he really liked the EP and wanted to take some copies to distribute. He was the first person to reply and this was the first step in opening up the wider world to me.

I remember being particularly interested in this specific release as Thurston Moore was going to be on it and I'd been a fan for many years. I'd had contact with him on a few occasions both by email and face to face. We were supposed to do a collaboration as well, but it fell by the wayside which is a shame. I don't think I got to hear anyone else's contributions before I chose which Kylie Minoise tracks to use for the release, which is the way it usually is with such releases. I didn't get any guidance from the label either, which again is standard. One of the great advantages with working with small labels is that they usually trust and respect you enough to give you total artistic freedom to just let you do what you do. Kylie Minoise tracks are influenced by whatever I am listening to, reading and watching at the time of recording, mostly subconsciously. These influences all go through the Kylie Minoise blender: turned up to 11, then drank down and puked out.

'Schwarze Polizei'/'Coming Undone'/'Retect'/ 'Got The Life'/'Grussverweigerung' Kommissar Hjuler/Mama Baer/Thurston Moore (Goaty Tapes, 2009)

Kommissar Hjuler: I worked as a police officer from when I was 16 years old. On the one hand, it never felt like the right job given my creative desires, but then again, due to a serious wish for normality, it was. The turning point for me was 1999 – it wasn't enough just to consume weird music, so I started creating my own and, having met my wife, she began to sing on my releases. The desire became to release LPs without needing the vinyl – only the cover. The covers became bigger works of art: paintings, collages, assemblages of various kinds. Some covers are very harsh stuff, bondage and violence, to annoy all those who wanted to teach me that art should never refer to anything pornographic in order to be rated 'good art'. Some covers are as big as paintings, others are handpainted, some are three-dimensional objects – there's one release labelled *KHj+F* consisting of 250 copies, each one with different, unique, handmade cover art. There's an LP where the cover is a player for 8mm films. The LP is attached to the bottom and the player works. I then created a series of LPs with film for cover art, so if you have the player and those LPs you can see the films.

Our contact with Thurston has been minimal. After he reviewed us in *Arthur* I looked up who he was, sent him a few of our records, then got a letter back from the Goaty Tapes label proposing a split cassette with him on one side, us on the other. His track was called 'Schwarze Polizei', which I believe was a reference to my work as a police officer – a dedication to us. It's a very simple guitar noise track. I went on to create an LP series called *FLUXUS +/–*, which mostly isn't our music. I select artists and invite them to contribute. If they provide several tracks then the next step is for me to select which I prefer, but often they've already made the selection and will send me one track only. I choose them literally because of my own expectations and feelings on what is good music and art. Some of them I know, some I like – for example, Jo Kondo, Jonathan Meese, Franz Kamin – but there's always a strong element of chance. On three *FLUXUS +/–* records I received music from Steve Dalachinsky, he made the selection, and the tracks featured Thurston playing as well: accident. Thurston contacted me again, a short message saying, "You have released my music, I'd like copies of them."

Mother/Groundhog
Chris Corsano/Mats Gustafsson/Thurston Moore/ Bill Nace
(Ecstatic Peace!/Open Mouth, 2010)

Bill Nace: This was the first and only time for this group. Thurston was doing a short East Coast tour with Mats and we were kind of all hanging out in between shows; Thurston just asked if me and Chris wanted to join for this show at The Middle East, so it was pretty last minute. Me, Chris and Thurston then had a show set up at The Rock Shop in Brooklyn, so we pressed up the set with Mats to sell at the gig.

Mats Gustafsson: A very noisy show. Of course, Chris is a fantastic drummer and great to communicate with, but when you add a drummer and one more guitar the sound gets denser – when it's just the two of us, you're a bit more free to move dynamically in any direction. If you add more people the music will likely go in a particular direction, which is not a comment on the quality of the resulting music, it's just a factor resulting from adding more people. I think it was an exceptional concert, it fit really well together. It was so smooth – you don't really think about what you're doing, you just do it, then you know it's working. The whole show felt like just five minutes.

We did seven or eight gigs that tour, driving around bringing our own amps, saxophones, guitars with us – that helps because then you know exactly what kind of sound it'll have. It was really easy and I love driving tours because you have time to talk, listen to music, plan new projects, think of new records to make or record shops to hit. Flying – checking in, security, there's a lot of time and stress connected with it. When you can avoid it and drive, there's another tempo built in and that's a better feeling. That's where everything started for me 25 years ago, driving tours because of budgetary restraints – but now it's because it helps the music and we can play on our own equipment. Plus, with the Internet, you can find good food now, you don't have to have a greasy burger every day on the autobahn – airports too don't have good food; my group Fire got food poisoned at Charles De Gaulle the other day.

Play Some Fucking Stooges
Mats Gustafsson/Thurston Moore
(Quasi Pop Records, 2012)

Mats Gustafsson: *Play Some Fucking Stooges* was a one-off thing, the guy [Edward Sol, Ukraine-based founder of Quasi Pop Records] running the label was really enthusiastic about making a vinyl LP and we have a soft spot for enthusiasts. Thurston and I did the Diskaholics tour in Japan then a lot of one-off shows, mainly because Sonic Youth always had total priority so there was never real space to do much real touring. So this US tour in 2009 is one of the few duo tours we did and we recorded most of those shows. The theme of the tour was to find the best junk food in the US, so we were driving around in Thurston's Volvo looking for the best doughnuts we could find, or the best pastrami sandwich, or the best Philly cheesesteak. We made a tour so we'd have really good record shops near every place we played – and really good junk food too. Then I wrote a few articles for a Swedish culture magazine about being on tour with Thurston, looking for food. It's bizarre but both me and Thurston are devoted to what we do and to life – we're way too enthusiastic as human beings so we're always looking for new kicks. We both collect records and books and all kinds of stuff that kicks our asses and minds, so it'd be weird for us to just focus on one thing when there's a load of other things for us to be inspired by. It takes energy, but it adds energy to what we're doing too.

'12 String Acoustik Regret'/'12 String Acoustik Suicide Pact With God'/'Of Death' Gravitons/Thurston Moore (Wintage Records & Tapes, 2010)

Kevin Crump: My desire to push local artists was always based around a core belief that these individuals were not getting the attention and respect they deserved, whether locally or on a national scale. One of my main rules is to document and ship away, always trying to get my copies as far away from Toronto as possible. Besides, I always hate finding my music in the local discount bin at the second-hand record shops.

I had a zany marketing scheme to promote the local artists I really loved. I started reaching out to more A-lister noise acts that I had befriended and started a tape subscription series in which the buyer received a split cassette in the mail along with a handcrafted box and two posters. I think I locked down the first three releases before promoting it online via Iheartnoise. Thurston was quick to respond about buying in on a subscription – I responded offering a free subscription in return for an original master to use as a future edition in the series. I drive a hard bargain! I am sure I had one of those dreams where I thought this was it! This release would turn Wintage into the next Sub Pop! Then I woke the next day and remembered it was a noise release.

Mani Mazinani: Myself and my partner, Jill Aston, last performed on November 16, 2015, around the time that our baby reached seven months of age. Prior to that we played on December 2, 2014, when Jill was in her seventh month of pregnancy. Not sure how many babies can claim to have forced their mother to perform with her guitar projected to the side *in utero*. The only thing that receives 100 percent of our attention now is Manasi, current candidate for the third member of Gravitons, our two-year-old daughter.

The first thing we had prepared was ready months before anything came from Thurston – but Kevin wanted us on the tape with Thurston, so instead of putting our stuff out earlier, with someone who had already submitted, he waited. Thankfully! It meant we got to make a new – and better – recording for it too. While our sound is very consistent, we're always evolving gradually. The new recording was purer both in a playing sense and in an audio sense. With this style of music you can't go backward in terms of style or musicianship. We play with a timer; if we decide it'll be 30 minutes we set it to start, on zero we're going and at 30 minutes we stop. That's generally our set-up – Jill plays electric guitar via a distortion pedal into an amp. I play a smaller jazz drum kit as opposed to a big rock kit. With Gravitons, I don't consider it free improvisation. The material we're playing in that moment is completely improvised but there's a form or energy that we push toward to accomplish what Gravitons is – and that to me is a composition. Every single performance of ours is really playing that composition but what changes are the circumstances, what instruments we have that day, the recording environment, duration. Beyond that it's just one piece.

A Ticket For Decay
Hat City Intuitive
(Ecstatic Peace!, 2010)

Hat City Intuitive: Hat City Intuitive coalesced around 1989–90 as a kind of music lab situation in Brookfield, Connecticut. We were into a lot of improv, contemporary classical and noise, then decided to try it out for ourselves; Todd Knapp, Chris Ludwig, John Howard, then Greg Vegas a few months later. It mutated over the years; Chris left, Larry Demming and Dave-O came and went, then eventually Gene Moore and Ernie Lattanzio came on board.

Gene Moore: Thurston and myself were in a local bar in Danbury, Connecticut when we spotted Todd Knapp from Hat City Intuitive. We got to talking and he invited me to sit in – guess they liked my strange ways on the guitar and kept me on for the duration.

Hat City Intuitive: For most of the nineties there was no place for a group like us to play and it seemed impossible that anyone would actually sit and listen. We'd play out once or twice a year and folks would sit, stare, and wonder what the fucking point was. We fit into no scene; we came from no scene; and we predated that 'New Weird America' bullshit by a good 10 or 11 years – our scene was always just us. Even with no prospects, we practised once a week for years then, after a long while, we came together if someone asked us to play a show or we got it in our noggins to record. We would build up tapes from shows and practices and use them to make the albums.

199

Thurston's brother, Gene, had been a member for years so the idea of recording sprang from that. We came together for two sessions at Ernie's house in Bethel, 2008. We referred to it on the album sleeve as 'The Lost Elms', but it was Ernie's basement with his water heater, furnace, clothes washer and dryer. One session was over an Easter weekend where the Moores and the rest of us needed an excuse to get away from the families for a few hours and make noise. Thurston's presence did not alter things; it was only occasionally that he sounded like 'Thurston', so he fitted right in. The dynamics of the group are unalterable; on a good Hat City Intuitive jam you cannot tell who played what. Even the track titles, we would sit around collectively brainstorming titles with the only justification being that they cracked us up or mystified us.

Suicide Notes For Acoustic Guitar
Thurston Moore
(Carbon Records, 2010)

Joe Tunis: When I started work at a department store, my boss was a huge music fan and collector. I ended up hearing these mix tapes he would make. One in particular had tracks from The Butthole Surfers, Soul Asylum, Pixies, Sinead O'Connor, 'Silver Rocket' from *Daydream Nation*. That kicked off my interest in Sonic Youth and Thurston. A couple years later, in college around 1991, I decided to start a band. I didn't know how to play anything but I had a beat-up bass from my brother and a new friend I met was playing guitar, so we spent a summer jamming every night. Fast-forward a couple years, as I'm graduating college I decide to start Carbon Records, using my pseudo-corporate job to fund the label. The daytime career definitely got in the way of any kind of touring, but it also enabled me to put out a bunch of records. The rise of the Internet and CD-R technology is what really drove the growth of Carbon. The trading culture at that point helped so much with regard to spreading the word, getting the label more exposure.

Thurston was probably one of the easiest people I've dealt with. I think we sent a couple emails back and forth, about the series it was going to be part of, and before I knew it there was a CD-R master in my mailbox. We really never talked about the material or its background. The only liner notes he gave me were the track titles and 'Recorded at Northampton

Studio for the Lost, August 2010'. I didn't know it was going to be acoustic, but I figured it was going to be out-there and interesting since I already had a bunch of solo releases by him. I never direct artists with regard to what they're going to submit to the label. If it's someone I already know, I trust what I'm going to get will be of high quality.

Putting out a release by Thurston definitely garnered some attention, and actually it helped legitimise the label a bit locally. I think most people in Rochester thought I was just putting out local bands, weirdo noise that they didn't understand. But once they heard I put out something from 'the guy in Sonic Youth', they were like, 'Oh wow, it's kind of a real label.'

Solo Acoustic Volume 5/12-String Meditations For Jack Rose
Thurston Moore
(Vin Du Select Qualitite, 2011)

Steve Lowenthal: I was working at the Hospital Productions store in NYC – Thurston would come to the store to shop for noise and black metal. The store was a beacon of the noise/cassette underground but when I went home I listened to a lot of acoustic music, so I wanted to somehow merge those interests in a natural way. Vin Du Select Qualitite was a desire to find other kinds of acoustic guitar records outside the standard blues/folk dynamic that much acoustic music evokes.

John Fahey was a huge influence on my label and on the instrument of the acoustic guitar in general. I began researching my book *Dance Of Death: The Life Of John Fahey, American Guitarist* at the same time, so I was immersed in Fahey research and actively sought out musicians who echoed his expansive ideology of the acoustic guitar. The thought was to make a uniform series of LPs that showcased the diversity of what can be done on an acoustic guitar. Instead of documenting a scene, we wanted to cull players from different generations and approaches.

I couldn't think of a Thurston record that was all acoustic and instrumental. I supposed it might be a unique entry into his catalogue and he'd fit perfectly into what Vin Du Select Qualitite was going for in terms of forward-thinking acoustic guitar playing. Thurston is remarkably distinctive as a player, especially when heard solo in this setting, acoustic and untreated with no overdubs. Take away all the pedals and effects and you hear him and only him – no other guitar player sounds like that. Not being a musician myself, I think there is a certain 'gunslinger' competitiveness in solo guitar, even non-traditional musicians want to be acknowledged for their skill and a solo acoustic album leaves nothing to hide behind. I think he absolutely understood and took the challenge to heart.

My label has a series called *Solo Acoustic*; Thurston provided the fifth instalment. The album is subtitled *12-String Meditations For Jack Rose* and has a 100-copy-only limited version signed by Thurston with different artwork. Thurston forgot the series had an artistic theme and asked Christina Carter and Bill Nace to do artwork. Rather than waste their efforts or break with the series artwork template, we did two versions. The limited version came on red vinyl with the artwork printed on heavy, rich cardstock. Thurston signed and numbered each cover in silver ink.

The idea to dedicate the album as a whole to Jack Rose was entirely Thurston's and I only knew about it when he sent in the final files. Jack Rose is a player who left a huge mark on the 21st-century acoustic guitar scene, so it was incredibly fitting that Thurston made such an intimate tribute on an acoustic label.

Patrick Best: I played music with Jack for over 20 years and he was a close personal friend. His development as an acoustic guitar player stunned everyone who knew him but did not surprise anyone who was close to him. In the end, his playing was magical.

Mike Gangloff: It's still hard for me to talk a lot about Jack – or hard for me to stop talking once I start, maybe, so I try to keep quiet. I'll just say that the *Whys Of Fire* session happened when Jack was near the start of the solo acoustic work that most people know him for. In hindsight, it was a good time for him to break his electric guitar.

Demolished Thoughts
Thurston Moore
(Matador, 2011)

Justin Pizzoferrato: When my first studio, Bank Row Recording, closed down, I had piles of gear that needed a home while I looked for my next studio space. I mentioned it to Thurston and he was receptive to allowing me to set up in his and Kim's living room. So he and I hauled my console and 16-track tape machine into their house, set up shop and started recording tracks for *Demolished Thoughts*. We recorded the acoustic guitar tracks and vocals for five songs. There was a weekend of recording scheduled to flesh out the tunes and record new ones. Unfortunately, it was cancelled last minute and the project was put on indefinite hold. It was picked back up with Beck in LA and I sent all of the files I had to Beck's engineer.

Thurston has books upon books of lyrics. It almost seems like he's coming up with them on the spot, but he's pulling them from these books he has. He was really excited by 12-string acoustic guitar at the time and I think the songs reflect that. They're beautiful and complex. I played Samara Lubelski some of them before she got involved and she couldn't believe that it was one single guitar. She assumed he'd been layering his parts.

Keith Wood: Thurston was getting into acoustic guitar and I mainly played acoustic for a long time, so I was just in the right place at the right time with the skill set to carry it out. Once we started the band it was full on; we practised three or four times before our first gig and even before that, me, John and Thurston did a local gig at a place called The Elevens and ran through some songs. I was in Chicago visiting some friends when he sent me the record, so I started figuring out the songs in standard tuning, which was really difficult, but I got them down. Then I got to his house for rehearsal and he showed me all the tunings and, wow, it was so much easier! I was very familiar with different tunings but to figure out three or four different tunings to learn a record is a lot to ask. Thurston uses a lot of harmonics and there are a lot of open strings. Most of the time, when I've played with him, we're only fretting two notes at a time and strumming fully – it comes right from the Glenn Branca days, these big chords ringing out and creating overtones. I had to learn to play guitar a different way because I've always fingerpicked; then with Thurston I started using picks again, and the amount of open strings ringing out… he was playing a 12-string acoustic, then with another six-string that's 18 strings vibrating.

John Moloney: Thurston asked me to play in his band for the *Demolished Thoughts* acoustic tour: myself, Mary Lattimore on harp, Samara Lubelski on violin, Keith Woods on acoustic guitar. When we started out it was really mellow; I played drums with brushes. Then, when we toured, our sound guy made me get rid of the brushes – no one could hear them.

Keith Wood: The violin and the harp were very important to that record – we had no bassist, the harp has a lot of strings so you can fill a lot of the sound with that, plus the low strings on the guitar were tuned to C or D which added a good bass sound. We'd always do little noise sections and working with an acoustic guitar with fuzz or distortion added is fun, because there's so many different ways to coax feedback out of an acoustic guitar. The Beatles do it at the beginning of 'Paperback Writer' but otherwise it hasn't been done a lot. We started trying to work out which pedals communicated with the acoustic guitars best. He was using his core set-up – big muff, ratt pedal, MXR phaser – but we were trying all sorts of pedals to see what the combinations of pedals would sound like together.

John Moloney: A lot of bands can be democracies, a lot of bands can be dictatorships – I always felt that Thurston knew what he was doing, I respected that, and I'd played in other bands where you do a few rehearsals and you get this feeling it's a colossal waste of time. There's always a good

Samara Lubelski and Thurston at the Ecstatic Peace! Poetry Night, White Columns Gallery, NYC, February 5, 2010.   *Credit – Louis Caldarola*

vibe with Thurston leading, there's never an emergency, he'll tell you what he wants but there's no stress about how the songs are played – he'd very rarely ask you to play something differently, he just trusted in the people he had with him. We all worked well together, we all laughed together – clowning around was the main activity of the day, then we'd play some music.

Voice Studies 05 – 'Lonely Charm'/'Love Song As A Lion'
Thurston Moore
(My Dance The Skull, 2011)

Marco Cazzella: Around 2009, I was obsessed with Alighiero Boetti. In the seventies, in an act he considered a work of art in its own right, he opened Hotel One in Kabul and ran it for a few years until the Russian invasion. His example drove me to start a label. At the very beginning it was Bethania Dick and myself; Tom White, Andrea Kearney and Dylan Nyoukis helped out too. Our aim was to promote contemporary artists whose work is inspired by the dangerous and convulsive beauty of everyday life. Sound wasn't the main driver, contemporary poetry was.

This was the starting point for the *Voice Studies* series. I wanted to keep things simple and to-the-point. The point was to get people to experiment with their own voice, or with other people's voices, or with found voices – so there simply wasn't a clearer title for what I wanted to do. There are no guidelines for the artists involved; I write to them, maybe suggest a couple of ideas and perhaps they'll come back with ideas of their own, a very natural back and forth. Ultimately, I want people to have absolute freedom because, as the title says, it's a 'study' after all.

In 2010, Bethania and I were working on publishing a book by Aleksandra Waliszewska and Matthew Wascovich from the band Scarcity Of Tanks. We'd only released four tapes at the time but Matthew told us that he had informed Thurston of the series and that he was interested in contributing to it. We ended up being invited to meet Thurston backstage at a show in London. A few months later he sent through the master – that was it! Two tracks, each 10 minutes long. They're not spoken word, they're truly wild noise – they're bordering on the kind of music Whitehouse used to create. It's like he's trapped in a cage, closed in and trying to get out – intense stuff. You can hear his voice trying to escape wherever he is, yet he never manages it. They're highly dramatic pieces.

Planning wise, it's hard work yet straightforward at the same time. Right at the very start I established the aesthetic of the project: plain white cards, the words *Voice Studies*, then the only details that change are the artist's name, the credit, the catalogue number. I handle getting the recordings mastered, then a company in Northern England produces the run of 100 tapes. I'm in the middle coordinating everything and, when I get the tapes back, out they go: a few to the media, copies to the artists, copies to fellow artists, just a few copies left to go on sale.

'Boogie X'/'Hot Date'/'Boogie Y'/'Gold Dime' Thurston Moore/Talk Normal (Fast Weapons, 2011)

Sarah Register: Powerful forces were pointing Andrya and I toward a profound friendship. In the mid-2000s, I asked her to keep an ear out for anybody looking for a somewhat amorphous additional bandmate. Eventually, she put me up as a possibility when Antonius Block needed a bass player; I craigslisted a cheap bass, auditioned – and voila! When it fizzled out, Andrya and I were both pretty clear on doing something together that would be the brainchild of the two of us.

Andrya Ambro: We wanted to be minimal. We wanted to be raw. Initially, we took great influence from old blues people like Geeshie Wiley and Son House. Of course, we were influenced by lots of other things, both mutually and sold separate. We also never wanted to be a duo, but no one else could hang I guess, or perhaps no one else made sense. I do understand how one could associate Talk Normal, on sound alone, with the no-wave movement. Sarah and I were very connected to the idea of making something from less, something from what many perceive as nothing, like, 'Let's make something crappy be awesome…' But I can honestly say we never had any intention of sounding like any of those no-wave bands. It may not be obvious but we were very much into song structure, practising our instruments, we were kinda serious minded and disciplined. We loved melody. And we wanted joy to be the undercurrent to all our music. Not that I want to make any sweeping generalizations of no wave, but these do not seem like defining characteristics.

Nathan Howdeshell: I thought the marriage of Talk Normal and Thurston for a single was cool, bridging the gap of no-wave time somehow. For me I thought, 'Wow, what an honour.' This release means a lot to me, but I gave away every copy I had so it's a beautiful memory.

Sarah Register: Nathan Howdeshell approached us about doing the seven-inch. We were stoked, I mean, Nathan is many things – not least a profound musical enthusiast and a way sick guitar player – and Talk Normal had been in touch with Thurston about various things, but I don't think we would have had the balls to ask him ourselves: "Hey man, wanna split a seven-inch?"

Andrya Ambro: Thurston had caught word of us – I have no idea what he had heard as this was prior to our first full length being released. I was shocked and elated. It wasn't until we played at Easthampton college while on a weekend tour with Red Dawn II and Tall Firs that we met him. I liked how nonchalant he was when chatting. Later that year, we saw him at another show we were playing in Brooklyn with Magik Markers. I overheard him specifically commenting to someone on the music being played – sounded as if he liked it. That someone told him it was a playlist; it was my playlist! I quietly blushed alone and patted myself on the back. Post our first full length, *Sugarland*, coming out, we played an Ecstatic Peace! showcase at SXSW and another showcase with Thurston where he only played acoustic guitar. It was then that he told us that Kim loved *Sugarland* and played it often at home. I could have died then. And of course it was way cool that Kim let us use her artwork for our 'M'lady' seven-inch.

For the single, the song 'Gold Dime' was initially incepted by Sarah, who had recorded a noise dirge all over a long monologue about not having enough money and our lousy (and often MIA) practice-space proprietor. She started off, "So I got this credit card my parents gave me for Christmas. It's got $100 on it." I was so very amused by the lyric and tone behind it. I then added some drums and sang some vocals. My vocals were pretty spur of the moment. But the image of the gold dime seemed fitting. I thought of it as just a little piece of the pie. That's all we want. I'm remembering that I even recited her initial monologue at a book/text reading thing our friend hosted – I think it confused a lot of people. We tried to incorporate a different version of 'Gold Dime' on our second album but we ran out of time and money. How poetic. Also, let me elaborate for a second: I know most people thought of Talk Normal as dark and intense – okay, yes, we were dark and intense, I accept this, but we were also just amusing ourselves, or each other. 'Gold Dime' is my case in point.

Nathan Howdeshell: The Thurston cover is amazing! It's a letter he wrote to a friend after first moving to NYC. He talks about discovering The Clash and how he wants to start a band.

Sarah Register: Thurston's artwork was an influence on ours in that we saw his as the deadline was approaching and loved the handwriting aspect. Ours is just the song lyrics, written alternatingly by Andrya and I. That song was the result of a free rant I'd recorded about craziness going on at our practice space and other 'life bullshit' at the time, over some drone with a pulsing beat. That is not something I'd ever done before, the recorded rant, and it ended up being very cathartic for me. Andrya created the soaring choruses and we both contributed to a busy arrangement of noises.

The seven-inch seemed like it was on and off the table a few times so, for a while, we were tinkering, not knowing if it would become real. At some point Nathan called out of the blue and was like, "Can I get that file in two days?" That was the perfect fire to force us to finalise a mix and send it off. If I'm remembering correctly, we didn't hear Thurston's contributions till the seven-inch came out, which didn't feel problematic. To me, the whole thing was ultimately a delight.

Caught On Tape
John Moloney/Thurston Moore
(Feeding Tube, 2012)

John Moloney: I was in a band called The Shit-Spangled Banner which started in '94 then petered out in 96–97, which is when we transitioned into The Sunburned Hand Of The Man with the same people – with a few more added. We had a cassette which Rich Pontius put together and gave to his girlfriend, who passed the tape to Thurston and Byron Coley at a show. They listened to the tape and liked it, so they asked if we'd want to put a record out. They were doing a series called the *Actuel Ass*

Run series that looked like the old BYG Actuel [French free jazz record label 1967–1972] jazz covers. So they put out the first LP I ever played on. We became friends, started playing the same little shows, or he'd be at the shows we'd play out in Western Massachusetts.

We were playing shows all the time and people would always ask, "Do you have a record?" It felt like something we had to do. We were recording everything we did when we got together, using a tape recorder we found in the trash; put two microphones into it and pressed 'record'. There was this place in town near Berklee College of Music, a production house that made dubbed cassettes and CD-Rs, semi-pro packaging, jewel cases and so on. We had this recording mastered; we took it down there and made 50 copies which we sold out on tour. It snowballed from there. I'd get emails from music distributors saying, 'Hey, I got some people asking for Sunburned Hand Of The Man CD-Rs, do you have any for sale? Can I buy 40?' That felt insane to me. Byron would order $200–$400 of CD-Rs off at me at once and I'd be thinking, 'Are you insane?' But that's how my Manhand label started, because of Byron. He made it a real thing for us – validated the label when we hadn't even planned on starting a label. It just turned into that kind of thing.

The title of the band with Thurston, Caught On Tape, comes from the Raymond Pettibon drawing that's on the first LP – it was a coincidence. Thurston and Eva [Prinz] were at Ray's art studio in California one time, it's floor to ceiling with art; art everywhere. So they're walking around and under Eva's foot is this little drawing, it's a butterfly and the words 'caught on tape'. Pettibon would do these collages of his own drawings, cut up his own work and put it together. So that was a piece – Pettibon just let Eva have it. Thurston showed the drawing to me and I suggested it should be the name of the band, so there it goes.

Fundamental Sunshine
John Moloney/Thurston Moore
(Manhand, 2012)

John Moloney: *Fundamental Sunshine*, the tape, came out first as a Manhand release. I did the artwork; I pulled a picture online, a Vietnam picture. We did a Thurston Moore solo band tour of Spain and Portugal in 2012. At the end of the tour, Thurston had four solo shows booked thanks to Carlos

Van Hijfte, his booking agent. He asked me if I wanted to come with me. We played those four shows in Rotterdam, Amsterdam, Antwerp and Paris. We had a little tape deck that I bought for touring, I'd put it on the stage and just record. So we recorded the whole tour, and that's where the release came from.

Acting The Maggot
John Moloney/Thurston Moore
(Feeding Tube, 2013)

Irish-American Prayer
John Moloney/Thurston Moore
(Manhand, 2013)

Banjaxed Blues
John Moloney/Thurston Moore
(Manhand, 2013)

John Moloney: We did another tour in December 2012 – four shows on the East Coast. *Acting The Maggot* is a one-off show in Cleveland in its entirety. The stuff for *Irish-American Prayer*, we booked ourselves a tour of Ireland, eight shows in January 2013; Thurston and I just wanted to do something, so I made a CD-R to take with us and turned it into a proper CD later on, but I hand-packaged it – that's just my vibe. I sent them to a CD printing place, sent them the artwork and they sent me back a spindle of CDs. The music is a collage I made and comes from the 2012 East Coast tour. I emailed Thurston, asked him to send me some spoken word, maybe something Irish-related. So he read some poems by an Irish writer, Dennis O'Driscoll, he sent me that and I edited the recording, slipped the poetry in wherever I felt it needed something to break it up. I did the collage because it's the kind of thing I would do with Sunburned and I was good at it by now – I just applied the same technique to these recordings. That CD-R never even got distributed, I made it purely for the merch table – I've still got a rack of them here unassembled. We recorded that whole Ireland tour and some of the *Banjaxed Blues* record is from that tour.

Full Bleed
John Moloney/Thurston Moore
(Northern Spy, 2015)

John Moloney: *Full Bleed* was a studio session. The label Northern Spy wanted us to make a record. We weren't so into the idea at first – Caught On Tape was just something for us to do for ourselves, we put the records out in conjunction with Feeding Tube Records, Ted Lee's label, a local record store in Northampton that Thurston was a silent partner of for a long time, along with Byron. We'd use the backroom as a venue and a practice space when we were writing songs for Chelsea Light Moving. So I said, "We don't need to put out a record on any label." But we ended up doing it – it was fun. They thought we would tour for it, go to SXSW, we had to halt all that, it wasn't what we were going to do. Caught On Tape is just a collaboration between two friends, we do it when we do it, we're not trying to make a go of it or make a name for ourselves.

Justin Pizzoferrato: The sessions for *Full Bleed* were booked way in advance, then postponed. There was almost no discussion about the session. We recorded for about four hours and mixed for about four hours. Thurston would say, "Let's do some quiet stuff!" Then they'd just end up playing loudly. The number one most important thing for me was to be 100 percent invisible. The performance depended on the energy in the room and, with strong forces like John and Thurston, you simply must stay out of their way. I wanted to capture things the way they happened. It's not easy to do that when the guitar is in every drum mic on the kit, but you find a way. Good music transcends technical limits; always has and always will!

The Tingle Of Casual Danger
The Sunburned Hand of The Man
(Manhand, 2012)

Samara Lubelski: *The Tingle Of Casual Danger* is live at Café Oto one night and was probably billed as a Sunburned Hand Of The Man gig. Everyone who was on tour during the *Demolished Thoughts* period was on-stage, including Aaron Mullan and Dave Mies from Tall Firs who were, I think, opening shows for us at the time.

211

Keith Wood: There was a *Wire* magazine article by David Keenan where he coined the phrase 'New Weird America' which included Devendra Banhart, Six Organs Of Admittance and a bunch of others. But before that I don't think we'd all thought about it – I hadn't. I went and bought *The Wire* the day after I'd played with Six OJrgans and we were driving up to the mountains and I saw the cover story; it was news to us! We all just kept crossing paths. The music was so different, it was noise music, it was improv, it was folk music, it was country. My relationship to it was just seeing everyone doing what they wanted, and how they wanted to, and people were willing to collaborate and have a good time doing what they love.

I'd always played in bands, so you open shows for people, you get their numbers, you stay in touch and they come through again; they stay at your house and vice versa. It's exactly the same as when Thurston and Mike Watt and all those guys did it in the early eighties. You build a network of people and when you're coming through town they'll put on a show for you; if they're coming through town you'll put on a show for them.

YokoKimThurston
Kim Gordon/Thurston Moore/Yoko Ono
(Chimera Music, 2012)

Thurston Moore: Sean Lennon was behind me doing a remix for Yoko ('Rising' on *Rising Mixes*, 1996). I went into a studio and had the engineer strip all the instrumentation out of the mix so I could just hear her voice. I could hear her making breathing sounds, clicking, spill sounds. I cranked it up loud until you could hear everything in her mouth. I had the engineer record a minute or two from all these different Japanese noise cassettes – Merzbow, Government Alpha, MSBR, Masonna – all of which got credit. I had her voice and every once in a while I'd bring up this wall of noise. I thought it was radical – but didn't hear anything back from her. So, we were in Australia in a hotel and I got a phone call from the reception, "Yoko Ono is on the line for you?" It was the first time I'd really talked to her. She said she just wanted to call and tell me I did a wonderful job.

The first time we met was when we were thrown together at an event that was happening outdoors at the Battery Park in New York: Yoko, DJ Spooky and myself improvising. I remember I was very sensitive to her being on-stage – I didn't want to blow her eardrums out – so we did this gentle improvised thing. So, afterward, she came up and said, "Wow, that's not what I expected!" I asked, "What did you expect?" She replied, "Well, seeing what you did at The Roxy, a full-on assault, I thought that's what you would do." I said, "I don't exclusively just play noise." We've had this relationship where neither of us quite knows what to expect of one another.

David Newgarden (Manager for Yoko Ono): In 2010–11, we did a series of special concerts with the new YOKO ONO PLASTIC ONO BAND with Cornelius band members, plus Harry Hosono, Yuka Honda, Nels Cline and Sean Lennon, along with a wild cast of special guests performing with her or covering her songs. Kim and Thurston played 'Mulberry' with Yoko in Brooklyn and Los Angeles. Interviewed backstage, Thurston mischievously managed to hot-dog a little attention away from the other illustrious guests by announcing news that he, Kim and Yoko were about to record an album together. This was big news, especially to Yoko and Kim, who knew nothing about it! Yoko laughed it off initially, I think slightly annoyed but half-admiring Thurston's chutzpah. After many months and a few cancellations, a recording date happened on February 26, 2011 at Sear Sound. The location was familiar and comfortable to all; Sear had a homey rec-room feel with wood panelling, worn carpets, old couches and lamps, and posters and cartoons on the walls.

Listening back to the *YokoKimThurston* album it feels like a late-night jam, but it was actually a cold Saturday morning. We set up vocal mics for all, guitar amps and drums. I picked up coffees and three copies of *The New York Times* at Yoko's request. The spoken words of the piece 'Early In The Morning' were snipped verbatim from the day's news; she instructed each person to privately select a list of phrases from the paper and the tape rolled. Making her previous album, I'd observed Yoko singing lyrics from a notebook, but that day she ran with the spontaneous free-improvisation spirit, and free-styled lyrics from her head. She was in amazing form. Kim moved excitedly around the studio from guitar to bass to drums. Thurston played electric and acoustic 12-string guitars seated on a folding chair. Of course, we had no idea that it would be Thurston and Kim's last collaboration together.

Thurston titled and sequenced six tracks for the CD, and suggested the entire session be released as a limited-edition three-LP set. Thurston mixed the tapes a month later at Sear, and then Yoko fine-tuned the mixes. Kim's vortex-like cover painting was made by spray painting through a Christmas wreath onto a canvas. We recreated the design with individually painted

Mats Gustafsson and Thurston take tea for two at Henie Onstad Kunstsenter, Høvikodden Norway, June 9, 2013.   *Credit – Martín Escalante*

boxes for the vinyl set, hiring a florist to make smaller 12" size wreaths and spray painting all day long in the ventilated painting room at Auto Dent Collision in Fort Hamilton, Brooklyn.

Yoko Ono: It was a wonderful recording. I've played some shows since then with both Kim and Thurston but miss them both.

Vi Är Alla Guds Slavar
Mats Gustafsson/Thurston Moore
(Otoroku, 2013)

Mats Gustafsson: At Café Oto they record the shows; most places these days ask if they can record, so there's almost always a board recording made now. So if you're planning to make a recording you can set up more professionally. We had a similar place in Stockholm that was active for a couple of years called Ugglan, 'The Owl', it was almost a copy of what Café Oto is now. Café Oto's attitude toward music, being determined not to do just one kind of jazz or one kind of noise, that's fantastic. There's a place in Warsaw called Pardon, To Tu, which is similar to Café Oto. You can have a two- or three-day residency – which is something Café Oto started with, resurrecting this old jazz tradition where you don't have to travel and you can play for a whole week, which really helps the music. Copenhagen Jazz House is another venue that's been transformed into a super-creative place, it's a jazz club but with a really interesting programme. In Berlin there are plenty of places to play but very little money to tour – it's all door money. A lot of the cultural funding has been falling all over Europe, but I have a feeling there are more places with a lot of enthusiasts producing concerts and smaller festivals. Of course, the competition to get the gigs is a lot higher than 20 years ago but the audiences seem higher, so something is going in the right direction.

Chris Corsano: I did have occasion to hear Thurston play in a duo with Mats Gustafsson around 2013, and I was totally blown away at how responsive Thurston's playing was without sacrificing an ounce of its wall-of-sound quality and forward momentum. Not that he wasn't amazing before, but it seems like he cracked some higher-level codes of simultaneous listening-playing/action-reaction.

Live At Henie Onstad Kunstsenter
Mats Gustafsson/Thurston Moore
(Prisma Records, 2015)

Lasse Marhaug: The Henie Onstad Kunstsenter – translates as 'Art Centre' and, for short, HOK – is situated 15 kilometres outside Oslo, on the peninsula called Høvikodden. The building itself rests comfortably in an idyllic, green sculpture park. Since its opening in 1968, HOK was the leading venue for modern art in Norway. Music was also the art centre's profile, and it played host to artists like John Cage, Iannis Xenaxis, Yoko Ono… Then somehow the art centre's focus shifted in the nineties, and music was not a priority. In 2008, Lars Mørch Finborud and I were employed to re-establish the centre as an arena for experimental music. We were given a limited budget but otherwise free rein to do what we wanted. It was hard work but also a success, and we had artists come to perform or work on commissioned pieces. We also resurrected the art centre's own record label, Prisma Records, and set about documenting selected performances as well as issuing archive recordings we unearthed. We booked Thurston and Mats to perform on the outdoor stage; being two of the busiest musicians in the world, it took three years to find a date that worked.

June 9, 2013 was a beautiful sunny Sunday afternoon, with the audience comfortably spread out across the natural amphitheatre grass. Thurston and Mats arrived early and devoured the current exhibitions and the bookshop contents with great enthusiasm. The soundcheck only took them about five minutes. The audience arrived early; many had brought their kids and were having a picnic. Then, at 2p.m., the duo blasted into an hour-long onslaught of full-on glorious noise. Mats didn't touch his saxophone for the first 20 minutes, just twiddled electronics while Thurston sat with the guitar flat on his lap, hitting it ferociously, trying to

Lasse Marhaug and Thurston at NyMusikk, Oslo, January 16, 2014.

Credit – Martín Escalante

find the missing link between Keith Rowe and Gorgoroth. But the HOK audience were not confused indie-rock or jazz fans, they knew what they were in for and they loved every squeak and screech the duo produced. Music that's normally experienced late at night in claustrophobic, dark basements, with the smell of alcohol and sweat in the air, had become the soundtrack to a leisurely Sunday afternoon on the Oslo fjord. Good noise music works like a mirror – what you bring to it is what you take from it. Less than two years later, I resigned from my job at the art centre and the very last thing I did was to release an LP of Thurston and Mats' noise picnic.

Last Notes
Joe McPhee/Thurston Moore/Bill Nace
(Open Mouth, 2013)

Bill Nace: The steps and changes kind of come in waves, there's slow and fast periods... but Northampton was a definite catalyst for me and kind of a foundation for a lot of what I do now. This show was something we had both talked about wanting to do for a long time and having the opportunity to play with Joe is still a highlight for me.

Joe McPhee: The concert came about as a result of an invitation from Thurston straight out of the blue, I never knew why and never asked. I certainly didn't know what to expect and, I suspect, neither did Thurston or Bill. I live in Poughkeepsie, New York, which for all intents and purposes might as well have been the other side of the universe with respect to what was happening on the Lower East Side of NYC in the eighties. In this case, past was not prologue; we were starting with a blank canvas and a full pallet.

What was known was the date, the time and place. Roulette is a marvellous performance space. It is a comfortable, acoustically inviting concert environment and a perfect setting for this first meeting. I had given some thought to my instrumentation and, again, I didn't want to go for the familiar. Not the tenor or soprano or trumpet this time, rather alto saxophone which is more challenging for me. I wanted to be out of my comfort zone – no muscle memory. We would be looking for the new, the unknown. This was as close to what might be best described as PO Music in practice; a 'Positive, Possible, Poetic Hypothesis' music unfolding in real time making discoveries along the way. We arrived, found our places on-stage and never once discussed what or how or why. The appointed time came; we started, listened and played. When it was finished, we stopped.

@
John Zorn/Thurston Moore
(Tzadik, 2013)

Marc Urselli: I've been engineering records since I was 17. I had a recording studio in Southern Italy where for a few years I was recording pretty much all the punk, hardcore and noise bands in a radius of 100 miles. Italy's scene was exciting and bustling but I wanted to do more, so I moved to NYC to pursue an internship at EastSide Sound, a recording studio that was opened by Lou Holtzman in 1972; now I run that same studio. I know EastSide Sound's room and collection of microphones and pre-amps inside out, so it's second nature for me to get good sounds. John simply tells me who the musicians are and what instrument they will be playing and I set up the mics, the console, the outboard and everything else.

It was just the three of us at the recording session and just me and Zorn at the mixing session. Zorn likes his sessions to be private, in order to avoid any kind of distraction from the music, so not even my assistants are in the studio once I hit the record button. It's part of my style to be as transparent as possible during recording sessions, so as to not interrupt or alter the creative flows in any way. Spending a day recording them playing together was a beautiful experience of communion and artistry.

Cause & Effect Vol.1
'Gleo' – Thurston Moore
(Joyful Noise, 2013)

Karl Hofstetter: I originally formed Joyful Noise purely so that my then-band would have a logo on the back of our CD, to create a false sense of legitimacy. I originally had no intention of actually forming a

218

label as I was all of 19. But I started realising that I had a better aptitude for label work than I did for drumming, so I started releasing my friends' bands, and then friends of friends, and it pretty much just continued from there. 2008 was a turning point, my 'fuck it' moment. I stopped looking to imitate what other labels had done in the past. I started reimagining the role of a label, which to me meant doing releases because they were fun and crazy. Strangely, this was the moment when the label actually got some traction.

I see elaborate packaging and a tactile aesthetic as increasingly important in the digital age. Back when physical media was invented it was utilitarian – you actually needed that physical record in order to hear the music. That's no longer the case, as all music is instantly available for free. What I have learned is that serious music fans still have the desire to collect music and experience it in a kind of ritualistic way. I think interesting physical formats enhance the music-listening experience; they communicate some humanity to the listener. Not that there isn't a place for casual Spotify listening, but having elaborate packaging and limited, unique physical media definitely makes for a special experience. And, ironically, this has created a record-buying atmosphere where expensive, elaborate vinyl releases sell better than those with the cheap packaging.

Andrya Ambro: Karl from Joyful Noise chose the connection. To be honest, I didn't think we were the appropriate fit. Okay yes, how grateful we are to receive that association, like wow. And yes, we had similar alternative guitar tunings; yes, we employed feedback; yes, perhaps we both attempted to draw from a mutual raw spirit. But it feels like we came at it with a very different approach than Thurston. I think I approach my expression from a place of feeling trapped and wanting to break free from that. That may sound clichéd but it is so very real for me and maybe Sarah too, whether that's being trapped as a woman or just as a social creature in this world. And I'm not sure Thurston pulls inspiration from that feeling. Or maybe he does, and I got it all wrong. But here's an observation: Thurston seems enamoured by and incredibly supportive of the female experience.

Karl Hofstetter: The introduction to Thurston was actually kind of funny in that we were never actually introduced – he just ordered a record from our site. We got all his info that way; luckily, we were correct that there wasn't more than one Thurston Moore living in New York City. We sent him a nice letter and care package with his order, and then I emailed him a few weeks later to take part in *Cause & Effect*.

The concept was a split seven-inch series with the 'influencer' on Side A and the one influenced on Side B. So we had some legendary trendsetter guys on Side A – Thurston Moore, Lou Barlow, David Yow – and new bands that resulted from their musical trailblazing on Side B – Talk Normal, Dumb Numbers, Child Bite. That release was a little involved. It's always more laborious when there are different entities on a single release.

Sarah Register: 'Shot This Time' was meant to be a barnstormer of a romp, with a big, keening guitar, a stadium beat, a growling ode to the crucifixion I was feeling at the time, plus the soul of Aretha Franklin-esque *wah-ooh*s in the chorus which Andrya expanded and performed. 'Shot This Time' was a whole different trip to 'Gold Dime', though again a dump of my own psychology. There's only a few other Talk Normal songs besides these that are pretty strictly from my point of view, lyrics-wise.

Keith Wood, John Moloney, Samara Lubelski and Thurston live, electric.

Credit – Eva Prinz

Chelsea Light Moving
Chelsea Light Moving
(Matador, 2013)

Keith Woods: After touring so much for *Demolished Thoughts*, we'd grown tired of acoustic guitars. We all wanted to plug in and rage a little bit. Mary Lattimore stopped playing because we were getting too loud for the harp. So, All Tomorrow's Parties asked us to play *Psychic Hearts* in Camden, the whole record, so we learnt it and we were doing some of the songs with acoustic but started going over to the electric because it sounded better. That's how the transition happened. Thurston kind of knew what tuning they were all in, then we went back and figured them all out from there.

It's a simple truth that anyone who comes to see Thurston play has some kind of history with Sonic Youth – the Thurston sound was so integral, though, that whatever he does will always have that within it. People would call out Sonic Youth songs at the shows and Thurston had the best response, he'd say, "Hey, we're not a cover band! We don't do covers!" He was moving forward. He's like a shark, he's got to keep moving.

John Moloney: We started adding a couple of songs from *Psychic Hearts*, a couple of songs from *Trees Outside The Academy* and it started to roll until eventually Thurston had an electric guitar that he'd break out for something on one of these tours – and that was where it started to morph into an electric band. I still refer to Chelsea Light Moving as The Thurston Moore Band, I lump those two bands together, in fact there was a time where I hadn't been at home longer than three weeks solid in over three years: March 2011 to January 1, 2014 – the last time we played.

Samara stayed on as bassist, me on drums, Keith and Thurston guitars. Thurston had the songs written, we did three together, then he came to studio rehearsals with a few more he had. We toured relentlessly on that record all over the world. We'd worked the songs up before we played them live. Normally, a band will record a record and then go play it live, while, back in another era that maybe only lives in my imagination, a band would write songs, tour them for a year, then record them when they're really hot and they've been tweaked and re-tweaked. I wish we could have recorded that record in the middle of the touring cycle – I feel there was a peak. We played some shows at SXSW where I remember thinking, 'I wish this was the record.' We were so hot!

221

Justin Pizzoferrato: A typical session with Thurston is to show up, set up, wait a few hours then work your ass off. It was the first time I'd been involved from start to finish with him; I was really excited and the sessions turned out to be a lot of fun, though they were whirlwind. John, Keith, Samara and I would show up to the studio, set up and wait for Thurston. He'd usually be a few hours late. He'd show up and we'd jump into tracking. It was really intense. Thurston would run eight takes, one after another – no breaks, no discussion – until the band got it tight enough. We set the entire band in one room with no isolation, no baffles, full bleed. Thurston's amp was extremely loud and John was hitting his drums really hard. It created an insane energy and really glued the sounds together. We had a hard time getting Keith and Thurston's guitars to blend correctly. They were pretty much playing the same part but it kind of had to sound like one mass of sound. Playback was not yielding that result, so Keith and I got into the studio one night and rerecorded all of his parts with a different amp. I finally figured out that it was a tone thing. Keith was more than happy to redo his parts and it worked like a charm.

Mixing was always much shorter than I wanted it to be. Thurston knew what he wanted and would ask for it. For example, he'd ask for reverb on his voice. I'd dial up my reverb and before I had a chance to twiddle any knobs, he'd tell me to turn it up until he liked it. And that was it. No time for nuance. That said, Chelsea Light Moving's record isn't one of nuance necessarily. The important thing about it was that it sounded heavy as fuck. There wasn't any fussing or time for anyone to make any revisions.

Untitled
Chelsea Light Moving/Merchandise
(No Label, 2013)

John Moloney: We did a tour cassette with some outtakes from a house party Matador put together, an album preview where we played in a basement. Matador put this contest together where, 'Hey, you can have Thurston Moore and his band, Chelsea Light Moving, play at your house.' I remember the press release had Thurston saying something about how we were going to come and destroy your house, your basement, your attic, wherever. We got all these offers – it had to be somewhere within a certain range of where we lived. There was a band house with a huge basement where even Thurston could stand up without having to lean over. Matador sent a film crew up, Justin Pizzoferrato came up and set up a live sound rig and we played almost the entire album, a scorching set. The music from the split cassette with Merchandise comes from that same night.

Justin had set up his mobile recording unit, so before we had people come in, before we had the film crew, we were just down there fucking around, doing improvised punk songs with Thurston singing while Justin was testing the equipment. Everything was recorded and I put together the split cassette myself. Merchandise were going to be the opening band on the tour, we became close friends; so, in the spirit of being DIY record people, I emailed Carson Cox and we agreed to do a cassette for the tour. They sent me a track, I pulled everything else from those punk songs in the basement, plus there was a second recording session we did for Chelsea Light Moving at Justin's studio. Matador wanted three or four more songs on top of what we put together in the first session. So a couple of months later, in December 2012, Thurston and I went into the studio as a duo and recorded The Germs' 'Communist Eyes' and 'Heavenmetal', which ended up on the album. But we also did some instrumental stuff that didn't make the album – all really cool songs though. So I pulled those and put them onto the split-cassette.

Comes Through In The Call Hold
Clark Coolidge/Thurston Moore/Anne Waldman
(Fast Speaking Music, 2013)

Ambrose Bye: I grew up around both the Poetry Project in NYC and Naropa University in Boulder, Colorado. Almost all of my life I have been in this world of art, poetry and music. I got into recording and production in my twenties and at some point it was logical to work with the people closest to me, friends and family members. I think of Fast Speaking Music more as an imprint, it's not really a label in the sense of being a business. It feels more like a bunch of independent projects that we sort of organise. The name of the 'label' came from the poem 'Fast Speaking Woman' by Anne Waldman; she's also my mother. I have been recording poets and musicians over the last six years at Naropa University – Anne and

Ambrose Bye and Thurston Moore, NYC, May 7, 2016.   *Credit – Anne Waldman*

Thurston happen to be two of those artists. The space for recording was once inhabited by Harry Smith, creator of *The Anthology Of American Folk Music*; he was brought out to the school by Allen Ginsberg in the late eighties. Anne has been at Naropa for 41 years and Thurston has been coming for the last four years.

Anne Waldman: The Jack Kerouac School is the generative literary wing of Naropa University, founded by a Tibetan Buddhist lama, Chogyam Trungpa, in 1974. The site is up against a backdrop of the Rocky Mountains and close to the Continental Divide. I co-founded the Kerouac School and shared directorship with Allen Ginsberg a number of years. Early faculty included William S. Burroughs, Gregory Corso, Diane di Prima, Philip Whalen, Amiri Baraka. There's a focus on the poetic 'outrider' tradition, cultural activism and performance. The month-long summers are wonderfully intense and generative in the realm of an engaged, worldly poetics and a deep discourse of history, archive, world issues and the particulars of a wild imagination.

Thurston is decidedly in the lineage of the Beats and the New American Poetry. Spontaneous, letting the work be guided as the mind is, instant upon instant. Nothing officially 'verse culture', or staid, or censored. Emotional ambiguity. Open. Witty. Genuine and ranging. And there's the identification with a very expansive poetics and the curiosity that the Beats had, that intervenes on the culture and moves across borders and across genres. The cultural importance and huge intervention of the Beat literary movement can never be underestimated, and Thurston is a part of that continuum.

For *Comes Through In The Call Hold* I provided text and improvised on the vocals – various Sprechstimme natural tendencies and rant – for 'Om Krim Kalyai Namah', a chant invoking Hindu goddess Kali, destroyer and sometimes preserver. The text is also a 'response' to the Devanagari Sanskrit alphabet, which contains all the sounds of the universe. This was free-form intensity, with poet Clark Coolidge on drums, Thurston on guitar, the three of us at close quarters and bouncing off a big mutual sound in the small Harry Smith Studio, my voice having to hold its own inside Clark and Thurston's barrage of interconnected energy-sound waves. The track 'History Will Decide' is an *homage* to Brion Gysin and William S. Burroughs incorporating some of their *Third Mind* lines. It's a polemical piece covering a range of current events: Nicolas Sarkozy, Bandar, Egypt's Tahrir – refrain with gusto, "The streets of the world!"

Anne Waldman, Clark Coolidge and Thurston in Boulder, Colorado, June 30, 2012.
Credit – Ambrose Bye

Oasis At Biskra
Ambrose Bye/Daniel Carter/Thurston Moore/
Eva Prinz/Anne Waldman/Devin Brahja Waldman
(Fast Speaking Music, 2014)

Ambrose Bye: A friend named Jef Mertens from Belgium contacted me about doing a limited cassette release. I sort of collaged the album together, but when I do that I work pretty spontaneously and fast to keep it as organic as the original performances. It's a blend of live improvised recordings and some added after-effects. With these more improvised projects I tend to mix and add things with a 'first thought, best thought' improvised approach, rather than being meticulous and striving for some unachievable perfection.

The most memorable part for me is at the beginning; the sound in the background is the wind blowing through the sound hole on an acoustic guitar and creating some weird harmonic on the string – I recorded it on top of a sand dune in southern Morocco. The rest of the track was recorded in Manhattan. My cousin Devin and Thurston were playing together while our friend Eva was making dinner. I pulled out a couple mics and hit 'record'. At the end you can hear Eva blowing the whistle for us to come eat. The poetry was added later. Thurston is unbelievably easy to work with; his approach is telepathic, ephemeral and efficient. His love for art and poetry and noise and life is ecstatic.

Soft Machine Sutra
Samara Lubelski/Thurston Moore/Gene Moore/
Tom Surgal/Anne Waldman
(Fast Speaking Music, 2014)

Samara Lubelski: This was at The Stone. It was a live event for the 100th birthday of William S. Burroughs. I recall there was also a 'question and answer' with Anne Waldman that Thurston did. I showed up to see the gig and Thurston sent me home to fetch my violin for the second set. I was along for the last-minute ride! I couldn't hear anything except for Tom Surgal while we played. No idea how that one turned out.

Keith Wood: Thurston's always been into collecting rare books. When we were on the road we'd hit bookstores and look for 1950s New York school poetry books – we spent hours in bookstores. Thurston's always been involved in countercultural activities so it's the same thing as collecting punk-zines – moving through layers of information.

Ambrose Bye: As far as The Stone goes there is no recording equipment there; it's a very modest and amazingly intimate place to hear music, I just put a few microphones around the room, it was really loud in there, not an ideal set-up but that's what was captured; to me what's important is just pushing 'record'. Particularly with musicians who just play and are constantly improvising, capturing what you can is the first step. Later on, you can hopefully clean it up and make it sound better through mixing and mastering. A shitty recording of a great performance will always be better than a great recording of a shitty performance.

Tiny People Having A Meeting
Ambrose Bye/Clark Coolidge/Max Davies/
Thurston Moore/Anne Waldman
(Fast Speaking Music, 2015)

Anne Waldman: I met Thurston in NYC probably over 20 years ago. He came to a reading with a pile of my books to sign. I was touched that a rocker was a reader, although he was known as such, and we've become really close in the last decade. It's been a great fit having him come to Naropa in the summers, giving classes on Ginsberg's relationship to music, or Burroughs', as well as helping students along with their own lyrics and music. And he also performs with others, and shares that rhizomic community spirit Naropa is famous for.

John Corbett: I think there's a direct lineage of DIY that leads back to three particular roots: Sun Ra and El Saturn Records; Charles Mingus, Max Roach and Debut Records; and Harry Partch and Gate 5 Records. These labels paved the way for artist-run labels of the punk and post-punk era. And that's a lineage that Thurston understands better than most people. It's much like the small-press poetry world, the self-production of pamphlets and staple-bound xeroxes and broadsides and chapbooks. Again, something that Thurston has mined incessantly. Jazz and poetry have inevitable connections to punk because they're dependent on the ambitions of putting things out for oneself, knowing that there isn't an infrastructure to issue your shit so you have to live by the credo that if you want anything done (right), you have to do it yourself. Who else can you rely on if you're making little scratch noises or singing songs in a scream? Nobody but yourself. As Albert Brooks said in *Modern Romance*, "We'll leave it up to us."

Anne Waldman: Thurston feels like family, a spirit familiar. His playing is the door to some kind of transcendent world where one inhabits magic trembling caves with walls of sounds, elemental ground path and fruition.

I thought of Thurston's playing when I visited India's Ajanta caves; here one can strike a pillar for a resonant, bell-like, insistent ringing, a centre of melodic rupture but also history seems to press in, prescient... I have heard him wild in the studio; the great finesse and modesty and concentration is always cohesive to alchemical shift, while guitar utterance leads me on, and a Sufi's spin. Thurston is also a wonderful poet, friend to poets, publisher and archivist, who values the ephemeral, mad rush and passion for zines and small press and poetry, everything. Was there ever another time like this when the conjuncts of music and poetry were so important? And to be on the same wavelength with one who holds all this so dear? We are so lucky in our lineage and 'the company of friends' (Bob Creeley's phrase). Bows and Kudos, Thurston Moore. Forever.

Live At Café Oto
Thurston Moore/Alex Ward
(Otoroku, 2013)

Alex Ward: Café Oto suggested releasing the duo set as a limited edition vinyl pressing as part of their fundraising drive and I was happy to go along with the idea – with the added stipulation that a digital version should also be made available, so that the music could be heard by those not in a position to make quite such a substantial financial donation.

I arrived at the venue about an hour before doors were set to open to set up. By the time I got there, Thurston had already gone off to get dinner. I did a bit of warming up and checked the mics, and then hung out until show time. Thurston arrived back immediately before the performance was set to start, made his way through the crowd and launched into a spoken introduction which segued into a reading of some of his poetry. He then announced the other poet for the evening, Tom Raworth, who proceeded to read a selection of his work.

Then it was time for our duo. We said a quick hello and shook hands – the first words we'd exchanged in person in over a decade. The duo set certainly felt very focused and, if not exactly introverted, then at least characterised by a high degree of concentration and even tension. With no percussion or bass instrument to provide support, the challenge to maintain musical continuity in such a performance can feel somewhat like a high-wire act. The trio in the second half with Steve Noble on drums also felt very intense, but in a more explosive, immersive and cathartic way.

One of the main differences in our approach is that Thurston often employs an element of drone tonality in his playing and uses tuning which facilitate this. Our similarities include a preference for a certain strength of gesture and a type of improvising where the individual personalities can still be clearly heard, as well as blending into a collective sound. With regard to the duo on the LP, it quickly became apparent there was a whole area of high frequencies where our instruments could blend and interact very interestingly. One of the challenges was then to find a way to explore that area to its full potential while not letting it dominate the music to the point of becoming one-dimensional and shrill.

James Nares and Thurston at the Metropolitan Museum of Art, NYC, April 15, 2013.
Credit – Elizabeth Blake

Sonic Street Chicago
Thurston Moore
(Corbett & Dempsey, 2014)

John Corbett: After the No Music Festival in 1998 we stayed in touch, saw each other from time to time at one festival or another. As a former guitarist, I'm very picky about other guitarists. He knows exactly how to build and dissipate energy, how to modulate texture, how to vary dynamic level and when to go for the kill shot.

We came to the idea of presenting the film, *Street*, as part of a whole night associated with Christopher Wool's retrospective at the Art Institute of Chicago. We had already done an evening like this at the Guggenheim, with a different line-up, and in this case we knew that we had an auditorium with a fantastic screen, so the notion of presenting [James] Nares and Moore was a ringer. I wanted a variety-show atmosphere, several different but complementary acts. Richard Hell had also read at the Guggenheim, where the event was titled *Nation Time* (after Joe McPhee's great record) but he read from the autobiography in Chicago; in NYC he had prepared a statement about Wool's work. McPhee played with Milford Graves, the first time they'd worked together. We had 850 people in the house and it was on fire.

James Nares: When I shot *Street*, I wasn't thinking of having any music at all. I was going to try and approach sound the way I had the visuals – to try and reveal something about sound by slowing it down. But I found that when I slowed down recorded sound it started to come across very 'digital' and it also seemed to weigh everything down. It amped up the slowness until it was like walking through a field of mud in big boots. So I gave up on that. Then I tried driving around the city with a shotgun mic poking out of the car window, so I could catch snippets of conversations – but that didn't really work. Then I tried taking all kinds of city sounds and making something with that, but it still wasn't working. Then, one day, we were looking at the footage and playing some music and suddenly I realised that the music really gave it something. The purist in me hadn't wanted to put music on – I thought if I put a layer of music over the whole thing it would become very controlling, manipulative. Watching the footage though, I started to realise that it worked pretty well.

So I decided I wanted a soundtrack by somebody who knew New York City, who was part of the city, someone whose music I loved, somebody I thought would 'get it'. So I thought of Thurston – but I wanted him to play solo, as a counterpoint to the cast of thousands in the film. I wanted to have the soundtrack as a parallel world, not just illustrating the film; instead, I wanted it to be a wandering instrument in the same way that I wandered through the city when I was making the film. I knew Thurston could improvise an interior wandering, and he did it fantastically well.

The music on the film is all solo acoustic 12-string guitar. I asked him if he'd do the music and he said that he was off on tour in a few days – so I pushed: "Can you get something done before then?" He gave me permission to use anything off his recent albums to make the soundtrack, so then, when I heard his record *12-String Meditations For Jack Rose*, it felt perfect. I asked him if I could use some of that, he said, "Sure, but let me give you some more stuff." So he went home with a copy of the film – but he wasn't watching it while he made the music – and over a couple of nights he recorded. I then took that music, plus a couple of pieces from the album, and with my sound guy, Bill Seery, we constructed a soundtrack out of them. The most important thing for me was that the music should have a rolling rhythm, like how certain music sounds good if you're in a car, a lolloping rhythm. I wanted the music to have that feel which Thurston kept in mind with the music he recorded. When we made the soundtrack we didn't lend emphasis to visual things, but we did craft it a bit so that it worked – and we did create something that has a structure, a beginning-middle-end, but it caught the wandering I wanted.

At the Metropolitan Museum of Art in New York, Thurston did the music live on an electric guitar, but he didn't watch the film – I didn't want that – he faced the audience. But he definitely has eyes in the back of his head because there were times what he was doing was so synced with what was happening on the screen! Next, Christopher Wool had a one-person show at the Chicago Art Institute and wanted to show some things concurrent with that in the cinema. So he asked if Thurston would do another live performance with *Street*, and that's the performance that's on the CD. With the Met show, the soundcheck was amazing, so when Thurston did the actual performance, it was a different energy in a big theatre full of people and he did something different. Everyone loved it but I was secretly thinking, 'Oh but the soundcheck was so fucking good...' In Chicago, he did something that was more as I imagined it should be. At the Met, at times, it became, for me, too abrasive, but that's a very minute criticism because it was still awesome to see the film with a real-time soundtrack. He could tell when it was the end of the film because, without needing to look at it, the screen went dark so he'd notice that – plus there's a vibe that comes off an audience when something is ending, you can feel it.

A while after, Thurston had this gig; he asked me if I'd do a duo with him. I got nervous but the night before the gig we jammed a bit; he said he thought he'd do it without any boxes; I agreed, thought it was a good idea to keep it clean and simple. Then he showed up at the gig with all these boxes and all I had was my guitar: "Thurston, I don't have anything!" I asked if I could borrow something and he passed me this box saying, "Use this, it's really great. It's got three buttons – if you press the first one, the thing just launches into this big sound… and if you press the second one then it just ramps it right up! Then the third one… just don't push the third one." So, of course, as soon as we started playing I went straight to the third one.

'Detonation'/'Germs Burn'
Thurston Moore
(Blank Editions, 2014)

James Sedwards: I first met Thurston properly when he lived in my house in Stoke Newington. When he first moved to London he took a room at my place for about a year. After a while I think he decided that he liked living in London, so he moved out and got his own flat just round the corner. A few months later he contacted me, saying that he had started writing some new material and wondered whether I would be interested in playing it with him. It sounded interesting so I gave it a go. There was already a gig lined up so we had to work fast. We did two rehearsals and learned about 45 minutes of material and then went and played. It was completely instrumental and quite abstract at times. We actually played twice that day, a matinee and an evening performance, and afterward we felt that it had gone well so we decided to do more.

Radieux Radio: My involvement in Thurston's music started when he moved to London – it's where I'm based and we'd been in touch, writing to one another, for a long time. He was moving into an area called Stoke Newington which has a beautiful history of non-conformism. At the time, I was in touch with an anarchist publisher called Stuart Christie who was a member of the Angry Brigade, who were based in that area. They were an organisation similar to the Baader-Meinhof Group, or the Weather Underground, but unlike those groups they were non-violent. They would use explosions as part of their message, accompanying them with communiqués explaining why they would destroy a piece of property such as an embassy, an office, a police station, the Ford Motor Company.

The first of Thurston's songs I wrote lyrics to was 'Detonation', it was inspired by Stuart Christie: when he was 18 he tried to assassinate Franco and his mother wrote a letter trying to get him out of jail in Spain. The song's lyrics talk about sit-ins and go-slows, wild-cat strikes and I mention a toy grenade at the end which is a reference to an incident where a group of Angry Brigade members and other activists stormed a meeting of City of London officials and asked to have a conversation about educational opportunities, strikers and other matters. Everyone remained and listened because there was a grenade on the table that they brought with them and – at some point – one of the members pulled out the key and everyone ran. I wrote it as a poem and showed it to Thurston.

The thing about doing something radical is that, hopefully, those kinds of messages become redundant as laws change and people are given the rights they deserve, as we move forward and achieve progress. In the lyrics I've written with Thurston, the messages that seem political, I hope there'll be a point in the future they're no longer relevant – that's the greatest hope when writing an activist statement.

David Blanco: N16, in and around North East London, there's a lot going on over here, has been for years. If you delve deep enough you'll find a rich history here.

Will Shutes and I met in late 2011. We soon fell into a conversation about how there's a lot of really good stuff happening on our doorstep but there wasn't a label that was tying it all together. The labels I found most memorable were those that presented their geographical location to the rest of the world; a regional sound that was a representation of their environment, of what their backyard was like. That's what Will and I wanted for Blank Editions. My daughter was born in February 2012, around the time we released our first record and pretty much the very worst timing ever to start up a label. We are kitchen table. I make the sleeves when my kids have gone to bed. We contact the record shops one by one. We wanted to build a label from the bottom up. Will and I have that conversation: "If you saw that would you buy it?" If we both say yes, then we have the discussion about whether we have enough money to do it justice.

Will and I noticed how many people in bands were recording stuff at home – to us that was really exciting because not only were those recordings not formulated for release, a lot of them were sketches or improvisations. So we made a list of bands we liked that were in the neighbourhood or lived in London. We then approached people in certain bands and offered them a chance to record a seven-inch. It's so easy to work with individuals; no management; no red tape; no record-industry bullshit.

My wife and I were shopping locally one evening and we saw Thurston in a shop – I found out later that he'd moved into the neighbourhood. A month after, I was out with my daughter who was a baby at the time – coincidentally, she had a Sub Pop T-shirt on – when I happened upon Thurston in the street. I initially thought, 'Should I introduce myself?' We were launching Douglas Hart's seven-inch at a pub called The Old Blue Last that very night, so I thought he might appreciate an invite. I went over, he saw my daughter's babygro, it amused him and I invited him. That night I gave him a copy of the Douglas Hart record – each one has a slight variation to the cover, Douglas and I had handmade them over a few months. So I let Thurston pick whichever one he liked the cover of most. I asked him if he would be interested in doing a seven-inch with us – he said, "Yes!"

When Thurston first moved into Stoke Newington he started playing local shows with James Sedwards, playing these loose arrangements; so, for the seven-inch, they took two of these pieces and fleshed them out with Thurston handling guitar, bass and vocals. It was all fairly spontaneous. Will has a friend who had some days available at his studio which slotted into Thurston being in town, so he headed over and recorded over eight hours. We figured out the deal over lunch – how many records he wanted, who would do what – we hadn't discussed it before, we were just excited. We hadn't figured out how we'd finance it, so he said he'd take X amount of records, we'd pay for everyone's lunch, minicabs and the recording – perfect for us! We had the conversation so everyone knew what to expect, we were able to shake hands with complete trust. A few days later rough mixes came through; Thurston went back in and tweaked it a little bit, then the final mix went straight off to the pressing plant.

Sun Gift Earth
Thurston Moore
(Blank Editions, 2014)

David Blanco: *Sun Gift Earth* came out in November 2014 to coincide with the landing on the comet, Rosetta. November 14 was the scheduled date a satellite was due to land on the comet, so we timed the release for that. Thurston approached us; I think he liked how easy we'd been to work with on the seven-inch so had us in mind. He had some songs he'd recorded with Chelsea Light Moving, asked us if we'd be interested.

Radieux Radio: This song was about a satellite – Rosetta – landing on a comet: the point of the mission was to gather dust from the comet in order to explore the history of our universe. All these scientists and astrophysicists were waiting hours for the moment when they were going to wake up a satellite that had travelled over ten years to get to this point – it was so exhilarating. It was a few hours after it was meant to wake up, so people were nervous if it would work: it was a very expensive risk – it had taken so much time and work to get it out there. When it said "Hello Earth," there were tears and applause. People around the planet were online, on a conference call, cheering together. It was a remarkable moment for planet Earth. So there are those meaning of life moments that are important for the planet – then there's sitting outside at a concert with your friends, listening to music together, and that's still the meaning of life.

Samara Lubelski: 'Rebellion Of Joy' was a riff of Thurston's that Chelsea Light Moving had been working on in soundchecks and rehearsal for a while. I had my joke that the guitar riff was inspired by Pink Floyd's 'Hey You'. We never quite nailed it, thus there's a bit of shakiness in the recording. 'Rosetta', meanwhile, was a jammer in the studio, fooling around in between tracking for the Chelsea Light Moving record. Everyone in the band had a heavy background with improvising, jamming, whatever, so it occurred pretty naturally while the vocals were definitely overdubbed.

Free improvising was my favourite part of playing with Thurston live. We always did a bit every night, usually coming in and out of 'Ono Soul'. He's a generous and inquisitive player, and coaxed us along the garden path when needed. There was an understanding that the band was under his leadership and that carried over to our live improvisations. I saw it as my

David Blanco and Thurston in Abney Park Cemetery, London, January 2014.

Credit – Peter Beste

role to meet him on the plane of existence. It could be jaw-dropping at times and worthy of thanks to the music gods; when we played our first duo gig together at White Columns, he played the entire set with his guitar on his lap, using the paper invite to the gig in place of his fingers or a pick.

Live At ZDB
Gabriel Ferrandini/Thurston Moore/Pedro Sousa
(Shhpuma, 2014)

Cristiano Nunes: ZDB, we are a non-profit organisation in a poor country, so most of the time we have to make special arrangements. We don't have enough money to get the most suitable technical conditions in terms of sound equipment, microphones, backline to cover all the different bands that we get – basically we always need to adapt. When you get used to struggling to make things happen it becomes normal, and because of this, in the end it's a normal day like any other. To me, ZDB is a style of living; a place where you can learn and share. It has the stress and frantic pace of a band on tour, mixed with the pleasure of having a huge melting pot of different art, people, sensations, feeling; where you can make new friends for life, see old friends dying, people falling in love, couples breaking up or getting married! We're a family with a lot of love to share and I think people can feel that when they're in the venue. It's a life-changing place.

Sérgio Hydalgo: Thurston sincerely likes Lisbon; he has a connection with the city – I don't know if it was because it was a time of his life when he was looking to find his own space, but he seemed to find it while touring with his friends. I think he was able to feel Lisbon was a kind of home, a cosmopolitan space where there's a strong community of musicians. He came back a few months later and spent a week or so, the first idea was to do a residency focusing on his poetry but then, the city and the vibe, he was having a good time, eating well, going to bookstores, record stores, soaking in our traditional Fado music.

I asked him if he wanted to play along with two very young Portuguese musicians, Gabriel Ferrandini and Pedro Sousa, and he accepted immediately and just did it. Those kids were about 23 years old, they mainly play improvised free jazz with a lot of nerve – they've played with all the best cats in Lisbon and have now toured and recorded all over Europe. I

Sérgio Hydalgo and Thurston at ZDB in Lisbon, March 13, 2012.

Credit – Vera Marmelo

knew it'd be a dream for them to play an open set with Thurston: fire jazz, intense, brutal – they play loud, they're young, full of life. I knew they could do it – sincerely, I think it helped that they feel respect but they're not starstruck. They had the nerve to play, to be genuine, to act on the same level with Thurston. My desire was to put these great young musicians in a position that the locals expecting Thurston to only play with major, huge figures would never have imagined. Putting him together with them would cast a different perspective on Gabriel and Pedro – and

239

I knew that, by not being too respectful of Thurston's reputation, they'd play their best and that the three of them would rock.

A Portuguese trio called Sunflare opened the show, they're pretty intense. Thurston was by our bookstore at the entrance and the guitar player, Guilherme Canhão, asked him 10 minutes before going on, "Hey, do you want to play with us for one song?" Again, Thurston said yes. I was surprised – he just accepted it, the openness is mind-blowing. He ran through the song with them once then he was out on-stage playing it with them.

The main show was insane! It was intense, physical, you had to be in front seeing their expressions, how they're sweating, how hard it is on them physically, how open and loud. It's impossible to capture that intensity. We were all there, mouths open – it was amazing and raw all at once. They hadn't even met until right before the show, the most they had time to say was, "Let's not start loud, let's start quietly," then a minute or two into the set someone hit the note and that was it – they never stopped or let up until the end. If you play a club or a venue like ZDB, it's so small and there's so many people, you're sweating every drop of water out of your body, it's really intense. I know the lighting is brutal too on that stage – it's an exhausting experience, not something you can just do and leave it. So combine that with music that's intense in itself, you're losing several pounds every show.

The Rust Within Their Throats
Margarida Garcia/Thurston Moore
(Headlights, 2014)

Margarida Garcia: Most music I do starts behind closed doors, and what I show in public is the distillation of that; no need to expose more. I prefer to record rather than to play live. During concerts, however, there is always an unspoken and spontaneous exchange with the public that I like; this makes me see other things in what I do. Sound is probably the only matter that can go through bodies, shake and vibrate them as it bounces through a room; that does something to the music, then, when it comes back, it does something to me.

I choose my concert partners based on some kind of feeling of affinity. I had met Thurston in NYC on occasion, we also shared friends and collaborators like Samara Lubelski and Loren Connors, but it was only when Sérgio Hydalgo showed Thurston my solo record that he indicated his interest in a possible collaboration. I trusted from the beginning that we would have an immediate, unspoken, mutual understanding.

On the day of the concert, my boyfriend and I had gone to the flea market. We fell in love with the hugest and craziest book I ever saw – it had a spine almost a half-metre tall! It was full of handmade – and very strange – collages of someone's life; after much thinking and negotiating, we didn't buy it because it was too expensive. But later, when we met Thurston, he immediately told us that he had bought the craziest book at the flea market and there it was! That made me think the concert would go well.

Manuel Mota: Margarida is a good friend of mine and she makes music through her bass that I find so unique, it really touches me. Margarida and Thurston both played very genuinely; they were committed, free, creative and simultaneously showed visible respect for each other. No poses, no strategies, just truly spontaneous music. This is rare and, for me, it is what's important in music; in society; in life. I was in the audience and felt the music they created was special. I told them that same evening I would be glad to put it out.

Sérgio Hydalgo: The show itself with Margarida was delicate, hard to describe. I'm a huge fan of Margarida – she's shy and not keen on promoting herself, so I knew she would never have approached Thurston. She deserves to be heard and I wanted to do something to help her music become better known. I felt they would each enjoy playing with one another and they'd be a good match. But there's always some aspects that you can't duplicate on a record. Live, if you move a little to the left maybe you're hearing more of one instrument – then you move over to the right and it's the hum of Thurston's amplifier. You can't replicate that live contact.

Margarida Garcia: I chose an old print from the Lisbon earthquake of 1755 for the cover of the record – it fit with my memory of the performance. Listening back, I'm amazed at how Thurston weaved it all – it sometimes sounds very composed, which was the exact opposite of the feelings I had during the concert. When I hear a recording of a concert it's always strange because the feeling of what happened is so completely different; it's like a stranger did it.

Manuel Mota: The poetic title and the artwork are wonderful, dark, deep and positive. Three hundred copies were released, then for distribution I sent an email to my list and waited for the orders which were, in this case, far higher than what's normal for Headlights; the record was soon almost sold out. But the investment when making an LP is much bigger than that required for a CD. I used money that I didn't have, I used my dangerous credit card for it and I think I'm still paying back the debt. A distributor from Glasgow ordered copies that I sent and never got paid for – of course, the numbers are small, but for a very small underground label like Headlights these things are important. It's better business to put out 50 copies on CD-R that one sells immediately, thus achieving a small profit, rather than making an LP where you invest much more and the return comes slowly.

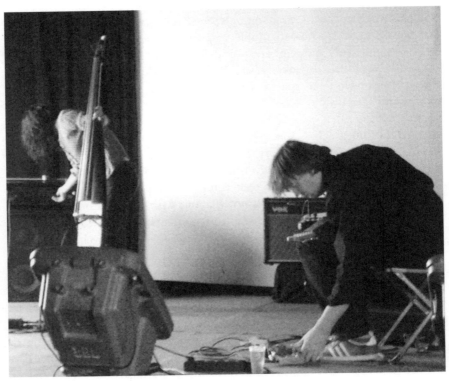

Margarida Garcia and Thurston at ZDB, Lisbon, April 23, 2013.

Credit – Björn Schmelzer

III: Beneath Trident's Tomb
Twilight
(Century Media, 2014)

Keith Wood: When Thurston was working on the Twilight project he was listening to a lot of black metal. He lent me his car while he was away and there was a whole bag-full of tapes and CDs in the car. He came back with a lot of heavier ideas – he'd copped a few black metal moves – but his playing anyway is related to that kind of sound. It's very textural, very ambient, and he'd been listening to black metal for a very long time.

Neill Jameson: *Daydream Nation* was a record that really changed my perspective on things. There are some riffs on that record that you could put side by side with a lot of the classic Norwegian black metal – there's stuff that would fit perfectly on Mayhem's *De Mysteriis Dom Sathanas*. Thurston knew more about underground black metal than most people who have been involved in the scene for 20–30 years. He'd bring out his laptop and show me recordings he'd picked up over the years – this was really fancy shit he was into, this wasn't casual fandom, he was going deep into the archives. He knew the history, the intentions, the aesthetic. He had a full appreciation of the genre and it was clear this wasn't some vanity project where someone comes into something they don't understand just to have people talk about it.

Stavros Giannopoulos: He would go to tons of black metal shows – a lot of people were undoubtedly looking at Thurston and thinking, 'What's this guy doing here?' or just wouldn't have recognised him. His lexicon of black metal was insane. He's so into being noisy and abrasive that it makes sense. Thurston told us that he had an idea of starting a cassette-only label focused on black metal where no one would know it, but he would do all the bands, just him. Hilarious that a super-prolific guy like Thurston would go that far to, more or less, have that joke on everybody! I've met people who are nowhere near Thurston's level but who think that they are so important – but there's Thurston hanging around with us, just asking us where the record stores are: "Hey, let's go get tacos! Margaritas!"

Sanford Parker: During the making of the second Twilight album, we were in a studio recording and the studio had a subscription to *Decibel* magazine. The new edition came in, I was flicking through, there was an interview with Thurston on his obsession with black metal. At the studio I owned at the time, my partner Jeremy Lemos was the sound guy for Sonic Youth. Thurston's literally name-checking everybody in the room – I joked about it, someone else said we should get him in on the next record and we laughed. Afterward, though, I thought it was a cool idea so I got his email from Jeremy, hit him up one day, told him who was in Twilight, asked if he'd want to get involved and he replied, "Yeah man, FUCK yeah! I totally want to do it."

Stavros Giannopoulos: We used to joke around because Jeremy was saying, "Thurston would love this!" We were very, "Sure, whatever; Thurston Moore is going to come to Chicago and record with our dumb asses?" Then lo and behold, there was an email chain going around between us all with Thurston.

Neill Jameson: We decided to do the record because we wanted to work with Thurston and we wanted to work with Sanford and Stavros again, so we just gritted our teeth and did it. We all had chaotic personal lives around the time of this record, so even for us to get together and do another Twilight record was difficult enough. The record title was something Jef and I came up with when we were talking about how there were initially three of us – a trident – and there wasn't going to be a band after this record. So it was a heavy-handed metaphor. The Twilight records are so diverse; there's no unifying sound beyond making something that was really ugly, dark and reflective of what was going on in our lives.

Sanford Parker: A big part of the Twilight sound is Jef Whitehead. He grew up in the Bay Area as much on shoegaze and post-punk as black metal. That guy is incredible. He can pick up any instrument; he can come up with the most bizarre, amazing riffs and patterns you've ever heard. I've seen him do it time and again.

Jef Whitehead: Ha! I played most of the bass and all the drums on those records but the core was always the vocals to me. I met Neill in 2004 when Krieg opened for Antaeus. I was well into Krieg, Weltmacht and his other work, so I was definitely excited to work with him. His music has always had a firm hold on the heart of what black metal is to me. In my opinion, the self-titled is the only Twilight that is a solely black metal record. *Monument To Time End* and *III: Beneath Trident's Tomb* seem much more experimental, for lack of a better term.

Stavros Giannopoulos: We did a week, maybe 10 days, before Thurston got there – we got some stuff down, all very unfinished and no vocals, then we took a week off. Then we did another week to 10 days later the same month, when we reconvened with Thurston and Neill to go over what we had down.

Sanford Parker: It'd start out with a loose idea, a riff, then Jef would go and record drums to a click-track. We'd arrange the drum parts, he'd lay down a bass track, then he or Stavros would lay down guitar and we'd build off of that. Then Neill would go out there and come up with some crazy-ass vocals over the top. If anybody had an idea we'd listen and try it, then decide if it was going anywhere. Everyone was involved in everything – if someone had an idea for a keyboard part I'd try it; otherwise, if I had an idea they'd let me just go for it.

Neill Jameson: I did the majority of the lyrics with Jef giving a huge contribution as well. I use the cut-up method, putting together lyrics as I'm singing them. I take pages and pages of lyrics and, while I'm going, I'll just pull out a line here or there, pull from different pages. Once a song was down I'd put the lyrics in order.

They'd done some skeleton tracks – Jef, Stavros and Sanford – then I flew in the same day Thurston did and we were there the last five-six days. That's when all the vocals were done – it was dynamic, not the usual relaxed environment. Everyone was constantly working, building our own parts, exchanging tons of ideas. It felt like a really collective work effort rather than something where you bring in your own ideas and work them out in isolation. We had expected that we would come in, do the record, then Thurston would throw some stuff over it. We didn't expect that he'd become a member of the band but that's what happened; it wasn't a guest appearance; he was intrinsic to this band – the first one in the studio every day and the last one out. He's part of every single second of that record. We would wake up, go to the studio and have coffee then we'd get to work until 11 at night, sometimes later, with minimal breaks.

Stavros Giannopoulos: I walked in with a couple of riffs but near everything else that I did was done on the spot. There were some things that we walked in with that were quite well put together; then there were things that Jef had in his head that he'd never even played. There was a lot of improvisation – it wasn't totally thought out or planned. Jef would be like, "This is the bass layer of it," and we'd be thinking, 'This sounds so stupid.' But the end result would be amazing. Thurston was on top of it all, he'd suddenly start doing things – I can't tell you how many times Sanford and I just stood staring, thinking, 'How is he making that work?'

Sanford Parker: When he walked into the studio I had all these amps set up, we hadn't talked a lot about what he wanted gear-wise. He just said, "Whatever, man," walked up to the first amp he saw: "This one will do." I had it mic'ed up, he plugged in – me, Jef and Neill just stood there watching as he went fucking insane, making all this crazy noise. I ran into the control room, whipped open ProTools, armed the track and hit 'record' as fast as I could. He did that for 20 minutes – he was standing on top of the amp, throwing his guitar around, jumping off. The very first thing he did – we hadn't even played him a track. We were in awe, just stood mouthing like, 'What the fuck…?' When he was done he looked over and just said, "I hope you got that." That was him just testing out an amp – it was like a show, I could have released just that and people would have loved it.

To me it was inspiring. When I've seen guitar players who try to come even remotely close to what he's done, they roll in with a suitcase full of effects pedals and these crazy handmade guitars – then to see him roll in with this beat-up Jazzmaster and just a Whole Foods shopping bag of generic guitar-centre pedals you could buy anywhere, then just watch him, with so little, make something that sounds amazing, it makes you realise it's nothing to do with the gear. You could hand him anything and he'd make it awesome.

Jef Whitehead: He nailed all his parts pretty much first-take. Pretty inspiring watching him play, especially on 'Oh, Wretched Sun'. Probably my favourite track on the record because of his soloing on the chorus. We were all in the control room when he was tracking and everyone just looked at each other: a unanimous "*YESSS!*"

Stavros Giannopoulos: Hot dogs are a big thing here in Chicago – there are a lot of late-night hot-dog places. So one night, Sanford, Thurston and I are hungry and we go out to this famous stand – nowhere to sit, just a window with a shelf where you can eat your food. So we're telling insane

246

tour stories. Sanford and I have our badges of honour, but Thurston starts talking about Neil Young doing this thing called the Bridge School Benefit where they play acoustic – Sonic Youth were playing and during their set he looks over and Paul McCartney is there. So Thurston ends up talking to Paul McCartney and brings up that they're all big fans of McCartney's brother who went under a different name, Mike McGear, and put out a weird psychedelic poetry record. Paul looked at him and said, "Y'know, in my entire career, no one has ever brought up my brother's record to me. I'm going to go give him a call – I've got to go do that!" So that's it, we're sat eating hot dogs and Thurston tells us about how he stumped Paul McCartney.

Neill Jameson: My favourite memory: the last night, Thurston was going to be heading home. Thurston, Jef and I shared a cab and Thurston had the idea of just stopping at a bar real quick – we did a shot to commemorate the end of the record. It was a really special moment where I could stop and see that we'd done something really important for ourselves, and it didn't matter what the reception would be. You just had to savour it.

Transient – 'Home'
Krieg
(Init Records, 2015)

Neill Jameson: We did 'Home', the song for Krieg, in 2014. My two passions are music and literature. I always like to try and blend the two together – so I'd written a long-form spoken-word piece, but I don't particularly like hearing myself speak. So I had the idea to take people who would be able to read it in a manner befitting what I'd written. Dwid Hellion from Integrity and Thurston are both very unique voices – Dwid was easy to get on, Thurston I waited. I was hesitant, then, eventually, I sent him the piece and asked him if he'd be willing to do this for me. He said yes and by the time we entered the studio the disc arrived. It's one of those moments where you give someone something you've done to see how they're going to work with it – and it matches exactly what you wanted. It was really important to me because I don't publish lyrics and I don't sing very clearly, and so this was one of the first times where I had something that was direct and clear and you could tell my intention and the point I was trying to get across. For him to take the time, take it seriously... it means more to me than most work I've done in 20 years.

The Best Day
Thurston Moore
(Matador, 2014)

Deb Googe: Recording the album was completely unexpected as far as I was concerned. I'd only really met Thurston properly a few days before. James Sedwards suggested me and Thurston messaged me to see if I would be interested in playing bass for them, and of course I was... it's Thurston Moore! I was really nervous and added to that James is no slouch, he's an absolutely amazing guitarist, so all in all I was pretty intimidated.

James Sedwards: We only had a few days to make the record. Thurston and me played the songs less than 10 times before the recording of the album took place. The biggest challenge was to get the rhythm section up to speed as quickly as possible because it was the first time Deb and Steve had played them. Even though Thurston and me had played the songs, they were constantly changing and even during the session the material was still developing. The structures were often changing take by take and new dynamics were being put in. Bringing in a rhythm section was obviously a big change, so new aspects of the songs were coming to light, plus there were a couple of songs that none of us had played – 'The Best Day' itself was worked up there and then. A few songs developed with everyone coming up with their parts and if a new direction we liked suddenly unfurled, then we went with it as there were few preconceived ideas as to how the songs should sound. When you hear that record it really is day one for the group.

Deb Googe: The thing that will always stick in my head is Thurston's teaching and conducting method. He would basically take us through parts of a song and give each part a label. Once he had shown us all the parts we would run through the song with him bellowing out the next part-name just before we needed to change, but obviously when it came to recording he couldn't shout because we didn't want the guitar mics to pick up his bellowing. So instead he just wrote letters on various scraps of paper, spread them on the floor and kind of conducted with his foot – while playing guitar. So I'm sat there desperately trying to remember how to play section 'C' while staring at his foot the whole time, waiting for the change. All of this was being recorded, that's how rehearsed we were. I knew that Steve [Shelley] was in London for a few days, I think he was on his way to start a tour with Lee [Ranaldo]. I thought the main priority in the studio was that Thurston wanted to try and get Steve to track some drums for the record. I thought maybe he just wanted to add some bass to give it a more live band feel and so Steve had a bass to play along to, but not necessarily that he would actually record the bass. On the first day, however, I didn't go into the studio, the others recorded a couple of ideas for tracks and sent me the links so I had a chance to listen to them overnight, but that was kind of it. So I turned up on my first day with no idea of what I was going to do and very little concept of what they were intending to do either!

James Sedwards: My guitar parts were loosely guided by Thurston in as much as he had written the initial riffs for each song, and it was my job to come up with an appropriate counterpoint. A lot of the time we were in unison because it seemed appropriate and we liked the power, simplicity and overtones that came from that. For the moments when we were playing diverging parts, there was never any particular direction from Thurston other than to say whether or not he liked what I was doing.

Radieux Radio: I had always been interested in Thurston's lyrical work and his poetry. He has a poetry imprint called Flowers And Cream and he published a poet called Cody-Rose Clevidence – she's transgender, as am I. Being transgender means being beyond titles like poetess or male or female – that's an important part of the message of my work, that it's genderless. Also I write a lot in French and Arabic: it's the sense of being apart from any sense of nation. If it were up to me, I don't think I'd choose English as the language these lyrics emerged in – but Thurston doesn't speak Arabic yet! I think English is in a terrible state of privilege right now, I don't believe it's the language we should be speaking – something referenced in the song 'Vocabularies' which is about being born into a generation of star-children who are here to teach us to move forward without borders and without this antiquated language that implies superiority. There's a mention of a woman being given away in marriage – which is a disgusting reference to our past, to people being thought of as possessions to be traded.

There's another song on that album: it's named for a woman called Grace Lake, she was a member of the Angry Brigade and a poet too. It's all instrumental but it's beautiful, just like she was. She studied poetry after she came out of jail – she was one of the Stoke Newington Eight, which was one of the longest trials in the history of the Old Bailey. There's so much work Thurston has recorded that's instrumental-only, that he doesn't have lyrics for. When he feels he needs something he'll call me, or text me from the studio, or play me something and ask if I have something for it. It's a collaboration – he's not a lonely person, he's a leader, a conductor, he wants to draw things in from everyone. *The Best Day*, interestingly, he just played some riffs for me – I took poetry I had already written, moved them around a bit, gave them to him and he moved them around a bit more. He still has this wonderful punk element, this chaos. Sometimes I would give him a lyric and he would ask me if we could sharpen it up – he would tell me if it was too gentle for him. He's a good editor that way. Living in Thurston's world things have to be dynamic, so sometimes I'm too 'peace and love' and he doesn't want just that – he wants ecstatic peace.

Deb Googe: Café Oto in August was the first gig with the four of us. Steve, James, Thurston and I. Steve had flown over from New York because we were supposed to be rehearsing for a tour. I think Thurston was just hanging out at Café Oto, as he does, when he realised they didn't have anything on, so he asked if we could rehearse there and the people at Café Oto were up for it. Then Thurston figured we might as well invite friends along, and then it was friends of friends, and then it was just open house really. The four of us hadn't played together since we recorded the album, three or four months before, so there was absolutely no preparation involved which was… interesting. In a lot of ways it was great, because I just didn't have time to worry about it too much and you can't really get a better way of practising for a tour than playing in front of an audience.

The Jeffrey Lee Pierce Sessions Project – *Axels & Sockets* – 'Shame And Pain'/'Nobody's City' Nick Cave/Jeffrey Lee Pierce/Iggy Pop/ Mark Stewart/Thurston Moore (Glitterhouse Records, 2014)

Jim Sclavunos: I knew individuals who were organising this Jeffrey Lee Pierce tribute project – they reached out to me for contacts and eventually asked, "Do you want to do something?" At that point the project needed fresh blood to push things along – that's where I came in: calling musicians in, mixing, producing, playing drums; they needed a lot of different roles filled at that point, so I helped push it to the finish line. The album was third in a series of albums based on unreleased demos Jeffrey recorded before he died.

When Thurston moved to London I saw him pretty shortly after he arrived and asked him if he wanted to play. He said, "Why not?" – didn't take much discussion. He added guitar parts to a song that I mixed and played drums on, 'Nobody's City', that has Nick Cave and Iggy Pop doing a vocal duet. There were already several tracks of other guitarists on the song, but Thurston's guitar parts were better tailored to the end result and were a unifying thing. All these musicians, they had never all played together on a record; I think it was a great tribute to Jeffrey. It was done for a charity set up by Jeffrey's sister, with considerable help from a fellow named Cypress Grove, a former collaborator of Jeffrey's.

The Polar Bear – 'Six, Two, Thirteen' Michael Chapman (Blast First Petite, 2014)

Michael Chapman: It started in Amherst, Massachusetts. I was playing at the Unitary Church and Thurston, with his whole band, came down to the gig and we had dinner afterward – which annoyed me a bit because we went to a vegetarian restaurant, which is not my style whatsoever! When I was talking to Thurston he said, "Do you know these people?" And he mentioned John Martyn, Mike Cooper, Ralph McTell, Roy Harper – all the English acoustic guitar players. "Yeah, I know those guys." He asked, "Can you ring 'em up then and see if they would send me recordings of three tracks and give me *carte blanche* to do whatever I want on them?" So I told him I'd give them a bell. I thought that was interesting, to give away control of your record to somebody you've never met before!

I rang round; in the end it was only me, Mike Cooper and Wizz Jones that sent him stuff. I got some rough mixes back a while later. Thurston was working with Jim O'Rourke and it sounded to me like they'd got a load of different guitars in a load of different tunings just leaning against amplifiers feeding back – then mixed it. I never asked if that's what happened but I did think it was pretty intriguing. Then they were working in downtown New York on 9/11, the studio was just a block away from Ground Zero and was wrapped in plastic for over a year because it was so contaminated, with the tapes still in there. Whether that's still the case or not, I don't know, but the whole thing ground to a halt.

He and I got closer musically and the outcome was the 2013 tour called *Acoustic Fire*, where we'd each play acoustic guitar then let it all turn into a big feedback jam at the end of each show. I'd never done that before. We didn't rehearse – we just plugged in and let fly; great! We'd play to people who had known me and known my playing for years, then see their shock when I did something completely different, expanding the parameters. People saying, "Hell, never thought we'd see you play like that!" I'd say, "Feeling's mutual, I never thought I'd see me play like that." It was all new so I enjoyed myself. Reactions were generally good – there were two guys at Colston Hall in Bristol [UK] who were incandescent with rage; who stormed out swearing at us. That was great! I should have paid them to do it every night!

The piece on *The Polar Bear*, I realised I had all these live tapes with Thurston so I just picked one – that was the end of the show, if we play like that there's nothing to follow that. The way it starts off, I play a guitar riff, recognisable as a riff, then Thurston destroys it and I keep dragging it back in because Thurston is very much anti-melody, while I'm about melody and rhythm. So to have my guitar riff demolished by Thurston was a fun concept. With improv sometimes you go see someone play and you don't know if they've started yet – are they just pissing about, tuning, or have they started? And how the hell are they going to stop? Mostly, people play too long because they don't know how to stop. I don't think Thurston and I intended to let that go for 12 minutes, but when you're having fun why give up? It's not like a written piece of music with a static ending and when you get that far you go home. We played on a 50/50 level. The first thing you do is leave your ego behind. I thoroughly expected to get the short end of the stick when it came to money because Thurston is a lot more famous than I am, so I asked what we were going to do and he came right back, "Straight split, Mick." It was the same on-stage.

Oh Michael Look What You've Done: Friends Play Michael Chapman – 'It Didn't Work Out' Thurston Moore (Tompkins Square, 2014)

Michael Chapman: The tribute record came from my wife, Andru. It took her two years to assemble that. It was for my 70th birthday – she spent two years phoning people I knew. She was going to do just 50 copies for myself and friends, it was just called *Happy Birthday*. Josh Rosenthal at Tompkin Square got hold of a copy somewhere and cherry-picked it. Lucinda Williams doing one of my songs, I'd never have dreamt life could get that good.

John Russell and Thurston on-stage for John's 60th Birthday at Café Oto, London, December 19, 2014.
Credit – Helen Petts

With... – 'The Second Half Of The Second Half'
John Russell
(Emanem, 2015)

John Russell: My earliest involvement with free improvisation was on electric guitar and at the time I was compared to an amalgam of Derek Bailey, Pete Townshend and Sonny Sharrock, but I wanted to find out more about the guitar itself, dig deeper into the nature of the instrument and find my own voice. That is why I ditched electric playing in 1976 and played solely acoustic. However, a few years ago I decided to get an electric guitar and have used it on quite a few occasions now. It really is quite a different animal with the biggest difference being response times. An electric is much slower than acoustic and it misses a lot of picking-hand subtleties. It also sounds different and it takes me longer to understand what I am hearing. In some ways, I have to let the guitar go its own way and play itself while I make adjustments to what is happening.

An old colleague and friend, the Swedish saxophonist Mats Gustafsson, was playing with Thurston at Café Oto in London and I was invited to join them. Thurston then invited me for a duo concert at the same venue some time afterward; just the two of us all evening on both electric and acoustic instruments. It was a good opportunity to get to know each other's musical identities and capabilities. I don't think I had any doubts about it working once we had started playing together. It quickly became clear that Thurston had a very open way of playing that left a lot of room for fellow musicians and that he knew how to listen. It may sound silly but a lot of players don't know how to do that when it comes to improvising. His playing feels a bit akin to folk music, maybe to do with different tunings and also the way he picks and strums the instrument. At the same time it's very rocky in an open way; a kind of free-pulse thing that Hendrix had rather than a tight 'math-rock' sort of thing. It makes for a welcoming, come-on-in-and-join-the-fun feel. For me, I try to use all elements of the guitar and listen to all the sounds, and in some ways try to frame or encapsulate the other musician's playing in a context that I feel brings out the best in the music. I suppose Thurston is saying, 'Come on in, the water's great,' and I'm saying, 'Don't worry, you aren't going to drown.'

For the CD and the concert we only had a short spot, and I was waiting for a quadruple heart bypass operation. I made a joke that the audience would have to imagine me jumping from speaker cabinets and playing the guitar behind my head, but apart from saying that I didn't make any concessions. I wanted something that was a contrast to the other groups I was playing in that evening, and also something that pointed back to my early days playing in a rock group. I love the noise, you know? On the gig, I remember Thurston was taking care of a lot of the detail and I was making more of the din, if you see what I mean!

My birthday falls on December 19 and every year I would get that thing of, "We bought you one big thing rather than two small ones and anyway, you need a new shirt for school." I've also been running this series of concerts, Mopomoso, for years and every year we have a Christmas party. I thought about doing something at that but then thought, 'I'm 60 and I want my own birthday party at least once in my life!' I got in touch with the venue and they were up for it. Then I had to go to hospital as I was having chest pains, breathing difficulties and swollen legs. That was October 22 and I was kept in for a month while tests were carried out. They found I had had a massive heart attack and that only 25 percent of my left ventricle was working, with all three arteries to the heart blocked. I had also told the doctors that I really needed to do the gig and to avoid that date for any surgery. This meant I was out and about for the day, after being stuck in a hospital, raring to go!

Thurston Moore: Even now, I'm still finding out about improvisational music – it's one of the most interesting forms of music I've ever dealt with, especially not coming out of any kind of academic playing or jazz schooling. Just the other night, seeing John Tilbury play with John Butcher and Thomas Lehn was amazing. It still intrigues me, informs me, inspires me.

Cuts Of Guilt, Cuts Deeper
Mats Gustafsson/Merzbow/Thurston Moore/ Balazs Pandi
(RareNoise Records, 2015)

Daniel Sandor: The biggest part of my job was to find the right place, that's where I contributed. I went to 20 studios before that where we could possibly record. I was looking for a place where it felt good to be – it had to be big, it had to have some kind of acoustics, but more than that I was thinking about the situation. I know Balazs and I know he'd survive at the North Pole, but for Masami [Akita] I was thinking about what he would feel when he entered each studio. Then I found this place! Park Studios in Wembley – a decent music studio, but the weird thing about it was there was an indoor skate park right next to it. It was a nice studio – nothing special, modern, very professional – but with this skate-park I felt it would sound like nothing else; it's like an aeroplane hangar, so acoustically it's interesting but also, just to go there, seeing the ramps – I felt that would be inspiring. So we brought a multicore cable and wired up the skate park, ready to set up the band there.

I had the chance to go a couple of days before, walk around, make drawings. I went there on the morning of the recording, met the in-house engineer who helped me set up the backline, the microphones, we checked the levels as best we could. Everyone arrived one by one, so over and over there was this, "Oh wow! What the fuck is this?!" That was important for the recording; they all left wherever they came from, just a normal day going to do some recording at a normal studio like any other – then they walked into the live room and, "Wow!"

Balazs Pandi: Everyone was really excited when they saw it. Masami is 60, he's sliding on his ass down the ramp to get to his equipment and it wasn't a small ramp! The amps were up at the top except for Thurston's – his was next to my drums so he could hear himself – while Masami's and Mats Gustafsson's amps were up on top.

Daniel Sandor: The ramp was a big, wooden, U-shaped structure about five metres high. It's shaped like a satellite dish, a bowl which focuses the sound. You have the drums within this structure creating a very powerful ambience, then, above this, a metal structure with completely different reverb and acoustic properties.

Balazs Pandi: It worked so well. I had no monitor – none of us did – but I could hear everything in perfect balance. We had headphones and all I asked was to get more of Thurston's amp because we were next to each other divided by a soundproof piece of Perspex, so my microphones wouldn't be audible in his microphones – which meant I had a hard time hearing him without assistance. I could hear everything else blasting in full detail.

Daniel Sandor: All I needed to do was sit back and listen, travel with the guys. My job, once they started, was not to disturb and to make sure the recording was running. I really believe in energies in recording situations – it's very dramatic sometimes, how much everything around you influences you, how certain people can make a very unique emotion appear in the room. Recording these four guys, you could feel that; they were travelling together, sharing the same moment.

Balazs Pandi: I played in London at an All Tomorrow's Parties night – Thurston played and afterward we hung out backstage, talking. We'd been on email: 'Do you want to do this?' 'Yes!' 'Can you do it on these dates?' 'No I can't.' This was the first time we could really talk. Thurston asked me whether we could do this thing with Masami and Mats – we had a gig booked as the trio. I told Thurston the date and that we had a day off before – which, coincidentally, was the only day he was free. He was coming in from Paris then the next day he'd fly out to the US. It was a miracle we could get together for that one day. Thurston could have asked to relax for that one day before flying but no, he said, "We have to do this record." Mats flew over. Masami took a day out while on tour when he could have been playing a show.

I landed from Budapest the day before so I could be there early to start on the drums. Masami played a show and so arrived by train. Mats came from Austria while Thurston had played Paris the night before so he got there last, about half an hour before the recording, checked his amp, then we played for hours. We had a lot of material to draw from by evening. It was intense. We played four-five hours, four takes – one of which was an hour and 10 minutes.

After the session I went to a restaurant with Mats and Masami and we couldn't even talk, we just sat there staring, our minds were totally dried out. We each walked back to the hotel, said, "Goodbye, see you tomorrow," and I think everyone passed out. You get really exhausted by the loudness of it. What I do is really physical. These are all long pieces, which means I don't stop at all – I just drum through, maybe, an hour at a time. It's heavy on the body over that many hours.

These kinds of recordings can be easily sabotaged, not by technical issues, but by ego issues. If you're open about everyone's ideas, then there isn't much that can go wrong. I like these musical situations where I feel I'm meditating: to reach it everyone needs to participate and not set anyone off. I'm addicted on a level that's in no way a conscious decision, but it happened to be that I didn't play written, structured music for years. Playing in situations like this is the most precious thing, and I always approach these situations with curiosity, as it's always interesting to see what changes will happen to my playing or more generally within me as a human being.

Then of course there are the off-stage times. Hanging with this quartet is always dead serious. Charity shops, bookstores, record stores – we hit 'em all. I feel like one of these small fish that cling to the big sharks, I'm eating up all the little chunks left over in the digging carnage. 'You know this? You got this? You MUST have this!' There are countless incredible records and books that I otherwise wouldn't have gotten to know, and a lot of inspiration that ends up in my playing too, so it's a double win whenever we team up.

Untitled
Jooklo Duo/Thurston Moore/Dylan Nyoukis
(Chocolate Monk, 2015)

Virginia Genta: That's the recording from the Brighton show. The first show, Nottingham, David [Vanzan] played drums so heavily that he got some bloody blisters. So as a result, the day after he couldn't play drums! He then decided to get a piano off the van that we just picked up in Leicester and he played that instead. So it was all totally improvised, definitely. Listening is the most important part. You must already know what could happen and what your answer could be.

Dylan Nyoukis: That was a real fun gig. David, the percussionist from Jooklo Duo, had played a fucking flyer the night before, blistered his hands like a goob! So the drums were out for the night, which in retrospect was a good thing. Jooklo dragged a vintage piano out of the back of their van. David got down on that. Thurston on guitar, Virginia – lungs of a legend – blew sax like a fucker, and I did tapes, voice and a wee bit of dancing. It got fruity!

Virginia Genta: The Nottingham show had worked out great from the very first minute. That was the first time we ever played with Thurston. It was pure joy. Something like six more bands played before us. The room was as hot as hell and the stage only had red lights. Everyone was waiting for a blast, so Thurston said, "Let's play a very quiet one!" and we agreed on that. But sure, after the first very quiet and meditative five minutes the guitar started getting nasty and I flew in it and then the drums got insane and from then on it just kept growing and growing! I think that it was natural to have a completely different show on the day after, since it couldn't get stronger than that and David had those nasty blisters. Dylan joined us in Brighton, so the whole vibe had changed; it got even more abstract there.

Me and David met at art school in 1999. We were both 15 years old at the time, growing up in a very depressed area located an hour west of Venice, a place where nothing ever happens. And that's definitely what brought us to find ways of escape like art and music. In 2003 I bought my first saxophone at a flea market, and while still in school I recorded my first release, a three-inch CD-R that I credited to Jooklo, and that's where we first used that word. In 2004 we played our first few shows as Jooklo Duo and a couple of years later we started touring massively, and never stopped since then.

We had our first contact with Thurston through underground cult label Qbico that put out a crazy amount of limited-edition vinyl between 2000–2010, with all sorts of handmade covers. Qbico released our first three records in 2007 and they put them in one of these 26 boxes that they used to do, numbered with the alphabet letters. I personally carved the front letters on all the Jooklo boxes and when we had to choose one for ourselves we picked 'T' for 'Troglosound', our own label. But Emanuele Pinotti, Qbico head, told me that he already reserved all 'T' letters of those boxes for a guy called Thurston Moore. So I was like, "Uh. All right, then we'll take the 'Z', never mind." That was a funny start!

In summer 2013, we happened to be playing as guests of German collective Metabolismus when they were opening for Chelsea Light Moving on a few German shows. One of those nights, Thurston told us he moved to London and he would like to play with us there some day. A couple of months later we performed at Colour Out of Space in Brighton and stayed at some friend of Dylan's, who had a very special piano at his place, really small and light, only five octaves, we'd never seen one like that before. So as soon as we flew back home from Brighton, David started looking for a piano like that on the web and found one in Leicester. We called the seller and bought it and then realised we had to pick it up somehow. So we started planning a tour that would allow us to drive from Italy to the UK and back, in order to get the piano! As the tour was building up, I asked Thurston if he still wanted to play together in London and he was up for it, but for some reason it couldn't work in London. So I wrote to Steve of Harbinger Sound in Nottingham and he said he would love to set up a show for us. Then I wrote Dylan that we were about to tour and I told him we were playing in Nottingham with Thurston, so he said he would love to do a Brighton show too and yeah, that's how we all got together and how we are all connected. All because of that piano! Life is magic...

Live At White Cube
London Sinfonietta/Christian Marclay/
Thurston Moore
(The Vinyl Factory, 2015)

Christian Marclay: In 1994, I made an acoustic guitar that had 12 music boxes embedded in its body and, in 2010, I invited Thurston to perform on that guitar at the Whitney Museum during my exhibition, entitled *Festival*. It was an amazing performance with a very intense energy; I thought he was going to break this fragile instrument. I took little, Swiss-made, 18-note, wind-up music-box mechanisms and mounted them within the guitar body. In the context of this exhibition – where I presented my graphic scores which were being interpreted daily in the galleries – I thought of this guitar not so much as a score, but as a way of providing an instrument that had limitations and built-in musical quotes, thereby influencing the performance; very much like my graphic scores which are open yet there's a structure that influences the performer. It's all about prompting a different type of performance.

An early influence was Fred Frith [British experimentalist and co-founder of the influential Henry Cow], who I'd seen in New York experimenting in the late seventies with his 'table-guitar' performances. He would place the guitar lying flat on a table and would operate on it, in a way, by applying different devices like a drill, an EBow or little motors, strings, brushes, whatever. It also comes from my belief in improvisation, and in music as a social activity that brings people together. It's what I love about music – it's a very social thing and that's the magic; to get up on-stage and just do it; to have this unpredictable communion with other performers. That, of course, never translates on a record; it becomes something else. On record it's been fixed, so you don't have the tension that arises when you're there experiencing a performance. There's a tension to performance that you can never capture on a recording. A record is a done deal – unless you scratch it, which is what I do.

My show at White Cube in London was a way to address these interests, providing a platform, a structure, something for music to happen in. It was my way to participate without actually performing much, still keeping the music open and free. The exhibition focused on the performance aspects of my work, so it was nice to invite all of these performers I've collaborated with, to get them to be part of it and also to celebrate them. We didn't have a budget to bring people from overseas, so if people were in town during those three months, or if they lived relatively close by in Europe and had another reason to come to London, then we'd chip in for airfare. As Thurston is in London a lot lately, he was one of my first guests.

The London Sinfonietta had approached me to create a piece, but instead I suggested they be the band in residence. It was great to offer a classically-trained ensemble as interpreters for these guest musicians and composers. The London Sinfonietta has very skilled musicians and most of the time they're asked to play written music, so for them it was also an interesting challenge to work with musicians who don't necessarily write notes and charts.

I wasn't involved in what Thurston chose to do – I just said, "Here's the ensemble, here's your slot, do whatever you want." But the context of the exhibition had an influence; there were all these glass vessels around, beer-drinking glasses. Also you could hear in the background the sounds of clinking glass from my video installation in the hallway, so it wasn't a silent environment or a neutral space, but these conditions could shape the music and I encouraged that. There were restrictions in that sense – the ambient sound, the resonant space of a concrete gallery and hard surfaces, which are not ideal. Those were the conditions and people did whatever they wanted – some people exploited them more than others. I did a piece with two musical saw players and a group of people rubbing the glasses with wet fingers, like a glass harmonica, and I asked Thurston to sit in. It sounded very ethereal and it's also on the LP.

Also satisfying was the diversity of the audience; the London Sinfonietta brought their audience and the improv scene brought theirs, rock fans as well as families. The art world came to see an exhibition but also encountered new music; usually they're very reluctant, but if they're confronted with this music in a familiar context they end up liking it. There were a lot of children, parents with babies deciding to cry as soon as there was a silence. All that stuff wound up on the recordings.

With The Vinyl Factory we built the first ever portable pressing plant, a hydraulic vinyl pressing machine that allowed us to press records in the gallery. We also had screen printers from Coriander Studio making the covers, which were collages I had designed. The idea was that if you came to a performance one weekend you could get the recording of it the following weekend. I had to constantly design covers for the next pressings, it was all very intense; all of this process was part of the exhibition. The recordings weren't always the best quality but that wasn't the point, it was about the spirit of the show, how these things happen, from live music to packaged vinyl.

Parallelogram
John Moloney/Thurston Moore
(Three Lobed, 2016)

Cory Rayborn: I wanted to do another big, multi-artist project that consisted more of 'separate' titles rather than a big, lidded box. I didn't want to do seven-inches so I felt that split LPs might be a good approach, especially if I could pair the right artists together. Getting the line-up together took about six months – getting the rest of the project together and into a finished collection you can have and hold took about another 18. Ha! Long enough for us to have a kid in the middle of the process!

John Moloney: Thurston and I did a show for Three Lobed recordings; they did a day festival in North Carolina so we went down and played a set. One piece of it was based around 'Ono Soul' from the *Psychic Hearts* record – the label really liked it so I helped them edit it down, made a few tweaks to the board recording. That same day, right after that, we did a trio with Merzbow that was also recorded – we wanted to put it out instead but we couldn't get in touch with Merzbow in time, so it was easier to use 'Ono Soul'.

Cory Rayborn: Thurston and John were among the earliest folks to say that they were going to be in the series. Their commitment was verbal and came about backstage following a Chelsea Light Moving set in Raleigh, North Carolina. Later that same year, Thurston and John turned in a

262

smoking live set at a day-long festival that I had assembled along with my friends at WXDU-FM.

Thurston and all of the Sonic Youth folks are exceptionally kind and big-hearted people. The thing that I admire about them all so much is that they are all so plugged in with the scene and, really, fans. They're out there at shows, catching sets, watching things that they enjoy and staying plugged into the pulse of what is going on. Thurston's enthusiasm never flags or wanes. Every encounter I've ever had with him has been exceptionally gracious and personable. No matter how many releases I put out, it will always be this old hobby project back in my law-school apartment in my mind. Thurston's involvement, especially in its constancy, has definitely served as a sort of personal validation of everything I've tried to do. I know that if I am doing something that interests him in putting out multiple things with me over a long stretch of time then I'm doing something right.

I don't think the sort of success or scale that some of those eighties and nineties labels achieved is necessarily achievable today. The nature of the business is a limiting factor for sure. Those labels got to live through the boomtime of CDs and indie distribution – these days they would have been fighting over digital streaming scraps and the remnants of vinyl culture. Changing technology has certainly made recording one's own work a lot easier, cheaper and efficient. There's a democratising upside to that – fewer barriers to entry, greater ability to evaluate one's own work – as well as a bit of a downside in that there is less of an editorial eye or ear cast on the recorded work. A total game-changer.

John Moloney: That was September 2013, at the beginning of a tour where we did three Caught On Tape shows – the festival, then another was on a rolling train exhibition across the country called *Station To Station*. They rented these luxury train cars and this one train made the journey all the way across country. Doug Aitken is the artist who put it together – it was really well executed, all these visual artists would come on and off the train, musicians would join and do a stint on the train, everyone doing things in conjunction with one another. We boarded at Washington DC and rode it all night to Pittsburgh, where the train stopped; at the station they had a big, multimedia art exhibition and we played a concert there. Then we got back on the train and rode it to Chicago, where we played at the station. The next day we got up and drove back to Pennsylvania, where we met up with the band and went on a Chelsea Light Moving tour that lasted a few weeks. Thurston and I did 'Schizophrenia' while on the train and there's a pro-shot video of us in one of the carriages performing on this moving train. We played it straight – it was wild for me. I said, "Steve Shelley's going to slit my throat when he sees this video!"

Marshmallow Moon Decorum
Thurston Moore/Frank Rosaly
(Corbett Vs. Dempsey, 2016)

Frank Rosaly: I was put in touch with Thurston because he was supposed to play with another drummer that night, but had to cancel. I was basically a last minute fill-in. I had a show earlier that night with the band Health&Beauty at a bar called The Whistler, and then ran across the street to play with Thurston. I still had that music in my head a bit when I switched gears and played with him. It was a great night, packed full with enthusiastic freaks hanging on everything we were playing. The room felt so charged and I felt really free to experiment. I remember feeling like I was playing without making much use of my developed language; it was more like gestures – reactive at times, but mostly just paralleling Thurston's sound. He was responsive to what I was doing and he gave me ample space to just be me. At times we aligned; at times we were foils against each other.

What made it a joyful performance for me? That's easy to answer: failure! Let me explain, this was my first time playing with one of my biggest musical heroes. It's easy to get into a head space of delivering, hanging, making it happen when you are playing with someone you admire. I was brave enough to not concern myself with that. I put my soul into gear and allowed myself to take chances, over and over, dancing with the idea that this next thing could fail miserably. 'Oh, pick up those chains and play with those... shit, this could go terribly wrong...' I kept taking chances. To me, when I see a musician really reaching for something maybe beyond their reach or comprehension, I feel the humanity in what they're doing, what we're all doing when we are at our best. I love playing like a child who isn't concerning themselves with the outcome. It's about experience and trying some new thing that might not work. Solving problems. Spontaneous discovery is real life, man.

'Feel It In Your Guts'
Thurston Moore/Bernie Sanders
(Joyful Noise, 2016)

Karl Hofstetter: The projects we've worked with Thurston on – *Cause & Effect, 50 Bands & A Cat For Indiana Equality*, the 2016 flexi-disc series and the Bernie Sanders single – were all conceptual releases which don't yield much, if any, money. Two of them are benefit releases, in fact. So Thurston's interactions with us have never been financially driven and it's been hugely inspiring to me to work with one of my idols for the fun and purpose of music.

We like to think that the work of the label is an expression of what individuals can achieve if they embrace a shared desire to create something good, something honest. Bernie Sanders' vision chimes with the beliefs we share over here: he inspires us to think the era of self-interest and money über alles can end. So we decided to speak through action, to use the skills and experience we have here, to show our support for what Sanders is saying. We considered the question, kicked the idea around and what have you, and decided Thurston Moore was the guy we wanted to ask to do this – there's an open spirit at work there we appreciated and felt was the right fit for what we hoped was a gesture of hopefulness and enthusiasm. Our gut feeling was confirmed, given that Thurston said yes almost immediately.

The next mountain to climb was how to set about getting a presidential candidate involved with the work of a weirdo indie-pop label out of Indiana. Again, it came down to people helping people – one of our employees was already friends with Bernie's campaign team. We said hello and told them what we were thinking… and, to our surprise, they not only responded but within a week we heard Bernie liked the idea very much. From there it was all pretty fast; we sketched the concept out and just let Thurston cut loose on it. We stuck to what we do best and made sure we could get a physically and artistically compelling item out into the world; 1,000 copies only on white vinyl. Our friend David Kloc created the portrait of Bernie for the cover. Instead of asking people to buy it, we just asked them to make a donation to Bernie's campaign and shoot us a photo of the receipt as proof. Wow… the whole lot went inside days.

Thurston and Adam Gołębiewski at Od:Zysk Squat, Poznań, Poland, May 20, 2014.
Credit — Eva Prinz

Heretics
Heretics
(Unsound, 2016)

Andy Moor: *Heretics* was an idea that Anne-James and I had on the shelf for several years. There's an advertising agency in Paris, L'Agence Herezie, that do slightly weird, unconventional adverts and list on their website all kinds of crazy pictures of heretical thinkers. Andrea Stillaci, the director, told us that if we wanted to make an album around the idea of heretics then they would fund it. At some point Anne-James asked me if there was someone I would really like to play with and I mentioned Thurston. Anne-James agreed and it took a while to set up but we managed to get together.

Anne-James Chaton: We worked together for almost two years to write this project. First, we started to play together on tour; Thurston performing solo, Andy Moor and I as a duo. Then, progressively, Thurston began playing on some parts of our duo. We gained a taste for it and decided that it would be even more exciting to play songs that we composed together. Thus we created *Heretics* through a desire to mix our respective universes: rock, improvisation, noise, poetry, reading and performance. We embarked on this project with the idea that each of us could be all things at once: singer, poet, guitarist. The first decision made by Thurston, Andy and myself was that everything should remain open; there was no division of labour like, 'You are the guitarist,' 'I am the poet.' Each of us brought our individual writings, riffs, books, images – and from that we extracted something more like a sound piece than an album, although it does consist of a number of titles. So, ultimately, I play the guitar for the first time in my life; Thurston performs text; Andy lends his voice to a song.

What I remember most is a certain rhythm of work, this back and forth of continuous exchanges, questions, proposals, numerous forms before reaching a final form. We searched until the last minute, passionately, without pressure, just desirous of making an object together.

Working with Thurston presented several challenges. It was the first time I had worked with another writer and another voice; it was also a dive into another culture, other influences. Even if we share some literary and musical loves, we don't necessarily perceive them in the same way. And it was also a new live presence, a voice, a gesture. We had to be able to agree, write and perform together, without flattening our different sensitivities. From my first writings I was fascinated by the great avant-garde of the 20th century, the Russian Futurists, Dada, the Surrealists, the Lettrists, both from a literary and pictorial point of view. Then came engagement with contemporary forms of these great ancestors: the sound poets, the performers of the literary scene in the late nineties.

Andy Moor: The agency, along with the local theatre and La Muse En Circuit (founded by Luc Ferrari) in Paris paid for us to go to a studio in Saint-Nazaire. Anne-James and I arrived on the first day, then Thurston joined us a day later by which time we had quite a few things already worked up for him to look at. We each brought ideas with us to the studio; it wasn't an improvisational recording or something we made up – we had material in mind for this and we built on it when we all got together. We then went to La Muse En Circuit in Paris – again with various people funding the recording – and put the record together.

Anne-James usually comes up with the concept and then I contribute ideas. We were looking for figures that we considered heretical, our own interpretation of what heresy is, so both me and Anne-James came up with people we wanted to do pieces on and Thurston added a few: Caravaggio; José Mujica of Uruguay; punk rock – Thurston's idea.

Anne-James and I have played together for years but Thurston just slotted into that; he's a very easy guy – not easy as in passive, he has a real force and he contributes something significant to it, but he's quite laidback and relaxed when you work with him. He's not a stressy, diva-type rock star or something – he's listening all the time and he has ideas. Also, he's really into poetry, he's fascinated by it – always has been but particularly at the moment. For him, it was a great pleasure to play with a sound poet from France. It was a twist to not just be playing with another guitar band; I think he really liked the combination.

Anne-James Chaton: A 56-minute documentary was shot by a young French director, Benoît Bourreau. He followed all the work, the residence time, the one performance we gave in the Theatre de Saint Nazaire in January. He's preparing a film about the meeting between three artists and three universes.

Mikrosession#11 'Transcendent Transaction' – The Thurston Moore Group (No Label, 2016)

Johannes Buff: I'd been working with Thurston as his live sound engineer for a year and felt I knew the band enough to invite them to Mikrokosm, our studio in Lyons. When I sent the invitation, they were about to record their second album. So another recording session was definitely not a priority. The invitation was accepted, cancelled, then rescheduled.

Benoit Bel: We had a project called *Mikrosession*, which is an invitation to record and be filmed at the same time – then we're free to edit what we want from it. So we got the studio ready; the band arrived around 1p.m. to record until 6p.m., just the right time to record a full song. Thurston entered the studio with just a simple riff. They jammed on it for 40 minutes with Thurston giving instructions. We took a short break in the control room, validated the sound, everything was okay so they started to record. Over those hours it became a song, lyrics shaped inside 15 minutes. Such a lesson in musicianship! The set-up was all of them in the live room with the drums, that way they could have the feeling they were playing like a real band: headphones on, bass amp in one booth and the two guitar amps in another to prevent leakage between sources. Then we just needed to add James' solo and Thurston's vocal as overdubs.

Johannes Buff: Thurston revealed the lyrics and the vocal melody only after the instrumental was tracked, leaving everyone in the dark about one of the most important aspects of his songwriting. That's a strange one to me, because his musicians could react to it if they knew what else was part of the equation. Maybe it's just me being slow to understand the song; maybe he doesn't know what it will be like at the time they're jamming the parts; maybe he processes them separately in his mind, it doesn't really matter. When he lays the vocals down on top of what sounds like a succession of parts, suddenly you have a song appearing that makes complete sense as a whole. That's a magical thing to witness.

Johannes Buff and Thurston outside Johannes' apartment in Paris, Spring 2015.
Credit – Eva Prinz

Disarm
Adam Gołębiewski/Thurston Moore
(Endless Happiness, 2017)

Adam Gołębiewski: In music there's a relationship between the object, the sound and the self–body, hands, touching it, feeling the vibrations. Generally in the language of music, there are a lot of metaphors about what sound is, what sound is pretending to be. In the percussion context we have the 'break', the 'shot', sound is described as 'crispy'. I don't like to pretend that the sound is something other than what it is. I really like this straight, harsh sound characteristic. When I work, when it sounds like I'm breaking something, then I'm really breaking something. A lot of the time it's not done on purpose; it's very much about the pressure of touch, sometimes very delicate but other times wood, metal, plastic objects break because of dense articulation, and it is authentic. What I'm describing is very timbrally orientated – if you want this rich sound you need to be merciless. If you have a basic drum, you've got this plastic skin, metal objects, wood, your hand. This creates a powerful tension where you're feeling your way around the borders of your capacity, the capacity of the instrument, the place of the listener in relation to these sounds on the edge of hearing.

The other side is the social background of the instrument. Obviously everybody knows that instruments are socially designed – some have long histories, a heavy cultural weight that you sometimes can't escape or other times you choose to reproduce. This is true of drums also. If you have cymbals, a snare drum, they're designed for a specific purpose; a particular sound characteristic. What I'm finding interesting is to try and step past those limits. Even within a musical structure I'm trying to apply unorthodox articulation, or maybe a traditional technique, but only to an extent that it becomes a transgression – where the instrument is behaving in a way that nobody designed it to. You have to find your own way through practice, a way to say that this is your sound and interpretation of reality. The first occasion to play with Thurston wasn't as a duo, it was as a trio with Yoko Ono at a relatively mainstream festival in Poznan´. Months before it took place, Yoko Ono and Thurston's duo performance was announced as the headliner. A few weeks before, I was invited by the person from New York who was curating it. I had to think first, 'Is this a really good situation for me?' but I agreed and it was good experience.

271

As far as I remember, as far as I remember, we only did about 10 minutes' rehearsal as a trio – then launched straight into the concert. But somehow he and I ended up playing together all day, trying to align ourselves, to match up. We'd worked all day at both our timemeasured playing and as an improvisational duo. Matching sounds was what we were aiming for, not just on a technical level but in terms of intonation, timbre, loudness, structural things. Thurston's tools were simple: amp, a small number of pedals, guitar; then me with my threepiece drum set with two cymbals. The results felt rich and authentic. I never felt I was dealing with a star so I enjoyed how natural it was performing with Thurston. Not pulling out, not being too quiet or hiding, never overwhelming – his work is very exact. Paradoxically, while experienced artists do that, it's not necessarily true of everyone you meet and work with. When it sounds good you can feel it inside – I sympathise with that guitar sound, I like its simplicity, its broad range, its subtleties and shades. It has a lot in common with my drum sound – heaviness or dense textures, or the sound of things being torn, broken, rubbed. Often, when we play together, we change direction very rapidly – it shows this focused presence that he has, that we have.

Since then, I think we've played together around five times – four times in Poland, once in London. After our initial meeting playing with Yoko Ono, we then played with Alex Ward, then as a duo in London at Café Oto and we worked with John Edwards in 2014. Some gigs took more sweat, more blood; after the duo sets the instrument was worn and I got some injuries to my hands but was still smiling.

Rock n Roll Consciousness
Thurston Moore
(Fiction/Universal, 2017)

Radieux Radio: Recording for *Rock n Roll Consciousness* in Paris was really fun and very different to how we worked together on *The Best Day*: we shared the recording studio, just the two of us writing on the spot with the music sometimes changing to fit the lyrics — the first time I've heard that happen. But then it's always different with Thurston, I don't think he likes things to stay the same: if he had to work in the same studio over and over or with the same people over and over, I don't know if that would be as exciting for him. He seems to prefer a dynamic life, no day similar to the day before — always different.

Deb Googe: By the time we recorded *Rock n Roll Consciousness* we'd been playing live together a lot. We really know each other's styles and strengths; I think that comes across on the record, this album sounds more cohesive, it sounds like an actual band.

There were no demos and no rehearsals. Some of them were developed during touring. Quite often during soundchecks, Thurston would just start playing something and we'd join in. But there were also some tracks that were totally new in the studio, to me anyway. Very much like *The Best Day*, Thurston would just play parts, we would play along until we were all happy and then, bit by bit, piece them together.

The actual recording sessions were pretty laidback. We generally started around midday and left around midnight maybe. The recording was mainly done at the Church Studios in London and the sessions were kind of squashed between gigs on the UK tour in May 2015. The bulk of it was done in one session which I think started on May 5. Then we had to pack everything down on May 9 because we had a show in Bedford. So the gear was packed down and loaded out of the Church Studios at 1p.m. and we went off to Bedford to play a show and then, the following day, we went to Oxford for another show and then we went back to the Church for a couple days beginning of the following week. Thurston hadn't done any vocals till that point, so that was quite exciting; up until then I had no idea how they were supposed to fit in or even if there were any, but I actually ended up doing some backing vocals too, which is a first for me. I think James and Thurston had one more session to do some overdubs but I was all done by the end of that session; then, on May 14, we headed down to Brighton to do a festival.

James Sedwards: *The Best Day* was recorded in two different studios over the course of three days and it was our first time playing together as a group. For *Rock n Roll Consciousness* we were able to remain in one studio for nearly two weeks (though we did leave the session at one point to do a couple of gigs) so there was definitely a better sense of purpose all round. Another big difference was that we had a producer and several engineers working with us. Also, the producer, engineers and recording console were with the band in the live room so it was a much more interactive experience in general.

The music was worked up in a similar way to *The Best Day*, but this time none of the band had played any of the songs before the session apart from one track. The recording took place in the middle of touring with three weeks of gigs either side of the session. In the first run of gigs we had partially worked up one of the songs in soundchecks and also played a version of it live on a radio show. We had also experimented with a couple of new riffs but not taken them any further. When we were in the studio, Thurston would show us the riffs and then we would start interpreting them with our own parts and would add ideas, so the songs would begin to take on a life of their own and often unexpected directions would emerge. At the time we all felt that it was more of a 'band' record and that everyone was more aware of what their role in the group was and what the material needed to sound good. For each of the songs we had to learn and develop the material in the studio and then work it into shape very quickly, there was never the opportunity to revisit any of the pieces after we moved on from them. We probably spent about half a day on each song and the takes that made it onto the record were either the third or fourth run-through of the piece so, without a doubt, the music is about as fresh as it gets!

Lydia Lunch: Thurston has a very specific trajectory and the stamina to play as much as he does. I think that was always there – always reaching for something different from the very start. I never felt, 'In five years he'll be better.' He was always amazing. A lot of us will play until we drop. It's about his character, the soul of the individual, of an artist – because he is a very unique artist, beyond the beyond. It's about the soul transmuting into the guitar strings then going into extra-stellar space where the sound is another dimension that transports the individual into space. Thurston wants to be transported to another place outside of dismal reality.

Deb Googe: Thurston has an astronomical appetite for life and the most phenomenal knowledge and love of music, poetry, books, film, news, culture…you name it. He's a very open and generous soul, so you never stop discovering new things when you're in his orbit, he's a very inspiring person to be around.

Contributors

Andrya Ambro is co-founder, percussionist and vocalist for the minimalist noise duo Talk Normal, as well as playing in various other projects. She has dedicated most of the last 14 years to music, currently creating under the title Gold Dime.

Josh Baer was director of the White Columns non-profit art space from 1979–83, and co-owned Neutral Records during this period. He ran the Josh Baer Gallery for a decade, was managing editor of *ZG Magazine*, continues to issue the *Baer Faxt* arts newsletter and is now a private art advisor. Josh has been a Professor of Graduate Studies at the Fashion Institute of Technology, a director of the Franklin Furnace Archive and the Andrew Glover Youth Program, and on the I Love NY Art Benefit Executive Committee, supporting victims of the World Trade Center attack.

Benoit Bel forged his musical and sonic identity in Iceland alongside his mentors, Valgeir Sigurdsson and Mio Thorrisson, at Greenhouse Studios, working with artists such as Björk, Bonnie 'Prince' Billy, Kate Nash and the creative Bedroom Community. Now in his own studios, Bel performs, writes and arranges mainly for albums, but also for cinema, live performance and contemporary art. His productions define a craft-oriented but demanding vision of music, highlighting tone, space and experimentation.

Patrick Best is the son of a fiddler father and pianist mother. He spent his teenhood playing in DC punk bands, then discovered dub and Indian classical music. Moving to Richmond, Virginia in '89, he dove into an art-punk scene and began playing in free-jazz bands until, through playing in a rock group called Ugly Head, he found himself performing with Jack Rose. Living just a few doors from Mike Gangloff, the trio forged a friendship alongside a drive to push music to the outer limits. Best and Rose joined Pelt in 1995.

Martin Bisi volunteered, aged 17, to work at CBGB, and also worked with the band Material. A chance encounter with Brian Eno led to the opportunity to start a studio. Bisi, Bill Laswell and Material, struck gold in recording Herbie Hancock's Grammy-winning hit, 'Rockit'. Bisi built and opened his own BC Studio in 1981, since which time he has realised albums by artists as diverse as Eno, Hancock, Helmet, U.S. Maple and Swans, among countless others. In his own eponymous band, he plays guitar and sings amid heavy post-rock and ambient soundscapes.

David Santiago Blanco is a British graphic designer and co-founder of Blank Editions. After graduating from art college, already well-versed in the local punk and hardcore scenes, Blanco set up his design practice in 2001 to concentrate on music and book packaging. After moving to Hackney, east London, in 2012, David co-founded Blank Editions with publisher and author Will Shutes, to document music and art emerging from the local area.

Phil Blankenship is a lifelong video maniac and horror fiend, committed to sharing harsh noise with the trash of humanity. Since 1997, he has released nearly 300 records, CDs and cassettes on his Troniks label, including recordings by John Wiese, Yellow Swans, The Rita, Hive Mind, Wolf Eyes and others. Based in Los Angeles, Phil spends his spare time petting cats, watching VHS and recording horrible sound art.

Alan Bloor is a Canadian experimental composer and sculptor. Based in Toronto, Ontario, Bloor has been performing harsh noise material as Knurl since 1994, the year of his seminal releases *Initial Shock* and *Nervescrap*. Knurl has released over 70 titles internationally and delved heavily into experimentation with found objects as sound sources, including fan blades, typewriters, scrap metal and car springs. Bloor has explored a less harsh side of noise music in his acclaimed ambient project, Pholde.

Benoît Bourreau was born in 1978; he lives and works in Paris as an artist and filmmaker. He has directed *Mieux partagés que nous ne sommes* (2006), a medium-length documentary screened at Festival Del Film Locarno and Montréal International Festival of Film on Art, and *Le chant des particules* (2011), a short film screened at Clermont-Ferrand International Short Film Festival, International Shortfilm

Festival in Dráma and Kasseler Dokumentarfilm und Videofest. His first feature documentary, *Making Heretics* (2016), was recently premiered at IndieLisboa International Independent Film Festival. Currently, he is directing his second feature documentary, about filmmaker Olivier Assayas, for the legendary *Cinéma, de notre temps* by André S. Labarthe. During the creation of this book, he granted access to his film of Thurston in the studio recording *Heretics*, plus the corresponding live footage.

Stuart Braithwaite is a guitarist, singer, multi-instrumentalist and founding member of Mogwai. The band formed in Glasgow in 1995, and a stream of critically-acclaimed releases followed. In 2013, their eighth album, *Rave Tapes*, was the first to crack the Top Ten, and their most recent record, *Atomic*, is the soundtrack to Mark Cousins' BBC Four documentary *Atomic: Living In Dread And Promise*. Braithwaite has collaborated with several artists outside of Mogwai, most recently as a member of Minor Victories, a new band formed with Slowdive's Rachel Goswell and Editors' Justin Lockey, whose debut album was released in 2016.

Glenn Branca has worked as a composer over the past 40 years, including music for experimental rock bands, large ensemble instrumentals for electric guitars, 16 symphonies, chamber ensemble pieces, an opera, a ballet, choral works, film music, 14 albums, dance, theatre and installation art. He is the inventor of the Harmonics Guitar, many of the instruments used in his pieces and a musical theory based on the harmonic series, as well as various tuning systems. His bands, Theoretical Girls and The Static, were crucial to 'no wave', and Branca is one of the most influential living composers in experimental rock and contemporary classical music.

Britt Brown is a native son of the Lone Star State and has devoted himself to supporting innovative independent artists for over a decade. Under the banners of the Not Not Fun and 100% Silk labels, which he co-runs, he has issued well over 400 music releases with scant regard for commercial success and an absolute focus on supporting artistic integrity. Britt has been a freelance writer for *The Wire* since 2011 and continues to perform in the drone-industrial duo Robedoor.

Johannes Buff is originally from the Basque Country. He has been in demand as an audio engineer since 2006, and is a self-taught, multifaceted enthusiast and inspired musician. His 2007 solo debut was *Last Ten Meters*, and he is gaining increasing recognition for his production work. Today, he splits his time between making records at

Mikrokosm Recording Studios in Lyon, France, and worldwide tours, working with artists such as avant-rock legend Thurston Moore, Chilean electro pioneer Matias Aguayo and French cosmic rockers Zombie Zombie, among many others.

Ambrose Bye is a musician and producer living in New York City. He is a co-founder of Fast Speaking Music. Recent projects featuring Thurston Moore have included *Tiny People Having A Meeting, Comes Through In The Call Hold, Oasis at Biskra, Harry's House Vol. 1, 2* and *3*, and *The Avant-Age Garde I Ams Of The Gal Luxury*.

Marco Cazzella is an artist based in London. He is known for his publishing work with My Dance The Skull, particularly the *Voice Studies* cassette tapes series. His artwork involves paintings, drawings, textiles, found objects and poetry, investigating themes such as childhood abuse, addictions and the father-son relationship at both an individual and collective level.

Michael Chapman signed to EMI's flagship Harvest label in the mid-sixties; his celebrated second album, *Fully Qualified Survivor*, has never been out of print since. He produced over 50 albums in the subsequent 50 years and has recently been touring with a cello and pedal steel trio. Michael continues to be at the forefront of the acoustic guitar/songwriter genre, touring and recording with many of the younger, cutting-edge guitarists of today; still pushing the envelope at 75.

Rhys Chatham is a composer, guitarist, trumpet and flute player from Manhattan, currently living in Paris. Chatham's instrumentation ranges from *Guitar Trio*, composed in 1977, to the evening-length work for 100 electric guitars, *An Angel Moves Too Fast to See*, composed in 1989, all the way to *A Crimson Grail* for 200 guitars and 16 basses. Along with the G100 and G3 programmes, he is currently offering a solo concert, an evening-length work with the composer performing on electric guitar, trumpets and bass, alto and C flutes. The record, *Pythagorean Dream*, was released in June 2016 on the UK Foom Label.

Anne-James Chaton is a French writer and artist. He has written a number of books published by Al Dante, and joined the German record label Raster-Noton in 2011. Chaton has given numerous performances internationally, worked with the Dutch band The Ex and released two albums with the English guitarist Andy Moor. He also appears on two albums with the German artist Carsten Nicolai (aka Alva Noto). In 2013, he started the trio project *Heretics* with Andy Moor and Thurston Moore – a book and CD mixing poetry and music from the three artists has been released on the Dutch label Unsounds.

Andrew Clare is a creative designer, artworker and art director based in Brighton, with numerous credits to his name including work for the UK Arts Council. In his youth, having written a fanzine for several years, he founded the Graphic Death Audio Products cassette label to release the work of his band, I'm Being Good, alongside other local exponents of experimental rock. The label halted around 1997, with his efforts being diverted to his Infinite Chug label which ran from the early nineties until the mid-2000s.

John Clement was born 1943, on a cold February 13. He grew up listening to his father's music, largely Bach, which he still loves. John then fell in love with blues, R&B, folk music and – being unable to afford a 12-string guitar – went home one Christmas to use his father's shop equipment to build his own. Then came the kazoo, to make the soundtrack to a movie about the Nihilist Party of London, Ontario, and from that grew The Spasm Band, wherein was explored sound and the conversations musicians can have via their instruments. John and his wife celebrated their 50th anniversary in June 2016; he is a proud father to three girls and a boy.

Nels Cline is a guitarist/composer who has played in the arenas of jazz, improvised music and rock globally for over three decades. He has played on over 200 recordings with innumerable fine musicians, including his periodic collaborations with Thurston Moore (Pillow Wand). Nels has led his own group, The Nels Cline Singers, for over 12 years and has made over 20 recordings of his own. He's probably best known these days for his work with Chicago-based band Wilco, with whom he has performed and recorded since 2004. Nels and his wife reside in New York City.

Byron Coley lives on an old dairy farm in western Massachusetts. He began buying records in the late pre-Beatles era. Coley has written for several periodicals over the years, including *Cretin Bull*, *The Fish Frau Gazette* and *Ball*. He lives with his wife, the inventor Lili Dwight, and enjoys working in the yard during the warmer months. In the winter, he skis.

Loren Connors has composed original guitar music for over four decades. In 1979, *Cadence* noted that he was "trying to extend the boundaries of sound and pitch of acoustic guitar, but he is unique in the utilization of blues in his work, one could almost say this is avant-garde blues. He's swimming in new waters." Connors names abstract expressionist painter Mark Rothko as a key influence. His music – which

279

embraces the aesthetics of blues, Irish airs, blues-based rock and other genres without rigid form – has been recorded on Family Vineyard, Northern Spy, Drag City and other labels.

Vice Cooler has enjoyed a wide-ranging life in the creative arts. As a musician, Vice was a founding member of XBXRX and Kit, as well as collaborating with Chicks On Speed, The Raincoats and producing Peaches' album *Rub*. He has directed videos for Lee Ranaldo, Feist, Mastodon, Adult Swim, Deerhoof and others, while also working as a photographer on projects including Kim Gordon's *Girl In A Band* biography and the *Body/Head* LP. Vice was part of the leadership at the NFJM and VCR labels, and is currently working toward the 2017 release of his first solo album.

John Corbett is a writer, producer and curator based in Chicago. He is co-owner of Corbett Vs Dempsey, an art gallery through which he produces CDs of jazz and improvised music, old and new. Corbett is the author of several books, including *Microgroove: Forays Into Other Music* (Duke University Press, 2015) and *A Listener's Guide To Free Improvisation* (University of Chicago Press, 2016).

Chris Corsano is a drummer who has been operating at the intersections of free improvisation, avant-rock and noise music since the late nineties. He has worked with saxophonists Paul Flaherty, Joe McPhee and Evan Parker, guitarists Sir Richard Bishop, Heather Leigh Murray and Michael Flower; and one-of-a-kind artists like Björk and Jandek. His style incorporates high-energy free improvising, more textural work and augmenting the drum kit with everything from cello strings stretched across the skins to disassembled saxophone parts.

Kevin Crump runs Wintage Records & Tapes and is an eternal cheerleader for the virtues of the local scene in Toronto, Canada. He has been an active participant and player in the experimental music scene for over a decade, performing under a variety of names.

Lin Culbertson is a musician and composer based in New York City. She is co-founder of the group White Out, and has performed and recorded with a wide range of artists including Jim O'Rourke, Thurston Moore, William Winant, Nels Cline, C. Spencer Yeh, Carlos Giffoni, Zeena Parkins and Mike Watt, among many others. Lin's recent sound work is informed by her experience as a graphic and media designer. She has started to incorporate visual elements into her compositions through the use of graphic scores, videoscreen grabs and image translation software. Lin also composes music for film and television.

Kylie Minoise (aka Lea Cummings) has unleashed a zodiac of unforgettable collisions over the last decade, while performing over 150 solo live aktions in over 20 countries, breaking hearts, microphones and minds. His recorded output provides limitless opportunity for bickering and confrontation, with over 50 releases on various international record labels including Harbinger Sound, Dirter Promotions and his own label, Kovorox Sound. His insistent aural savagery has made him a hero of young and old alike, and a great number of exotic members of the animal kingdom admire his dedication to absolute antisocial provocation as a life force.

Warren Defever was born in 1969; by age five he was performing country music, polkas and waltzes, accompanying his grandfather on guitar, fiddle, lap steel and accordion. By age 21 he had engineered the first Gories album, toured the US in the rockabilly band Elvis Hitler and under the alias His Name Is Alive, at which point the latter enjoyed a 13-year run with famed British label 4AD. All of this has been followed by a successful studio career working on records for Michael Hurley, Iggy & The Stooges and Genesis P-Orridge, and producing a Grammy-nominated series of children's music albums for Smithsonian Folkways.

Cris Deison has been involved in the noise/rock electronic area since 1990, and approached the world of sound via self-released cassette collages with tape recorders, turntables and objects. He established a small label (Loud!) and began to collaborate with other artists. Influenced by electro-acoustics/ambient minimal electronics as well as digital music and sound design, he operated with samplers and field recordings. New releases display the new sound direction taken by Deison: calm waves of looping, deep ambient scapes, penetrated by sample fragments and light additional noise-ambient textures to form a minimal framework. Deison also co-owns the Final Muzik label.

Don Dietrich is a musician, sculptor and painter living in West Nyack, NY. He graduated from Parsons School of Design in 1976 with a BA in sculpture, and has participated in numerous solo and group exhibitions of painting and sculpture. In 1983, he received a prestigious Edward F. Albee Foundation Fellowship. In 1979, Dietrich co-founded Borbetomagus with Donald Miller and Jim Sauter. The group has a vast discography and has performed internationally. Later, in 2008, he founded New Monuments with C. Spencer Yeh and Ben Hall, issuing releases on Important and Bocian Records. Dietrich has also performed in a duo with Hall.

Aaron Dilloway is a native of Brighton, Michigan, who started performing as a member of Galen in the mid-nineties. In 1998, he became a member of free-improv group Universal Indians while also co-founding industrial-noise outfit Wolf Eyes. Dilloway works as an improviser and composer, primarily focused on the manipulation of eight-track tape loops combined with tape delays, electronic sound effects, organic sources of sonic material and voice. He left Wolf Eyes in 2005 and now runs the Hanson Records store in Oberlin, Ohio, and the associated mail-order and distribution network.

Shayna Dulberger has been actively playing bass since 2001 and has recorded three albums under her own name: *TheKillMeTrio* (2006), *The Basement Recordings* (2011) and *Ache And Flutter* (2013). She also plays in the band Cellular Chaos, with Admiral Grey and Weasel Walter, and in Hot Date, with Chris Welcome. She has been active in the free-jazz scene for over a decade and has performed with numerous individuals of note from across the world of music. Since 2005, Dulberger has enjoyed sparking a love of music among young students at a private school in Queens.

Jim Dunbar has been into music since time immemorial as a gig-goer, record librarian, DJ, radio presenter, band manager, A&R executive, film-music supervisor and record producer. Dunbar's early influences include his uncle (Russ Gibb of Detroit's Grande Ballroom), *San Francisco Chronicle* critic John Wasserman, KSAN DJ Richard Gossett and his childhood next-door neighbour, composer and visual artist Harley Gaber.

Hanin Elias was born in in Wittlich, Germany, in a hospital near where Holger Meins of the Red Army Faction was on hunger strike. A bomb threat led to Hanin, still in an incubator, being evacuated. At age 15 she rebelled against normality and ran away from home to live in squats, while making music. She co-founded the band Atari Teenage Riot and, dissatisfied with the male-dominated music world, opened the Fatal Recordings label for female artists. She has recorded numerous albums, her latest projects being the Fantome record *It All Makes Sense*, in 2014, and her EP *Hold Me*, in 2016.

Paul Flaherty is a New England saxophone improviser who has devoted his artistic expression to free-form music, both in concert and on recordings. This process has gone on for 40 years and 60-plus recordings. He has worked with two main drummers, Randall Colbourne and Chris Corsano, releasing over 15 albums with each. Flaherty's first recording was with a free group called Orange in 1978, followed by other free-form releases over the next 37 years with various musicians embracing the concept of 'no preconceived plan beforehand, just follow the music'.

Don Fleming is the singer and guitarist for Velvet Monkeys, B.A.L.L. and Gumball, and has been a member of Half Japanese, the *Backbeat* band (1994 Beatles biopic), Wylde Ratttz (1998 film *Velvet Goldmine*), Dim Stars and The Nasty Bits (2016 TV series *Vinyl* on HBO). As a music producer he has worked with Sonic Youth, Teenage Fanclub, Screaming Trees, The Posies, Hole, Joan Jett, Alice Cooper, Pete Yorn and Andrew W.K. Don has also been an archivist for the estates of Alan Lomax, Hunter S. Thompson, Ken Kesey, Tuli Kupferberg, George Harrison and Lou Reed.

Tim Foljahn has spent three decades in music, with a career spanning his role as a founding member of Two Dollar Guitar, work with artists including Cat Power, Thurston Moore and Half Japanese, and his part in the fictional band Sideboob on the TV series *Orange Is The New Black*, alongside his solo endeavours. He resides in Hoboken, New Jersey, where he paints, writes an advice column and continues to navigate the complex relationships and enthralling beauty that make up this world of ours. His latest release, *Fucking Love Songs*, is a cracked, unique and darkly romantic affair meditating on love.

Jon Forss is a graphic designer and the British half of multi–award-winning design partnership Non-Format, which he co-founded in London, 2000, with Kjell Ekhorn (the Norwegian half). Non-Format has designed music packaging for many record labels, including more than 100 releases for the British label Lo Recordings. Between 2001 and 2005, the duo were the designers of *The Wire* magazine. In 2007, Forss emigrated to the United States and, in 2015, Non-Format merged with the Norwegian design firm ANTI. He continues to collaborate with Ekhorn and ANTI from his studio in Saint Paul, Minnesota, despite seven timezones between them.

Marco Fusinato is a visual artist and musician. His work has been included in the Venice Biennale of Art, 2015, the first ever exhibition of sound at the Museum of Modern Art, New York, 2013, a range of projects for the Sao Paulo Biennale, 2012, and in the book/music package *Sonic Youth: Sensational Fix*. Fusinato performs regularly in the experimental music underground. His ongoing series of long-duration noise-guitar performances, *Spectral Arrows*, described as "a monumental aural sculpture", was first performed at the Glasgow International Arts Festival, 2012, followed by performances all around the world.

283

Mike Gangloff founded Pelt and Black Twig Pickers, and now rocks the Appalachian freedom drone in a duo with his wife, Cara Gangloff.

Margarida Garcia is a musician and visual artist who developed in the Lisbon scene and now practises her art worldwide in the company of musicians including Manuel Mota, John Tilbury, Otomo Yoshihide and others. She studied at the Parsons School of Design, New School University in New York City. The double bass is her main instrument but her creative efforts combine sound, video and drawing.

Stavros Giannopoulos grew up on a diet of metal, grunge, hardcore, hip hop and whatever else caught his ear. The beating wings of his creative urge belong to the mighty Atlas Moth. Stavros has lent the raging ecstasy of his guitar and voice to The Atlas Moth for nearly a decade, over three albums: *A Glorified Piece Of Blue-Sky*, *An Ache For The Distance* and *The Old Believer*. Stavros felt blessed to be a Twilight brother, and has also provided visual art for Leviathan and Corrections House. He's currently enjoying tearing stages to charred matchwood and preparing the latest Atlas Moth album.

Carlos Giffoni is a Venezuelan experimental musician; he was also previously the founder and director of the No Fun Fest and the No Fun Productions record label in New York City. Carlos currently lives in Los Angeles, where he splits his time between production for video games, musical creativity and improvisation... and the beach. Looking back over the innumerable performances he has taken part in, Carlos says that his favourites remain those shared with Thurston, alongside the respective Japanese tours with Merzbow and Jim O'Rourke.

Michael Gira is primarily known for his work with his musical group, Swans.

Adam Gołębiewski was born in 1984 and lives in Poznań, Poland. He is a percussionist, improviser, musicologist and sociologist. Adam has mainly played within the realms of free jazz, improvised and experimental music. Within his work, he focuses on the ultimate potential extension of the drum set and percussion instruments to anatomy, sound and expressiveness, which results in a direct and intense sound language. Among his many endeavours, Adam has played and collaborated with numerous icons of experimental art and music, and has authored a variety of site-specific sound-installation projects.

Chris Gollon has exhibited in St Paul's Cathedral with Bill Viola (a contemporary video artist), and has works in major museum collections including the British Museum. His work is attracting increasing acclaim and was featured on Alan Yentob's BBC1 programme, *Imagine*. The book on his life and work, *Chris Gollon: Humanity In Art* by art historian Tamsin Pickeral, endorsed by Bill Bryson OBE, was published in 2010. Song lyrics often lead him to new imagery, as with his ongoing collaboration with singer-songwriter Eleanor McEvoy including her album *Naked Music* (2016). His official website is: www.chrisgollon.com.

Deb Googe embraced the DIY movement of the late seventies, forming anarcho-punk band Bikini Mutants, who, along with The Mob, started the *All The Madmen* fanzine and record label. Deb spent a decade from 1985–95 as a member of My Bloody Valentine, before leaving to form Snowpony with Katharine Gifford (ex-Stereolab), releasing three albums and four EPs together. The last few years have been a blizzard of activity: she rejoined MBV in 2008, was announced as Primal Scream's bassist in 2012, performed with Joybabe, Rockhard and Pimmel, and, from May 2014, brought her talents to The Thurston Moore Band.

The Grassy Knoll (aka Nolan Green) fuses the technical terrorism of The Bomb Squad with the organic impact of Miles Davis' Jack Johnson – industrial-strength beats vying with serpentine sax solos, ambient-noir atmospheres cloaking coiled aggression... cut-and-paste style, it effectively blurs the line between Birdland and clubland. Green's latest release, *Electric Verdeland Volume One* featuring Vernon Reid, Jon Dee Graham, Jesse Dayton and James Rotondi, was recorded at his home studio in Austin, Texas. "Bands like The Grassy Knoll manage to make music that's compelling, communal, fun and beautiful without it ever sounding fake and aloof." (Shirley Manson, *NME*)

Mats Gustafsson works primarily with saxophones and live electronics as an improviser and composer, his work taking place in a solo context and with groups including The Thing, Fire!, NU-ensemble and Fire! Orchestra. His collaborations have spanned the creative arts – dance, theatre, visual art – as well as the realms of noise, electronica, rock, contemporary music and free jazz. He has produced and curated a number of festivals and tours, and runs record labels such as Slottet, Crazy Wisdom, Olof Bright Editions, Blue Tower Records and TROTS. Mats is a self-confessed diskaholic and is striving to stay addicted.

Jeff Hartford established his reputation in the realm of noise and experimental sound under the aliases Noise Nomads and Moose Jaw. He continues to run the Bonescraper Recordings cassette label, putting out his own music and that which interests him.

Rob Hayler is the editor of the radiofreemidwich blog, which publishes entertaining writing on experimental music. He also records as midwich, runs the micro-label fencing flatworm recordings and originated the term 'no-audience underground' to describe the self-sufficient, DIY, noise scene that he documents.

Pascal Hector (born 1982) is a founder of the music label Meudiademorte, a member of the experimental music group Datashock, and has been active in the German underground since the early 2000s. Besides recording and releasing music, he works as a visual artist and is studying Sound Art at the Academy of Fine Arts (HBKsaar) in Saarbrücken.

Richard Hell was a founding member of the early CBGB bands Television, The Heartbreakers and Richard Hell & The Voidoids. His 1977 Voidoids album *Blank Generation* is generally acknowledged as seminal to punk. Hell retired from music in 1984. He is the author of the autobiography, *I Dreamed I Was A Very Clean Tramp*, and the novels *Go Now* and *Godlike*, as well as a collection of essays, journals and lyrics, *Hot And Cold*. His most recent book is *Massive Pissed Love: Nonfiction 2001–2014*. He lives in New York and is at work on a new novel.

Karl Hofstetter founded Indianapolis, Indiana-based music label Joyful Noise Recordings at age 19. He christened it as a statement of intent, a pure expression of what he hoped to help birth. From 2010, with the support of his band of comrades, the label's mission became the creation of strictly limited editions where the individual aspects of a musical release are valued and appreciated. Fighting for music as more than 'aural fast food', something beyond mass market product, each Joyful Noise release is a unique object passed from the music lovers at the label to the music lovers listening.

William Hooker is an artistic whole, a vast circle of vision and execution. A body of uninterrupted work beginning in the mid-seventies defines him as one of the most important composers and players in jazz. As bandleader, Hooker has fielded ensembles in a diverse array of configurations, with each collaboration seriously investigating his compositional agenda and the science of modern drum kits. As a player, he is known for the persuasive power of his relationship with his instrument. A disciplined, adaptive and energetic approach to his medium insures his *oeuvre* continues to grow thicker and richer. (*Written by Thomas Stanley.*)

Nathaniel Howdeshell is a 35-year-old farmer from Arkansas. He runs a record label called Fast Weapons.

Sérgio Hydalgo has been a music curator at ZDB since 2007. ZDB is an independent art centre in Lisbon which initiates the creation, production and promotion of all forms of contemporary art; Sérgio has initiated a curative process based around artistic residencies. Thurston Moore joined ZDB for residencies in Lisbon, on the island of Madeira and in the Azores, primarily focused on his talents as a writer; Liz Harris, aka Grouper, spent a week in Aljezur, southern Portugal, which resulted in her latest, highly acclaimed album, *Ruins*. Recently, Angel Olsen started a two-week residency in Lisbon.

Neill Jameson has been one of the loudest, most polarising voices in the American black metal underground for over 20 years now. Splitting his time between his main project, Krieg, and various other collaborations such as Twilight, he also manages to find time to irritate people using the written word and has contributed to *Decibel* magazine, *Noisey* and *No Clean Singing*, among others. Spanning multiple genres musically, he finds people who have a dogmatic dedication to one simply boring.

Jooklo Duo (Virginia Genta on reeds, flutes, piano, percussion and David Vanzan on drums) have been blowing minds all over the world since 2004, with hundreds of charming performances and some cult records. They keep spreading their powerful and uniquely vibrant sound, deeply rooted in the free-jazz avant-garde but heavily influenced by traditional folk music and, at the same time, open to extreme sound experiments. Over the years, the perpetual search for new and challenging combinations has led Genta and Vanzan to form a large variety of ensembles and to collaborate with numerous artists.

Terri Kapsalis is the author of *Jane Addams' Travel Medicine Kit*, *The Hysterical Alphabet* and *Public Privates*. Along with John Corbett and Anthony Elms, she co-edited *Traveling The Spaceways: Sun Ra, The Astro Black, And Other Solar Myths* and *Pathways to Unknown Worlds: Sun Ra, El Saturn, And Chicago's Afro-futurist Underground*, and co-curated the touring exhibition *Pathways To Unknown Worlds*. As an improvising violinist, Kapsalis has a discography that includes work with Tony Conrad, David Grubbs and Mats Gustafsson. She is also a founding member of Theater Oobleck, and teaches at the School of the Art Institute of Chicago.

David Keay played drums with The Coachmen, various early Moore/Gordon projects, Elodie Lauten, Harry Toledo, Richard Lloyd, The Vipers, Marcel Monroe, etc. In 1999, he self-published the novel *Fake Book*, which Richard Kostelanetz included in his *Dictionary Of The Avant-Gardes, Volume Three*. In 2007, with his wife, Laura Feathers, Rick

Clarahan and Dan Hill, he released the vinyl double album *A Jumpin' Jackpot Of Melody* by The Daycare Centre. As The Kiosk, in which he plays various instruments, DIY duo Keay and Feathers have produced five CDs, and word has it that he's mixing *Volume 6* on their Tascam at time of writing.

Leslie Keffer is an Ohio native who has been releasing music and touring since 2003. She also created and wrote *Noisebloid*, the first and only noise tabloid blog (running since 2005). She is a member of The Laundry Room Squelchers, Ohio Giants, and has collaborated with Rodger Stella, Sharkiface, Unicorn Hard-On and Nautical Almanac. Keffer also booked shows at Betty's in Nashville 2007 to 2013, and currently resides in Denver, Colorado. She has released on Ecstatic Peace!, Tusco/Embassy, HereSee, No Kings and more.

Richard Kern, photographer and filmmaker, remains first and foremost a portraitist. For more than two decades, Kern has worked with a shifting band of accomplices – including Lydia Lunch, David Wojnarowicz, Karen Finley, Rita Ackermann, Lucy McKenzie, Marilyn Manson and Indochine – to seek out, unravel and illuminate the complex and often darker sides of human nature. Kern makes the psychological space between the sitter, photographer and viewer his subject. With his dry, matter-of-fact approach, he underlines the absurdity of 'truth' and 'objectivity' in photography while playing with our reliance upon taxonomies surrounding sexual representation. (*Written by Matthew Higgs.*)

J.D. King is a writer, graphic artist and musician. His short stories and poetry have appeared in: *Splice Today*, *Sensitive Skin* and *Obsolete Magazine* (*OM*). Recent graphics have been created for: *The New York Times*, *Fortune*, *The Boston Globe*, *The USPS*, *Audubon*, *Nickelodeon*, *Women's Wear Daily*, *The Smithsonian*, *Consumer Reports* and *The Washington Post*. His band, J.D. King & The Coachmen, have two albums out on Ecstatic Peace! He's currently shopping around his novel, *Copenhagen Or Bust*.

Brian Kinsman is an experimental musician who has been writing, performing and recording music for nearly two decades. His work with percussion has gained the most attention in recent years, via productions such as The Boredoms' BoaDrum88 event at LACMA and Doug Aitken's *Happening* at MOCA LA. Brian's songwriting has featured in *Snakes On A Plane*, among other sci-fi and horror films, and he currently performs in the experimental rap trio True Neutral Crew – alongside Signor Benedick The Moor, Margot Padilla and Grammy winner Daveed Diggs.

288

He also runs the Deathbomb Arc label and PR boutique Kinsman And Meng.

Campbell Kneale has been bashing a left-of-centre path since the mid-eighties but came to the attention of... er, somebody (anybody?) in the late nineties with the birthing of Birchville Cat Motel, fusing the gravelly growl of the New Zealand 'busted-amp' scene with the higher-plane trajectories of droning minimalism and the lower-plane sludge of blackened metal. After exhausting every permutation of electrified sound within this format, with literally hundreds of releases under his belt, Campbell chucked it all in, transforming into Our Love Will Destroy The World in order to rethink everything he had learned. He currently resides in small-town New Zealand and is still thinking.

Kommissar Hjuler began his adult life as a police officer in the town of Flensburg, a German town on the border with Denmark. His musical and artistic tastes soon became all-consuming and he has since devoted his energies fulltime to the creation of visual art, film and sound art. He works regularly with his wife, Mama Baer, with neo-Dada ideas incorporating concepts from Fluxus and art brut. He has an extensive musical discography.

Amanda Kramer has been co-owner and art director for over a decade of Not Not Fun Records, an influential independent label that has spearheaded a number of underground musical movements. She is also owner and creative director of 100% Silk, a dance music label that's been featured in *L.A. Weekly, Pitchfork, Vogue, i-D, Tank, Spin* and *The Guardian*. In addition to her curatorial work, she is a founding member of Pocahaunted and performs live as LA Vampires – a retro-futuristic take on sensual house anthems. Kramer is also the producer of *SILK*, a full-length documentary about contemporary underground dance music culture.

Adam Kriney is a Brooklyn, New York–based musician and composer. Currently, he can be found drumming and singing in his psychedelic heavy rock band, The Golden Grass. He was also the leader of legendary free-jazz outfit Owl Xounds and prog/psych/space-metal warriors La Otracina (both groups RIP).

Colin Langenus has travelled the world playing his music, with such bands as Usaisamonster, Colin L. Orchestra, CSC Funk Band, Bullroarer and Alien Whale. His ambitious creative trajectory entails upward of 100 recordings since 1994, released by esteemed labels such as Fat Beats, Load, FPE, Northern Spy and his own long-running Mass Dist. Colin also records and produces other artists including Jonny Fritz, Jimmy Cousins and Erin Durant. Nowadays, he spends most of his time in New York playing piano and working on recordings.

Ron Lessard is the founder and proprietor of the RRRecords shop in Lowell, Massachusetts. A devoted champion of new artists, Ron founded the RRRecords label – and a number of sub-labels and related series – to bring the work of underground musicians to the world. Starting in the early eighties, RRRecords was the first American record label to focus on noise music, a furrow the label has continued to plough for several decades and over hundreds of releases.

Alan Licht is a New York-based musician and writer, and a founding member of Love Child and Run On. He has performed with artists including Tom Verlaine, Arthur Lee's Love and Royal Trux. Currently playing with Lee Ranaldo & The Dust, he also co-created the Text Of Light ensemble that improvises alongside avant-garde cinema screenings. Alan has released eight albums of experimental guitar, including *Sink The Aging Process*, *A New York Minute*, and *Four Years Older*. He is the author of *An Emotional Memoir Of Martha Quinn* and *Sound Art: Beyond Music Between Categories*, and edited *Will Oldham On Bonnie Prince Billy*.

Steve Lowenthal lives in New York City and is the author of *Dance Of Death: The Life Of John Fahey – American Guitarist* (Chicago Review Press, 2014). He runs the label VDSQ Records and is currently the director of operations at Black Editions.

Samara Lubelski is a player of multiple instruments within the broad waters of song, abstract improvisation and long-form drone. Best known as a solo artist with seven full-length releases, she has also been involved in numerous art-music provocations and recordings. Her experimental violin record, *String Cycle*, was released by Ultra Eczema in spring 2014. *The Gilded Raid*, a solo song record based on an insular and pastoral walk through the decline of western civilisation, is her most recent release.

Lydia Lunch is passionate, confrontational and bold. Whether attacking the patriarchy and their pornographic warmongering, turning the sexual into the political or whispering a love song to the broken-hearted, her fierce energy and rapid-fire delivery lend testament to her warrior nature. She has released too many musical projects to tally, been on tour for decades, published dozens of articles and half a dozen books, and simply refuses to shut up. Brooklyn's Akashic Books have published her recent anthology, *Will Work For Drugs*, as well as her outrageous memoir of sexual insanity, *Paradoxia, A Predator's Diary*.

Andrew MacGregor (Gown) spent half of the first 30 years of his life playing, selling and participating in music. He currently lives in semi-rural Nova Scotia, Canada, with his wife, daughter, dog and cat, where he continues to make music, achieves certain self-set goals and occasionally (but rarely) plays live. His most recent releases are *The Old Line*, which was released on vinyl by Divorce Records, and *The Sound Of Time*, released on cassette by Arachnidiscs.

Toshi Makihara has dedicated his life to the potential within percussion for understanding the role repetition and variation can play in developing and bringing forth new sounds. He combines the use of a range of percussion instruments alongside found objects and everyday materials, and has played in numerous musical contexts, including a significant focus on dance.

Christian Marclay is well known for his work in sculpture, video, photography, collage and performance. For over 30 years he has explored the connections between the visual and the audible, creating works in which these two distinct sensibilities enrich and challenge each other. As a pioneering turntablist, performing music since 1979, his work made a significant impact on the new music scene. He has performed internationally, alone or in collaboration with musicians such as John Zorn, Zeena Parkins, Butch Morris, Christian Wolff, Shelley Hirsh, Günter Müller, Kronos Quartet and others. His artworks are in numerous, prestigious, public and private collections.

Lasse Marhaug has been active in the Norwegian experimental music scene since the early 1990s. As a performer and composer he has contributed to over 300 CD, vinyl and cassette releases over the years, as well as extensively touring across all continents of the world. Marhaug has collaborated with several artists in the music scene, as well as working with music and sound for theatre, dance, installations, film and visual arts. He runs the label Pica Disk and in 2011 started his publishing imprint, Marhaug Forlag, including the interview fanzine *Personal Best*.

David Markey has sustained a truly independent career as a filmmaker, photographer and musician for over three decades. His body of work represents a unique record of the California punk scene: his films include the Sonic Youth/Nirvana tour documentary *1991: The Year Punk Broke*, LA punk-scene classics *The Slog Movie* and *Desperate Teenage Lovedolls*, international film festival favourite *The Reinactors* and the documentary on legendary punk band Circle Jerks, *My Career As A Jerk*. Markey has also directed numerous music videos and created the critically-acclaimed book *We Got Power! Hardcore Punk Scenes From 1980s Southern California*.

Mani Mazinani makes artworks in multiple media including installation, video, film, photography, painting, printmaking, multiples, sound and music. His work directs attention to the physicality and logic of his subject medium. Mazinani's current interests include the origins of ancient philosophical thought, the perceptual limitations of humans and hip hop culture. In music, he is an improviser and composer with a long-standing presence in Toronto's free-improvisation scene, performing in various groups and as a soloist playing turntable, synthesizer, piano, drums and guitar. Mazinani also plays in Gravitons with Jill Aston, and collaborates with artists including Michael Snow/CCMC and Not The Wind Not The Flag.

Joe McPhee, born 1939 in Miami, Florida, is a multi-instrumentalist, composer, improviser, conceptualist and theoretician. He evolved the concept of 'Po Music' – developed through his interest in Pauline Oliveros' Deep Listening theories and Edward De Bono's book *Lateral Thinking: A Textbook Of Creativity* – which he summarises as "a Positive, Possible, Poetic Hypothesis", applied to creative improvisation as a process helping him discover new ideas. McPhee's career spans 50 years and over 100 recordings, ranging from his work with Clifford Thornton in 1969 through to Survival Unit III, a trio founded in 2004 with Fred Lonberg-Holm and Michael Zerang.

Robert Meijer: owner of Luettgenmeijer gallery in Berlin between 2008–15; publisher of records and art projects under EN/OF; publisher of records under Bottrop-Boy and Semishigure; currently doing quite uninteresting things.

Paul D. Miller (aka DJ Spooky) is a composer, multimedia artist and author. His DJ Mixer iPad app was downloaded 12 million times in 2014. In 2012–13, he was the first artist in residence at the Metropolitan Museum of Art, NYC. Miller is also executive editor of *Origin Magazine* and a contributing editor to *C-Theory*. His book, *Sound Unbound*, is a bestseller for MIT Press and in 2011 he released a graphic design project, *The Book Of Ice*, exploring the impact of climate change on Antarctica via a book, multimedia installation and music composition for string quartet.

Phil Milstein is the founder of the Velvet Underground Appreciation Society and the American Song-Poem Music Archives. He is the producer of an eclectic range of albums, from the beatnik novelties of

Stone Age Woo: The Zorch Sounds Of Nervous Norvus to the somniloquy recordings of *Dion McGregor Dreams Again*. As musician, he was a member of Uzi (with Thalia Zedek) and has released several solo-ish recordings under his own name and that of Pep Lester. Launched in 2005, his *Probe Is Turning-On The People* might be the world's longest-running music downloads site.

Heath Moerland (aka Sick Llama) is the boss of the Michigan-based label Fag Tapes. Keeping it rude as a musician and visual artist, he has performed and exhibited artwork worldwide. Besides various solo projects Heath is also involved in many musical configurations: to name a few, Tyvek, The Intended, Slither, Roachclip and Mirror II Rorrim.

John Moloney entered the world via Malden, Massachusetts in November 1971. John was a founding member of, and drummer for, psychedelic art-music collective Sunburned Hand Of The Man, which has been active since 1994 and continues its creative journey to this day. As a drummer, John has performed and/or recorded with Thurston Moore, J Mascis, Hush Arbors, MV&EE, Vibracathedral Orchestra, Six Organs Of Admittance, Sunroof!, Paul Flaherty, Egg,Eggs, World Domination, Boredoms, Howling Rain and many more. His visual art has featured in numerous group exhibitions and he has contributed artwork to many recording artists over the years.

Monster Dudes (Jeremy and Venec Miller) was born in a basement in the cold of Idaho winter, 2003–04. A father and four-year-old son, the duo did more than just play music: they created improvised theatre, wrestling on stage, performing often confounding acts of heroism in a free-for-all brawl – with youth often triumphant. The line-up and instrumentation morphed constantly, sometimes within the context of a single song. Today, Monster Dudes continues but gone is the propensity for encouraging chaos, instead more geared toward their enjoyment of making music, both together and in the members' separate endeavours.

Jean–Marc Montera is a French guitarist specialising in free improvisation and sound experimentation. He co-founded *les Groupe de Recherche et d'Improvisation Musicales* in 1978 and, in 1999, joined forces with stage director Hubert Colas to found Montévidéo, a centre for contemporary art creation in Marseille. In 2001 he created *l'Ensemble d'Improvisateurs Européens*, an ensemble specialising in graphic scores and work commissioned from young composers. Jean-Marc performs with a number of groups including AMP (a guitar trio with Noël Akchoté and Jean-François Pauvros), The Room (a duo with Sophie Gonthier) and

Meditrio (with medievalist musicians Julien Ferrando and Jean-Michel Robert.)

Andy Moor began his career in Edinburgh, Scotland, with the multi-faceted Dog Faced Hermans, before moving to the Netherlands in 1990 to join The Ex. In recent years, Andy has collaborated with musicians from a wide range of backgrounds including Yannis Kyriakides, with whom he performed a set of *rebetika* songs (urban Greek tunes from the twenties and thirties), sound poet Anne-James Chaton, DJ/Rupture, John Butcher and Thomas Lehn, Lean Left (quartet with Ken Vandermark, Terrie Ex and Paal Nilssen-Love) and Heretics (trio with Thurston Moore and Anne-James Chaton), as well as his continued work with The Ex.

Gene Moore started out on a white Hagstrom 2 guitar back in 1969, mostly played on the porch of his friend Peter Ross's house. Having served in the US Air Force from 1975, Gene got married and became a proud father of two. His musical horizons expanded while based at McQuire AFB, New Jersey, where he would get to see numerous bands; meanwhile, he accompanied younger brother Thurston to a lot of NYC gigs. In the mid-2000s, Gene was invited to join Hat City Intuitive and, subsequently, he joined forces with Todd Knapp and Matt Sekel to form Prana Bindu.

Tom Moore is an artist and educator based in Roanoke, Virginia. He created and runs Throne Heap records and tapes.

Thomas Mortigan is an American musician and artist specialising in black metal and modular synthesis. He resides in Houston, Texas and has been involved in such noteworthy bands and projects as Octagon, RU-486, Valefor (USA), Tellurian Fields and Vicious Beast, and also performs modular synthesis under his own name. Mortigan also ran the DIY cassette tape label Destructive Industries, which put out many cassette releases from such acts as Rudolf Eb.er, Thurston Moore, Jarboe (ex-Swans), Grinning Death's Head, Militia, Castevet and others.

Manuel Mota was born in 1970 and has been performing publicly since 1990. He is based in Lisbon, where he gained a degree in architecture and taught himself guitar. Improvisation is his main focus and creative process, and the field he considers the most complete, challenging and free. Manuel founded the label Headlights in 1998, and it's through this that he has, almost exclusively, released his musical works.

Bill Nace is an artist and musician based in Western Massachusetts. He has collaborated with an extraordinary range of musicians including

Michael Morley, Chris Cooper, John Truscinski, Jake Meginsky, Jessica Rylan and Kim Gordon, with whom he regularly plays as one half of the duo Body/Head. He has performed at a wide variety of venues and featured at festivals such as ATP, Colour Out of Space, Supersonic Festival, International Festival Musique Actuelle and Homegrown. Nace's range has been described as "veering from sculptural, almost Remko-Scha-esque chime to Loren Connors-style elegance in only a few short moves" (Mimaroglu Music, 2010).

James Nares' paintings seek to capture the moment of their own creation. They are most frequently made in a single brushstroke, recording a gestural passage of time and motion across the canvas. Using brushes of his own design, he repeatedly creates and erases his strokes, over and over, until he feels he has made one that represents a precision of balance between intent and improvisation. Nares' films reference many of the same preoccupations with movement, rhythm and repetition, while also ranging further afield. In 2014, Rizzoli published the first monograph on Nares' work over the last four decades.

The New Blockaders embraced Luigi Russolo's Art of Noise manifesto, becoming merchants of 'anti-music', taking his work to a new level by using noise to develop a complex language capable of subtleties of shade and nuance, without sacrificing any of its feral power or ability to unlock repressed personae in the listener. Their 1982 manifesto proclaims: 'Blockade is resistance. It is our duty to blockade and induce others to blockade; anti-music, anti-art, anti-books, anti-films, anti-communications. We will make anti-statements about anything and everything. We will make a point of being pointless.' Everything about The New Blockaders entails refusal – art, replaced by nothing.

David Newgarden met Thurston selling used records on Astor Place, and suffered permanent damage to his left ear at CBGB on June 10, 1984, at the first of dozens of Sonic Youth gigs he attended. From 1985–94, Newgarden was music/programme director at WFMU radio, New Jersey, where he organised a 1991 benefit concert featuring Sonic Youth, John Zorn's Painkiller and Dim Stars. He assisted Sonic Death in 1993–94 and Tzadik Records between 1994–97, and helped start up the performance space Tonic in 1998. Newgarden has also managed Guided By Voices for over 20 years, along with other performers including Yoko Ono.

Pete Nolan plays drums in The Magik Markers, sings and plays guitar in Spectre Folk, and released a record last year under his own name entitled *Easy*. He's a dude from a cornfield in Michigan but has

295

called Brooklyn his home for a number of years, where he's been lucky enough to play with a lot of forward-thinking improvisers and art-rock types. He currently resides in Northampton, Massachusetts with his wife Julie and two daughters, Violet Ray and Gala My. He's recently become re-obsessed with the first two Stooges LPs.

Cristiano Nunes is a freelance sound technician, a simple guy who has been privileged to work with Zé dos Bois Gallery (ZDB) – a cultural association located in Lisbon, Portugal – since May 2008. The core of his job consists of operating and recording live concerts. Cristiano is a dedicated music lover working with heart, soul and huge respect for the artists. Some people believe that he feeds on musicians' happiness!

Dylan Nyoukis is a proud son of Scotland and a conjurer of avant-garde creation in all its misbegotten forms. Nearly 300 releases on his label, Chocolate Monk, testify to his desire to champion kindred spirits and their personal envisioning of what DIY experimentation can yield. Dylan started out performing as Prick Decay/Decaer Pinga with Dora Doll, before becoming one half of Blood Stereo with Karen Constance. He regularly cavorts under his own name; one current delight lies in the use of vocal gibber as raw meat for improvisation and sound manipulation. The Colour Out of Space music festival will return...

John Olson was born in 1972 in Bismarck, North Dakota. Since the early nineties, he has been pasting together a multicoloured body of work consisting of insane sound, mash-up words, nebulous paintings and mangled glossy-magazine moments. Trained as a painter, printmaker, soprano saxophonist and electrician, Olson is best known for being one third of the seminal avant-garde trip-metal act Wolf Eyes, and for his prolific mail-order record label American Tapes, which released 1,000+ musically and visually inzane artefacts from 1993–2015. His book of 365 record reviews, *Life Is A Rip Off!*, was published by Third Man Press.

My Cat Is An Alien (MCIAA) is the outsider duo of experimental, instantaneous composers and intermedia artists formed by brothers Maurizio and Roberto Opalio in Torino, Italy, 1998, before moving to a secret region of the Western Alps. MCIAA act through music, shamanic live audiovisual performance, cinematic poetry films and videos, painting, design, photography, installation, poetic writing and phonographic art editions. MCIAA's aim is to subvert the rules and principles of contemporary music and visual art, through a massive and highly innovative, poetic and philosophical body of work – a mission that earned them the cover of *The Wire*.

Balazs Pandi hails from Budapest, Hungary. Since emerging from the thrash metal and hardcore scene in the south side of Pest, he has made music his home. Balazs has thrived within a wide variety of collaborative situations, ranging from avant-jazz alongside Wadada Leo Smith and Arthur Doyle to free electronics with Masami Akita (aka Merzbow); with contemporary musicians such as Trevor Dunn and Joe Morris; with sludge-rockers Porn and genre-benders including Justin Broadrick (aka Godflesh), Mats Gustafsson and Thurston Moore. Balazs is employed as a music, arts and culture journalist, while maintaining a heartfelt commitment to the grassroots, DIY work aesthetic.

Evan Parker has been rewriting the sonic limits of the saxophone for nearly half a century. He has developed a post-Coltrane technique allowing him to play counterpoint on what was designed as a single-line instrument. Exploding its potential, he generates electronic-like textures acoustically and has built a personal soundscape that retains its own arresting lyricism while eschewing conventional tunes. Parker has worked with comparable revolutionaries including Cecil Taylor, Paul Bley, John Zorn and Anthony Braxton, performing within experimental electro-acoustic groups and contemporary classical ensembles as well as adding a razor-sharp edge to more orthodox line-ups and recording groups.

Sanford Parker has a body of work which should not be considered a mere collection of loose sheets – in which case his *oeuvre* would approach phonebook dimensions and could effortlessly crush a cockroach. Over the past decade and a half, anyone lowering their ear into the realm of metal and industrial will likely have come into contact with Sanford's work, either through his wide-ranging involvement as a producer and sound technician, or as a musician. His musical projects have included Buried At Sea, Corrections House, Minsk and Nachtmystium. As a producer he has lent his skills to Pelican, Eyehategod, Rwake and Voivod, among many others.

Justin Pizzoferrato is an audio engineer/producer living and working in the Pioneer Valley of Massachusetts. Shortly after moving to western Massachusetts, Justin met and began working with J Mascis at his home studio Bisquiteen. That job led to work with Sonic Youth, Kim Gordon and Thurston Moore, as well as many others unconnected with the band. Much of it followed him to Sonelab, the studio he's owned and operated since 2012.

Robert Poss has performed and recorded with Rhys Chatham, Nicolas Collins, Phill Niblock, Susan Stenger and Bruce Gilbert, and has composed and performed music for choreographers Sally Gross, Gerald Casel and Alexandra Beller. In 1986, he formed the influential wall-of-guitars group Band Of Susans. Reviewing his 2010 solo release, *Settings: Music For Dance, Film, Fashion And Industry*, *The Wire* wrote that Poss's "abiding love for electric guitar is no casual dalliance or detached Platonic infatuation; it's an erotic commitment, an obsessive plunge into the instrument's metallic churn and enveloping drone". He continues to perform his guitar and electronics pieces worldwide.

Chris Pottinger has lived a life dedicated to music, to visual art, to ongoing and unending creativity; art as life. Chris performs solo as Cotton Museum, a project commenced in 2002, utilising synthesizers, unusual electronic instruments and the saxophone to explore the world of experimental sound. He runs his own label, Tasty Soil Records, to bring work he finds interesting (and his own creations) into the world, while his music has graced numerous other releases worldwide. The name 'Cotton Museum' stems from the deformed, bulbous creatures he has created to adorn album covers and which inspire his music.

Walter Prati is a professor at the Conservatorio di Latina and Istituto Europeo di Design in Milan. As a composer and musician, his focus is on interaction between traditional and new electronic instruments, specifically through the application of informatics to music. This creative direction led him, in 1987, to the Centre for Computational Sonology at the University of Padova where he used the System 4i, one of the first computers designed for real-time synthesis and transformation of sound. Walter is a founder of Studio MM&T for musical research. He has performed at numerous festivals and venues with a wide range of artists.

Massimo Pupillo is a bass player, composer and improviser who has played on more than 50 albums and pariticipated in over 2,000 concerts. He founded the band Zu, whose albums came out on Mike Patton's Ipecac Recordings, and has collaborated with numerous musicians including The Melvins, Oren Ambarchi, Peter Brötzmann, Ken Vandermark, Stephen O'Malley and Damo Suzuki, among others. He has composed soundtracks for a number of feature films and for dance and theatre companies – most notably for Romeo Castellucci's Societas Raffaello Sanzio.

Jack Rabid has spent 36 years as editor and publisher of music magazine *The Big Takeover*, while also writing for publications including *Spin*, *The Village Voice*, *Alternative Press*, *Interview* and others. For the last eight years he's also hosted *The Big Takeover Show* online, now on realpunkradio.com. He performs with reunited nineties shoe-gaze band Springhouse, having previously played with Even Worse, LA band Leaving Trains and Last Burning Embers. Jack gained his bachelor degree in economics from New York University and lives in Brooklyn with his wife, Mary, and children, Jim and Caroline.

Newton (pronounced: NOO-tən) is the moniker of experimental musician and sound artist **Mat Rademan**. Rademan has created a prolific and profound catalogue of recordings, performances, films and installations since the project's inception in 1995. His sound is a singular blend of electronics, pedals, voice, cassette recorders, contact microphones and occasional non-musical devices. Seamlessly incorporating techniques from *musique concrète*, noise, turntablism, Fluxus, anti-music, field recording, glitch and sometimes performance art, the result is a tightly-composed sonic assault steeped in both theory and practice as can only be achieved by a seasoned veteran. Rademan runs the prolific Philadelphia label Breathmint, founded in 1995.

Radieux Radio is a poet, musician and activist based in London. During Thurston's 2016 Residency at the Louvre in Paris, Radieux and Thurston recorded their first album entitled *Les Tendances* (forthcoming). Thurston's electric and 12-string acoustic guitars accompany Radieux's vocals (in Arabic and French), cello and typewriter.

Hal Rammel has been involved in the creative arts and music for the past 45 years. As a composer and improviser he utilises musical instruments of his own design and construction, releasing many recordings on his own Penumbra Music label. During the eighties, he was an active member of Chicago's experimental and improvised music scene. In 2013, 14 instruments designed and built by Hal Rammel were included in the permanent collection of the National Music Museum in Vermillion, South Dakota, including many acoustic instruments built in the early nineties that figured prominently in his work with Chicago improvisers.

Lee Ranaldo has spent three and a half decades as an artist, encompassing numerous musical recordings and performances, poetry books and journals, visual art, music production and composition. Active in the New York music scene from 1979 and a co-founder of Sonic Youth, recent highlights of Lee's work include the *contre-jour* sound/light in-the-round performances with his partner Leah Singer; and his *Hurricane Transcriptions* based on wind recordings made during Hurricane Sandy in 2012, written for the Berlin Kaleidoscope String Ensemble and recently performed by Brooklyn's Dither Electric Guitar Quartet. His *Lost Highway* drawings and *Black Noise* prints have been exhibited across the US and Europe.

Kim Rancourt is a musician, promoter and photographer. He has fronted the bands When People Were Shorter And Lived Near The Water, After That It's All Gravy and Shapir-O'Rama, and is currently recording a solo album with a new band produced by Don Fleming. For many years, Kim was music curator of Sideshows By The Seashore in Coney Island. He is a freelance tour guide in New York City and is currently giving the arts and architecture tour at the Lincoln Center for the Performing Arts; he is also the official tour guide for Coney Island.

Cory Rayborn is an attorney by day who runs Three Lobed Recordings by night, with the assistance of his family's cats. He will always stop what he is doing any time that 'Elegy For All The Dead Rock Stars' starts playing in his immediate vicinity.

Alan Read ran Krayon Recordings, a now-defunct record label which was based in Bournemouth, UK. During its lifespan it put out records and put on gigs by artists such as Astral Social Club, Bridget Hayden, Duncan Harrison & Dylan Nyoukis, Eli Keszler, Harappian Night Recordings, High Wolf, MoHa, Moon Unit, Noxagt, Oren Ambarchi, Part Wild Horses Mane On Both Sides, Paul Flaherty/Chris Corsano/C. Spencer Yeh, Sylvester Anfang II and Vibracathedral Orchestra, to name just a few.

Sarah Register is a musician and mastering engineer working in NYC since 1997. In Talk Normal she played guitar and bass, and sang.

Dr Claire Robins is currently Reader in Art and Education, as well as Programme Leader for the MA Art and Design in Education at UCL, Institute of Education. She is on the editorial board of *engage*: the national association for gallery educators. She studied Fine Art at St Martins School of Art and has taught in numerous colleges, schools and galleries while continuing to work as an artist.

Brett Robinson is an archivist, poet and performance artist based in Easthampton, Massachusetts. He is a founding member of Radioactive Prostitute and Egg,Eggs. He can often be found lost in the Pioneer Valley woods.

Frank Rosaly is a drummer and composer living in Chicago and Amsterdam. He has been involved in the improvised/experimental music community since 2001, becoming an integral part of the contemporary music fabric and navigating a fine line between the vibrant improvised music, experimental, rock, jazz and multidisciplinary communities. He contributes much of his time to performing, composing, teaching and organising events, while also touring regularly. Frank has collaborated with Bobby Bradford, Frode Gjerstad, Peter Brötzmann, Tony Malaby, Roscoe Mitchell, Anthony Coleman, Paul Flaherty, Marshall Allen, Eric Boeren, Fennesz, David Daniell, Doug McCombs, Michael Moore and Jaap Blonk, among others.

John Russell was born in 1954 and started playing the guitar in 1966. His first experiences of playing free improvised music were around 1971–72 and he has been doing it ever since, over the years working with many of the music's greatest players in various countries around the world. He founded Mopomoso to promote and increase the understanding of the music, and is also co-founder of the Weekertoft label with Irish musician Paul G. Smyth.

Matthew Saint-Germain: lifelong Minnesota resident; 1984, Mondale. Owner of Freedom From. Loves balls of all kinds and "arguing with everyone and using your fucking debate shit to confuse me". UMN BA in psychology pending. Writes about food and baseball.

Daniel Sandor is a London-based music producer and audiovisual consultant. His diverse work history includes recordings for clients ranging from Valerie June to Merzbow, Keiji Haino and Thurston Moore; lighting design for opera and contemporary music performances; or technical management of high-profile events. Whenever he's not working, he likes to write songs in his studio for his own band, Volkova Sisters.

Jim Sauter was born in Nyack, New Jersey, a suburb of New York City, where he took up the saxophone in public school and met lifelong friend and collaborator Don Dietrich. He has played as part of the groundbreaking trio Borbetomagus for several decades, as well as appearing on recordings by God Is My Co-Pilot, Scarcity Of Tanks and Rudolph Grey. His ongoing partnership with drummer Kid Millions has produced several outstanding albums. For close to 40 years, Sauter has worked as a professional museum exhibition designer and is currently exhibits specialist at the Franklin D. Roosevelt Presidential Library.

Jane Scarpantoni is a cellist/composer/arranger who has performed and recorded with the late, great Lou Reed, The Lounge Lizards (NYC), and Patti Smith, among others. She also has appeared on many and various recordings, with artists including the Yeah Yeah Yeahs, Martha and

Rufus Wainwright, and Springsteen. She is also the DMV Band's secret weapon. DMV – Jane, Exene Cervenka and Shivaree – play the songs of Duke McVinnie and have just finished an insane country album with him. Jane also continues work, as always, on her own music and art, as well as other collaborative projects.

Giancarlo Schiaffini is a composer, trombonist and tubist who has recorded over 160 records. Self-taught, he played in Italy's first free-jazz concerts and compositions in the mid-sixties, then studied at Darmstadt with Stockhausen, Ligeti and Globokar. He formed the contemporary ensemble Nuove Forme Sonore and collaborated with the Gruppo di Improvvisazione di Nuova Consonanza. Giancarlo has given numerous seminars across the globe and taught at the conservatories in l'Aquila and Siena. Having worked with Cage, Armitage, Nono and Scelsi, his treatise on trombone techniques was published by Ricordi and a further work on improvisation and listening by Auditorium (Milan).

Jim Sclavunos is a multi-instrumentalist, producer and writer. He has been a member of Nick Cave & The Bad Seeds since 1994. Alongside Lydia Lunch, he was an integral part of the no-wave scene in the bands Teenage Jesus & The Jerks, Beirut Slump and 8 Eyed Spy, before joining Sonic Youth. Since then, Sclavunos has recorded with a diverse host of artists including Grinderman, The Cramps, Marianne Faithfull and Iggy Pop, along with solo albums such as *The Vanity Set*. In 2012 he presented *Faustian Pact*, a live adaptation of Murnau's film *Faust*, at the Perth International Arts Festival.

James Sedwards is the leader, guitarist and main composer of the avant-rock band Nøught, whose music combines visceral intensity and attack with extreme structural complexity. Amongst his other projects are The Devil, a collaboration with Ben Wallers and Sophie Politowicz of Country Teasers (of which Sedwards has also been a member), and Deadly Orgone Radiation, an improvising trio featuring Weasel Walter and Alex Ward. The Devil released their debut album on Copy Records in 2013 and Deadly Orgone Radiation released *Power Trips* on Copepod in 2015.

Wally Shoup plays unfettered, emotion-laden alto saxophone and has been involved in freely improvised music since the mid-seventies. He has worked with a wide array of musicians, including Thurston Moore, Nels Cline, Evan Parker, Davey Williams, Jack Wright, Bill Horist, Paul Flaherty, Chris Corsano, Nate Wooley, Dennis Rea, Daniel Carter and many others. His current Seattle projects include the noir-jazz Wally Shoup Quartet, the skronk-free jazz trio Spider Trio, the Wally Shoup

Sax Trio +1 and the Kelley/Campbell/Shoup Trio. He was named one of Seattle's 50 Most Influential Musicians by *Seattle Metropolitan Magazine* in 2009.

Paul Smith co-founded the Doublevision video label with Cabaret Voltaire before starting Blast First, which went on to release records by artists including Sonic Youth, Steve Albini, Butthole Surfers and Dinosaur Jr. In the nineties he started the King Mob spoken-word label, releasing recordings by the Black Panthers, Charles Bukowski and Ken Kesey among others. The Blast First Petite label sprang to life in 2004 and continues to this day. Paul regularly acts as an arts producer for a number of cultural entities and as a self-proclaimed Curator of Rock Antiquities, restarting the careers of Wire, Throbbing Gristle, Magazine and The Pop Group.

Tom Smith (To Live And Shave In LA) prefers not to use the third person. He must leave for Hamburg Flughafen in less than six hours so he will now go to bed.

Dagobert Sondervan has been a lifelong explorer of music, starting with piano lessons, study of classical percussion, studies at the Jazz-Studio College of Antwerp and participation in numerous rock and punk bands. From 1995 he was resident DJ at the Fuse club in Brussels, among other locations, before making his first release under the name Anton Price, followed by the album *The Collapse Of The State Vector* in 2000. Recently he has been involved in music coding, working as a specialist for Nord, Focusrite, Novation and Roli.

Susan Stenger has bridged the rock and art music worlds since her youth in Buffalo, NY, where she both played in bands and studied experimental music. After classical flute training in Prague, she joined the NYC-based SEM Ensemble to specialise in John Cage, Christian Wolff, Julius Eastman and Phill Niblock. She was a founder of Band Of Susans and all-bass band Big Bottom, and has performed with Rhys Chatham, FM Einheit, Siouxsie Sioux, John Cale and Nick Cave. Stenger has composed several film soundtracks and exhibited at MOCA Lyon, Sketch Gallery, AV Festival, Toronto Nuit Blanche and Stockholm Music and Art.

Tom Surgal is a filmmaker/musician who has directed a number of adventurous music videos for leading alternative bands like Sonic Youth, Pavement and The Blues Explosion. He is currently in production on a documentary entitled *Fire Music: A History Of The Free Jazz Revolution*. Tom was previously a member of The Blue Humans and is a longtime collaborator of Thurston Moore's. He is also a co-founder of the band White Out. A native New Yorker, he currently resides in his hometown.

JG Thirlwell is a composer/producer/performer based in Brooklyn. He has released over 30 albums under his own name as well as pseudonyms, including Manorexia, Foetus, Steroid Maximus, Baby Zizanie, Clint Ruin and Wiseblood. Thirlwell has featured as producer, remixer or arranger for many artists, including Karen O, Zola Jesus, Tony Oursler, The Melvins, Swans, Lydia Lunch, Coil and many more. He has also completed commissions for Kronos Quartet, Bang On A Can and others, and is a member of the Freq_Out sound-art collective. JG also created the score of TV shows *The Venture Bros* and *Archer*, and several film scores.

Wharton Tiers was born in Philadelphia in the year of the Stratocaster, and has been recording, composing and playing music his entire life. He moved to NYC in 1976, playing with Theoretical Girls and Laurie Anderson before starting Fun City studio. This led to a recording career of over 200 releases. In 1996, Wharton returned to playing with The Wharton Tiers Ensemble, an instrumental, symphonic, surf-guitar group. He started Fun City Recordings in 2011 and is currently revising his symphonic works, preparing to release a jazz record and a piano recording, *Political Sonatas 2016*, alongside new ensemble music.

Rafael Toral, born in Lisbon, 1967, is a music performer and composer active since 1984. Formerly known for his drone/ambient work with guitar and electronics, and acclaimed records such as *Wave Field* (1994) or *Violence Of Discovery And Calm Of Acceptance* (2000), he radically renewed his approach to music in 2004: electronic music inspired by post-free-jazz. Whether performing his *Space Program* compositions or in numerous collaborations, he has been touring the US, Europe and Japan. In 2014, he relocated to the mountains in central Portugal for a more sustainable life.

James Toth is a writer, recording artist, and musician currently based in Richmond, Virginia. He has written about music and culture for *The Wire*, *NPR*, *Stereogum*, *Salon*, *Relix* and *Aquarium Drunkard*, among others. Toth appears, under the moniker Wooden Wand and in countless collaborations, on over 100 records. In 2015 he co-founded (with his wife, Leah) the experimental label Footfalls Records.

Trumans Water continued after Kirk and Kevin Branstetter moved with Kevin Cascell to Portland. Cascell left the band after 10 years and is now a prolific collage artist in Portland. The brothers then hooked up with bassist Mike Coumatos (The Bugs) and drummer Geoff Soule

(Fuck, Sad Horse). Shortly after moving to Portland, Kevin moved to France where he still lives. Trumans releases have become rarer due to the geographical separation, but they continue. Kevin also tours Europe as a one-man band called Worlds Dirtiest Sport.

Joe Tunis was introduced to interesting music by his boss at a department-store job back in high school, and remains forever in his debt. In college Joe learned to play bass and drums, and started a band before deciding to start a label. Carbon Records commenced in 1994, with over 230 releases to date including national and international artists such as Tom Carter, Loren Connors and Gate. Joe also plays in numerous projects including Pengo, Tuurd, Crush The Junta, Tumul and Entente Cordiale, as well as solo under the names Joe+N and Bruise Halo.

Jon Tye has a history stretching from school bands to punk bands to post-punk bands... XS, The Fans, Missing Chemicals... supporting The Damned, A Certain Ratio and Red Krayola... mid-eighties sound-clash group Giant and a left turn into electronic library music leading to acid house, ambient and the formation of Lo Recordings, and an epic sweep of collaboration involving Lol Coxhill, Luke Vibert, Aphex Twin, Stereolab and Grimes, along with personal projects like Twisted Science, Hairy Butter and Milky Globe. Now half of Seahawks, Jon also records as Cherry Garcia, Brain Machine and Captain Sunshine & The Valley People. He's resident in Cornwall, high on the hill.

Marc Urselli is a five-times nominated/three-times Grammy Award-winning engineer, producer, mixer, composer and sound designer who writes, produces and records artists. He lives in NYC and has recorded over 50 albums by John Zorn, also working with Les Paul, Lou Reed, Laurie Anderson, Sting, Joss Stone, The Beach Boys, Lila Downs, Eric Clapton, Jeff Beck, Faith No More's Mike Patton, Keith Richards, Buddy Guy, Bon Jovi's Richie Sambora, Goo Goo Dolls' Johnny Rzeznick, ZZ Top, Sam Cooke, The Black Crowes, Aerosmith's Joe Perry, Simply Red's Mick Hucknall, Luther Vandross, Simple Minds and many more.

Carlos Van Hijfte was born in 1954 on a farm in Zeeland, the Netherlands. In the early sixties his family moved to a house with electricity, where he soon bought his first record player. In the late seventies, Van Hijfte started a record store in Eindhoven, where he would meet Lee Ranaldo in '81. That summer he started promoting shows, and in June '83 he presented his first Sonic Youth show, after which he was their European agent until the end. Carlos also booked European shows for others, including Cat Power, Shellac and Dinosaur Jr.

305

Greg Vegas is a Connecticut native currently living in Brooklyn, NYC, working in the music industry as an artist and record label manager. He played guitar in nineties indie-rock band Monsterland, and then guitar and tenor sax in the long-running Hat City Intuitive. Greg can now occasionally be found sitting in on sax with bands like SAVAK, Obits, Goat, Graveyard, Suuns and many improv incarnations, when he has the time.

Sonny Vincent formed punk rock band Testors in 1975, who were a key part of the NYC scene until disbanding in 1981, earning a cult following that continues to this very day. In the eighties his bands included Sonny Vincent & The Extreme, Model Prisoners and Shotgun Rationale. Vincent has released 20 albums under his own name and spent nine years touring with Maureen Tucker (ex-Velvet Underground), as well as forming a band with Scott Asheton (The Stooges) and Captain Sensible (The Damned). He continues to work creatively in music, film, multimedia art and writing.

Anne Waldman has spent her life seeking out, and creating, poetic communities, and ensuring the archival salvation of precious literary histories. Deemed a "counter cultural giant" by *Publisher's Weekly*, her work transcends creative forms and encompasses her extensive poetry, performance pieces, feminist criticism, editorial roles, art/poetic and music/poetic collaborations, including an opera on the life of Ezra Pound and films. Author of over 40 books (publishers include Penguin and Coffee House Press) and recently a recipient of the Before Columbus Book Award for lifetime achievement, Waldman also co-founded the Jack Kerouac School of Disembodied Poetics at Naropa University and continues to direct its summer writing programme.

Frans de Waard has been producing music since 1984 and is primarily known for 'Kapotte Muziek', as described in 2008 documentary *What You See Is What You Hear*. He has played with numerous individuals in formal arrangements (including Roel Meelkop, Freek Kinkelaar and Peter Duimelinks), performed improvised music with whoever is available and worked under a variety of names including Beequeen, Goem, Zebra and Freiband. Frans founded and continues to run *Vital Weekly*, the online magazine for underground music. His latest endeavours include The Tobacconists with Scott Foust, Ezdanitoff with Wouter Jaspers and his own lo-fi/noise identity, Modelbau.

Alex Ward is a composer, improviser and performing musician, primarily on clarinet and guitar, based in London. In the nineties he co-led the band Camp Blackfoot; since 2007, he and drummer Jem Doulton have worked as the duo Dead Days Beyond Help, in which Ward plays guitar, sings and co-writes the material. Besides his involvement in DDBH and a wide range of improvised collaborations, Alex currently leads the bands Predicate, Forebrace and The Alex Ward Quintet/Sextet, and plays guitar in the rock band God's Mama. He co-runs the record label Copepod with Luke Barlow. (alexward.org.uk)

Byron Westbrook is an artist and musician based in Brooklyn, NYC. He works with the dynamics of perception, often in the form of multi-channel audio performances or via installations using video or lighting. His work has been shown internationally at venues including the ICA (London), ISSUE Project Room, PS1, Fridman Gallery (New York), Disjecta (Portland), Human Resources (Los Angeles) and *Instants Chavirés* (Paris), among others. He holds an MFA from Bard College and has been an artist in residence at the Civitella Ranieri Foundation, Clocktower Gallery and Diapason Gallery for Sound. He has made numerous audio releases and is currently visiting in faculty at the Pratt Institute.

Jef Whitehead, multi-instrumentalist, is a native of Stanton, California. In his teens, he began drumming in bands while also riding as a sponsored amateur skateboarder for Concrete Jungle and Speed Wheels (among others). As an artist, besides his work for countless bands, his iconic images have also been commissioned by numerous skateboard companies and he created Thunder Trucks' 'Heart/Grenade' emblem. He also has more than a quarter-century's experience as a top-level tattooist. Jef's main music projects are Leviathan and Lurker Of Chalice, and he has played on over 30 albums. With his wife, Stevie, and daughter, Grail, the Whitehead family devote every day to the creation of art and music.

John Wiese is an LA-based artist and composer. A highly-respected presence in the academic world of contemporary sound-art as well as the noise/experimental underground, he specialises in the fields of sound for installations, multi-channel diffusions and large ensemble scores. His expertise in composition and texture is on display in works under his own name (many on his label Helicopter), as well as his influential *concrète* grindcore outfit, Sissy Spacek, and his extreme electronics unit, LHD. Wiese is also an accomplished visual and graphic artist with exhibitions and publications across the globe.

William Winant, a 2014 Grammy-nominated percussionist, has performed with some of the most innovative and creative musicians of our time, including John Cage, Iannis Xenakis, Keith Jarrett, Anthony Braxton, James Tenney, Cecil Taylor, George Lewis, Steve Reich, Jean-

Philippe Collard, Frederic Rzewski, Ursula Oppens, Joan La Barbara, Annea Lockwood, Oingo Boingo and Kronos Quartet.

Keith Wood launched Hush Arbors in 2001 and has released 12 solo records, including *Since We Have Fallen* (Harvest), *Landscape Of Bone* (Three Lobed), *Hush Arbors* (Ecstatic Peace!) and *Yankee Reality* (Ecstatic Peace!), the latter produced by Dinosaur Jr.'s J Mascis. As a fan of self-releases, experiments and rarities, he regularly makes tour-only CDs, live recordings and split releases with various friends. In addition to Hush Arbors, Wood has toured extensively as a guitarist with Wooden Wand, Six Organs Of Admittance, Jack Rose, Voice Of The Seven Woods, Current 93 and Thurston Moore.

Discography

While my completist tendencies have driven me to aim for perfection, it seems that every time I turn around I locate another song Thurston Moore has contributed to a compilation, another collaborative effort released under a whimsical band name, another document of a wild night on-stage with him at the epicentre. I find that as awe-inspiring as it is entertaining.

This discography only notes the first issue of any release and does not record reissues, promo editions and alternative versions; neither does it record remixes or production roles. Entries are listed chronologically, specifying album titles in italics, 'songs' (in the guest appearances by Moore on others' albums, or on compilations of original material), artists and/or other participants in the recording, then label and year of release in brackets.

Thurston Moore 1981–Autumn 2016

Failure To Thrive – The Coachmen (New Alliance Records, recorded 1980/ released 1988)

Just Another Asshole – 'Fucking Youth Of Today' – Thurston Moore (no label, 1981)

Noise Fest – 'Untitled' – Sonic Youth (ZG, 1982)

Who You Staring At? – 'Music For The Dance Bad Smells Choreographed By Twyla Tharp' – Glenn Branca/John Giorno (Giorno Poetry Systems, 1982)

Symphony No. 2 (The Peak Of The Sacred) – Glenn Branca (Atavistic, recorded 1982/released 1992)

'Leaving'/'One Night Stand' – Even Worse (Autonomy Records, recorded 1982/released 1988)

Body To Body, Job To Job – Swans (Young God Records, recorded *c.* 1982–85/released 1990)

Symphony No. 1 (Tonal Plexus) – Glenn Branca (ROIR, 1983)

Symphony No. 3 Gloria – Glenn Branca (Neutral, 1983)

Hard Rock – Michael Gira/Lydia Lunch (Ecstatic Peace!, 1984). *While this was the first Ecstatic Peace! release, and Moore recorded, designed and issued this release he did not perform on it.*

In Limbo – Lydia Lunch (Doublevision, 1984)

Thurston believes there was a recording around this time with the band ARTLESS; however, despite the kind support of Mykel Board and John Hall, no data can currently be located.

Tellus #10: All Guitars – 'Skrewer Boy' – Thurston Moore (Tellus, 1985)

Young, Popular And Sexy – 'Pope' – Thick Pigeon (Factory, 1987)

Honeymoon In Red – Lydia Lunch (Widowspeak Productions, 1987)

The Crumb – Lydia Lunch/Thurston Moore (Widowspeak Productions, 1988)

The End Of Music (As We Know It) – 'European Son' – Thurston Moore (ROIR, 1988)

Roll Out The Barrel – **'King Kong'** – Jad Fair/Kramer (Shimmy Disc, 1988)

Barefoot In The Head – Don Dietrich/Thurston Moore/Jim Sauter (Forced Exposure, recorded 1988/released 1990)

Life In Exile After Abdication – Maureen Tucker (50,000,000, etc., 1989)

'Hey Mersh!'/'Talk So Mean – Alternate Non-LP Mix'/'Talk So Mean – Alternate Non-LP Mix' (12") – Maureen Tucker (50,000,000, etc., 1989)

Joggers And Smoggers – 'Gentlemen' – The Ex (Ex Records, 1989)

Mono! Stereo: Sgt. Shonen's Exploding Plastic Eastman Band Request – 'Telephone Piece' – Thurston M. Miserable/Pat Fear (Giant Records, 1989)

Rake – Velvet Monkeys (Rough Trade, 1990)

'Rock The Nation'/'Why Don't We Do It In The Road?' – Velvet Monkeys (Sub Pop, 1991)

Special Kiss – Gumball (Paperhouse Records, 1991)

Dim Stars EP (3x7") – Dim Stars (Paperhouse Records, 1991)

Guitarrorists – 'Blues For Spacegirl' – Thurston Moore (No. 6 Records, 1991)

Mask Of Light – Rudolph Grey (New Alliance Records/Ecstatic Peace!, 1991)

Dim Stars – Dim Stars (Paperhouse Records, 1992)

Clear To Higher Time – The Blue Humans (New Alliance Records, 1992)

'Electric Pen'/'Gum' – Mirror/Dash (Ecstatic Peace!, 1992)

Fortune Cookie Prize – 'Black Candy' – Kim Gordon/Thurston Moore/Epic Soundtracks (Simple Machines Records, 1992)

Outlaw Blues – 'Sitting On A Barbed Wire Fence' – Kim Gordon/Thurston Moore/Epic Soundtracks (Imaginary Records, 1992)

Fourteen Songs For Greg Sage And The Wipers – 'Pushing The Extreme' – Keith Nealy/Thurston Moore (Tim/Kerr Records, 1992)

'Starfield Wild'/'Earth/Amp' – Thurston Moore (Table Of The Elements, 1993)

Rock Animals – 'Butterfly Boy' – Shonen Knife (August Records, 1993)

Shamballa – William Hooker/Thurston Moore/Elliott Sharp (Knitting Factory Works, 1994)

Your Invitation To Suicide – 'Speed Queen' – Two Virgins/White Flag (Munster Records, 1994)

Backbeat (soundtrack) – The Backbeat Band (Virgin, 1994)

Monster – 'Crush With Eyeliner' – R.E.M. (Warner Bros, 1994)

Our Band Could Be Your Life: A Tribute To D. Boon & The Minutemen – 'Shit You Hear at Parties' – Thurston Moore (little brother records, 1994)

Skins, Brains And Guts EP – Society's Ills (Ecstatic Peace!, 1994)

US Tour 95 – 'Live 9/27/95 Knitting Factory' – Violent Onsen Geisha (Japan Oversea, 1995)

Wavelength Infinity – 'Cosmic Equation' – Ezra La Plante/Thurston Moore (Rastascan Records, 1995)

Psychic Hearts – Thurston Moore (Geffen, 1995)

'The Church Should Be For The Outcasts – Not A Church That Casts People Out'/'Thoodblirsty Thesbians' – Male Slut (Stomach Ache, 1995)

Milktrain To Paydirt – 'Asleep Sneeze' – Trumans Water (Homestead, 1995)

Klangfarbenmelodie And The Colorist Strikes Primitiv – Thurston Moore/Tom Surgal (Corpus Hermeticum, 1995)

'Cindy (Rotten Tanx)'/'Teenage Buddhist Daydream' – Thurston Moore (DGC, 1995)

Instress Vol. 2 – 'Just Tell Her That I Really Like Her'/'Deirdre Of The Sorrows' – Loren Connors/Thurston Moore (Road Cone, 1995)

Not Me – Thurston Moore/Tom Surgal (Fourth Dimension, 1996)

Piece For Jetsun Dolma – Thurston Moore/Tom Surgal/William Winant (Les Disques Victo, 1996)

Piece For Yvonne Rainer – Thurston Moore (Destroy All Music, 1996)

Please Just Leave Me (My Paul Desmond) – Thurston Moore (Pure, 1996)

Electricity Vs Insects – Prick Decay/Thurston Moore (Chocolate Monk, 1996)

We'll Sail Out Far... Maybe A Little Too Far – 'Winter Johnny' – Thurston Moore (Apartment Records, 1996)

Heavy (soundtrack) – 'Victor And Callie'/'Undertow'/'Kissing On The Bridge'/'Spinning Goodbye'/'Culinary Institute' – Thurston Moore (TVT, 1996)

United Mutations – 'Yvonne/Thaw' – Infrastructure/Thurston Moore (Lo Recordings, 1996)

Godz Is Not A Put-On – 'Quack, I'm A Quack' – Male Slut (Lissy's Records, 1996)

Germs Tribute: A Small Circle Of Friends – 'Now I Hear the Laughter' – Puzzled Panthers (Grass Records, 1996)

Songs We Taught The Lord Vol. 1 – Phil X. Milstein/Thurston Moore (download, recorded 1996/released 2015)

Songs We Taught The Lord Vol. 2 – Phil X. Milstein/Thurston Moore (Hot Cars Warp, 1997)

Legend Of The Blood Yeti – 13 Ghosts/Derek Bailey/Thurston Moore (Infinite Chug, 1997)

Pillow Wand – Nels Cline/Thurston Moore (little brother records, 1997)

In Store – Nels Cline/Thurston Moore (Father Yod, 1997)

MMMR – Loren Connors/Jean-Marc Montera/Thurston Moore/Lee Ranaldo (Xeric, Numero Zero, 1997)

Kerouac: Kicks Joy Darkness – 'The Last Hotel' – Lenny Kaye/Patti Smith/Thurston Moore (Rykodisc, 1997)

'Telstar'/'Sputnik' – Don Fleming/Thurston Moore/Experimental Audio Research (Via Satellite, 1997)

'I Hate The Nineties'/'Tube Tops Forever'/'Cellphone Madness' – Rodney & The Tube Tops (Sympathy For The Record Industry, 1997)

Further Mutations – 'Careful With That Rake Eugene' – Eugene Chadbourne/Thurston Moore (Lo Recordings, 1997)

Waiting To Be Old – 'April's Shower' – Thurston Moore (Opprobrium, 1997)

Smiling Pets – 'Here Today' – Thurston Moore (Sony, 1998)

Foot – Foot (God Bless Records, 1998)

Riddim Warfare – 'Dialectical Transformation III (Soylent Green)' – DJ Spooky (Outpost Recordings, 1998)

Root – Thurston Moore (Lo Recordings, 1998)

Vision Volume One: Vision Festival 1997 Compiled – 'Fuzz Against Junk' – Jon Voigt/Lawrence Cook/Thurston Moore (AUM Fidelity, 1998)

Resonance Volume 7 Number 1: Maverika – 'Concerto For Guitar And Posthumous Scratch Orchestra' – Thurston Moore (London Musicians' Collective, 1998)

Dirty Windows – Lee Ranaldo (Barooni, 1998)

RRR 500 – 'Untitled' – Thurston Moore (RRRecords, 1998)

Velvet Goldmine (soundtrack) – Wylde Rattz (London Records, 1998)

A Possible Dawn – Loren Connors (hatNOIR, 1998)

No Music Festival (boxset) (Entartete Kunst Records, 1998)

III – The Grassy Knoll (Antilles, 1998)

The Revolution Of Everyday Life – 'Needled'/'Ex Novo' – Echo Park (Lo Recordings, 1998)

Strings & Stings – 'Millionaire Dream' – Ultra Milkmaids/Thurston Moore (FBWL, 1999)

Color In Absence Sound – 'Punk Eye' – Thurston Moore (Hell's Half Halo, 1999)

Pearl + Umbra – 'Causes Causes Causes' – Russell Mills/Undark (Bella Union, 1999)

Subliminal Minded: The EP – 'Dialectical Transformation III Peace In Rwanda Mix' – DJ Spooky (Outpost Recordings, 1999)

The Promise – Thurston Moore/Walter Prati/Evan Parker (Materiali Sonori, 1999)

'G.Neurus'/'Super Tuscan'/'Super Tuscan Deisonic Rmx: Sollo Un Minuto' – Deison/Thurston Moore (Loud! Sin, 1999)

'Apple Seeds'/'Inverse Ratio Or "The Vanishing Voice"'/'Halloween 99' – Golden Calves Century Band/Dr Gretchen's Musical Weightlifting Program/Thurston Moore (Polyamory, 1999)

This Is NeMocore – Foot (Instant Mayhem, 1999)

Jeg Gleder Meg Til År 2000 – 'Armageddon' – Foot (Universal, 1999)

Live At The Cooler – Foot (Breathmint, 1999)

Fringe Benefits – The Walter Sears (Instant Mayhem, 1999)

Hurricane Floyd – Toshi Makihara/Thurston Moore/Wally Shoup (Sublingual, 1999)

Lost To The City/Noise To Nowhere – Thurston Moore/Tom Surgal/William Winant (Intakt Records, 2000)

Blackbean And Placenta – 'French' – Thurston Moore (Blackbean And Placenta Tape Club, 2000)

Analogous Indirect – 'O Michigan' – Thurston Moore (Public Eyesore, 2000)

4 Compilation – 'Akihabara Nightnurse' – Thurston Moore (MSBR Records, 2000)

Up From The Archives – 'Untitled' – Thurston Moore (Sub Rosa, 2000)

TM/MF – Marco Fusinato/Thurston Moore (Freewaysound, 2000)

Fuck Shit Up – Christian Marclay/Thurston Moore/Lee Ranaldo (Les Disques Victo, 2000)

Record Player (DVD) – Christian Marclay (Intermezzo Films, 2000)

Kill Any/All Spin *Personnel* – Beck Hansen/Thurston Moore/Tom Surgal (Freedom From, 2000)

New York – *Ystad* (or *Black Box*) – Mats Gustafsson/Thurston Moore/Lee Ranaldo/Steve Shelley (Olof Bright, 2000)

Moonlanding Vol. 1–2 – 'Mouse' – Thurston Moore (Helicopter, 2000)

Naked In The Afternoon: A Tribute to Jandek – 'Painted My Teeth' – Dapper (Summersteps Records, 2000)

The Revolution Of Everyday Life – Black Pig Liberation Front (Fringecore, 2000)

Opus: Three Incredible Ideas – Thurston Moore/Walter Prati/Giancarlo Schiaffini (Auditorium Edizioni, 2001)

Dapper (cassette) – Dapper (oTo, 2001)

Live At Easthampton Town Hall – Nels Cline/Thurston Moore/Zeena Parkins (JMZ Records, 2001)

Four Guitars Live – Nels Cline/Carlos Giffoni/Thurston Moore/Lee Ranaldo (Important, recorded 2001/released 2006)

Untitled – Diskaholics Anonymous Trio (Crazy Wisdom, 2001)

Hanging From The Devil's Tree – 'The Widow' – Thurston Moore (Your Flesh, 2001)

Bully (soundtrack) – 'Intro – Kill The Bully'/'Blood On My Shirt'/'Shut The F★★k Up Donny'/'Outro – Get Your Story Together' – Thurston Moore (OCF Entertainment, 2001)

Corona Classics Volume 1 – 'Oh You Fine Bird!' – Dapper (E.F. Tapes, 2002)

'Yellow Label Silence'/'Come Back Archimedes Badkar, All Is Forgiven' (12") – Diskaholics Anonymous Trio (no label, 2002)

You've Got Your Order Volume I 'Like A Ghost On Fire' Mike Watt/Thurston Moore/Thalia Ferriera (Chrome Peeler Records, 2002)

Weapons of Ass Destruction – Diskaholics Anonymous Trio (Smalltown Superjazz, recorded 2002/released 2006)

Live in Japan Vol. 1 – Diskaholics Anonymous Trio (Load, recorded 2002/ released 2006)

45'18 – '4'33' – Thurston Moore (Korm Plastics, 2002)

Neon Meate Dream Of A Octafish: A Tribute To Captain Beefheart & His Magic Band – 'Beatle Bones 'N Smokin' Stones' – Dapper (Animal World Recordings, 2003)

Live At Tonic – Chris Corsano/Paul Flaherty/Thurston Moore/Wally Shoup (Leo Records, 2003)

G2, 44+/x2 – Phill Niblock (Moikai, 2003)

Tribute To Martin Luther King Jr. – Thurston Moore/Moz (Breathmint, 2003)

The Vietnam Songbook – 'Fourth Day Of July' (download) – Thurston Moore (no label, 2003)

The Good, The Bad And The Ugly – 'South Beach' – Sonny Vincent (Munster Records, 2003)

'Sweetface'/'Rom Supply Co.' – Mirror/Dash (En/Of, 2003)

The Whys Of Fire – Dredd Foole & The Din (Ecstatic Peace!, 2003)

Season Of The Western Witch (book/CD) – Georganne Deen/Viggo Mortensen/Thurston Moore (Perceval Press, 2003)

For The Dead In Space: Volumes II & III – 'Fourth Day Of July' – Mike Watt/Thurston Moore (Secret Eye Records, 2003)

Dr. Eugene Chadbourne's Adventures At The Guitar Festival/Greetings Fellow Pickers – Dr. Eugene Chadbourne (Leo Records, 2003)

Åke Hodell: Friends Of The Bumblebee – 'Tennis Sisters' – Thurston Moore (Håll Tjäften, 2003)

Tracks & Fields – 'Industrial Noise Blues' – Male Slut (Kill Rock Stars, 2004)

Nancy Sinatra – 'Momma's Boy' – Nancy Sinatra (EMI, 2004)

From The Earth To The Spheres Vol. 1 – Thurston Moore/My Cat Is An Alien (Opax, 2004)

Future Noir – 'In My Room' – Hanin Elias (Fatal Recordings, 2004)

Kapotte Muziek By Thurston Moore – Kapotte Muziek (Korm Plastics, 2004)

'Jong'/'New Wave Dust' – Thurston Moore/John Wiese (Troniks, 2004)

Make No Mistake About It – Carlos Giffoni/Thurston Moore/Dylan Nyoukis (Gold Sounz, 2004)

'Messy Mystery'/'New Vietnam Blues' – Can't/Nipple Creek (U-Sound Archive, 2005)

Noise Hello Kitty – 'Hello Kitty Is Back!' – Coco Moore (no label, 2005)

Mercersound – 'Sleeping Pill' – Thurston Moore (Mercer Union, 2005)

'Do They Know It's Hallowe'en?' – North American Hallowe'en Prevention Initiative (Vice Records, 2005)

Dialects – 'The Ancients ★Swingset Live 2005★' – Electric Kulintang (Plastic Records, 2006)

Secrets From The Clock House – 'Nuclear War' – Future Pilot AKA (Creeping Bent, 2006)

STRP1: – Reactions To The Music Of Dick Raaijmakers – 'Pianoforte' – Thurston Moore (Basta, 2006)

I Don't Think The Dirt Belongs To The Grass – 'Anal Cry' – Thurston Moore (Carbon Records, 2006)

Viva Negativa!: A Tribute To The New Blockaders Volume 1 – 'Corion Sound for T.N.B.' – Thurston Moore (Vinyl On Demand, 2006)

A Raga For Peter Walker – 'Dirt Raga' – Thurston Moore (Tompkins Square, 2006)

'Untitled' – Mirror/Dash (AA Records, 2006)

'Female Body Inspector'/'Monster Tape' (cassette) – Monster Dudes (Deathbomb Arc, 2006)

D.D.T. (cassette) – Aaron Dilloway/Charlie Draheim/Thurston Moore (Tuskie Skull, 2006)

Blood Shadow Rampage – Dream Aktion Unit (Volcanic Tongue, 2006)

Indeterminate Activity Of Resultant Masses (Music For Ten Guitars And Drums) – Glenn Branca (Atavistic, 2006)

I Can't Be Bought – Mirror/Dash (Three Lobed Recordings, 2006)

Flipped Out Bride – Thurston Moore (Blossoming Noise, 2006)

Noise (DVD compilation) – 'Hotel Athiti' – Mirror/Dash (MK2, 2006)

Noon And Eternity – To Live And Shave In LA (Menlo Park Recordings, 2006)

Horóscopo: Sanatorio De Molière – To Live And Shave In LA (Blossoming Noise, 2006)

Insertion/Untitled – Cotton Museum/Thurston Moore (Tasty Soil, 2006)

Free/Love (cassette) – Thurston Moore (Throne Heap, 2007)

The Voloptulist – 'Corion Sound For T.N.B.'/'840 Seconds Over' – The New Blockaders/Thurston Moore/Jim O'Rourke/Chris Corsano (Hospital Productions, 2006)

The Roadhouse Session Vol. 1 – Chris Corsano/Paul Flaherty/Thurston Moore/Wally Shoup (Columbia, 2007)

'Touch You' (10") – Thurston Moore (Endleseries, 2007)

Visionaire No. 53: Sound (compilation) – 'Intermittent Overload Of Electric Toothbrush And Hairdryer' – Kim Gordon/Thurston Moore (Visionaire, 2007)

Untitled (compilation) – 'Dickraymakerz' – Thurston Moore (Public Guilt, 2007)

X-Plural U.S. (compilation) – 'Black Metal Boyfriend' – Mirror/Dash (Mystra Records, 2007)

Black Weeds/White Death (cassette) – Thurston Moore (Meudiademorte, 2007)

Action/Extra Action (book/DVD) – Richard Kern (Taschen, 2007)

AM500 – 'Noh Neighbors'/'Noise Complaint' (boxset) – Thurston Moore (American Tapes, 2007)

Touch The Iceberg (CD-R) – Owl Xounds Exploding Galaxy (Fuck It Tapes, 2007)

LP – The Bark Haze (Important, 2007)

Total Joke Era – The Bark Haze (Important, 2007)

McCannabis (cassette) – The Bark Haze (Arbor, 2007)

Northampton Wools (cassette) – Northampton Wools (Bonescraper Recordings, 2007)

Untitled – Paul Flaherty/Thurston Moore/Bill Nace (Ecstatic Peace!, 2007)

The First Original Silence – Original Silence (Smalltown Superjazz, 2007)

Trees Outside The Academy – Thurston Moore (Ecstatic Peace!, 2007)

'Mature, Lonely And Out Of Control'/'Alternative Hair Styles' – Graham Moore/Thurston Moore (Nihilist, 2007)

Kumpiny Night (CD-R) – Elisa Ambrogio/Ben Chasny/Zac Davis/Dredd Foole/Kim Gordon/Gown/Matt Krefting/Thurston Moore/Bill Nace/Jessi Leigh Swenson (no label, 2007)

Thrash Sabbatical (boxset) – 'Unzipped'/'Petite Bone'/'Creamsikkle' – Thurston Moore (Deathbomb Arc, 2007)

One For Merz – The Bark Haze (Three Lobed Recordings, 2008)

Basement Psychosis (cassette) – The Bark Haze (Ecstatic Peace!, 2008)

Live (CD-R) – Zac Davis/Thurston Moore (Maim & Disfigure, 2008)

Maison Hantee – 'Chamber 20' – Mike Ladd/Alexandre Pierrepont (Rogueart, 2008)

Time Machine (CD-R) – Peeper (Manhand, 2008)

'Western Mass Hardcore Rules OK'/'Untitled' – Paul Flaherty/Thurston Moore/Slither (Not Not Fun, 2008)

Guitar Trio Is My Life! (boxset) – Rhys Chatham & His Guitar Trio All-Stars (Radium, 2008)

Sensitive/Lethal – Thurston Moore (No Fun Productions, 2008)

Blindfold (cassette) – Thurston Moore (Destructive Industries, 2008)

Keffer Gordon Moore (cassette) – Kim Gordon/Leslie Keffer/Thurston Moore (Ecstatic Peace!, 2008)

Built For Lovin' – Thurston Moore (Lost Treasures Of The Underworld, 2008)

'Blues For Proposition Joe'/'Sign Stars'/'101 On Semlow'/'Seychelles' – Mirror/Dash, Kit (Nothing Fancy Just Music, 2008)

'Come Across' (CD-R) – Mirror/Dash (Schunck/Glaspaleis, 2008)

'Unzipped'/'Paved Fury'/'Motor Hands' – Kevin Shields/Thurston Moore (Deathbomb Arc, 2008)

Now And Forever (boxset) – The Thing (Smalltown Superjazz, 2008)

Monolith: Jupiter – The Bark Haze/Traum (Music Fellowship, 2008)

The Second Original Silence – Original Silence (Smalltown Superjazz, 2008)

Strange Songbook (Tribute To Haruomi Hosono 2) – 'Gradiated Grey' – Thurston Moore (Commons, 2008)

'Aeresol'/'Ivan' – Steve Shelley/Thurston Moore (no label, 2008)

'Noise Virgin'/'CCTV Laceration'/'Free Twisted Filth'/'I'/'II'/'III'/ 'Spirithenge' (CD-R) – Kylie Minoise/Thurston Moore/Tusco Terror/Wether (Insult Recordings, 2009)

'Schwarze Polizei'/'Coming Undone'/'Retect'/'Got The Life'/'Grussver-weigerung' (cassette) – Kommissar Hjuler/Mama Baer/Thurston Moore (Goaty Tapes, 2009)

Uppers And Downers – 'Hang Up The Pin Up' – Cobra Killer (Monika Enterprise, 2009)

The Secret Song – 'Known Unknowns' – DJ Spooky (Thirsty Ear, 2009)

Break It Up – Jemina Pearl (Universal/Ecstatic Peace!, 2009)

Deaf In The Valley (cassette) – 'Aerosol' – Thurston Moore (905 Tapes, 2009)

The Blasting Concept (compilation) – 'Three Collectors Of Bird Note' – Thurston Moore (Smalltown Superjazz, 2009)

Senso – White Out/Thurston Moore/Jim O'Rourke (Ecstatic Peace!, 2009)

Wild And Free (CD-R) – The Bark Haze (no label, 2009)

'Can We Just Talk Instead?'/'Sadnessfinalamen' – The Bark Haze/Our Love Will Destroy the World (Krayon Recordings, 2009)

Valley Of Shame – Northampton Wools (Open Mouth, 2009)

Mother/Groundhog – Chris Corsano/Bill Nace/Mats Gustafsson/Thurston Moore (Ecstatic Peace!/Open Mouth, 2010)

'12 String Acoustik Regret'/'12 String Acoustik Suicide Pact With God'/'Of Death' (cassette) – Gravitons/Thurston Moore (Wintage Records & Tapes, 2010)

A Ticket For Decay – Hat City Initiative (Ecstatic Peace!, 2010)

Suicide Notes For Acoustic Guitar (CD-R) – Thurston Moore (Carbon Records, 2010)

All Kinds Of People: Love Burt Bacharach – 'Always Something There To Remind Me' – Jim O'Rourke (AWDR/LR2, 2010)

Sing For Your Meat: A Tribute To Guided By Voices – 'Stabbing A Star' – Thurston Moore (No More Fake Labels, 2011)

Live At All Tomorrow's Parties 2010 (download) – Northampton Wools (Digital Music Archive, 2010)

Les Anges Du Péché – Jean-Marc Montera/Thurston Moore/Lee Ranaldo (Dysmusie, 2011)

Solo Acoustic Volume 5/12-String Meditations For Jack Rose – Thurston Moore (Vin du Select Qualitite, 2011)

Demolished Thoughts – Thurston Moore (Matador, 2011)

Voice Studies 05 (cassette) – 'Lonely Charm'/'Love Song As A Lion' – Thurston Moore (My Dance The Skull, 2011)

'Boogie X'/'Hot Date'/'Boogie Y'/'Gold Dime' – Thurston Moore/Talk Normal (Fast Weapons, 2011)

Caught On Tape – John Moloney/Thurston Moore (Feeding Tube, 2012)

Fundamental Sunshine (cassette) – John Moloney/Thurston Moore (Manhand, 2012)

The Tingle Of Casual Danger (CD-R) – The Sunburned Hand Of The Man (Manhand, 2012

YokoKimThurston – Kim Gordon/Thurston Moore/Yoko Ono (Chimera Music, 2012)

Play Some Fucking Stooges – Mats Gustafsson/Thurston Moore (Quasi Pop Records, 2012)

Mind Wars (cassette/seven-inch) – 'Untitled'/'Untitled' – Beck (Fonograf, 2012)

Lifers (cassette) – 'Home/Dream' – Thurston Moore (Life Like, 2012)

Xavier's Birds – 'F/E' – Joshua Burkett (Time-Lag Records, 2013)

Tarp (boxset) – 'Grey Matter Books, April 2010' – Conrad Capistran/ Joshua Burkett/Joe Malinowski/Northampton Wools (Feeding Tube, 2013)

Ultramafic – 'South Beach (Sonic Version)' – Sonny Vincent (No Balls Records, 2013)

Shot/Extra Shot (book/DVD) – Richard Kern (Taschen, 2013)

The Grief That Shrieked To Multiply – To Live And Shave In LA (Monotype Records) – 2013

'Ghost Dance' (download) – Anne Waldman/Ambrose Bye/Thurston Moore (Fast Speaking Music, 2013)

'Dinner Bell' (download) – Thurston Moore/Devin Brahja Waldman/ Ambrose Bye/Eva Prinz (Fast Speaking Music, 2013)

Comes Through In The Call Hold – Clark Coolidge/Thurston Moore/Anne Waldman (Fast Speaking Music, 2013)

Live At Café Oto – Thurston Moore/Alex Ward (Otoroku, 2013)

Last Notes – Joe McPhee/Thurston Moore/Bill Nace (Open Mouth, 2013)

@ – John Zorn/Thurston Moore (Tzadik, 2013)

The Only Way To Go Is Straight Through – Loren Connors/Thurston Moore (Northern Spy, 2013)

Vi Är Alla Guds Slavar – Mats Gustafsson/Thurston Moore (Otoroku, 2013)

Banjaxed Blues – John Moloney/Thurston Moore (Manhand, 2013)

Cause & Effect Vol. 1 – 'Gleo' – Thurston Moore (Joyful Noise, 2013)

Acting The Maggot (CD-R) – John Moloney/Thurston Moore (Feeding Tube, 2013)

Irish-American Prayer (CD-R) – John Moloney/Thurston Moore (Manhand, 2013)

Chelsea Light Moving – Chelsea Light Moving (Matador, 2013)

Untitled (cassette) – Chelsea Light Moving/Merchandise (no label, 2013)

Harry's House Vol. 1 – 'A # Of Times' – Thurston Moore (Fast Speaking Music 2013)

Sonic Street Chicago – Thurston Moore (Corbett Vs. Dempsey, 2014)

'Detonation'/'Germs Burn' – Thurston Moore (Blank Editions, 2014)

Sun Gift Earth (cassette) – Thurston Moore (Blank Editions, 2014)

Live At ZDB – Gabriel Ferrandini/Thurston Moore/Pedro Sousa (Shhpuma, 2014)

The Rust Within Their Throats – Margarida Garcia/Thurston Moore (Headlights, 2014)

Oasis At Biskra (cassette) – Ambrose Bye/Daniel Carter/Thurston Moore/ Eva Prinz/Anne Waldman/Devin Brahja Waldman (Fast Speaking Music, 2014)

Soft Machine Sutra – Samara Lubelski/Thurston Moore/Gene Moore/Tom Surgal/Anne Waldman (Fast Speaking Music, 2014)

Live – The Thing (The Thing Records, 2014)

III: Beneath Trident's Tomb – Twilight (Century Media, 2014)

The Best Day – Thurston Moore (Matador, 2014)

Sonic Protest 2014 – '?Kollektr SK'M!' – Thurston Moore (Sonic Protest, 2014)

The Jeffrey Lee Pierce Sessions Project: Axels & Sockets – 'Shame And Pain'/'Nobody's City' –Mark Stewart/Jeffrey Lee Pierce, Iggy Pop/ Nick Cave (Glitterhouse Records, 2014)

The Polar Bear – 'Six, Two, Thirteen' – Michael Chapman (Blast First Petite, 2014)

Oh Michael Look What You've Done: Friends Play Michael Chapman – 'It Didn't Work Out' – Thurston Moore (Tompkins Square, 2014)

Harry's House Vol. 2 – 'Sunstroke' – Marty Ehrlich/Thurston Moore (Fast Speaking Music, 2014)

Absence Blots Us Out – To Live And Shave In LA (Blossoming Noise, 2015)

Too Live: In Shame In M.I.A. (VHS/CD-R) – Thurston Moore (Obsolete Video Formats, 2015)

Transient – 'Home' – Krieg (Init Records, 2015)

Harry's House Vol. 3 – 'Olympia' – Thurston Moore (Fast Speaking Music, 2015)

The Avant-Age Garde I Ams Of The Gal Luxury – 'Secret Heroes R U 'A'/'Slow Limos And Meteorites' – Heroes Are Gang Leaders (Fast Speaking Music, 2015)

Hit The Wall! – Mats Gustafsson/Thurston Moore (Smalltown Superjazz, 2015)

Full Bleed – John Moloney/Thurston Moore (Northern Spy, 2015)

Fluxuus Aan De Waanzin – 'For Mary' – Steve Dalachinsky/Tom Surgal/ Thurston Moore (Psych.KG, 2015)

Fluxus – 'In The Book Of Ice' – Steve Dalachinsky/Tom Surgal/Thurston Moore (Psych.KG, 2015)

FLUXblonk LUFTessl Weibel – 'Glissandos' – Steve Dalachinsky/Thurston Moore (Psych.KG, 2015)

With… – 'The Second Half Of The Second Half' – John Russell (Emanem, 2015)

Cuts Of Guilt, Cuts Deeper – Mats Gustafsson/Merzbow/Thurston Moore/ Balazs Pandi (RareNoise Records, 2015)

Untitled (CD-R) – Jooklo Duo/Thurston Moore/Dylan Nyoukis (Chocolate Monk, 2015)

Live At White Cube – London Sinfonietta/Christian Marclay/Thurston Moore (The Vinyl Factory, 2015)

Live At Henie Onstad Kunstsenter – Mats Gustafsson/Thurston Moore (Prisma Records, 2015)

Tiny People Having A Meeting – Ambrose Bye/Clark Coolidge/Max Davies/ Thurston Moore/Anne Waldman (Fast Speaking Music, 2015)

50 Bands And A Cat For Indiana Equality (download) – 'The Best Day (Live)' – The Thurston Moore Band (Joyful Noise, 2015)

Parallelogram (boxset) – John Moloney/Thurston Moore (Three Lobed, 2016)

Marshmallow Moon Decorum – Frank Rosaly/Thurston Moore (Corbett Vs. Dempsey, 2016)

Heretics – Heretics (Unsound, 2016)

'Metal Moments' (seven-inch flexi) – Thurston Moore (Joyful Noise, 2016)

'Feel It In Your Guts' (seven-inch flexi) – Thurston Moore/Bernie Sanders (Joyful Noise, 2016)

Free Chelsea Manning (cassette) – 'Chelsea's Kiss'/'Sad Saturday' – Thurston Moore (Blank Editions, 2016)

Offerings – Radieux Radio/Cameron Jamie/Thurston Moore (12fr, 2016)

Mikrosession#11 'Transcendent Transaction' – The Thurston Moore Group (no label, 2016)

London Live (Cassette) - Sick Llama/Thurston Moore (Fag Tapes, 2016)

Disarm – Adam Gołębiewski/Thurston Moore (Endless Happiness, 2017)

Songs We Taught The Lord Vol.1 – Thurston Moore/Phil X. Milstein (Feeding Tube Records, 2017)

Rock n Roll Consciousness – Thurston Moore (Fiction/Universal, 2017)